Jason Schneider On
Camera Collecting
Book Two

*A fully illustrated handbook of articles
originally published in MODERN PHOTOGRAPHY.*
With Current Prices

Other books by Jason Schneider
  Jason Schneider on Camera Collecting

Library of Congress
Catalog Number 81-40485

ISBN 0-87069-419-7

Copyright © 1982
Jason Schneider

Second Printing, 1985

Published by

Wallace-Homestead Book Company
580 Waters Edge
Lombard, Illinois 60148

One of the
ABC PUBLISHING
Companies

Dedication

To my wife Glenda for putting up with innumerable ancient cameras strewn about the house, and to Herbert Keppler, Fred Spira, Bernie Danis, Ken Hansen, Sam Engler, Robert Olden and others too numerous to mention for their aid, assistance and encouragement in the preparation of this volume. I take full blame for any errors, omissions, or misemphases that may appear herein, and extend full credit to the above-mentioned for their unfailing helpfulness and good cheer.

Introduction

Like its predecessor, Jason Schneider On Camera Collecting, this book consists largely of a compilation of columns previously published monthly in Modern Photography magazine under the heading, "The Camera Collector", and is offered in response to numerous requests from photographic collectors and enthusiasts. In addition, I have included chapters on How To Sell Your Camera, Filter Sizes For Collectible Cameras, and, against my better judgment but by shrill and persistent popular demand, a brief (hence incomplete) Collectible Camera Price Guide.

In writing The Camera Collector columns, my objective has been unwavering—to provide sound information about collectible, mechanically and/or aesthetically fascinating photographic hardware in a readable and entertaining fashion. While their freewheeling style may displease some punctilious historians and catalogers, it does succeed in conveying some of the essence of photographic collecting—the thrill of discovery, the consternation of ignorance, the humble appreciation of mechanical genius, and the snickerings attendant on the idiosyncracies manifest in many a quaint and curious camera design.

While there *is* an index (at the back) to aid you in locating facts and impressions on specific cameras ranging from the pedestrian to the priceless, this book is emphatically not a comprehensive listing of collectible cameras, nor does it purport to be one. There are simply too many obvious gaps and peculiar inclusions.

In any event this second volume contains entirely new material than the first and thus complements, rather than supplants it. It is particularly suited to dipping into now and then and I hope you'll find its contents informative as well as entertaining.

Contents

International potpourri: Ilford Witness, Ensignette, Leica-inspired Elettra I from Italy

A stillborn English "system" 35, another pride of the British Empire, and an inscrutable Italian "Leica."

Every once in a while one of my readers comes through in a big way and practically sends me an instant, ready-to-run column covering a unique, peculiar, fascinating and rare camera I've never even heard of, much less seen. Now that's fairly easy to do if you happen to unearth a moldy old view camera with a funny shutter made in 1884, but to completely amaze me with a post-World War II rangefinder 35 takes a bit of doing. And so, this month's "Confound the Collector" award of one unexpired (but discontinued) roll of Verichrome Pan 116 film goes to Robert Wolters of Deerfield, Ill. for having done so with one of the rarest of rare birds, the Ilford Witness (ca. 1950).

A brilliant flop, Ilford's Witness was an advanced "system" 35 antedating Leica M3.

Now, the first thing that struck me as a bit odd about this interchangeable-lens, coupled-superimposed-image rangefinder 35 is its utter lack of any "Ilford" marking, or "Made in England" stamping anywhere on the camera body. Indeed the only reference to Ilford in the printed loose-leaf instruction manual is a penned notation that the "special flash gun" is supplied by Ilford Ltd. In fact, that isn't the only hand-inscribed erratum or addendum contained therein. Entire passages referring to the lens name, the operation of the slow-shutter dial and the entire section on special Witness cassettes (never produced) were

either deleted or changed by someone with a neat deliberate manner and impeccable penmanship. Do you somehow get the feeling that the Witness was essentially a prototype that never got off the ground? Bob Wolter's claim that only 120 of these beasts were ever produced certainly seems to imply as much.

In any event, it's kind of sad that Ilford never "got it together" with this Leica-and-Contax-inspired creation, as it appears to be carefully thought-out and quite advanced for its day. The body is described as "precision die-cast" and the back-and-bottom cover is removable *a la* Contax with twist locks on both ends of the bottom plate. The shutter is apparently a Leica-derived horizontal cloth focal-plane with slow speeds (of 1-1/25 sec.) set on a Leica-style, front-mounted click-stopped dial. However, you set fast speeds (1-1/25-1/1000 sec.) on a top-mounted, non-rotating click-stopped dial placed with its knurled edge overhanging the back edge of the camera top for convenient manipulation. Furthermore, the booklet asserts that "intermediate speed settings" are possible with the latter, a feature that has only lately become commonplace.

The Witness rangefinder is a single-window, combined range-viewfinder patch in a contrasting gold color. While the viewfinder eyepiece is a bit on the dinky side and the finder lacks any frame lines or parallax-compensation markings, the focusing and viewing systems are very well executed—about on the level of a Contax IIa.

As usual, I've saved all the interesting stuff for last. First, there's the little matter of setting the flash-sync delay (which includes zero delay for strobe as well as setting for various bulbs). This is accomplished by turning a little dial found on the bottom of the main body section when the camera back is removed. Obviously, this means you'd better decide which type of flash you're going to use before you load the camera, and you can't switch to strobe in mid-roll! Then, there's the close-focusing range of the normal 50mm f/1.9 Dallmeyer lens, which you select by pushing the "near focus catch" and simply focusing closer—to 18 in., to be exact. Of course, the rangefinder no longer functions at these close distances, but it sure antedates Leitz's Dual-Range Summicron by a few years.

Curiouser and curiouser features

One Witness feature that Leitz never caught up with (because they probably rejected the idea) is its unique lens mount. Would you believe an interrupted screw thread (shades of Professional Camera Repair's Pentax adaptations) which allows you to bayonet in the "normal"

Dallmeyer objective, but also lets you screw in Leica screw-thread lenses and achieves full rangefinder coupling with the latter? There's even a spring-loaded lens-removal catch complete with red line (on the camera) and dot (on the lens)—orientation marks for mounting, just like on a modern SLR. Regrettably, this clever system only works with the 50mm Dallmeyer, the sole optic ever supplied for the Witness.

Now you might think that all this innovation was quite sufficient for a camera that was essentially stillborn. But no, being English the designers couldn't resist a final mechanical fillip—a spring-loaded dust cover built into the recessed, centrally placed accessory shoe! How photographic slobs like us have managed to put up with dusty accessory shoes for so long has always eluded me.

But seriously, whatever you may think of Ilford's design priorities, you've got to give them credit for devising a solid, competent, forward-looking machine that is anything but nutty in the classic British tradition. While it's arguable whether the Witness could have successfully competed with the re-emerging Leica and Contax in 1950 (and against photographers' ingrained prejudices in favor of them), the hefty, nicely finished Witness clearly didn't deserve to languish in such obscurity that its name evokes a puzzled stare even from veteran camera collectors. Of course, it's an ill wind that blows nobody any good, and the camera's system-oriented finesse, combined with its unheralded status and extremely low production figures, assures it a hallowed place in anybody's 35mm collection (even in British Museum's, if they've got one). What's it worth on the open market? I'd say a grand at least, but you should nab one in the flesh, the chances are excellent that its owner won't have the foggiest notion what it is and offer it for a pittance.

Born in '14 at start of the Great War, Ensignette was flag-bedecked, foldable.

Turning now to a much simpler but equally lovable English product, we have the cute little Ensign No. 2 I ran across at Olden Camera in New York City. One of the most foldable cameras ever conceived, this black-enamel-finished creation extends its front to shooting position on

two hinged nickel-chrome struts. So what starts out as a flat, pocketable box measuring about 5x2½x1 in. is magically transformed into a 5x2½x4½-in. camera. To unfold it you grab two side tabs on the front panel and just pull straight out until the struts click into position.

Aside from its foldability and a nice Union Jack motif on the left side of the front standard, the Ensign's features are pretty pedestrian. A fixed-focus design, it sports a meniscus lens with apertures of f/11, f/16 and f/22 which are set by rotating the brass front ring around the lens. This turns a circular plate with three Waterhouse-type stops in front of the lens. The shutter is a simple "ever-set" type with T and I (instantaneous) settings, the latter equivalent to about 1/25 sec. Unfortunately, the little selector lever which presumably pointed to T or L on the lower left part of the front standard is missing.

At any rate, the little Ensignette (from the World War I era) is one of very few cameras that folds to the size of a Kodak Instamatic yet made six whopping 1⅞x3-in. negatives per roll of long-discontinued 129 film. While its "brilliant" reflex finder above the lens is so-so, the weird format alone seems to justify its $30-$40 price among collectors.

A strange blend of crudeness and precision, Elettra I was a Leica "A" takeoff.

While it isn't even remotely British, I can't resist concluding this month's festivities with another camera I ran into while browsing around Olden's—a little Italian "Leica copy" called the Elettra I, a presumably late-30's product of Sirio Firenze, whoever they were. Obviously, the contours of this rangefinder-less scale-focusing 35 are Leitz-derived, but the shutter sure isn't. Incredibly, this camera sports a nicely machined double-helical focusing arrangement (1.2m to infinity), which is controlled by a beautifully finished knurled ring. And at the business end of this nice alloy focusing tube sits a 50mm f/8 doublet lens in a simple everset shutter! Yep, the front knurled ring lets you set speeds of only 1/25-1/200 sec. plus T, while you can select but four apertures (f/8 to f/22) by grabbing and turning two little pins around the lens. Oh well, the viewfinder is bright and usable, the bottom comes off and the spool pulls out just like a Leica, and the symbols for "open" and "closed" opposite the bottom-mounted slide lock are cute—an open and closed padlock. Why those inscrutable Italians would want to design a camera like this remains a mystery, but maybe there was a higher-priced Elettra II with an f/3.5 lens. Whatever the case, I'd peg the apparently rare but comparatively unsought Elettra at about $100 on the collectors' market, but given the acquisitive instincts of Leica-copy collectors, who knows?

Nagels of the 1930s

You may never have heard of Dr. August Nagel, but you've undoubtedly seen cameras made in his American-owned factory.

Few American photographers would be conversant with the products of the erstwhile Dr. August Nagel factory in Stuttgart (despite its enviable reputation for sound, beautifully designed, nicely finished cameras), were it not for a singular event that took place sometime in 1932—namely, the factory's acquisition by the Eastman Kodak Co. who changed its title to Kodak AG. From that time forward, Retinas, Recomars and, to a lesser extent, Pupilles and Vollendas became familiar names on the American photographic scene, though understandably most of our countrymen thought of them as "German Kodaks" rather than "Nagels." In any case, their importation came to an abrupt end in 1939, and while Kodak AG was reconstituted in the same virtually intact factory after the war (to produce a seemingly endless succession of postwar 35's—Retinas, Retina Reflexes and Retinettes), things weren't quite the same.

If there is anything that bespeaks the Nagel-Kodak era of the 30's, it's their elegantly designed roll-film and sheet-film cameras. The Nagel factory was justly famous for its nickel and nickel-chrome finishes and exceptionally fine black lacquer which adorned many of their "styled" creations. While the following quartet of Nagel-Kodak cameras (culled from the extensive collection of John Kowalak of River Edge, N.J.) isn't truly representative of their "restrained art deco-ish" appearance, all have one thing in common—they're rare. And as you'll see from their estimated values, all but the first are quite valuable.

When Dr. Nagel, the former head of Contessa-Nettel, resigned as director of production of the newly formed (1926) Zeiss-Ikon company in 1928, one of the first products of his own fledgling firm was the Nagel #10, one of

Plain but portentous, Nagel #10 hinted at firm's future grandeur.

Anything but rank, the Ranca was one of the rarest early roll-film Nagels.

the few pedestrian cameras Nagel ever made. It was basically a stripped-down 6.5x9cm pack camera quite typical of its day, and notable chiefly as being the precursor of the spiffy Kodak Recomar 18 of the late 30's

Unlike the Recomar, the #10 (and its larger 9x12cm cousin, the #14) lacked any lateral or vertical movement of the front standard. To focus the 10.5cm f/6.8 Nagel Anastigmat lens (which stopped down to f/36), you grabbed onto two knurled lugs on the underside of the lens board and pulled the whole business outwards until a metal pointer coincided with the proper distance (1.5m to "Ferne," i.e., distant, or infinity). You could then lock the distance setting by pushing in a tab emerging from the front standard's bottom right side. The shutter, an everset Pronto (with speeds of 1/25-1/100 sec. plus B and T) was equally primitive.

Now you notice that I said "primitive," not chintzy or ill-conceived. Inexpensive and derivative the Nagel #10 certainly was; poorly constructed or finished it emphatically was not. The nickel-chrome focusing rails and side struts were gorgeous. Ditto for the slide-out ground-glass focusing unit, its spring-loaded metal catch, and the black enameling adorning the rest of the camera. The hexagonal cutout in the middle of the front section between the focusing rails and elongated hexagonal chrome bezel around the focusing scale pointed toward future Nagel elegance. Incidentally, the total production run of #10 and #14 film-pack Nagels consisted of 2,500 units, and they were the only non-Kodak Nagels to be marketed for two years after the Kodak takeover in 1932. Obviously, then, the #10 is rare, but since it's not in great demand among collectors, its current value is only $50-$75.

Our second camera, however, is both rare and valuable—a true collector's prize. The little pocketable Ranca is a split-frame job, producing 16 1⅝x1¼-in. negs per roll of 127 film. As you may have guessed, this was accomplished by the traditional "two ruby window" method—you placed each frame number in window 1 and then in window 2. As camera cognoscenti are aware, this format—indeed the Ranca's entire appearance—parallels the much snazzier and jazzier Nagel-Kodak Pupilles, which featured helical focusing, first-rate optics (Tessar, Xenars and Xenons) and Compur shutters. The humbler but much rarer Ranca had none of these things, but its place in history is eloquently attested to by its nameplate, which bears the legend, "Kodak-AG Dr. NagelWerk Stuttgart."

You "unfolded" your Ranca by grabbing onto a knurled ring and turning it 90° counterclockwise until the helically geared lens tube locked into shooting position. You then focused (3.5 ft. to infinity) by turning the 5cm f/4.5 Nagel Anastigmat's front element. Like the #10 Nagel, the relatively inexpensive Ranca sported a Pronto everset shutter with speeds of 1/25-1/100 sec. plus B and T, but this one was also fitted with a self-timer controlled by a little lever to the right of the shutter-speed wheel.

Two Puppille features shared by the Ranca were its clever lift-out film-holder insert, which was actually integral with the top of the camera body, and its good-quality

flip-up finder, an inversed Galilean type. The Ranca originally sold for a hefty $60.50 and is presently worth about three or four times that—hardly surprising in view of its limited 1932-1934 production run, few of which reached these shores.

Perhaps the supreme achievement of the Nagel factory in the limited-production field was a camera called, appropriately enough, the Suprema. This meticulously crafted beast deserves another, more dubious title: "The world's most over-designed scale-focusing camera ever to accept 620 roll film." Imagine a rangefinderless 6x6cm-format creation larger than a Zeiss Super Ikonta B incorporating a unit-focusing (1 meter to infinity) 8cm f/3.5 (to f/22) Schneider Xenar lens in a Compar-Rapid (1-1/400 sec. plus B) shutter, and then shake your head and ask, "Why bother?"

Overdone? Suprema had more features than any other scale-focusing "620" folder.

Granted, the huge scissors-type nickel-chrome side struts (plus an additional satin-chrome locating strut on the right-hand side) assured precise lens-to-film-plane alignment, and the automatic film stop (which required that you set number one in the ruby window and then slide its cover closed) was another welcome feature. But since there was never a rangefinder Suprema, it all seems, in retrospect, so much technological overkill.

Oh well, as a work of art, the Suprema's supremacy has seldom been surpassed. The tooled leather coverings and acres of satin chrome were all in the finest Nagel tradition, and excellent "minor" features abounded. The body shutter release incorporated built-in double-exposure prevention, while the front shutter release didn't; the top

Conceptually brilliant, the rangefinder Duo lacked the Super Ikonta's rigidity.

matically popped into viewing position as you pressed the button to open the camera!

The Suprema was produced in very small quantities in 1938, was never imported into the U.S., and is virtually unknown even in Germany. As a consequence, I'd place the value of this near-mint-condition example at about $400. Incidentally, Nagel finally *did* get around to producing an equally monumental rangefinder folder, the Kodak Regent, but it wasn't based on the Suprema.

Now that you are throughly convinced of the absurdity of the Suprema's "rangefinderlessness," let's turn to our final Nagel Kodak, the rare rangefinder version of the more familiar Duo 620, many of which found their way into the U.S. Like the scale-focusing Duo 620, this one produced 16 1⅝x2¼-in. images per roll of 620 film and had a unit-focusing 7.5cm f/3.5 (to f/22) Kodak Anastigmat lens (a Tessar type) mounted in a Compur-Rapid (1-1/500 sec. plus B) shutter. Its automatic filmstop system was similar to the Suprema's, though this much smaller camera lacked the latter's front shutter release and its special knob atop the camera for resetting the automatic film counter.

Of course, these minor lacks were more than offset by the Duo's combined, coupled, superimposed-image rangefinder, which was nice and contrasty and accurate down to its 4-ft. minimum distance.

Although beautifully finished in the Nagel tradition, this camera suffered from the same disease (in milder form) that afflicted its scale-focusing counterpart—its side bracing was not the most rigid in the world (though it was somewhat better than many other folders). Still, in terms of overall construction, metallurgy and design, you'd have to rank it as one of the finest folding roll-film rangefinder cameras ever made, a worthy, if less famous, rival of the Zeiss Super Ikonta A. What's Kowalak's slightly marred rangefinder Duo worth? Well, he says he wouldn't sell it for under a grand, but I think I'll test his mettle by offering him a fast $200.

plate sported a depth-of-field scale on the left side; a built-in support foot adorned the bottom of the main body section; and the shutter incorporated a built-in self-timer. The minuscule optical viewfinder looked sadly out of place atop this magnificent beast, but it was actually quite a good one. Amazingly, this finder *partially* nested when you pushed down on it after folding the camera, and auto-

Cartridge-to-cartridge compacts; a rewindless saga

35mm manufacturers, unite and cast off your rewind knobs? Many tried and lost their shirts, but the result is this fascinating quartet.

Virtually every brilliant invention is plagued with a few lurking foibles, and 35mm photography is certainly no exception. Indeed, few common oversights in the world are more maddening than 35mm photography's big three: forgetting to put film in the camera, failing to check whether it's properly advancing, and opening the camera back before you've rewound the film into the cartridge. As

a direct result of these ubiquitous disasters legions of engineers and inventors have spent decades in the quest for an idiot-proof film-loading system.

True, they finally attained a measure of success with Kodak's introduction of the 126 cartridge in 1963, but this hardly assuaged the world's 35mm buffs. Of course, there was Agfa's earlier cartridge-to-cartridge Rapid system, but aside from ultimately falling on its face financially, it was also rather unoriginal. And to prove this latter bold assertion, I've selected a collector's cache of pre-Rapid "rapids" to regale you with.

America's half-frame success, the Memo combined spartan simplicity with style.

Lomb Anastigmat lens in a Betax No. X shutter (a three-bladed everset affair with speeds of ½ to 1/100 sec. plus B and T). Incidentally, you set the lens opening and shutter speeds by means of tabs emerging from the bottom and top of the recessed lensboard, and the frame counter advanced as you pressed the shutter-release lever on the camera's right side. The most popular Memo had a fixed-focus f/6.3 lens and currently fetches about $50-$60 as a collector's item. I'd, therefore, estimate the value of our focusing f/3.5-lensed model at $150. All Memos were decent, if unspectacular, picture takers and are usable today if you've got the cartridges.

Plastic and pocketable, Korelle's 35 had world's simplest film counter—you!

While I'm not prepared to go out on a limb and state that the American-made Ansco Memo was the very first cartridge-to-cartridge 35mm, it was certainly one of the first commercially successful ones. An oblong half-frame-format (18x24mm) creation measuring about 4x2¼x2 in. (excluding the round optional finder perched unceremoniously on its top), the Memo was introduced back in 1927, enjoyed a measure of popularity and consequently, had a long production run (10 or 12 yrs.). It was a lovable leather-clad beast of commendable simplicity. Once you moved the sliding catch behind the finder to the right and lifted the back off, loading was very straightforward. You placed a fresh D-shaped cartridge (Pat. No. 1,799,184) into the top receptacle, slid the non-tongued end of 35mm film into the felt lips of an identical cartridge placed in the bottom receptacle, closed the back and set the film counter (above the lens on the front of the camera) to zero. You could then advance the film a frame at a time with a single downward stroke of the spring-loaded film-advance knob built into the back plate. As you did so, a little claw on either side of the spring-loaded pressure plate engaged the film's perforations and moved it along—with nary a sprocket wheel in sight.

While this system was ingenious—you couldn't close the camera back if you put a cartridge in the wrong way—it wasn't foolproof. Film would occasionally jam if the cartridge were slightly bent, had lost its felt, or if the film refused to assume an ever tightening curl due to overloading.

The Memo was, however, very aesthetic in a spartan sort of way, especially the deluxe model (pictured) which sported a front-element-focusing (to 3 ft.) f/3.5 Bausch and

Of course there's no saying you can't design a vertical format everyman's half-frame 35 using the standard 35mm cartridge for cartridge-to-cartridge feed, and that's exactly what Korelle (the famous German 2¼ SLR folks) did in 1932. Aside from looking cute in deep burgundy brown plastic, the 3½x2½x1⅞ in. little Korelle 35 seems quite conventional. I say "seems" because the right-handed film-wind knob is as ordinary as any, there's obviously no rewind knob or button required, and a single sprocket wheel under the hinged pressure plate engages the film perforations. But can that knob to the right of the dinky (but clear) optical finder really be nothing more than a film length reminder dial calibrated in frames-per-roll? Apparently so, because the damn thing doesn't move as you wind film through the camera. How did it work? You simply tallied exposures in your head or stopped taking pictures as soon as you felt film tension—surely the simplest "end of film" reminder yet conceived.

Wait, that's not all. Did you ever hear of a half-frame 35 with a 50mm f/4.5 (Schneider Radionar triplet) lens? It would appear to be a bit long for a supposedly "normal" optic. And while the two-bladed everset Vario interlens shutter (with speeds of 1/25-1/100 sec. plus B and T) is conventional enough, the aperture scale below the lens bears the legend "Welta Kamera Werke." Funny, I thought they were one of Korelle's arch rivals. At any rate, the camera's certainly appealing enough and rare enough, which I suppose is why its owner shelled out $45 to acquire it. Current value: $75-100.

Presentiamo Duca

Moving on a bit in time to 1948, we come to a name familiar to most American darkroom workers, Durst of Bolzano, Italy. Would you believe they had the temerity to come up with an 8-millimeterish looking creation called the Duca which used a pair of genuine vertically arrayed Agfa Rapid cartridges and provided full-frame 24 x 36mm exposures on 35mm film by the simple expedient of a curved film plane? Yep—just lift the lid off the side cover, lift out the curved pressure plate, insert a pair of film-connected Agfa cartridges into the panel bottom compartment, close the cover, set the film counter (an integral part of the upward-moving film-advance crank on the Duca's left side) and you were ready to go—for 12 exposures, at any rate. As with the Memo, the Duca's sprocketless advance system consisted of perforation-engaging claws—and the Duca's pair is weirdly curvilinear in shape.

And by what optical legerdemain did those wily Italians compensate for a curved film plane? Simple, they employed a 2-in. f/11 Ducar lens (looks like a doublet) guaranteed to obviate the problem with oodles of depth-of-field. Hell, this optic even focused from 3 ft. to infinity, which I guess partially made up for the camera's two measly shutter speeds—T (actually B!) and I (about 1/50 sec.)—controlled by a sliding tab under the top-mounted vertically-arrayed optical finder. At any rate, the black-crinkle-finished all-metal Duca is a very nicely integrated mechanical design and it certainly qualifies as an oddball.

What hath Durst wrought? Not an 8mm, but a full-frame 35 with weird film plane.

Maybe that's why its present owner went slightly batty and paid $35 for it at a garage sale despite its original under-$15 price!

But perhaps we've slighted the Germans in all this. After all, they were the most persistent and (at least locally) successful opponents of the rewind crank. So without further ado, let's conclude with a genuine (but not Agfa) Rapid camera—the 1965 Penti, an East German product of the everstrange Welta factory. Now the first thing that strikes you about this decorous 2¾x1¾x2½ in. beast is its gold metalwork, accented by cream-colored plastic—there's even a buff-colored wriststrap hanging off its right side.

An elegant East German, the Penti was technically innovative, color-coordinated.

Obviously conceived as a ladies' camera, the Penti is no technological slouch either. Emerging from its left side (after you press the top-mounted shutter-release button) is a most ungainly looking protuberance also finished in stunning gold. This, friends, is the film advance and shutter-cocking shaft (shades of the Voigtländer Vitessa). By removing the camera back (held in place by a crummy-looking spring clip on either side) you can see how this devilishy clever contraption works. As you push it in, you're simply cocking the shutter and at the same time hooking the film-advance claw (under the hinged pressure plate) into an unspecting sprocket hole. As soon as you release your finger from the shutter button after taking a picture, zap—the claw grabs the film, advances it to the next frame, and the film advance shaft springs back out at you—nice!

By comparison, the rest of the Penti is almost anticlimactic. On the left side top of the camera is a manually-resettable film counter (you can't reach the milled setting wheel unless you remove the camera back) and a recessed PC flash contact. The vertically-arrayed optical finder is bright and clear, and there's a swivelling "cartridge-fall-out-guard" above the right-hand cartridge only. Optically, the Penti is fairly competent with a coated single-helical unit-focusing 30mm f/3.5 Meyer Trioplan (triplet) lens which stops down to f/22 and focuses to 1 meter. The two-bladed shutter even provides speeds of 1/30-1/125 plus B.

Clearly though, the Penti's raison d'etre is petite elegance—a somewhat surprising set of parameters for an East German machine of the 60's. At $35 its current owner

couldn't resist its charms either, a wise decision in my opinion. Current value: $50-75.

Many thanks to John Kowalak of River Edge, N.J., for supplying the quartet of fascinating rewindless minis for this particular column. Without his kind cooperation, this chapter wouldn't have been possible.

Kodak's 35mm cheapies: Made in U.S.A.

Kodak's "popularly priced" 35's never set the world on fire, but at least they were "Made in U.S.A."

Remember the good old 1950's, when you could still choose from a relatively plentiful selection of modestly priced 35mm cameras bearing the legend "Made in U.S.A."? Well, apparently those halcyon days are gone forever, expunged by the high costs of materials, development and labor plus an increasingly sophisticated American photographic public. Today the demand is primarily for 35mm SLR's with optical interchangeability and highly developed metering systems on the one hand, and compact rangefinder 35's with convenience features and exposure automation on the other. In short, the nature of 35mm photography itself has so changed that the holiday snapshooters and family portraitists who once flocked to the Argus C-3's and Bolsey Jubiless of the world have deserted 35mm and gone the way of the cartridge-loading Kodak Instamatic camera (pocket-sized and otherwise) and their many imitators. Speaking of Eastman Kodak Co.,

they too had a moderately successful fling with medium- and low-priced 35mm cameras in decades past and that just happens to be the subject of this chapter.

Back in 1938, Kodak finally decided to get its corporate feet wet and enter the 35mm fray with a neat, sleek and spartan entry named, rather unceremoniously, the Kodak 35. This rounded-edged plastic-bodied creation was pleasant-looking and decently made in an uninspired sort of way, but you certainly couldn't complain about its $18.50 price—even at the tail end of the Depression. Conceived as the bare minimum in a scale-focusing 35 (to compete with such stalwarts as the Argus A), it featured a front-element-focusing 50mm f/5.6 Kodak Anastigmat lens (with apertures from f/5.6 to f/16 mounted in a five-bladed Kodex No. 1 shutter, a non-sync "everset" type with speeds of 1/25-1/100 sec. plus T and B.

In addition, the Kodak 35 was adorned with a flip-up optical finder of reasonable (though hardly noteworthy) brightness and size, automatic film stop (of the notorious push-the-botton-before-you-wind variety familiar to Argus C-3 owners), a lensboard-mounted shutter release, removable back, and knurled plastic wind and rewind knobs. Then there were those distinctive minor accouterments familiar to all Kodak fanciers; a bright chrome pressure plate, beautifully made straight-cut steel film wind gears (visible after removing the camera back), and a never-to-be-seen-again metal strip atop the fixed lens barrel which read, "Made in U.S.A." in neat script.

Philately will get you nowhere

Now the interesting thing about the Kodak 35 is the proliferation of models with minor variations which were produced—a boon to the "philatelists" among camera collectors. Shortly after the aforementioned bare-bones model, Kodak unleashed a four-speed (1/25-1/150 sec. plus B and T) type with a 50mm f/4.5 Kodak Anastigmat lens for a blistering $29.50 (it was also produced in a highly desirable olive-drab military model now worth $60-$75), and a five-speed (1/10-1/200 sec. plus B and T) model with a Flash Kodamatic shutter incorporating a built-in self-timer and a front-element-focusing 50mm f/3.5 Kodak Anastig-

Competently spartan, this Kodak 35 has sharp Anastigmat Special lens.

13

mat Special lens, a Tessar-type optic. This latter version naturally had the built-in steadying foot below the lens barrel's midsection (a feature common to all Kodak 35's), a top-mounted accessory shoe and vertically-striated metal film wind and rewind knobs. In addition, later (1946-48) versions of this fancy beast sported a parallax-compensation wheel (calibrated from 4 ft. to infinity) behind the flip-up optical finder, and an ASA bayonet-type flash contact located at about seven o'clock just behind the shutter-speed dial. The deluxe Kodak 35 pictured is also fairly unusual in having a coated Kodak Anastigmat Special lens—most of the coated versions of this optic are labeled Kodak Anastar, the revised nomenclature for Kodak's high-quality front-element-focusing optics. Of course, the rewind knobs of all these relatively high-priced ($50 list) creatures were adorned with film-type reminder dials, listing such exotica as Kodachrome (both daylight and type A) and Super-XX (high-speed) film.

While scale-focusing Kodak 35's enjoyed a relatively long production run (1938-51) they were virtually a "dead-letter" after 1948. Despite reasonably good sales throughout their lifetime, the last three years of their manufacture saw the Kodak 35's eclipsed by several American rangefinder 35's offering more features and equivalent or lower prices, and then by the re-emerging foreigners, especially the German and Japanese. Today, Kodak 35's in good condition bring prices ranging from $30-50 among collectors scouring the used-camera market. Primitive but lovable, most are surprisingly good picture takers, especially the better-lensed models.

It was only two years after the introduction of the Kodak 35—in 1940, to be exact—that some marketing genius at Kodak decided to stick a separate-but-coupled split-image rangefinder atop the basic Kodak 35's body, producing, in effect, one of the ugliest 35's ever made by Kodak or anyone else. However, the two cameras' body shells were so similar that the same back would fit each one without a hitch!

Ugly but accurate, Kodak rangefinder 35 has split-image focusing.

Grafted atop the fairly pedestrian Kodak 35 chassis was (center stage) an ordinary inversed Galilean optical finder (about half life-size) plus (about 1¼ in. to the left of the camera's upper backside) a separate window revealing (of all things) a life-size split-image rangefinder operable over the camera's complete focusing range (4 ft. to infinity). Aside from providing a distinctive three-front-window array, this arrangement offered decent viewing combined with excellent focusing accuracy controlled by a milled wheel to the left of the lens). Minor features were quite similar to the non-rangefinder Kodak 35, including a bar-shaped lens-mount shutter release, automatic film stop (this time including true double-exposure prevention), self-timer, and a front-element-focusing (4 ft. to infinity) 50mm f/3.5 Kodak Anastigmat Special lens. While the model pictured has milled film-advance and rewind knobs *a la* Leica, the "latest" Kodak Rangefinder 35's had a chromed rangefinder window cover piece and vertically-striated chrome knobs atop the camera. The latest list price of the camera pictured was $70.60 (it's also unusual in that it has a factory-coated Kodak Anastigmat Special lens) and the last model (discontinued in 1951) had the same (coated) lens, but its name was changed to Anastar. Incidentally, most later Kodak rangefinder 35's were fitted with the identical Flash Kodamatic shutter (1/10-1/200 sec. plus B and T) found on the fancier non-rangefinder Kodak 35's, but it's also possible to stumble across "transition" models with a plain old non-sync Kodamatic shutter and coated Kodak Anastigmat Special 50mm f/3.5 lenses. At any rate, Kodak rangefinder 35's presently fetch about $30-$50 in decent shape, irrespective of minor variations.

This brings me to my all-time favorite among "popularly priced" Kodak 35's the original Kodak Signet 35 (born early in 1951, deceased in 1958). Admittedly, the Signet's chunky dimensions and the post-art-deco striations cast into its alloy body shell take some getting used to. Also somewhat out of character for a rather expensive ($99.50 list) instrument is the need to manually cock the Kodak Synchro 300 shutter (a two-bladed affair with speeds of 1/25-1/300 sec. plus B) before each exposure, with the ever-present possibility of making accidental double exposures. Of course, the beast did sport an automatic film stop (you kept track of the number of the exposure via a manually-reset circular frame counter smack in the middle of the camera top), but this is hardly a deluxe feature.

What you did get for your money was a nice bright, contrasty, coupled combined range/viewfinder which focused the lens down to a surprisingly close 2 ft. (though the smallish viewfinder was certainly afflicted with parallax at this distance) and a beautifully smooth focusing helical. If you're wondering how Kodak achieved this Leica-like silkiness, there's a succinct answer; the focusing mechanism incorporated 34 ball bearings which, according to my spies at E.K., were selected and manually counted by Kodak's camera assemblers using a long tube which they plunged into a barrel of bearings—somehow a pleasant thought in these days of totally automated production.

While the Signet's bottom plate was high-quality plas-

Clunky, chunky, and dated, Kodak Signet's fitted with amazing Ektar lens, excellent rangefinder, but mediocre shutter.

tic, that incredibly thick cast alloy body was and is a paragon of rigidity and strength. I've seen more than one Signet dropped with nary a scratch, much less a dent, resulting on its tanklike armored exterior. However, the Signet's *raison d'etre* is its lens, a 44mm f/3.5 Ektar which must rank as one of the finest unsung optics ever to grace a rangefinder 35. It's sharp and contrasty to the corners of the field even at maximum aperture, and stopped down to f/8 or so, it'll outperform many optical classics. Yet, when you remove the Signet's back (after ogling at the fairly straightforward exposure calculator consisting of sliding plates affixed to its backside) and look inside, you can't help noticing how crude-looking it is by comparison with the outside. Oh, the chrome pressure plate is nice and the film-guide rails are properly done, but that "quality look" is nevertheless absent.

Interestingly, the Signet was also produced in a black and olive-drab Army Signal Corps model which is worth considerably more than the $40-$50 you'll pay for a clean non-military model. Despite their mediocre shutters, all original-model Signets are fine picture takers, which is more than you can say for the plastic-bodied Signet 30, 40, 50 and 80 which followed them. Actually, the later Signets are not all that rotten (especially the highly-collectible model 80, which is the only leaf-shuttered interchangeable-lensed Kodak ever made in this country), but their Ektanar and Ektanon lenses are certainly eclipsed by the original Signet's unit-focusing Ektar.

Of course, the scale-focusing Kodak 35 also had offspring of sorts in the form of the well-known Kodak Pony series. These more modestly conceived 35's were manufactured in five distinct versions starting in 1950 and terminating in 1962. All were plastic-bodied cameras with front-element-focusing lenses, relatively simple shutters, and commendably bright viewfinders. The original model (1950-54) had an f/4.5 Anaston lens, Flash 200 shutter, and sold for $34.95; the model B (so marked) was basically the

same camera, but sold for a couple of bucks more (1953-55); and then came the odd Pony II (1957-1962), which had a better (four-element) 44mm f/3.5 Anastar lens but a single-speed shutter, scale focusing to 2½ ft., and an aperture ring calibrated in EV numbers (9-15) only.

Limited but lovable, this plastic Pony IV's optically satisfying, too.

My favorite Pony is the sleek-looking Pony IV (pictured) which was introduced in 1957 but went out of production before the Pony II (in 1961). Its 44mm f/3.5 Anastar lens is calibrated in f/stops and its conventional shutter buttom is nicer than the model II's plastic shutter-firing lever. It's also got shutter speeds of 1/30-1/250 sec. courtesy of its Flash 250 shutter, and it last sold for $43.95. The last of the Pony 35mm series was the fairly uncommon Model C (1955-58), which had an f/3.5 Anaston lens and Flash 300 shutter and sold for $32.75. And finally to eliminate a flood of letters, there was indeed a Pony 828 ($29.95) which, as its name implies took 828 roll film (providing a 28 x 40mm format) and was fitted with an f/4.5 Anaston lens in a Flash 200 shutter. While none of the Kodak Ponies has yet attained the status of a true collector's prize, and few seem destined to do so, they are nonetheless pleasant reminders that we once made some cheap, competent, "everyman's 35's" in this country. That, coupled with their more-than-adequate photographic performance (particularly the Anastar-lensed models) and their affordable prices ($15-$30), has finally extricated them from the bargain bin and placed them squarely in the camera showcase.

All in all, Kodak's 35's of the 50's illustrate what happens when a knowledgeable design team is saddled with the task of producing capable but "featureless" 35's. Still, they did try to compete, and whatever their failings, Kodak's "reasonably priced" 35's still had more "soul" per cc than their present assembly-line-produced pocketsized automatons.

15

The Sept: A French "still" 35 that made movies

Which French 35 antedates the Leica, takes and projects movies and stills? I'll give you seven guesses.

For some strange reason, the conventional wisdom regarding 35mm cameras has persistently accorded the Leica pioneer status as the world's first commercially successful 35mm still camera. Well, as many cameraphiles and collectors already know, it just ain't so. The American Tourist Multiple and (rare) Simplex, the Swiss Sico and French Sept were all capable of making still pictures on standard double-perforated 35mm motion-picture film (18x24mm cine frame format), and all antedated the 1924-25 introduction of Leitz's masterpiece, the first by over a decade, So while the Leica and its creator, Oskar Barnack, deserve our undying plaudits for establishing the 24x36mm format out of necessity and the first practical "minicam" by dint of brilliant engineering, first-still-35 laurels should probably go to an American (though precisely which American is a matter of some dispute).

Versatile, complicated, and very French.

Now the French, being a very proud and photographically oriented bunch, were hardly content to observe these newfangled, vertically oblong, hundreds-of-pictures-per-roll, still 35mm creations from across the pond—they were determined to create something better, or at least more versatile. And so it came to pass that, in 1922, the Societe' Francaise Sept of Paris unveiled the Sept, surely one of the most multi-faceted 35mm cameras of all time. If you think I'm overstating the case, just try to think of another 35, even a modern one, capable of taking 35mm movies as well as rapid-sequence still pictures, or one that can be operated as a contact printer, enlarger or projector as well! Diabolical eh? Perhaps that's why its maker, Etablissements Andre' Debris of Paris thought it appropriate to devise a logo consisting of a camera-wielding devil with his tail wrapped around the number "7" (spelled "sept" in French).

Sept logo?: Devil as cinematographer!

As you can see from its portrait, the Sept follows the then-established pattern of a vertically arrayed scale-focusing 35 with a separate optical finder. Also *de rigeur* for its time is its 250-exposure (on the 18x24mm format) film capacity, which also enables it to take 16-sec. (or so) motion-picture vignettes. Perhaps the severest limitation of the Sept's design is its single instantaneous shutter speed of around 1/60 sec.—fine for movies but a bit spartan for still shooting. Fortunately, the pictured model's 50mm f/3.5 Roussel Stylor (Paris) lens has apertures to f/32, which partially makes up for it, and this quite sharp uncoated lens also focuses to a closest marked distance of 4 ft.

As long as as we're raking this really very nice camera over the coals, we may as well get the final annoyance out of the way by stating that the Sept's viewfinder is a masterpiece of misplaced ingenuity. Look down through what looks like a conventional small reflex finder (top right) and you see a beautifully clear viewing image even after all these years. There's only one problem—it's upside-down because the front glass is the minus lens of a direct optical, alias Newtonian, viewfinder. Okay, now you get smart and pull a little tab which slides the front glass to the right of the camera body, and then pull the rear peepsight into place. *Voila*, you've got a direct vision finder all right, but its focusing point is such that you have to hold the camera 4 in. in front of your face to see a clear image. Oh well, at least the rest of the camera's execution is virtually flawless.

Open the Sept's left side (in shooting position) and you're greeted by two cassettes that look like enlarged Leica, Contax, Nikon or Canon items of the rangefinder 35 era. In concept, they're almost identical, too—their feltless light traps open by means of engaging tabs, but only when you turn two knobs on the outside of the (hopefully closed) camera body to the "open" position. Other interesting interior features are a hinged "pressure frame" in lieu of a pressure plate, a monumentally oversized sprocket wheel, large-diameter gears and a pawl to operate the 250-exposure counter (which reads out on the camera back), and directly behind the pressure frame, a square felt aperture.

If you close the camera (by sliding the locking tab on the left side to "closed") and direct your attention to the back of the camera, the purpose of the felt trap and open "pressure frame" becomes apparent. Directly above the exposure counter is a knurled round screw cap which, when removed, lets you install a light source behind this aperture for enlarging or projection. To do so, you've got

to open the shutter, of course, and for that purpose there's a knurled chrome lift-and-set ring on the side of the curved-top motor with settings marked "C" (continuous run), "I" (instantaneous still) and "P" (presumably "project"). The shutter release is a large lovely button emerging from the top of the spring motor unit. Press it down and leftward, and it pops up when released; push it down and to the right, and it locks in place in the down position. The "P" setting can thereby provide a "B" setting or a "T" setting for picture taking or projection.

Of course, describing the Sept's ingenious features is one thing; actually using the beast to make pictures is quite another. It's all brass body construction makes it weigh a heavy 4 lb. 4 oz. *sans* film, and while it's remarkably easy to hand-hold despite its ungainly shape, you'll need powerful digits to wind the spring motor. Incidentally, the motor (which came in two versions, the one shown being the heavy-duty round-topped job, as opposed to the original, less hefty, square-topped type) is easily detachable by means of three knurled screws on its side. This permits you to install the projection module conveniently.

Okay, let's open the cassettes, set the loaded camera on "C," and make a "moviette." The first thing you'll notice is that the Sept's rotary-sector shutter sets up a fearful racket, though any motor-induced vibration is easily damped by the camera's ample weight. You say you'd like to try a bit of slow motion? Easy, just take that small screwdriver out of your pocket and turn a little collared screw (marked "rapid") on the motor's side clockwise.

As you might imagine, the bench-assembled Sept was a rather costly item that debuted in the U.S. in 1923 at $225. However, the little devil made such a hit on these shores with pros and wealthy amateurs that production economies were introduced enabling it to be sold for a mere hundred bucks in 1928. Funny, while there are many Septs in operable condition still kicking around today

Movie style controls include crank, mode selector (right), frame counter (left).

Pressure "frame" and back are hinged.

17

among camera collectors, those beautifully made special plated brass cassettes are so rare, I've heard of a bunch of them which recently sold for more than the camera, which is itself worth about $200 (in good condition) to an interested collector. It's rather a shame, for, as I discovered, the Sept is an eminently usable classic even today, despite its ornery viewfinder and noisy motor.

For all its versatility, the Sept is a mediocre ("flickery") projector and a rather silly motion-picture camera. Nevertheless, it represents a remarkably integrated design for its day and its concepts of automatic spring-motor film advance, continuous run and rotary-sector shutter were destined to be combined with more compact Leica-like dimensions to form the redoubtable Robots, which are still with us, at least in surveillance trim.

Many thanks to Edward J. Szalkowski of Seven Hill, Ohio, for kindly furnishing the Sept pictured in (and "field tested" in conjunction with) this chapter. Without his generous cooperation this commentary wouldn't have been possible.

Modern's Photo Trivia Contest Questions

Enter MODERN's First Annual Photographic Trivia Contest and go pleasantly nuts competing for Schneider's prize bomb!

Fabulous Flexaret: A trivial grand prize?

And now, ladies and gentlemen, step right up to the First Annual Photo Trivia Contest—a competition so dia-

bolically insignificant that nobody, but nobody, is going to come up with every piece of photographic minutiae requested. Still, what's a contest without a prize—right? So, to the earliest postmarked entry with the largest number of correct answers, I will award my nice clean Flexaret VII (complete with leather case). While the Flexaret is neither so trivial nor weird as most of the following questions, I may as well inform you that it's a ghastly gray Czech-made twin-lens reflex that takes very nice pictures on 120 film and dates from about 1965. Oh yes, in the interest of preserving my sanity and preventing your writer's cramp, please don't repeat the question on your entries—numbers and answers will suffice. And now to your respective cogitation corners, and may the "nitpickiest" cameraphile win.

Photo Trivia Contest Questions

(Please note: Most of the following questions have simple factual answers, but, to separate the true "triviamaniacs" from the competent catalogers, some don't. Occasionally, more than one answer is correct, but fair warning; this is not often the case.)

1. (a) What is the oldest proprietary film developer still being sold? (b) When was it introduced?

2. What was 235 film?

3. What was Type F (Kodak designation) color film?

4. Which f/stop corresponds numerically to its equivalent U.S. (Uniform System) stop?

5. When were the following Kodak film-size designations introduced? (a) 110 (b) 126

6. What format is provided by a whole-plate camera?

7. (a) What famous American optical company made lenses for the Leica during and just after World War II? (b) Name two speed and focal-length combinations they offered at the time.

8. How could you get alternate black and clear frames on an entire roll of 35mm Kodacolor even though your camera was in perfect working order?

9. What does the "C" in Hasselblad 500C stand for?

10. Who in New York State can legally use Agfa Rodinal developer in the prescribed manner?

11. Name an Italian rangefinder camera with a non-interchangeable, collapsible, six-element f/2 normal-focal-length lens.

12. Name two five-element f/1.9 normal lenses that were fitted to full-frame 35mm cameras.

13. What is Pinakryptol green?

14. (a) What color is a Kodak Wratten Zero filter? (b) What is it used for?

15. Presuming 6x7cm to be the nominal "ideal format" these days, what was the very first ideal-format camera sold to the general public?

16. What is the manufacturer's listed format size for the most common version of the Micropress Technical camera?

17. What movie camera had a "self-timer" in which you inserted a card under a "finger" and waited for it to fall?

18. What year is ordinarily given as the birthdate of photography?

19. (a) What lens had a spinning blade in front of it? (b) What was its purpose?

20. Which discontinued TLR had the numbers on its Compur shutter-speed ring engraved in mirror image?

21. What's the rarest and most expensive lens to be found on a Voigtländer Bessa II?

22. Which 35mm slide projector has a straight tray which automatically reset itself to "start"?

23. (a) Which lens was supplied for the original Leitz Valoy enlarger? (b) How was it calibrated?

24. Name four watch companies that got involved in manufacturing or selling photographic equipment.

25. Which 35mm developing tank takes the least amount of solution?

26. What was the name of the first negative-positive photographic process?

27. What was the speed of the fastest photographic lens in general use prior to 1850?

28. (a) What was the original name of the Graflex Co.? (b) What major SLR-mechanism patent did they hold?

29. (a) Which 35mm SLR had the first instant-return mirror? (b) Which had the first pentaprism?

30. With which 35mm SLR's would it be conceivable to mistakenly take a picture with the lens cap on?

31. What 35mm SLR was first made in Italy and later in Lichtenstein?

32. What is a Purma camera and why is it so special?

33. What was the name and focal length of the Optika IIa's normal lens? (Hint: It is a 2¼x3¼-format Japanese SLR of the early 60's.)

34. (a) Which emulsions in what classic roll-film sizes bit the dust in 1976? (b) Name the sole, larger-than- 2½-in.-wide paper-backed roll film being offered by Kodak *after* 1976.

35. Which companies offer or offered the following *interchangeable* lens speeds and focal lengths. And what were the names of the lenses? 35mm f/3.2; 21mm f/3.3; 50mm f/2.2; 55mm f/3; 60mm f/1.2; 60mm f/1.5; 70mm f/2; 75mm f/3.8; 100mm f/3.4; 100mm f/4.2; 105mm f/6.3; 28mm f/5.6; 30mm f/4; 37.5mm f/2.8; 40mm f/1.9; 45mm f/1.5.

36. Which cameras were fitted with the following non-interchangeable optical oddities, and what were their names? 50mm f/2.4; 44mm f/3.5; 114mm f/4.5; 26mm f/9.5; 42mm f/2; 35mm f/2; 47mm f/8; 50mm f/3.9; 60mm f/3.5; 75mm f/3.8; 50mm f/2.5; 170mm f/6.3; 100mm f/1.8; 40mm f/1.9; 15mm f/3.5; 163mm f/7.9; 25mm f/3.5; 35mm f/1.7.

37. Which camera companies originated the following trademarks? Brownie, Hawkeye, Match-matic, Vacublitz, Pergrano.

38. (a) What's the slowest Kodak emulsion currently available? (b) What is its nominal ASA rating?

39. (a) Which Exakta deserves the title of "late 30's low-light champ?" (b) What was its nickname, and what was its lens?

40. Name two flash sync devices you could've fitted to your new Leica IIIC.

41. What did the Leicas made for the German Air Force during World War II say on them to prove it? (b) What were two additional identification points?

42. What famous early-focal-plane shutter rangefinder 35 pioneered the non-rotating shutter-speed dial?

43. What was the top marked shutter speed on the American made Mercury 1 half-frame 35?

44. How many frames did a short roll of 35mm film have prior to World War II?

45. Which famous 35mm camera could be made into a twin-lens reflex? (b) How?

46. What was an Essenkay adapter?

47. What happened if you inserted a flashbulb into your Kalart-Flash-Synchronizer-equipped flashgun without winding the synchronizer?

48. Name two twin-lens reflexes with focal-plane shutters.

49. Which folding roll-film camera incorporated parallax-compensating frames in the viewfinder which also corrected for field size?

50. What was the first camera fitted with an electronically controlled shutter?

52. What is the difference between a cartridge and a cassette?

53. Why did Railway Express Co. refuse to ship factory-loaded, original-model Kodak cameras to and from Rochester, N.Y.?

54. What was the first aperture-preferred, auto-exposure still camera and what was unique about its auto-exposure system?

55. Which folding rangefinder roll-film camera focused by moving the film place rather than the lens? Name two other cameras that focused the same way.

56. What was the lousiest lens ever fitted to a Rolleiflex TLR?

57. Name two single-lens reflex roll-film cameras with front-element-focusing lenses.

58. What was the fastest lens you could have obtained for your Leica in 1937 (without special adaptations)?

59. Name a twin-lens reflex with built-in motor drive.

60. Identify the first smaller-than-half-frame-format, single-lens reflex camera offered for sale.

Rollei Classics, both two- and three-lensed

A gaggle of two- and three-lensed Rollei classics, including the legend of how the Rolleiflex got its shape!

If you just can't resist the temptation to ogle at a collection of classic Rollei cameras under glass, one of the better places in the U.S. to do so is at Rollei of America's new headquarters in Fairfield, N.J. In fact, I recently had the privilege of being escorted around their neo-Bauhaus premises by none other than ROA's president. Fred Weitz, who was kind enough to unlock a few of the display cabinets containing the company's choicest photographic treasures.

As many of you are aware, the original 1929 Rolleiflex twin-lens reflex was designed and produced by Franke & Heidecke of Braunschweig, Germany. But few collectors know that Paul Franke was the businessman and his partner, Reinhold Heidecke, the engineering genius (whose name is enshrined in the Heidoscop viewing lenses found on virtually every twin-lens Rollei ever made). Another arcane bit of Rollei lore is that their twin-lens reflex roll-film camera—by far the firm's most famous product—was not their first camera. That honor (in 1921) belongs to the stereo Heidoscop (pictured), which was offered in 45x107mm and 6x13cm sizes and featured an f/4.5 Tessar taking lenses (ours are 50mm) and a pair of specially developed, pneumatically timed leaf shutters with speeds of 1-1/300 sec. plus B.

Revolutionary Rolleiflex of late 20's was first successful roll-film TLR.

Still used by some pros, Heidoscop stereo was first Rollei-made camera.

20

Engineering similarities found in both the Heidoscop and later Rollei TLR's include a mirror placed at a 45° angle behind the viewing lens (which, in the Heidoscop, sat smack in the middle of the taking lenses) and a flip-up viewing hood fitted with hinged built-in magnifier. Incidentally, the lever above the middle lens cocked the shutter, the knurled wheel over the left lens set both iris diaphragms, the knob to the right of the right lens was for setting shutter speeds, the knob placed symmetrically on the left was for focusing, and the shutter-release button was atop the right lens and slightly to the right. The Heidoscop is clearly a superbly integrated design, extremely well-made, and quite rare these days despite its continuing popularity among a small group of professional stereo slide makers. Would you believe that the current collectors' value of the camera pictured is about $700? Oh well, the larger (6x13cm) version is a bit scarcer and therefore fetches about $1,000 per copy.

But perhaps your taste runs to the original "Rollei" Rollei—to wit, the Rolleidoscop of about 1925, which looks suspiciously like the Heidoscop except for its rounded ends and hinged triple lens cap. Aside from producing 2.2-in. pairs of stereo images on 120 roll film, its operation is quite similar, too (note the disposition of the shutter-speed and focusing knobs). However, its paired f/4.5 Tessar lenses are 55mm instead of 50mm and its current collectors' value is $700, down from its $800 price tag of a few years ago.

So long as we've presented a brace of three-lensed Rollei creations, I thought I'd cater to the many Franke and Heidecke fans in the audience by including portraits of the original models of the two twin-lens stalwarts—the Rolleiflex and the Rolleicord—but first a legend entitled "How the classic Rollei got its shape." It seems that back in 1928, when Franke and Heidecke were mere upstarts among camera manufacturers and merrily producing small quantities of Heidoscops and Rolleidoscops, one of their brilliant (unnamed) engineers got a brainstorm. Why not saw a Rolleidoscop in thirds and place the viewing lens on top of one of the taking lenses?

Why not, indeed, and that's exactly what he proceeded to do. The resulting lash-up (details of the film-transport mechanism have not come down to us, but it must have presented quite a problem!) so pleased Messrs. F and H that they promptly hopped aboard Franke's motorcycle and drove to the Photo Lange camera shop in Braunschweig where they showed off their new prototype. Herr Lange, the proprietor, was sufficiently impressed with the fledgling design to order five "Rolleiflexes" on the spot—and so began one of the longest running and most successful camera designs in history. Parenthetically, this original Rolleiflex was emphatically not the first focusing twin-lens reflex, but *was* the earliest TLR to use paper-backed roll film

The 1929 Flex (pictured) features a very early rim-set Compur shutter with speeds of 1-1/300 sec. plus T and B, a 75mm f/3.8 Tessar taking lens and a 75mm f/3.1 Heidoscop-Anastigmat viewing lens. Beautifully constructed but

Who put the "roll" in Rollei? It was this elegant stereo Rolleidoscop!

Prettiest Rollei ever? I'll give my vote to this original 1931 Rolleicord despite its so-so Triotar lens.

spartan, the original Rolleiflex had a manually cocked shutter, "ruby window" frame counter, dismal focusing image and cable-release holder on the front panel. Incidentally, it's the only Rollei designed to take long-gone 117 film—basically, six exposures of 2½-in. wide—120 film on a narrower spool. And despite its obvious landmark status, the original Rollei TLR is worth only about $200 among collectors.

Turning now to my personal nomination for the snazziest Rollei ever, we have the original diamond-pattern-finish Rolleicord of 1931. Beneath its "art-deco" exterior is the Rolleicord we know and love with its familiar side-to-side-action shutter-cocking/shutter-release lever and standard Rollei control layout. True, the 75mm f/4.5 Triotar (triplet) lens is no match for the Tessar, the 'Cord's viewing image is typically prewar (adequate in the center and rotten at the edges), and there's no automatic film stop. However, like all Rolleis, even the earliest Rolleicord is a usable classic with a convenient (120 roll-film), film supply and decent, if not outstanding, photographic performance. While this user-collector would ordinarily lean toward the Rolleiflex's superior optics, I must admit to having a soft spot for that natty first Rolleicord—at this point, I might even shell out the necessary $100-150 to acquire a clean one.

While all these old Rolleis of the 20's and 30's are mechanically, aesthetically and optically impressive, seasoned collectors will immediately notice one peculiar fact—they're not super-valuable considering what they are. For example, a Leica produced in as limited quantity as a 6x13 Heidoscop would bring $3,000 not $700, and even such an obvious landmark as the original Rollei TLR only fetches a "C-note." As more than one expert has remarked to me, "There's basically no market for old Rolleis, and I can't understand why." The implicit message to would-be Rollei collectors is clear; now's the time to grab 'em. And for you Rollei fanciers lamenting over the lack of four-figure prices, be on the lookout for the super-rare 9x9cm Rollei which made 3¼x3¼-in. images on 122 roll film and looks like a giant Rollei 2¼ TLR. Its current price: A cool two grand.

Modern's Photo Trivia Contest Answers

Nitpicker's delight: Answers to all the questions in MODERN's First Annual Photographic Trivia Contest!

All you photographic triviamaniacs who've waited patiently on tenterhooks as I meandered over ancient Rollei lore can now relax. Here at last are the answers to all 60 of those magnificently insignificant, occasionally tricky questions posed in MODERN's First Annual Photographic Trivia Contest. You'll have to wait to find out who won the fabulous Flexaret (TLR) prize, but I've at least had the foresight to include the original question in the answers that follow. To all who entered, best of luck; and to the rest, I hope you find that following meaningless minutiae fascinating.

Ask a trivial question, and . . .

1. (a) The oldest proprietary (i.e., brand name) developer still being sold is Agfa Rodinal. (b) It was introduced in 1891.

2. Kodak's 235 film designation referred to a paper-wrapped "daylight load" of 35mm film designed to fit Contax (rangefinder model) cassettes. It's long discontinued.

3. Type F (Kodak designation) refers to transparency film balanced for clear flashbulbs (discontinued).

4. The only f/stop that corresponds to its U.S. system equivalent is "16".

5. (a) The original 110 film size (5-in.-wide roll film providing 5x4-in. negatives) was introduced by Kodak in 1898. (b) The original 126 (providing 4¼x6½-in. negs) debuted in 1906. Both are long gone.

6. The format provided by a whole plate camera is 6½x8½ in. Cameras of this type were most popular in the late 19th century.

7. (a) Wollensak is the famous American optical company that made Leica screw-thread lenses during World War II. (b) They offered a 50mm f/3.5, 50mm f/2.8 (rare), 90mm f/4.5 and 127mm f/4.5

8. You can get alternate black and clear frames on an entire roll of Kodacolor (or most other films) even though your camera is working properly by mistakenly leaving the shutter set on "T".

9. The "C" in Hasselblad 500C stands for Compur, that little ol' shutter maker.

10. In New York state, only qualified medical personnel (such as medical doctors and registered nurses) and diabetics can use Rodinal developer in the prescribed way. This requires a hypodermic syringe and needle, which are illegal to possess in New York unless you're one of the above.

11. The only Italian rangefinder 35 I can think of with a collapsible six-element f/2 lens is the Galileo Condor of the 50's, which was fitted with a 50mm f/2 Eliog.

12. Two five-element f/1.9 normal lenses fitted to full-frame 35mm cameras are the 58mm f/1.9 Meyer Primotar (in Praktica/Pentax mount) and the 45mm f/1.9 Hexanon found on the Konica auto S2. There are others, too.

13. Pinakryptol Green is a desensitizing agent added to the developer prior to inspecting partially developed black-and-white negatives in the darkroom. It was most popular in the late 30's.

14. (a) A Kodak Wratten Zero filter is basically a clear gel. (b) It is used as a dummy filter, for example, in setting up scientific apparatus where the focus point is quite critical and would be altered slightly if a filter were later added to the system.

15. The first 6x7cm or "ideal format" camera offered to the general public was the original Omega 120 press camera.

16. The manufacturer's listed size for the commonest Micropress Technical camera is 5x4 in. It's an English beast, and the convention over there is to list the larger dimension first.

17. The movie camera with a "dropping card" self-timer signal was the Zeiss Movikon 16, a deluxe German movie camera of the 30's.

18. The year ordinarily given as the birthdate of photography is 1839, the date of the earliest surviving daguerreotype.

19. (a) The lens with the spinning blade in front of it is the famous old Goerz Hypergon extreme wide angle. (b) The blade's purpose was to even out the exposure across the field, compensating mechanically for the inevitable light falloff due to the "cosine to the fourth power" law.

20. The discontinued TLR with its Compur shutter number engraved in mirror image is the well-known Voightänder Superb of the 30's with its tilting, parallax-compensating viewing lens. The numbers on the flat shutter scale were reflected upwards (for convenient chest-level viewing) by means of a little prism, so they had to be engraved in reverse.

21. The rarest and most expensive lens found on Voightländer Bessa II's is the 105mm f/4.5 Apo-Lanthar.

22. The straight-tray 35mm slide projector which reset the tray to "start" automatically was the Kodak Cavalcade Repeater.

23. (a) The lens supplied for the original Leitz Valoy enlarger was the 50mm f/3.5 Varob. (b) It was calibrated in an odd sequence of arbitrary numbers; to wit, 1, 2, 4, 6 and 10.

Photographic watches?

24. Among the watch companies that got involved in making or selling photographic equipment (I asked for four) were: Jaeger Le Coultre (Compass camera makers), Seikosha (Seiko shutters), Citizen (also watch and shutter makers), Wittnauer (of cine twin fame), Bulova (onetime importers of 8mm movie cameras) and Ricoh.

25. The 35mm developing tanks that take the least amount of solution (1⅓ oz.) are those in which the cartridge itself is immersed. Among these are the Sigeel, also

marketed as the Brooks Pixmat and currently sold by Porter's Camera Store.

26. The first negative-positive process was the Talbotype (also known as Calotype), patented by Fox Talbot in 1841.

27. The fastest photographic lens in general use prior to 1850 was the Petzval Portrait lens which (depending on focal length) provided apertures up to f/3.6.

28. (a) The original name of the Graflex Co. was Folmer & Schwing. (b) The major SLR-mechanism patent they held (and allowed to lapse) covered the automatic lens diaphragm (actually a semi-automatic type by today's standards, since you had to cock it).

29. (a) The first 35mm SLR with an instant-return mirror was the Asahiflex (1955). (b) The first 35mm SLR with a pentaprism finder was the Contax D (1949-50).

30. It would be possible to accidentally take a picture with the lens cap on using the following SLR's fitted with auxiliary direct optical finders: the original model Alpa 4 (also sold as the Bolsey Reflex), and the Praktina FX and Asahiflex I's and II's.

31. The only 35mm SLR (or camera, for that matter) first made in Italy—later in Lichtenstein—was the Rectaflex.

32. A Purma camera is a small English roll-film camera of the 30's which changes shutter speeds depending on which way you hold it for shooting!

33. The normal lens furnished on the Optika IIa roll-film SLR was a 105mm f/3.5 Musashino Koki Luminant. During the course of its production, the name was changed to just plain Luminon.

34. Classic emulsions and sizes that bit the dust in '76 were Verichrome Pan 116 and 616. The only wider-than-2¼-in. paper-backed roll films offered by Kodak after '76 are Kodacolor II 116 and 616. Note: The original question implied that only one such film is being offered after '76.

35. Interchangeable lenses in speeds and focal lengths requested are as follows; 35mm f/3.2 Canon (screw mount for rfdr.), 21mm f/3.3 Yashinon for Yashica SLR's, 50mm f/2.2 Takumar (early Pentax), 55mm f/3 Quantaray Macro lens (current), 60mm f/1.2 Fujinon in Leica screw thread, 60mm f/1.5 Zuiko for Olympus Pen FT, 70mm f/2 Zuiko for Olympus Pen FT, 75mm f/3.8 Tele-Xenar for Robot, 100mm f/3.4 Dynarex for Voigtländer Vitessa T, 100mm f/4.2 Anticomar for Plaubel Makina, 105mm f/6.3 Elmar for Leica (30's), 28mm f/6.3 Hektor for Leica screw thread, 28mm f/5.6 Hektor for Leica screw thread 30mm f/4 Xenogon for screw-thread Robot, 37.5mm f/2.8 Tessar for screw-thread Robot, 40mm f/1.9 Xenon ditto, and 45mm f/1.5 Coral for Aires V.

On to the fixed optics

36. Herewith the non-interchangeable optical oddities and the cameras they're permanently attached to: 50mm f/2.4 Colinar on Arco 35, 44mm f/3.5 Ektar on Kodak Signet, 114mm f/4.5 Tominon on Polaroid 180, 26mm f/9.5 "no-name" on Kodak Pocket Instamatic 20, 42mm f/2 (or f/1.8) Zuiko on Olympus Auto, 35mm f/2 Zuiko on Olympus Wide S, 47mm f/8 Super Angulon on Brooks

Veriwide, 50mm f/3.9 Anaston on Kodak Pony 828, 60mm f/3.5 Xenar on Rolleiflex 4x4, 75mm f/3.8 Tessar on many old Rolleis, 50mm f/2.5 Hektor in Leica screw-thread or Nikkor on Nikkorex 35 (original model), 170mm f/6.3 B & L Tessar on 3A Kodak Special, 100mm f/1.8 (or f/2) Ernostar on Ermanox of 20's, 40mm f/1.9 Highkor on Lord 5D, 15mm f/3.5 Complan on Minox, 163mm f/7.9 Kodar on 3A Kodaks, 25mm f/3.5 "no-names" on Viewmaster Personal stereo 35, and 35mm f/1.7 Rikenon on Ricoh Auto Half SL (not imported to U.S.).

37. The companies that originated the trademarks listed are as follows: Brownie, Eastman Kodak Co.; Hawkeye, Blair Camera Co. (later taken over by EK); Matchmatic, Argus (late version of C3); Vacublitz, Osram (Germany); Pergrano, Perutz (Germany) for slow film.

38. The slowest emulsion listed in Kodak's scientific film catalog (P-315) is a super-high-resolution glass plate, Type 649-F. Its nominal meter setting value is ASA .02!

39. The "low light" Exakta of the 30's was a black-body version of the model B vest-pocket Exakta which took 127 roll film. It was fitted with a 75mm f/2 Biotar and nicknamed the "Nacht (night) Exakta."

40. Two flash sync devices you could have fitted to your new Leica IIIC are the Geiss Kontakt and Hakosyn synchronizer.

41. (a) German World War II air force Leicas were (mostly) engraved "Luftwaffen Eigentum" (property of the Luftwaffe). (b) Additional identification points were gray enamel finish and K on red shutter curtain.

42. The famous early (focal-plane-shuttered) 35mm rangefinder camera that pioneered the non-rotating shutter-speed dial was the Contessa-Nettel.

43. The Mercury I 35's top marked shutter speed was 1/1500 sec.

44. Prior to World War II, a short roll of 35mm film had but 18 exposures.

45. (a) The famous 35mm camera that could be made into a twin-lens reflex was the screw-mount Leica (many models), although the Japanese Arco 35 of the 50's could also be adapted. (b) The Leica was transformed into a TLR by fitting it with a De Mornay-Budd reflex finder.

46. An Essankay adapter allowed you to use your Korelle Reflex with 828 roll film.

Zap your digits with a bulb?

47. If you were foolish enough to insert a flashbulb into your Kalart Synchronizer-equipped flashgun without winding the thing, the bulb went off in your hand!

48. Two twin-lens reflex cameras with focal-plane shutters were the Contax 35mm TLR and the Fothflex, both of the late 30's.

49. The only folding roll-film camera with parallax-compensating finder frames which also adjusted for field size was the Konica Pearl IV of 1958.

50. The first camera on the market with silicon blue cells was the Fujica ST 701.

51. The first (production) still camera with an electronically controlled shutter was the Polaroid 900 (1960).

52. The difference between a cartridge and a cassette *in terms of photography* is nonexistent. The terms are well nigh interchangeable when applied to either standard 35mm or super 8 "film containers."

53. Legend has it that Railway Express Co. once refused to ship original model No. 1 Kodak cameras to and from Rochester when a few of their freight cars containing them blew up! Why? The film base (1890's) was highly explosive cellulose nitrate.

54. The first aperture-preferred auto-exposure still camera sold was the Agfa Automatic 66, which featured the novelty of pneumatically controlled speeds.

55. One folding rangefinder roll-film camera that featured film-plane focusing was the Mamiya Six. Other cameras that focused the same way were the Richard Verascope and the Revere, both stereo 35's.

56. By general consensus, the lousiest lens ever fitted to the Rolleiflex TLR was the 80mm f/2.8 Tessar of 1949.

57. Two roll-film SLR's with front-element focusing were the Pilot 6 of the 30's and the 127-format Komaflex-S of the 60's.

58. The fastest lens you could have bought for your Leica in 1937 was the 50mm f/1.5 Schneider Xenon.

59. The only TLR with built-in motor drive is the current Tessina (gotcha!)

60. The first (and probably the only) smaller-than-half-frame SLR still camera is the Russian Narcissus 16mm.

Kodak's 828:
Sic Transit Gloria Mundi

The transient glory of 828, Kodak's mass-market-oriented scheme to banish the 35's rewind knob forever.

While I'm still in the midst of mulling over many a

quaint and curious Trivia Contest entry (the official winner will be announced later), it seems as good a time as any to hold forth on one my favorite weird formats—the one known affectionately as Bantam size and, more clinically, as 828 roll film. Now, before the knowledgeable among us start to snicker at Kodak's Great Commercial Folly or make wry comments about EK's solicitude in supplying its small but devoted band of followers with no less than four different emulsion types as late as 1975, let's look at it from the Jolly Yellow Giant's point of view.

It's 1935 and out of the depths of the Great Depression emerges this cinematic refugee known as 35mm still film. It's beginning to make commercial inroads despite the fact that you can't even buy it in commercially loaded cartridges. So you ask youself why, and you come up with a few logical explanations. First of all, with the 24x36mm format of 35mm you can obviously make smaller cam-

Elegance personified: Kodak Bantam Special of '41 was entirely U.S.-made.

eras—minicams they're called and they're all the rage. Sprocketed film also permits you to dispense with ye olde red window without complex film length measuring mechanisms, and the short focal lengths of 35mm camera lenses allow relatively wide apertures and/or increased depth-of-field.

Engagingly petite: Kodak's Flash Bantam of late 40's had Tessar-type lens.

So far so good, but there are a few snags. If these minuscule 35mm cameras are ever going to appeal to the average snapshooter, as well as the photographic hobbyist, you've got to offer convenient film loading; and that doesn't mean unwrapping a "daylight load" of 35mm film and inserting it into a special cartridge in the darkroom. Besides, 18 or 36 exposures are too many—you're liable to wind up with Christmas and Easter pictures on the same roll with the inevitable substandard results. Such must have been some of the thoughts running around the brains of Kodak's technical geniuses back in the mid-30's. And while their resulting plan to create a limitless amateur market based on 35mm and capture it for Kodak proved to be illusory, it was nevertheless brilliant.

To make a long tale shorter, in 1935 Kodak decided to take the plunge. They sliced 35mm-wide unperforated motion-picture stock into short lengths, perforated it once every 43mm along the top edge, and furnished it in tiny 8-exposure rolls of paper-backed 828 roll film. Thus, they gave the amateur a pocketable camera with a film-loading system and number of exposures-per-roll he was used to and, at the same time, relegated the red window to the role of an auxiliary frame counter (on most models, at any rate).

What a tab can do

This latter feat was ingeniously accomplished by cutting a slot into the top of the paper backing (just before the first frame) which allows a knife-edged forked tab affixed to the camera back to slip in and directly contact the upper edge of the film from the back. A small metal finger attached next to the film-wind shaft simultaneously engages the perforations from the other side, providing automatic first-frame positioning and automatic film stop for all subsequent frames on the roll. The genius of this system is that it required only a couple of inexpensive parts to produce these "modern" features. Of course, it meant that you had to push a little button on the back of your Bantam to disengage the trapped sprocket before you wound to the next frame.

A Depression cheapie: Bantam F8 of '36 has pop-out lens, mostly plastic body.

Unfortunately, I was unable to obtain an original 1935 Kodak Bantam—the one with the f/12.5 doublet lens—for this column, but I did latch onto its reasonably close relative, the 1938 Kodak Bantam F8 (pictured). Like all Kodak Bantams, the F8 (named after the speed of its lens, natch) produces eight 28 x 40mm images per roll. You can tell it's a cheapie by noting its mostly plastic construction, flip-up glassless frame finder, and pop-out front panel containing the only 40mm f/8 Kodalinear lens I've ever seen. Like most Bantams, it has a removable back, and you can't fire the single-speed Everset shutter until you press in a tab allowing the front to pop out.

Since the F8 lacks the usual scissors struts and mini-bellows folding system, perhaps you're wondering how it collapses. Look through the open back and pop it out to shooting position and you'll see the darndest looking coiled steel spring directly in front of the film aperture placed concentrically around the rear lens element! The F8 is modest all right, but rather rare, which is why I'd peg this one at about $40 today.

However lukewarm the public's reaction to Kodak's Bantams proved to be, they were a rather long-running act (1935-1957) and obviously went through several generations. I'll, therefore, skim over my 1938 Bantam with the 50mm f/5.6 Kodak Anastigmat lens, mentioning only that it's the sole model I've seen which has its film-advance knob on the bottom and loads left to right. Much nicer, in my opinion, is the Kodak Flash Bantam made 10 years later. Though some may disagree, I'd say that this model, and the f/4.5 Bantam (with the angular ends) that preceded it, are the finest examples of "Bantamry," the super deluxe Kodak Bantam Special notwithstanding. Let's take a closer look at the flash synced model (pictured).

In small packages comes . . .

A nattily attired little fellow finished in black enamel, brushed alloy, and good quality leatherette, the Flash Bantam's lensboard pops out on spring-loaded stainless steel struts placed above and below its tiny bellows. This reveals a shutter-cocking tab on top and exposes an ASA flash contact on the right side of the front section (in shooting position). Presuming the camera's loaded, you now flip up the folding optical finder (decent but not exceptional) and direct your attention to the camera's exposure and focusing controls, all of which are grouped fairly conveniently around the lens. The lens itself is a 48mm f/4.5 Kodak Anastar, a coated front-cell-focusing Tessar-type optic with apertures to f/16 and focusing down to 2½ ft. (Actually the selfsame optic in uncoated form and labelled Kodak Anastigmat Special debuted on the previous non-flash f/4.5 Bantam.) Shutter speeds cover a modest 1/25-1/200 sec. range plus the usual T and B.

Now, from these bald technical specifications, you might conclude that, barring its nice finish and styling for an American camera, the "FB" is nothing to get too excited over. And yet these little gems which recently sold for as

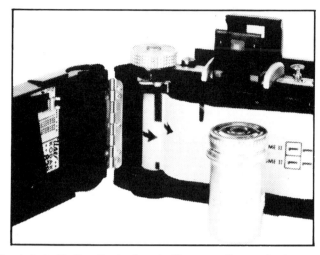

Simple but effective: Bantam's auto film stop relies on slot in paper backing (to left of film cam), knife-edged fork (to left of hinge) and a sprocket-locating finger (under film wind knob).

little as $10-$12 are now fetching $60-$75 even though finding film for them is virtually impossible. Why? Well, you might say that they were the Rollei or Minox 35's of their day.

To conclude the Kodak Bantam saga, what more glorious note to end on than Kodak's fabulous Bantam Special, first introduced (with uncoated f/2 Ektar Anastigmat lens in Compur-Rapid shutter) in 1936. The specific object of our adulation is the all-American Bantam Special of 1941 which has a coated(!) 45mm f/2 Ektar and Kodak's very own Supermatic No. 0 shutter with speeds of 1-1/400 sec., T and B. No matter which model it is, the Bantam Special is a Yankee tour de force—the kind of dream camera every box-Brownie-toting lad hoped some day to own.

Without a doubt, at least part of the Bantam Special's appeal was due to its elegant art deco appearance—would you believe finely applied jet black cloisonné in a horizontally-striped pattern? Even folded, its chunky shape has grace.

Fortunately for the well-heeled folks who plunked down $116.75 (with case) to own one in 1941, the Special was not all promise and no performance. It was fitted with a superbly bright coupled (but separate) split-image rangefinder with a long 1¾ in. base length and a whopping 8X magnification which remains unsurpassed even today. And while the Ektar lens is a bit soft at maximum aperture (or at the camera's 3 ft. minimum focusing distance) by modern standards, it's still a creditable performer at more common f/stop and distance settings.

In a way it's almost carping to subject the chic Bantam Special to any criticism. There were, indeed, few cameras in its day that could outperform it as a picture-taking machine and even fewer that did so with as much style. It stands as a monument to Kodak's perseverance with their brilliant but disappointing film size, and it's a collector's item *par excellence* currently valued at around $200 in decent condition.

Non-Kodak 828 roll-film cameras

Kodak's 828 cameras may have been a sales flop, but that didn't stop others from joining the fray.

We left little doubt that Kodak's brilliant "35mm roll film" concept, also known as the 828 or Bantam format, was not exactly an unqualified sales success. However, this hardly meant that the rest of the world's camera makers thought likewise at the time. Indeed, bunches (if not exactly hordes) of cameras accepting 828 roll film were produced by various manufacturers from the mid-30's well into the 50's. Furthermore, the Germans, English and Japanese got into the act as well as as numerous American camera producers. This month we'll stick with the Yanks and the Japanese.

Pepsodent toothpaste users of the early 40's sent in their boxtops and 15 cents to get this plastic disaster called a Cub.

Interestingly, many of these Bantam-sized 828-format creations are quite rare. Why? The vast majority of them were undistinguished box cameras with simple lenses and few adjustments to speak of. As a result, they were cast into various trash bins by owners and dealers alike who felt they weren't worth the trouble to resurrect or sell. But this doesn't necessarily make old non-Kodak 828 roll film cameras super-valuable, since the demand for them is presently as low (or lower) than the supply. In the long run, the prices of many of these "junk-tiques" are likely to rise dramatically, and folks like John Kowalak and Simon Marino, who furnished this month's quintet, will cash in.

As long as I've brought up the subject of "junk," let's present for your delectation what is undoubtedly the cheapest, most miserable camera ever to grace this column—the Cub, a late 30's product of the American Advertising and Research Corp. of Chicago. No, you couldn't run down to your neighborhood camera store to purchase one of these cheapies since the Cub is what was known as a "premium camera." In short, if you were gullible or foolish enough to want one of these gems, you bought a tube of Pepsodent toothpaste and sent in carton, along with fifteen cents, to get one! (Actually, "premium cameras" made for, or modified by, advertisers are still popular and rate a column on their own.)

What you got was an all-plastic (except for the shutter) disaster with a glassless frame finder, red window film-advance system, and with a single, instantaneous-shutter-speed setting. The removable back was so badly made that it barely fits the camera, and the red-knurled-plastic film-advance knob is no model of precision either. But at least the everset shutter still works and the single-glass meniscus lens is no worse than others of its type. For rescuing this photographic waif from the incinerator, John Kowalak has the satisfaction of owning a really rare Bantam-format camera, currently worth about ten bucks (since he's got the original instruction leaflet).

Sleekly styled but spartan, the Argus Minca was a box camera pure and simple.

Most American-made non-Kodak 828 cameras share one feature—or rather, lack of feature. They don't have Kodak's patented automatic-film-stop system. In other words, you've got to use ye olde red window. However, not all the cameras were as chintzy as the Cub. Take the Argus Minca, alias Camro (for the foreign market). The

Where have you seen a Camro before! See picture of its twin, the Minca.

Minca 28 is a pleasant 1940's creation that's nicely finished in bakelite-type plastic with alloy trim. Its lens is a 47mm f/9.7 Lumar, a doublet, and its interlens-everset shutter has two speeds. I (about 1/25 sec.) and T (which actually operates as B).

The Minca/Camro's optical viewfinder is decent but unexceptional, and both versions (which are identical except for the nameplates) have three aperture settings atop the lens barrel—to wit "Bright, Cloudy, and Color." These are controlled, Kodak-Brownie fashion, by a metal plate behind the front lens which has three different-sized perforations. Oh well, at least both members of this pedestrian pair are nicely styled, incorporate standard ¼-in. tripod sockets on their bottoms and reputedly take decent pictures. Like most Kodak Bantams the backs are removable, and their scarcity has finally been rewarded by a collector's price of around $25-35, irrespective of the nameplate affixed.

Regrettably, I was unable to latch onto any German or British 828's to regale you with, but I did find two very curious Japanese creations of the 1950's which are so weird they almost make up for it. Take the Museflex for example, a camera so rare it's not even pictured in the Japanese camera catalogs. Our Model M is an early 50's disaster bearing the legend "Muse Optical, Tokyo Japan." Although shaped like a twin-lens reflex, it's really a non-focusing box camera with shutter-speed settings of Instantaneous and B, and Waterhouse-style apertures of f/5.6, 6.3, and 8. These settings are controlled by twin-knurled knobs placed below the taking lens on either side. Aside from a dismal viewing image and a PC flash contact to the right of the lenses, the Museflex has two fascinating features—a peculiar 27x27mm square format on 828 film, and the darndest automatic film stop you ever saw. This latter device operates in conjunction with an ordinary knurled film-advance knob on the camera's right side, which turns the same number of degrees each time (whence it is stopped by a spring-loaded catch built into the camera). While this curious system results in a wider space between succeeding frames as you move along the roll, at

Classical in name only, the Museflex was a glorified Japanese box camera of the 50's.

It looks pretty good, but the Ebony Deluxe IIS was a toylike, tinny box camera.

least it eliminates the necessity of glancing at the red window each time. However, one thing it doesn't eliminate is the possibility of multiple exposures—you *can* fire the Museflex as many times as you like on the same frame. While the Museflex is sufficiently rare that there's no established collector's price, I'd peg its value at $40-60 at present.

Finally, we present the cute-but-spartan Ebony Deluxe 35 of the 50's which, like the Museflex, features a curved film plane. A metal and plastic non-focusing box-type camera, the Ebony IIS (was there a model I?) sports a 50mm f/8 Hoei lens with Waterhouse-type f/8 and f/11 apertures, an everset I and B shutter, and a PC flash con-

tact. Interestingly, the Ebony incorporates a threaded collar below the shutter-release button, a la Nikon and Leica! If this fails to impress, how about a hinged back, mediocre optical finder and an accessory shoe?

Crummy it may well be, but the little Ebony has its points. Like the Museflex, it's got a sliding cover for the rear window and—surprise of surprises, the leather case furnished with this tinny toylike creation is made of real leather and resembles the case sold with the super-deluxe Nagel-Kodak Pupille. Again, we're really in the dark as to its true worth, but I'll bet you can pay $25-30 for an Ebony with case should you stumble across one in your travels.

Trivia Contest Winner gets his trivial prize—plus some British classics

A winner announced, his peculiar prize described, and a brief foray into the realm of British classics.

To all those loyal readers who've been waiting with bated breath as I pondered over many a quaint and curious Photo Trivia Contest entry, I announce with pride that we've finally got a winner. He's none other than Robert Des Verney of the Bronx (N.Y.), the sole entrant out of a

total of 100 to correctly answer 38 of the 60 mischievous questions posed. MODERN readers with long memories may recall that he's the selfsame chap who wrote a few articles for us on collectible cameras back in the dark days (pre-October '69) before the Camera Collector column was even conceived.

Now, before I get a flood of letters charging me with nepotism and worse, let me quickly add that friend Bob not only won fair and square, he did so with a minimum of research (i.e., he left many easily researchable questions blank). And while this clearly identifies him as a trivialist par excellence (it's no longer trivial if you have to go to the library to look up the answers), it brings up an interesting conjecture. Could it be that there really are hordes of knowledgeable photo-maniacs out there who failed to enter this silly contest for fear of looking ridiculous? Perish the thought—and do feel free to take the plunge when we run Son of Trivia again.

Speaking of ridiculousness, perhaps you've fogotten by now that the prize for winning this strange contest is a distinctly odd Czechoslovakian twin-lens reflex—to wit, a Flexaret VI circa 1963. Actually, it's neither ridiculous nor trivial in the strictest sense, but it certainly looks different in its herringbone-textured gray plastic covering offset with black enamel areas, and its features are anything but ordinary. Actually this isn't too surprising, as the Flexaret is the product of the Meopta works, a state-owned optical firm specializing, it would appear, in making unusual cameras and optical instruments that actually work reasonably well. Among their more notable achievements are the Opema 35, a rangefinder-Leica-inspired creation with a 24 x 32mm format, the stereo-Mikroma, the only ultra-miniature (16mm) 3D camera I've ever seen, and the Opemus enlargers which offer quite good performance at

A cleverly weird TLR, this Flexaret went to MODERN'S Trivia Contest winner.

reasonable cost (if you can find them).

Getting back to our prize TLR, Meopta unleashed the original Flexaret on an unsuspecting world back in '49, and its signal feature was (and is) helicoid focusing, a fancy tag for a system in which the taking and viewing lenses travel back and forth in unison as you move a lever (below the lensboard) from side to side. The advantages obtained? You can focus with either hand (a boon for southpaws and northpaws alike), and you'll never suffer from focus-finger cramp, a disease known to Rolleiflex owners whose non-adjustible "left-handed" flash brackets get in the way of the focusing knob. At any rate, Minolta Camera Co. was sufficiently impressed to incorporate a similar system into practically every 6 x 6cm format twin-lens reflex camera they ever made (the sole exception being the original Minoltaflex of 1950).

Victorian TLR? Ross Twin Lens of c. 1890 with "accessory" shutter qualifies!

Of course by the time Flexaret model numbers had grown to VI, other clever little oddments were bound to creep in, so let's take a gander at some of the more obvious ones. To start with, our Flexaret VI was designed to accept either 120 roll film or 35mm cartridges without further modification (though regrettably our prize camera lacks the proper film-frame mask and cartridge adapters that came with the camera). Obviously, the camera's 80mm f/3.5 Meopta Belar lens (a 4-element Tessar formula optic) functions as a medium tele when using 35mm film, but the other built-in adaptations are fascinating. For example,

when you install a 35mm cartridge along with the appropriate spacers and mask, the extra pressure on the spring-loaded pressure plate inside the camera automatically changes the number in a little window on the camera back from 60 (2¼ square format) to "35". And as you switch your glance to the right side of the beast, you'll notice two circular frame counters placed side-by-side under the film-wind knob. Would you believe that the right-hand one does the actual counting while the left-hand one is manually set and has only four click-stopped settings 0, 1, 2 and 3? As you may have guessed, the second counter automatically resets the first one to "1" as you manually switch the second counter to a higher number and there's a red "11" in the first counter to remind you to do this at the right time. The sole purpose of this curious arrangement is to provide "semi-automatic" frame counting when shooting 35mm film!

Czech these weird features

As parting shots, we'll note that our Flexaret's shutter is a Czech-made Metax, a leaf type (with speeds of 1-1/400 sec. plus B) that appears to be of conventional design. Defiantly unconventional is the spring-loaded push-to-open catch which unlocks the swing-down back and locks it with utter security when you screw in the knurled end of its little actuating knob as far as it will go.

Oh yes—Meopta could hardly miss the opportunity to make dual use of the helicoid focusing lever below the taking lens so they turned it into a double ended "chopper" engraved with pairs of f/stops. It serves as a depth-of-field scale when used in conjunction with the dual (metric and footage) focusing scales engraved on a plate behind it.

Naturally, the Flexaret incorporates such amenities as a frame-type sportsfinder convertible for 35mm viewing built into the focusing hood, a self-timer, and a smooth-action lockable shutter release. Somewhat surprising is its softish, relatively dim focusing image, the product of a non-Fresnal viewing system. Oh well, you certainly got more than you paid for at $89.50 back in '63 and the taking lens was a good, if unspectacular, performer. Today a clean Flexaret of similar vintage will fetch about $60-75, qualifying it as a welcome, yet appropriately trivial grand prize.

Turning now to the sceptered isle, let's have a look at a few incredible English cameras I was fortunate enough to stumble across at Morgan Camera Co., 160 Tottenham Court Rd., London W1. Actually, stumble is perhaps the wrong word, since I had met Morgan's proprietor, Bob Nicklin, and his wife Janet at the Photokina exposition in Cologne, whence I was enticed to their little shop specializing in collectible photographica. To Bob, then, goes the credit for much of the following historical data, and the prices as well, which are furnished in rapidly deflating pounds sterling ($1.57 each at last count).

We commence with the remarkable Ross Twin Lens camera, a 4¼x3¼ in. format creation incorporating all the hallmarks of much later TLR's except one—a shutter!

Baby Sibyl. Its distinguished maker gave it a super finish, utterly silent shutter.

Reputedly Princess Alexandra's favorite camera, this c. 1890 beast focused via a knurled knob on its right side and sliced time into convenient segments by means of a Thorton-Pickard patent cloth focal-plane shutter mounted over the taking lens.

This latter device provides various instantaneous speeds depending on how many times you wind its spring—five to fifteen turns cover a 1/15 to 1/90 sec. range. Lenses are identical 6-in. Ross Rapid Symmetrical lenses with iris diaphragms that stop down to f/45. Inside, there's a bellows behind the bottom taking lens and the traditional 45° angled mirror behind the viewing lens, which reveals (naturally) an erect but laterally reversed viewing image.

According to Bob, this particular Ross TLR is a very early one and quite rare. The proof: most had two hinged cover doors to protect the lenses, while this one's only got one. Luckily, I was able to dredge up the original price of the 1897 Ross TLR (sans shutter). It was £17, a far cry from the £350 or so Morgans was asking for theirs.

Much more to my personal taste were a brace of Sibyls, both WWI-era sheetfilm cameras produced by the illustrious firm of Newman and Guardia of London.

The Baby Sibyl (pictured) featured the now-fashionable 4½x6 cm (1⅝x2¼ in.) format and incorporated three Sibyl hallmarks—a pair of "garden gate" folding side-struts, scale focusing from "two-yards" to infinity via a lateral-movement tab below the front standard and the famous Sibyl shutter, which provided speeds of ½ to 1/200 sec. and is virtually noiseless.

To quote from the original brochure of 1913, "The Sibyl shutters found on every model are encased in dustproof, non-corrosive metal boxes . . . are pneumatically con-

trolled and of simple and therefore reliable construction and design. All the working components being of brass or German silver, they cannot easily get out of order and are not affected by any change of climate." If that last bit sounds like an extravagant claim for a pneumatic shutter, get a load of this, "All speeds marked on index may be counted on to be absolutely correct since they are engraved from actual readings taken through our special shutter testing machine." I'd love to have seen it!

New Special Sibyl. Baby's big brother.

Promotional "hype" aside the Baby Sibyl is a lovely looking camera of excellent finish and construction, and its 65mm f/4.5 Ross Xpres lens (a 4-element Tessar type) was undoubtedly a good performer. It ought to be at Morgan's £110 asking price.

Our final camera is the Baby's big brother, the New Special Sibyl which is virtually identical except for its 2¼x3¼ in. format. Its shutter's a bit slower on both ends of the scale, covering a 2 to 1/150 sec. (plus B and T) range, and its Ross Xpres lens is a 112mm f/4.5 which stops down to f/45 and also focuses to 2 yds. The *piece de resistance* of this beast is, funnily enough, its small reflex finder, which has got to be the only one in the world to incorporate horizontal *and* vertical bubble levels nestled in its top plate *and* vertical movement of its front lens for parallax compensation. (Note the 0, 1 and 2 index marks on either side of the finder.) In my opinion, this majestic folder qualifies as a usable bargain at a paltry £80.

British classics mingle with a pair of funny folders

Egad! Another English triumvirate in the classic tradition, plus a brace of funky folders just for a chuckle.

I left you all hanging precariously from the parallax-adjustable reflex finder of Newman and Guardia's sensational Sibyl, a meticulously crafted roll-film folder made in England. For this episode, we return to Morgan Camera Co.'s unpretentious shop (at 160 Tottenham Court Rd., London W1) to sample some more of proprietor Bob Nicklin's mouthwatering British delights.

The first such treasure is a nicely finished "no-name" 4¼x3¼ view camera constructed of beautifully lacquered hardwood. Indeed, the woodwork is reminiscent of Sanderson, a fine English maker of "hand and stand" cameras, that flourished in the late 19th and early 20th centuries. Though devoid of any manufacturer's imprint, this little beastie is affixed with a plate bearing the names of Sands, Hunter & Co., most probably the retailer.

The legendary Una? Nope, but this nice little "unknown" is a pretty good copy.

Actually, if you squinted out of one eye or gave it a quick glance, this pleasantly straightforward, glass-plate camera could easily be mistaken for the lengendary Sin-clair Una (a true collector's prize and one of the most gorgeous wooden cameras ever produced in England). However, Bob prefers to play it safe, calling it a "Una type." Whatever you call it, it's got the typical British trap-door above the top, back portion of its red "Russian leather" bellows, which provides clearance for the relatively long, vertical adjustment of the front standard. It focuses by turning a knurled wheel on the right, and locks the focus by means of a cute brass "crank" below the lens.

Speaking of optics, the Una-type lens, most probably the original, is an f/6.8 Cooke Series III of unspecified focal length. It is mounted in a manually-cocked German Koilos leaf shutter, providing speeds of 1-1/300 sec. plus T and B. Interestingly, there are two f/stop scales on the plate below the lens, the top one bearing the legend "EXT". Usually such second scales indicate the f/stop when one half of a "convertible" lens is used as a moderate tele. In this case, however, the top set of digits probably refer to the effective aperture with the bellows fully extended.

Copy or not, the Una-type is a lovely turn-of-the-century camera in its own right, and probably a good picture taker even by contemporary standards. Perhaps that's why Morgan's has theirs priced at £180 (about $340 at last count).

The real Una? Yep, but this one's the less aesthetic large-format version.

As long as we've regaled you with the niceties of a Una-type camera, how about taking a look at the original Una itself? While Morgan's half plate (4¾x6½-in. format) version isn't quite as aesthetic looking (or valuable) as its smaller brethren, the magnificent woodwork and beautiful brass fittings are certainly of the same high caliber—almost in a class by themselves. Even the heads of the brass screws that hold the Una together have been aligned!

A product of the James A. Sinclair Co. of London, the Una is pictured in its fully raised position, clearly demonstrating the function of the trap door above the rear portion of the bellows. However, the use of the front-tilt control, to the right of the lens, and a similar knurled knob, to the left (which permits vertical movement of the lens itself, irrespective of the position of the main lensboard), are not as evident. There's even a marked three-position scale along the left side of the lensboard allowing you to repeat vertical shift settings.

While the bellows on our Una looks to be made of shiny leatherette (and therefore may not be the original), the lens/shutter unit is certainly in keeping with the camera's overall quality. It's a "7x5-in." Rodenstock Euryplan Anastigmat, mounted in the well-known Compound (Deckel) shutter which is marked 1, T, 2, 5, 10, on up to 1/100 and 1/150 sec. (funny to put the T in between the 1 and ½ sec. settings!). If that curious focal length designation has you stumped, bear in mind that it was common practice to mark lenses in formats rather than in focal lengths back in those days. In fact, it was common practice for marking large-format cameras' lenses right through the 20's, although this commendable camera dates from around 1900.

Actually, when you consider that the Una is a usable classic even today (with the suitable 4 x 5 back, that is) and has an excellent pedigree, Morgan's price is hardly outrageous at £110 (about $210).

Super-foldable Eclipse was a great buy.

Turning yet to another venerable British half-plate camera, elegantly constructed of superbly finished hardwood, we have the Eclipse, circa 1890, which managed to fold to remarkably compact dimensions. However, it completely *eclipsed* one major feature—the viewfinder, in favor of

(would you believe) a spirit level! Not that the Eclipse, produced by J.F. Shew & Co. of London, was devoid of clever features, one of the most intriguing of which was how it folded. You just swung away both hinged side panels, which released the tabs on each edge of the front panel from their respective grooves, pushed the lensboard back into the camera body, and folded the two perforated side panels over each other so the lens stuck out in the middle. Obviously, to erect this curious creature for picture taking, you did just the reverse.

This brings up the interesting question of focusing. "How?" you ask. "Not necessarily at all," is the reply. You see, the first version of the Eclipse (1886) was, despite its relatively large 4¼x3¼-in. format, a fixed-focus camera. True, the folks at Shew did eventually incorporate turn-the-lens type helical focusing into the Eclipse, but the camera's chief charm (and historical significance) is its well developed foldability, a feature later copied and improved upon by a certain company in Rochester, N.Y.

This simple "aim-and-shoot" camera managed to cram in one more fascinating feature, an early and successful version of the rotary sector shutter, in both its focusing and non-focusing version. This unlikely looking device was powered by a long, externally-mounted, flat coil

Spartan snapshooter by Dallmeyer had few adjustments, but pretty good lens.

spring. To cock it you grabbed onto the knurled edge of a wheel, emerging from a slot behind the lens, and turned it clockwise, against spring pressure, until it clicked into position. When you releasd it with a lever, it obviously rotated in the reverse direction, and a wedge-shaped opening passed in back of the lens, exposing the film. Alongside the shutter disc, concentrically placed, is the aperture control—actually a wheel perforated with Waterhouse-type stops. Considering its technical and historical status, Morgan's Eclipse is fairly priced at a mere £80 (about $150).

Finally, to go from the sublime to the (almost) ridiculous, we'll conclude with a pair of, for lack of a better term, folding box cameras in the nutty British tradition.

Undeniably English, the Hawkette was a folding box camera by Kodak, Ltd.

The first is the unceremoniously named Snapshot Camera, a metal, crinkle-finish late 20's and early 30's product of Dallmeyer, the famous old London optical house. Its signal features include—mammoth springs on both upper and lower sets of folding struts, a reflex finder atop the lens that "flips out" for horizontal viewing and camera control settings as spartan as the rest of the camera.

As you can see in its portrait the lens turns to "near, medium, and distant" focusing positions, apertures are "bright" and "dull" (take your pick), and the non-cocking shutter offers speeds of "fast, slow and time." Oh well, the f/6 Dallmeyer Anastigmat lens was probably better than those found on most cameras of this elementary type, and Morgan's £25 (about $50) price is certainly affordable.

Prettier looking—if you're fond of brownish wood-textured Bakelite, is a 30's vintage Kodak of England product, the No. 2 Hawkette. Curiously, this 120 roll-film folder, which also collapses on a pair of two-legged struts, was offered solely as a premium for chocolate and cigarette coupons! This model has a simple time-and-instantaneous shutter, Waterhouse-type stops on the time-honored pull-up metal tab and a reflex finder.

So what's so fascinating, you ask? Well, I kind of like the No. 2's hinged back (which opens to the left in the picture), its funky marble-pattern finish (which reminds me of the fascia panel of my late lamented Singer Gazelle —a car only an Englishman can love, or keep in tune) and, last and least, its £5 (about $10) price.

Argus 35s:
Simple, lovable, and American

Three little ol' Argus 35's. Elegant they ain't, but they're affordable, available and, above all, American.

Two straight chapters of exotic British cameras is enough for even the staunchest anglophile I'd say, so this time I've decided to do a complete about-face and present three distinct varieties of a lovably common, home-grown product—namely Argus 35mm cameras. Now before the high falutin collectors among us start to groan in unison, they should note (perhaps with a twinge of nostalgia) that for all their manifest shortcomings, Argus cameras generally performed well enough to start many a tyro down the primrose photography path for life. (I'd like to have a nickel for every Nikon-toting "advanced amateur" who cut his photographic teeth on an Argus C-3.) The second nice thing about them is that they were manufactured in the U.S.A. (Ann Arbor, Michigan, to be exact), which is more than you can say for any current 35 but Keystone's.

Devoid of frills, the original Argus A focused like few other 35's before or since.

If the design engineers at Argus, Inc., excelled at anything, it was in knowing their market. That's why they were able to compete so effectively (from the late 30's to the early 50's at any rate) with the likes of Eastman Kodak and numerous smaller American manufacturers. And while U.S.-made Argus cameras were never as elegant or refined as their European counterparts, they were invariably straightforward, workable and cheap. Indeed, producing an affordable camera, simple and rugged enough to stand up to American tyro's manhandling, is as succinct a statement of the company's philosophy as I have ever run across.

Perhaps the best exemplar of this approach is the company's first 35—the Argus A, born in 1936 and produced in various guises into the 50's. It is almost unique in being two-position-focusing 35 with a 50mm f/4.5 lens, but it sort of makes up for it by having a collapsible lens barrel. To bring your "A" into shooting position, grab the protruding part of the lens/shutter unit, turn it clockwise a bit to disengage three tabs from their retaining slots, and the lens springs out into shooting position. You then orient the lens so each tab is located directly in front of its respective slot (detent position) for near shots, or rotate it a bit farther for distant shots. The shutter release "falls readily to hand" in either position.

The materials used in the Argus A are a curious mixture by today's standards. The lens barrel and the round metal plate at the rear of the lens are very nicely chromed, the main body is molded of Bakelite-type plastic, and the removable back is pressed aluminum. Inside, the left-handed film take-up shaft and topside-only single sprocket wheel are made of brass, while the film-wind knob and bottom-mounted rewind knob are alloy castings.

Two infamous Argus features that made an early appearance here were the spring-catch back lock (none too secure even on the C-3's hinged back), and the "semiautomatic" automatic film stop and frame counting system. This latter abomination required the user to press down on a spring-loaded finger atop the camera, start to wind the film to the next frame, and then release it. It provided no blank or double-exposure prevention, but allowed the Argus to be among the few 35's without a rewind button of any sort.

Of course, there are also some nice things about the "A." Its optical viewfinder is decent, if unremarkable; its three-bladed everset Argus-Ilex-Precise shutter (with speeds of 1/25-1/200 plus T and B) is quiet and still works after all these years, and the camera's rounded front edges nestle comfortably in your hands. I still can't figure out how you were supposed to shoot portraits at f/4.5 with a two-position-focusing Anastigmat lens, but I suppose you could stop down to f/11 (the minimum aperture) and put the beast on a tripod. Granted, this was only possible with late model "A"—our early one lacks a tripod socket. Still looking for something really wonderful amidst this trivia? How about a 1941 price of $13.35, only $10-15 lower than its present value?

Evidently, even those Depression-starved amateurs thought that the A's minimal focusing arrangements constituted something of an oversight because Argus brought out the Model AF in 1937. As you may have guessed, it's basically an "A" (same lens, shutter, basic body shell and film-advance system) with helical-type scale focusing. Unfortunately, the AF's focusing mechanism is inconveniently placed on a helical at the rear of the lens tube where its knurled ring is hard to grab. However, the Argus engineers made at least one virtue of this necessity by providing close focusing capability—down to 1½ ft. Regrettably, two rather nice internal features that bit the dust in the AF (at least on the one in the photo) were the brass film take-up shaft and sprocket wheel. Those in the AF are made of unlovely pot metal (though the single sprocket metal has been transformed into a normal shaft with top and bottom sprockets).

How did those folks in the 30's react to this technological tour de force? Apparently without much relish, for the AF was discontinued in 1938. However, to be fair, it cost

Focusing to 1½ ft. was the Argus AF's main feature. In other respects, it was an "A."

Most popular 35 ever? Probably. The Argus C-3 sold in the millions despite obvious defects. Operation was clumsy and slow.

only $15 (about half its current collector's value) and its focusing arrangement was incorporated into the Argus A2F of 1939-1941, which also had an extinction-type meter next to the viewfinder and (remarkably) the same selling price.

If all these cute, but pedestrian scale-focusing Arguses leave you cold, here's some relief in the form of a true photographic legend—the Argus C-3, affectionately known as "the brick" for reasons too obvious to mention. Although I lack actual sales figures, I think it's pretty safe to say that the C-3 was one of the most popular 35's of all time (millions were sold). It figures, because this coupled-rangefinder 35 enjoyed one of the longest production runs of any camera—1935-1965—in basically unchanged form. Its predecessors, the rare model C of 1938 (boxy shape, rangefinder but no flash sync) and the model C-2 of the same year (coupled rangefinder, but no flash sync), gave scant indication of the fantastic popularity in store for it. In 1939 everything seemed to click, especially the burgeoning ranks of its amateur owners. While its formula for success will undoubtedly seem dated by today's standards, let's examine a classic postwar C-3 and see precisely what it was.

The first thing that strikes you when picking up an Argus C-3 is what I call its "styling image." Oh, it's got nicely chromed metal edges on its cast alloy front and back plates that almost make you forget that the body shell in the middle is pure Bakelite-type plastic. However, you can't really call it "styled" in the accepted sense of that term. What it is is a camera that exudes "cameraness." In fact, it is the epitome of what a "good camera" should look like to an amateur photographer—complicated enough so you might have to read the instruction book, but not really intimidating. In short, the C-3 has what the marketing folks call a "perceived value" which is much greater than its modest price ($69.50 even as late as 1958).

Inside the beloved brick

Of course, you can't take pictures with a clever (if inadvertent) marketing image, and the C-3 had to perform reasonably well in order to sell in such incredible numbers. Here I must confess that I'm a bit stumped, for while "the brick" had a mediocre triplet lens (the well-known 50mm f/3.5 Argus Cintar which was pretty crummy wide open but adequate from f/5.6 to f/16) it was undoubtedly one of the most infuriatingly inconvenient rangefinder 35's ever produced. I've already blasted its finicky back lock and complete lack of double and blank-exposure prevention in discussing the model A. Add to these non-features a stiff-focusing (but interchangeable!) lens mount, a "squinty" viewfinder and a separate (but decent) superimposed plus-split-image rangefinder, and you've pretty well got the whole plot.

Inside, the C-3 looks very much like the AF, except that the C-3's pressure plate is a sprung metal affair instead of a piece of plastic affixed directly to the back with rubber strips! However, about an inch above the film aperture are two round little windows, the left-hand one being the aforementioned dinky viewfinder, the other the rangefinder. The rangefinder was actually one of the C-3's more agreeable features. Like the Agfa Karomat the focusing images are of the superimposed type, but vertically displaced so the advantages of the coincident and split-image types are combined. Also, the fixed image appears in aqua, while the moving focusing image is in a contrasting pinkish hue, and it'll get you down to the usual 3 ft.

Moving to the C-3's top plate, you've got (on the right side) a body shutter release that works in conjunction with the famous shutter-cocking lever on the front of the camera. The shutter itself is a three-bladed, behind-lens leaf type with speeds of 1/10-1/300 sec. No B setting? Yes, turn the collar around the shutter button from I to B and you've got it. On the left side of the C-3's top plate is the time-honored left-handed film-advance knob (as with the "A" series, the rewind knob is on the right side of the bottom plate).

Perhaps C-3's most interesting and least used feature is its lens interchangeability, courtesy of its externally geared focusing mechanism. To remove the normal lens, you select the closest focusing distance, then unscrew the cover plate from the straight-cut "idler" gear that connects the gear around the edge of the circular rangefinder window with the straight-cut geared section at the rear of the lens mount. You can then lift the middle gear off its shaft and unscrew the lens from its screw-thread mount (you get a good view of the C-3's shutter mechanism in passing). Remounting a lens was an even more delightful experience. You first screw the lens all the way in, set the rangefinder to infinity, insert the little connecting gear, turn the lens to minimum focusing distance and screw in the connecting gear's retaining cover—whew!

Understandably, interchangeable lenses for the Argus C-3 were never brisk sellers, though Argus themselves offered a 35mm wide angle and 100mm tele, and Soligor (among several others) marketed lenses up to 135mm in the C-3 mount. Ultimately, lens interchangeability was really beyond this modest camera's essential identity—by the time its owner felt the need for extra lenses the faithful C-3 was traded in on one of the more glamorous (and capable) imports, or relegated to some obscure corner of the attic. The resulting glut of C-3s on the used-camera market has made the camera something of a standing joke among used-camera salesmen for years. But there's hope friends—the lowly "brick" that used to languish on the dealer's shelf under a $10-$15 price tag has recently been selling more briskly at $30-$40 for an example in nice condition.

Argus Epic continued

The Argus epic evolves, with a couple of ubiquitous postwar cheapies and an enterprising but unsung rangefinder 35.

In deference to the multitude of Argus owners who might feel slighted if I didn't give at least a passing nod to their particular model, I've decided to transform the Argus chapter into an ongoing saga and continue with an argosy of postwar Arguses. As I implied previously, Argus cameras of any sort are not held in especially high regard by hardcore camera collectors, but fortunately I'm a soft-core collector who appreciates their not-so-subtle blend of straightforward mechanical design and distinctively American appearance. As a matter of fact, the C-44—flagship of the Argus 35mm line—qualifies as one of the better rangefinder 35's ever made in this country. And, unlike the fabled Kodak Ektra or Bell & Howell Foton, the average photographer could (and can) actually afford to buy one.

Let's commence with the only non-35mm camera we'll talk about—the ever-popular Argoflex, a Bakelite-bodied twin-lens reflex. Introduced shortly before World War II

as the Argoflex E, the one pictured is a model EM of 1948, which is identical to the "E" except for having a *coated* 75mm f/4.5 Argus Varex taking lens. All Argoflexes featured that famous trademark—externally geared focusing, and all models provided a 2¼ x 2¼ in. format on 620 film. Our EM, like its predecessors, had an everset leaf shutter with speeds of 1/10 to 1/200 sec. plus B and T, and no flash sync. And curiously, its aperture scale is calibrated in an odd "semi-continental" sequence of f/stops—4.5, 6.3, 9, 12.7 (!) and 18.

Flip up the EM's viewing hood and focusing magnifier and you are greeted with one of the dimmest viewing images in creation, complemented by a central clear spot. Since the spot is non-focusing, it was probably included to help you find the subject! At any rate, Argus improved the view on subsequent models by fitting an f/3.5 viewing lens in place of the EM's f/4.5 Anastigmat. One Argoflex feature they never changed was its find-the-number-in-the-red-window film-stop system. Oh well, at least the film-advance knob turned smoothly, and the window had a spring-loaded cover to prevent fogged film.

You'll find few other noteworthy features on this spartan beast. Admittedly, the sportsfinder (which works with the focusing magnifier in stored position) is cute, as is the two-finger, spring-loaded back lock. But neither of these qualifies as a real blockbuster. It's even questionable whether the Argoflex was a great buy at $56 (plus $8 Federal Excise Tax) in 1948. However, the Argoflex was, and is, a decent and dependable picture taker—well worth

A Bakelite beauty, the Argoflex had 2¼ square format on 620 roll film.

Simplicity personified, Argus a-four was light, fully manual, affordable.

the $25—30 you'll presently pay for one in good shape.

Even more pedestrian than the Argoflex is the Argus a-four, a scale-focusing, plastic-bodied 35. As a matter of fact, it's got only two significant features that mark it as a mid-50's creation—built-in flash sync, and true double-exposure prevention. In keeping with earlier Kodak practice, its lens is a coated, semi-wide-angle; in this case a 44mm f/3.5 Argus Cintar. However, the shutter is a German Pronto (by Gauthier), a manually cocked leaf type with speeds of 1/25-1/200 plus B.

Like the original Argus A of the late 30's, the a-four has a single-wheel film-transport sprocket instead of the more conventional double-ended sprocketed shaft. It's also positioned rather oddly above the center of the film aperture. More in keeping with its era (1953-1956) are the two push-in flash sync sockets on the camera's left side (in shooting position). These sockets are designed to accept a towering BC flashgun for #5 flash bulbs, which would only work at the a-four's 1/25 sec. flash setting.

Do these specifications leave you unimpressed? Well, the Argus a-four is certainly light (12 oz.) and handy. It has a reasonably good lens which stops down to f/22 and focuses to 2.5 ft. Most importantly, the little a-four was precisely aimed at the budding amateur market with a list price of $39.50 (plus $4.25 FET). It might be a somewhat lackluster collector's item, but it's worth its present price of $15—20.

Successor to the C3? That was the plan, but Argus C4 never quite achieved it.

Now that you're starting to yawn, let's turn to something really exciting. First, we'll skip ever so lightly over the Argus C4; a fixed-lens, combined range/viewfinder 35 designed as the famous C3's successor. The C4, which was born in 1951 and deceased in 1958, had rounded sides, a 50mm f/2.8 Cintar lens, a 1/10-1/300 sec. shutter with built-in flash sync and true double-exposure prevention. It had a relatively long production run (1951-58) and was dubbed the C-4R in its last version, which had speeds down to ⅛ sec. For the record, it was priced at $84.50 and it's worth a bit less than half that figure today.

Perhaps the best thing about the C4 was that it provided the basic chassis for the deluxe C44, one of the few bayonet-mount, interchangeable-lens rangefinder 35's ever made in this country. The C44 boasted a die-cast alloy body with a removable back and featured the same general layout and appearance as the C4. You set shutter speeds of

1/10 to 1/3000 sec. (plus B) on a round knurled shutter-speed dial on the camera's front, and focused with Argus's traditional externally geared milled wheel. The C-44's bright, contrasty, combined and coupled range/viewfinder got you down to 3½ ft. with the C44's four-element 50mm f/2.8 Cintagon lens.

So far, nothing earthshaking—so let's turn to the C44's *raison d'etre*: lens interchangeability. In addition to the normal lens, you could get a 35mm f/4.5 Cintagon wide angle and a 100mm f/3.5 Cintagon medium tele. Like the 50, both were beautifully finished in shiny chrome and furnished in a nicely machined three-claw bayonet mount, reminiscent of Exakta's. To remove a lens, you set the focusing scale to infinity, pushed the lens-release catch below the lens, turned the barrel about a quarter turn counterclockwise and lifted it off. To remount the lens you match the dots and bayonet it in.

All the C44's lenses had click-stopped aperture rings—a nice touch back in the late 50's and early 60's—but the way they focus is considerably more interesting. Unlike Leica lenses (and optics for most other interchangeable-lens rangefinder 35's), the C44's lenses do *not* incorporate a precision machined cam at the rear of each lens (which is connected to the rangefinder by means of a spring-loaded follower arm). Instead, the rangefinder is coupled "directly and permanently to the revolving lens mount a la Contax. So, if you turn the C44's focusing ring with the lens removed, you'll still be able to focus the rangefinder.

An ingenious mount: Tab (at arrows) fits slot in lens for rangefinder coupling.

Now comes the clever part. Before you mount a lens on the C44, you have to set the lens to infinity and turn the focusing wheel so that a little tab (that runs in an arcuate groove outboard of the bayonet mount itself) is aligned with a fixed red dot. This enables a groove cut into the rear of the focusing ring (at the rear of each lens) to fit over the tab. As a result, when you turn the focusing wheel, the distance scale at the rear of the lens rotates within, and independently of, the front part of the lens barrel. This arrangement is not only ingenious, it has a practical advantage: The aperture scale remains conveniently visible atop the fixed front part of the lens barrel, irrespective of the focusing distance.

An all-American design?

I wish I could say that the Argus C44 was an all-American triumph in addition to being an under-appreciated classic, but that's not entirely true. According to heretofore reliable but as yet unconfirmed sources, its entire optical array was a product of the ever-fascinating Enna factory of Munich. That, of course, doesn't include the C44's "Variable Power Viewfinder, a slide-on accessory which has a wheel with settings for 35, 50 and 100mm on its left side, a parallax-compensation wheel on its right and a flash-sync socket below the frame selector! The C44's designers were evidently proud of their hot-flash shoe and didn't want you to lose its advantages merely because you decided to shoot with a wide angle or tele. So, when you slide the Variable Power Finder in place, a contact on its bottom mates with the hot-shoe connection, transferring the sync capability to the side of the finder—cute.

The works: Late Argus C44R complete with tele, turret finder, coupled meter.

The original Argus C44 had a relatively short production run—1956-57—despite its attractive price of $99.50. In 1958 it was replaced by the C44R, which is basically the same animal with a few minor changes. In place of the original knurled, metal film wind and rewind knobs, the "R" sports a rapid-advance lever and "pull out" rewind crank. And, at some time during the camera's production, it lost its nice, bright, Variable Power Finder accessory which was replaced with a more conventional three-lens turret job. Finally, some genius decided to update the whole plot with an unseemly looking cylindrically shaped selenium meter which fit over and coupled to the shutter-speed dial. Fortunately, these last two appendages were conveniently removable if you wanted to restore your C44R to its rather sleek, handsome, unadorned self. Finally, in the early 60's and until it went out of production in 1962, you could have ordered your C44R with a 50mm f/1.9 Cintagon lens with case and flash for $170, precisely $50 more than it cost with the f/2.8.

A Japanese casualty?

Since the Japanese camera invasion was already in full swing by 1962, it is tempting to regard the mostly-American C44 as one of its early casualities. However, I doubt whether this is actually the case. Granted, the Argus lacked slow speeds, fast speeds above 1/300 sec. and a self-timer—all of which were present on the Minoltas, Olympuses and Konicas of the day—but in truth, the C44 was never a great sales success despite its lens interchangeability and very good overall performance. What probably killed the relatively posh C44 was the name Argus, which had long been associated in the public mind with cheap cameras for the novice photographer. So, while the C44 was certainly substantial enough as a camera, its image was not, and the sophisticated camera buyer generally rejected it on that account. But, as usual, the manufacturer's despair is the camera collector's joy, and today a complete C44 outfit qualifies as a usable collector's prize worth in the region of $200—250.

Ugly Americans: The Mercury 35s

Leave it to the Americans to build a giant half-frame 35, then revise it to take standard cartridges.

For some strange reason, my recent column on American-made 35mm cameras has scared an interesting, hitherto unknown, breed of cameraphiles out of the woodwork.

They all write asking me the same question, "Why don't you write something about the Mercury 35—I've got one and it's weird/a beaut/a dog, or all of the above. Well I've certainly had enough impassioned pleas to convince me that there must be a fair number of these round-domed beasts lurking about the countryside. And so, without further ado, we present Mercury Memoirs, subtitled "Can

Ugly American? Perhaps, but original Mercury of '38 had pizzazz beyond its price.

American ingenuity and unskilled labor produce a $25 precision 35?"

One company with an affirmative answer to that question is the Universal Camera Corp. of New York (23rd St. in Manhattan) and Hollywood, Calif., purveyor of $5.95 and $8.95 Univex 8mm movies cameras to a Depression-pinched public. But could they possibly lure the wary and impoverished camera buyer away from the affordable Argus 35s on the one hand and the posh, feature-laden German imports on the other? Well, Universal certainly tried to implement this strategy with the original Univex Mercury of 1938, and by all accounts they were reasonably successful. True, it took an unfashionably automated (for its day) production line (manned and womaned by so-called semi-skilled personnel) to do it, but the resulting camera was as remarkably sophisticated for its price as it was ungainly looking.

The original Mercury, like the postwar Mercury II, is a scale-focusing half-frame 35 with hinged back and a cast-alloy body. Its distinctive "gadgety" appearance is a direct result of its most singular technical feature—a true, rotary sector shutter placed a few millimeters in front of the film plane. The use of two large, thick, circular-section blades allowed Universal to endow the Mercury's shutter with a wide range of speeds (1/20-1/1000 sec. plus B and T), despite its having a single-speed gear train. Different speeds were obtained by varying the angle of the wedge-shaped opening between the two blades—a reasonably inexpensive and accurate way to get faster shutter speeds than the competition. This plan also permitted the company to draw on their considerable experience manufacturing movie-camera shutters of similar design. Indeed, the concept would almost qualify as elegant except for one minor cosmetic problem—it necessitates crowning the camera body with an arch-shaped channel to contain those large, revolving shutter blades.

Although the Mercury's "crown" can be charitably described as peculiar in appearance, the camera's makers

were undaunted, and promptly adorned it with a similarly shaped depth-of-field scale, erroneously labelled. "Depth of Focus." Just below it is an early "hot shoe" that worked in conjunction with a specially designed "Photo-Flash Unit"—a bulb-type flashgun. Beneath the shoe are two knurled knobs—the one on the right is a shutter-speed dial that revolves as the shutter fires; the one on the left winds the film, counts the number of exposures and cocks the shutter simultaneously as you turn it clockwise.

Hands-on demonstration

Here's how it all works. Grab onto the left-hand dial and wind it one complete turn until it stops. This advances the frame counter at the rear of the dial one notch, and just before the dial stops the shutter dial moves clockwise a bit to read out the shutter speed you've set opposite the index line. You now press the conventionally located shutter-release button, and the shutter fires to the accompaniment of a low pitched whirring noise.

For the record, the original Mercury was fitted with an interchangeable 35mm f/3.5 Tricor lens—a three-element optic (made by Wollensak) that stopped down to f/22. Its screw-thread mount measures 23mm in diameter, and for a measly $19.95, you could have ordered a 3 in. f/3.5 Mercury Telephoto lens as part of your outfit. The standard lens focused down to a rather close 1½ ft. (on all Mercury models) by means of a knurled focusing helical permanently mounted on the camera body. The helical is fitted with a little, protruding, knurled focusing knob which makes things easier on the digits. How do you compensate for parallax at such a close distance? Well, the camera's decent-but-ordinary optical finder has a pair of parallax compensation markings.

As you can see, the Mercury I is really a much more straightforward rig than its outward appearance might indicate. The first shock comes when you try to load the thing—it's a 35mm camera all right, but it won't accept standard cartridges! Instead, it was designed for—you guessed it—Univex 35mm film which was available in ortho, medium and fast types. All three came specially packaged in mercury cartridges, which had grooved bottoms and felt light traps, and resembled Robot cartridges. And why would anyone afflict a basically pleasant machine with this limited film supply? Why to sell film, of course! Indeed, this was a Universal Camera Corp. tradition that had been carried forth with some success with practically every one of their previous Univex still and movie cameras. The film itself was produced by Gevaert (of Belgium and the U.S.) but, as with "special" film types and sizes before and since, distribution was a problem and this began to put a damper on sales of the camera.

Actually this was kind of a shame because the postwar Mercury II grew about ½ in. in height and ¼ in. in width (to 3 13/16 x 5⅝ x 2⅛ in.) and 5 oz. heavier (1 lb. 7 oz.) in order to accommodate standard 35mm cartridges. The switch to standard film cassettes also necessitated the installation of a rewind knob, rewind switch (below and to the left of the lens), and a take-up spool in place of the model I's rewindless system of cartridge-to-cartridge feed. In the updating process the II's lens was changed from the uncoated Wollensak-made f/3.5 Tricor to a coated f/2.7 lens of the same 35mm focal length, but made by Universal Camera Corp. themselves. However, it was still a triplet design furnished in 23mm screw-thread mount and it still stopped down to f/22. The only other visible change was the enlargement of both film wind and shutter-setting knobs—a move which made them a bit easier to turn.

Postwar Mercury II (shown with extinction meter) took regular 35mm cartridges.

Perhaps this is as good a place as any to say something about Mercury's format. It's most often listed as "half-frame," and that's correct up to a point. Actually, most Japanese half-frame cameras of the 60's produce 17-point-something x 24mm negs, while the Mercury's size is close to 19 x 24mm. The obvious result is that either Mercury gets fewer pictures per roll—65 per 36-exposure roll rather than 72. Other arcane Mercury lore includes the rather rare Wollensak-made 35mm f/2 Hexar super-speed lens which was available for the model II, a seldom-seen 1939 version of the model I which had a marked top shutter speed of 1/1500 sec. (with allegedly no internal shutter changes to justify this optimistic figure!) and, of course, the lovable Mercury Rapid Winder (pictured), an accessory reminiscent of the Konica 111A's vertical rapid-wind lever.

Now to answer the most common Mercurial queries in one convenient place: Yes, most Tricor lenses were decent picture takers despite their modest designs. Yes, I'm not surprised that your Mercury's shutter is still working, and I'm even less surprised that the speeds it provides aren't too terribly accurate. Finally, yes the metal finish on your model I is a bit better than that on the II; yes, both cameras are very solid and reasonably well constructed to roughly the same tolerances, and no, nobody will guarantee a Mercury shutter repair, and you can't get parts except by cannibalization.

Incidentally, to prove that inflation has reared its ugly head in times other than our own, the lovely $25 Mercury I was selling for $30 just before the war broke out, and by 1946 the model II was listed at $79.50. The last suggested retail price I could find for it was $82.90 in 1949. Presently, the Mercury's fascinating appearance and peculiar features have rewarded it with a collector's price of $60-$75

Rapid winder offered for Mercury I mated with geared end of film-wind knob.

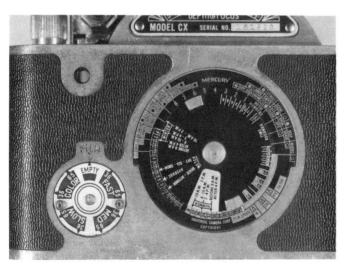

Bewildering exposure calculator (center) was calibrated for time of day, season, etc.

(it doesn't seem to matter which model you choose). Experienced collectors may snicker, but I have the feeling that these usable minor classics may soon fetch considerably more as the once plentiful supply is gobbled up by connoisseurs of U.S.-made cameras.

The Vidax:
Classic American press camera

The venerable Vidax—a tragic tale of America's postwar attempt to promote the world's most adaptable press camera.

Having regaled you with fascinating-but-budget-priced American cameras, I think it's about time to wave the flag a bit and prove that us Yanks were occasionally geniuses at designing cameras as well as marketing them. And what better way to present the vaunted Vidax, surely one of the most ingenious and ambitious 2¼ x 3¼-in. press cameras ever produced. Since what follows is basically a rave review, I may as well get the bad news out of the way and inform you that the Vidax's manufacturer, the Vidmar Camera Co. of New York, came to an ultimely end, folding shortly after producing a measly 200 (or so) of these magnificent beasts. As you may have guessed, this makes the Vidax a collector's item par excellence—a shame in a way because as you'll see it's a delightfully usable machine.

Press photog's delight? Undoubtedly, but the Vidax fell victim to a common ill.

The first nice thing about the Vidax is that it represents a clever response to a genuine need—the need for a portable, handholdable, roll-film press camera, comprehensive and flexible enough to satisfy the working pro. Back in '48 when the Vidax made its debut, pressmen in search of such an instrument had few choices. On the one hand, there was the heavy-but-lovable 2¼ x 3¼ Speed Graphic which added roll-film capability as an afterthought. It coupled different focal-length lenses to its rangefinder with difficulty, or not at all. On the other hand, there was the marvelous Medalist by Kodak, a 2¼ x 3¼ roll-film camera, equally as heavy as, but more compact than the little Graphic, but lacking lens interchangeability of any sort. So, along came the Vidax, with easily interchangeable, rangefinder-coupled lenses and sheetfilm and multiple-roll film formats, promising to be a working photographer's dream.

To begin with, the Vidax is a bellows-type folding camera, constructed largely of alloy castings. So while it isn't really tiny (2⅞ x 5½ x 7½ in. folded) it's extremely sturdy and remarkably light in weight for a camera of its type (a shade under 3 lb. 7 oz. with normal 101 mm f/4.5 Wollensak Raptar lens). Push a button below the circular rangefinder window, pull down the camera bed, and you're greeted by a pair of hefty, spring-loaded, channeled struts that lock in place very positively. Now, before pulling out the front standard, if you turn the focusing wheel on the left side of the bed you'll notice a few curious things.

Triple track and back

The focusing track rides on dual racks and pinions, which is nice but nothing unusual. However, there are no less than five pairs of detents for the spring-loaded fingers (at the bottom of the front standard) to lock into; two positions for cut film and three for roll film, depending on the focal length of the lens fitted. Then, at the right-hand end of the track is a little hook attached to a finely braided, plastic-coated steel cable that runs around a pulley and into the right-hand section of the camera body. Its function, as you may have suspected, is to physically couple the rangefinder with the focusing system. Finally, the little knob on the right side of the camera bed locks the focusing track in place.

O.K. let's pull the lens out to the red set of detents (to match the red dot on the normal 101mm's lensboard) and direct our attention to the back of the camera. With the roll-film back in place, you're greeted by three round, covered windows, marked 8, 12, and 16, each surrounded by a knurled bezel. Grab onto the knurling and turn any of them counterclockwise and the metal cover lifts to reveal—of all things—ye olde red windows. Yep, although the Vidax was the last word in sophistication for its day (or even today), you advanced your 620 or 120 roll film by turning the knob on its lower right end, and stopped when the next number came up in the little window. Yes, but how did you know which window to use?

Well, let's push the little latch-lifting button on the side of the roll-film back, lift it off and take a peek inside. Initially, everything appears quite ordinary inside. On the left is a film chamber with its spring-loaded, spool-retainer shaft on the bottom. On the right is the take-up-spool compartment with its spring clip on the top. In the middle is the 2¼ x 3¼ in. film aperture, framed on either side by film rollers. It's all perfectly conventional until you notice the metal channels above and below the center of the film aperture, the three pairs of color-coded dots near the bottom, and the flat, spring-steel clip directly below them.

Swift format switching was one of many Vidax tricks. Just release spring catch and you can "pull in the curtains."

Can it be? Yes! Pull down on either end of the clip and this releases a little pin. If, at the same time, you now grab onto the appropriate side of the film aperture, you can slide it forward in its groove and lock it in to red-dot, or green-dot positions. Obviously you must also do the same with the other end of the spring clip and the other side of the film aperture to mask the film aperture for 2¼ x 2¼-in. (12 exposures per roll) and 1⅝ x 2¼-in. (16 exposures per roll) formats. As you pull the metal frames in place to select either format, cloth blinds (affixed to the edges of both sliding frames) unroll, completing the light-tight masking system, while maintaining the opening in the center of the frame. Also, since the film plane remains in precisely the same orientation with respect to the lens, irrespective of the format selected, accurate focusing is assured at all times, and there are no separate finder masks to go astray. All in all, I'd award the Vidax top honors in the built-in-format-switching department—at any rate, I've never seen a similar system that was better conceived or executed.

That brings us to rangefinder coupling, a sticky problem encountered by every interchangeable-lens

rangefinder camera. Here too Vidax shines, with its elegantly simple system of rangefinder adjustment to accommodate lenses ranging from 65-127mm. Just twirl the knurled wheel to the right of the circular rangefinder window and observe the moving scale in a small oval window above the Vidax name inscribed on the front of the camera. When the red index line is just above the marked focal length of the mounted lens, you're in focus when the rangefinder so indicates (provided you select the right lensboard detents on the focusing track and the lens's actual focal length doesn't differ markedly from the one inscribed on the lens ring). Admittedly, that rangefinder-adjustment wheel isn't exactly conveniently located or easy to turn.

What about the range-viewfinder, you ask? Well, the front viewfinder glass is tinted blue while the circular rangefinder image is tinted magenta for improved contrast. And while the overall brightness and separation of the rangefinder is not quite up to standards set by the Leica M-3, it's nevertheless very good indeed. The viewfinder is also commendably large and clear for a camera of its era, but not quite as bright as those in some contemporary rangefinder cameras. In any event, the suffering press photographers of the day must have been impressed with the performance of the Vidax's finder system.

Quick change mount. Turn screws atop bar and it springs up, releasing lens.

Of course, a brilliant, multi-focal rangefinder and switchable formats aren't much use without a reasonably facile system for interchanging lenses, and the designers thought of that, too. While the Vidax is no match for your bayonet-mount SLR in this respect, it's considerably swifter than the lens changing system used on most press cameras before and since. Just turn two knurled wheels atop the front standard counterclockwise a few turns, releasing the spring-loaded clamp below them, and the lens and lensboard practically fall out forward into your waiting hand. Now you simply switch lenses, note the color of the dot on the lensboard, grab the locking fingers under the lensboard, and slide the front standard until it locks in place in the properly color-coded grooves. A system of adapting the viewfinder to cover different focal-length lenses (or format sizes, for that matter) was about the only thing Vidmar's engineers left out. Judging by the grooved channel on either side of the front finder glass, the various lens/format combinations were evidently provided for by the somewhat chintzy method of slide-in masks.

But nobody says you have to view your Vidax through the separate optical finder. Just snap off the roll-film back and snap on the sheet-film back and presto, you've got all the virtues and liabilities of a groundglass-focusing camera with a Graflok-style spring back. Does this mean you can't use the rangefinder? Of course not—remember there are a pair of rangefinder-coupling detents covering sheet-film operation with either normal or wide-angle lenses. In fact, the rangefinder couples down to 2½ ft. with normal (101 or 105mm) lenses, and the camera's 6-in. (bellows extension permits 1:1 and greater magnification with short focal-length lenses, but only by focusing via the groundglass.

Speaking of lenses, for this report I was fortunate indeed to obtain a Vidax with both backs and all three lenses —a 65mm f/6.8 Graflex Optar in 1-1/400 sec. (plus B and T) Graphex synchro shutter, the aforementioned 101mm f/4.5 Wollensak Raptar in similarly speeded Rapax synchro shutter and a 127mm f/4.5 Wollensak Raptar (which stops down to f/45 rather than f/32 like the other two) in a 1-1/100 sec. Alphax Synchro-Matic shutter. Each of these units is fitted with the classical American double-prong flash contact that fits the detachable socket built into the Vidax.

As you can now appreciate, the Vidax is as ingeniously

A back to end all backs, Vidax's had a red window for each of three roll-film formats.

conceived an American press camera as ever came down the pike. Not only that, but it was built like a tank without weighing like a tank, was as usable in the field as it was impressive on the drawing board, and indeed performed very well according to the few Vidax users I've managed to chat with. Certainly the very small number made before the factory went belly up were eagerly snapped up by knowledgeable press photographers who knew a good thing when they saw one.

As we mentioned at the beginning, this appealing, potentially revolutionary camera was killed by that sneaky businessman's disease known as undercapitalization. The result is that a camera that should have been noted for its many picture credits is known instead as an oddball, also-ran. But as ever, the manufacturer's nightmare is the camera collector's delight, and the basic Vidax I've detailed would now fetch about $500 on the collectors' market, quite a bit more than the $271.93 it listed for back in '48 with 105mm f/3.5 Schneider Xenar lens in Synchro-compur shutter.

Japanese oddballs:
A brace of Aires 35s, Fuji's Mini

A potpourri of seemingly pedestrian Japanese machinery from the camera collector's most recent cache.

It seems that the vast preponderance of cameras I've palavered about of late have come from other people's collections. Mind you, I'm not complaining—it should be obvious to my regular readers that writing these monthly meanderings would hardly be possible without the generous cooperation of fellow camera accumulators. What I'm

getting around to in my inimitably oblique fashion is this—I've recently shelled out for three fascinating Japanese cameras and made them part of my own collection.

The first of these gems is an Aires Automat of 1952, a rather conventional-looking, 2¼-square, twin-lens reflex. However, the condition in which I received it is anything but ordinary—it came brand new, in its original box with leather case and instruction book and wrapped in its original packing affixed with a "JIS Export Standard" (precursor of JCII) sticker. Where it had been languishing lo these

Pleasant but unexciting? Examine Aires TLR closely and you'll change your mind.

25 years is anyone's guess, but it proved to be in perfect operating condition—a pristine machine.

This nicely finished, good quality beast is a frank imitation of the fabulous Rolleiflex, down to the crosshatched knurling on spring-loaded film-retaining pins on its right, and the hinged, sliding lock on its bottom. The Aires lacks its more expensive cousin's automatic, first-frame positioning (you've got to line up the arrows on the paper backing with red dots on the sides of the film aperture), and there's no auto parallax compensation in the waist-level finder, but it's got a Rollei-style, single-throw, film-advance crank on the left, and a smooth-operating focusing knob on the right that'll get you down to a marked 2⅔ ft.

The Automat's exposure controls are arrayed on the front in the manner of a Rolleicord, with both apertures and shutter speeds controlled by knobs attached to levers running in curved slots on either side of the taking lens. However, there's no little window above the viewing lens where these are read out—you have to tilt the camera upward (in shooting position) to read your settings. Equally primitive is the focusing image, which is reasonably clear, but quite dim at the edges due to the absence of any Fresnel lens.

Guess who made it?

By now you're probably wondering what's so special about this camera to have captured this jaded collector's fancy. No, it wasn't the cute, double-hinged, light-excluding focusing magnifier that collapses at the touch of a little lever on its side—it wasn't even the admirable Seikosha-Rapid shutter with speeds of 1-1/500 sec. plus B, calibrated in the old non-geometric sequence of 1, ½, 1/5, 1/10, etc. What really caused me to part with my hard-earned shekels was the Aires' lenses—a matched 75mm f/3.5 Nikkor QC taking lens and 75mm f/3.2 View-Nikkor C on top! Can it be? Yep—back in those days Nippon Kogaku (Nikon) wasn't too proud to sell their fine lenses to small or medium-sized Japanese manufacturers with the requisite cash, and the Aires is one of a very small number of TLR brands to have benefited from such largesse.

Incidentally, the taking lens is a standard Tessar (four-element, three-group) formula, albeit a very well-made one, and the whole Aires TLR outfit cost me a fast 40 bucks—roughly 25 percent of its current value.

Believe it or not, the second camera to decimate my wallet was also an Aires—the model 35-V I'd been seeking for quite a while. Can you imagine a Japanese leaf-shutter 35mm rangefinder camera of the late 50's fitted with an interchangeable 45mm f/1.5 lens? Neither could I as I drooled over its picture as a penniless adolescent. Alas, it was the classic story—by the time I could afford to buy one, it had long since vanished from the marketplace. I was hoping to simply find the camera in decent shape some day, so I could hardly believe it when I saw an almost-complete Aires outfit with all three lenses on display in Olden Camera's glass case. I had to have it.

As with many long-nurtured dreams, the Aires 35-V proved something of a disappointment in reality, though it's undeniably an interesting camera and not really a bomb. As expected, its appearance is really neat with lots of knurled dials and angular corners. And residing majestically in the middle is the great big 4.5cm f/1.5 S Coral lens, a seven-element job of Aires' own manufacture—pretty good for 1958.

As you might expect, the camera abounds in curious features. For example, the little dial to the left of the round rangefinder window has positions for advance (A), rewind (R) and multiple exposures (D). To the right of the circular rangefinder window is a frosted, light-collecting window for the dual (45mm and 100mm), noncompensating, projected framelines which are constantly visible in the finder. Then, to the right of the actual viewfinder window is the selenium cell for the built-in uncoupled meter. You adjust it according to the position of the meter needle atop the camera, using a knurled ring placed concentrically around the rewind crank. The meter still works perfectly on my jewel, incidentally, and I was surprised to see that its film-speed settings go up to ASA 800.

Actually, the range/view finder is one of the 35-V's more agreeable components. It's reasonably large, quite bright, and the dual, field frames are not terribly obtrusive. Rangefinder contrast is also quite good, and focusing

A complete Aires 35-V outfit. Nice, so why is the camera collector complaining?

is smooth, at least with the normal lens, but one wonders whether the short 45mm rangefinder base is sufficiently accurate for such a fast lens. Oh well, the shutter release is smooth and predictable, the rapid-wind lever has a short stroke, and the Seikoska MX shutter provides speeds from 1/400 sec. plus B. Even the inside of the camera is quite pleasant to look at when you swing open the hinged back. So why am I complaining?

Well, I'll tell you—it's the lenses. Push a chrome button on the bottom of the f/1.5 as you twist it about ⅛ turn counterclockwise and you can lift it off, revealing the Aires' nicely machined three-claw bayonet mount. Now let's mount another lens. Set the focusing scale (which is integral with the camera) to infinity, line up the dot on the rearmost knurled ring on the lens with the one on the rangefinder-coupling tab (wide angle) or focusing ring (tele) and bayonet the lens in. With the 100mm f/3.5 Tele Coral there are two disappointments—it's a wobbly fit on the camera (even with everything in proper adjustment) and it focuses to a blistering 6½ ft. or so. The 35mm f/3.2 W Coral is better on the latter count—it'll get you down to 2⅔ ft. like the normal lens—but it still wobbles excessively so far as I'm concerned.

Admittedly, any hard feelings I might have are considerably assuaged by the Aires' nice finish, unique specs and low price—$99 for the whole outfit including slightly tattered, fitted, leather compartment case. I'd peg the average collector's value of this fairly scarce rig at about $150-$200.

The "mini-est" half-frame?

To go from the sublimely overextended to the merely minuscule, consider my final purchase—a Fujica Mini, which I believe qualifies as the tiniest camera ever to espouse the standard half frame (18 x 24mm) 35mm format. Measuring in at a sub-compact 3⅜ x 1 9/16 x 2⅛ in., the Mini's lens is a fixed-focus 25mm f/2.8 Fujinar-K, which lives behind an unremovable skylight filter covering the circular selenium-meter grid around the lens. This filter tuns as you move a lever attached to its underside, and this causes the meter needle in a little window atop the camera to deflect. Set the film speed (ASA 25-200) opposite one of the color-coded cut glass jewels (!) in front of the meter scale and you match the moving needle with a fixed index line, which sets the proper-exposure aperture. Not surprising is the Mini's single fixed shutter speed of approximately 1/60 sec.—a feature that places it in the snapshot class.

Smallest half-frame ever? Probably, but Fujica Mini's tricks don't end there.

Other features present on this 10-oz., mid-60's Japanese classic include: removable back, hinged pressure plate, plain frame-line finder (quite good, actually), and nicely applied black finish. Unique is the Mini's film-advance system—to get to the next frame you grab the camera vertically with your index finger on the flat, knurled wheel above the Fujica nameplate and place your thumb in a little dished indentation on the camera's bottom directly below. You now grab the camera's other end with your left hand and wind the *camera body* clockwise about 90°! Lovely, but the nicest thing about my Fujica Mini is still the price—a whopping nine bucks complete with pouch case at New York's 47th Street Photo. (They thought the meter was on the fritz, but it wasn't.) I haven't really seen too many Fujica Mini's on the loose lately, but I'd estimate its current value at $30-50. Oh yes, don't believe the cock and bull story that it was copied from a one-off 35 made for King Farouk!

"Leica" from Detroit plus the Graphic Electric

What strange beasts are these that should have been snared before? Why, an American "Leica" from the 30's and a three-volt Graphic!

As historians and prison designers are well aware, human ingenuity is an insidious thing to try to delimit or contain. Even when you attempt the seemingly simple task of defining a category of man-made artifacts—35mm cameras, for example—you will invariably run across a few that make a shambles of your classifications and others that simply slip through your analytical net. This time we'll deal with two fascinating examples of the latter variety—a pair of 35mm cameras that, to be consistent, I should have covered in previous columns. And just to prove that consistency isn't always "the hobgoblin of small minds," both happen to be rangefinder cameras bearing American trademarks.

A Detroit-made Leica? Hardly, but the Detrola was cheap and built like a tank.

The first turns out to be a 1939 answer to that ever-popular question. "Did we ever make a decent Leica copy in this country?" Well, I already burbled on at length about that topic when I covered the fabulous Kardon, Premier Instrument Company's "imitation Leica." (You remember, the project for the Signal Corps that never got off the ground until World War II was practically over.) But in many ways the Detrola 400, made by the Detrola Corp. of (you guessed it) Detroit, Mich., was more interesting. For one thing, it was a more original design, and for another, it was conceived as a "Leica" for the semi-affluent

Depression masses, something the original Leica could never hope to be. Suffice it to say that the 400 was the poshest of Detrola's handful of different models. It was the company's only serious attempt to break into the "luxury" 35mm market, and it sold at a somewhat reasonable price (for the time) of $69.50.

Well, to dispel any illusions before they arise, your 7/10 of a C-note—easily two weeks' wages in those days—couldn't buy anything resembling a Leica even then. But you've got to admit, the Detrola 400 does succeed in capturing the "Leica look" without being a slavish imitation. As a matter of fact, if you can forget the Leica for a moment and judge the Detrola solely on its own merits, it turns out to be a pretty good camera despite a few minor failings.

As you can see by gazing at its portrait, the Detrola 400 is a rangefinder 35. As it turns out, it's also a coupled rangefinder 35 with separate rangefinder and viewfinder windows about 9/16 in. apart (near the top of its backside). It has a screw-thread interchangeable lens on the front, and a horizontal, cloth focal-plane shutter inside—just like you know what. Its normal lens is a 50mm f/3.5 Wollensak Velostrigmat (a triplet type), its rangefinder base length is about 1⅜ in., its format is the standard 24 x 36mm and its shutter's marked speeds range from 1-1/1500 sec., including such Wetzlarian favorites as 1/75 and 1/200 sec. So much for the more pedestrian stuff.

Perhaps you're wondering how Detrola managed to get 1/1500 sec. out of an "ordinary" focal-plane shutter? Answer: they didn't—it's a figment of some ad man's imagination and you were lucky indeed if this setting provided a true 1/1000 sec. speed, or thereabouts. But the Detroit beast had its good points too—a slide-off back for easier loading, a reasonably contrasty and accurate rangefinder (with the circular focusing patch in a contrasting greenish color) and a remarkably good satin chrome finish to complement the body's commendable structural integrity.

Heavy duty? You bet!

The Detrola's rugged body construction was achieved in typically straightforward American fashion—by using heavily plated, rolled-metal construction, held together at various places with rivets (!) as well as screws. And you can rest assured that lots of brass resides under that heavy plating—despite its svelte Leica-like dimensions (5¼ x2⅝ x 2¾ in.) the 400 weighs a tad over 1 lb. 7 oz. with lens. Even its fictitiously marked shutter has a couple of grace-saving virtues. Unlike its expensive German mentor's, the Detrola's slow shutter-speed dial (1-1/10 sec.) is placed conveniently atop the camera (about an inch to the left of the main shutter dial), and you get slow speeds by simply turning the dial until the arrow points to any setting but that one marked "Out," *irrespective of the "fast" speed set on the main dial.*

Rounding out the Detrola's niceties are a small but usable viewfinder to the right of both rangefinder windows, a reasonably smooth-operating film-wind knob, an odd, front-mounted rewind button that many folks mistake for a self-timer and a folding rewind handle that nests in a round recess in the camera top to the right of the accessory shoe. "Not so niceties" include a narrow, semi-high-pressure shutter-release button, and—the final heartbreaker— a non-standard screw-thread lens mount. Yes, you can screw the Detrola's lens into your screw-thread Leica despite the fact that its thread is finer than the Leica's and a bit narrower at 38mm rather than 39. But alas, you can't focus it farther than about 5 ft.—the brass cam at the rear of the Wollensak optic won't couple properly. As for getting an Elmar or other Leitz lens on your Detrola, it simply won't fit—period.

Oh well, these days such tribulations matter little, for the Detrola 400's status as a collector's item far outstrips its value as a usable camera. In fact, I'd say it just about qualifies as being rare, which is why I'd peg a clean one at $150-200 today. I know, you just nabbed one for $29.50 and I'm responsible for creeping "camera inflation."

Interchangeable lenses? Sure, but that's not this Graphic's main attraction.

Turning now to something not quite as obscure but equally weird, we have the Graphic 35 Electric, a camera that should have concluded my December 1975 ruminations on the demise of the Graphic-Graflex company. Like the spartan Stereo Graphic, the Electric was actually made by Iloca, a West German firm, and, as you might suspect, it featured electric motor drive—a pretty nifty commodity back in '59 when the camera first came out. Unscrew the chrome cover on the camera's bottom, lift off an additional plastic cover and you're greeted by two penlight batteries. Their job? To advance the film and cock the shutter at speeds up to 1 frame per sec. The designers apparently

had sufficient faith in the motor to delete the conventional film-advance lever.

O.K. Let's insert a fresh pair of AA's and put this baby through its paces. To load the Electric pull back on the right side of the camera body and its comes off in your hand—peculiar. You now push a ridged catch on the lower right side of the back to release the bottom-mounted rewind crank, pull the crank down and insert a fresh roll of film. The take-up spool's on the left side, but it's not really a spool, it's a drum with one measly slot. Now insert the leader into this lone slot, wind the drum manually to make sure that film engages securely, line up a red dot inside the camera with one on the back and snap it shut. Oops, I almost forgot, you're supposed to set the manual frame-counter wheel (above the film aperture inside the camera) *before* you close the back, so let's turn it until the red signal appears in the little window below the selenium meter grid on the front of the camera. This sets the subtractive film counter for a standard 36-exposure roll.

When you push the shutter-release button in to advance the film to the first frame you finally get to experience something exciting—the classic "click-whirr" of the electric motor-drive camera. Furthermore, unlike many early cameras of this type, the Graphic Electric will advance film continuously, as long as you keep the shutter button depressed. Granted, you can advance film just as fast (if not faster) using an ordinary, manual, rapid-wind lever, but the Graphic lets you hold the camera a lot steadier while you shoot.

Now, you might think that this would exhaust the Graphic's more outrageous features, but it isn't so. Push a spring-loaded button below the normal 50mm f/1.9 Steinheil Iloca-Quinon lens and it bayonets off in a quick leftward twist. This reveals a three-lobed bayonet mount, a Synchro-Compur 1-1/500 sec. MX sync shutter in the middle and a flimsy-looking spring-loaded pin positioned at about 7:30. Amazingly, this last device is the rangefinder-coupling arm that "reads out" the rotary motion of each lens's focusing cam. This is located in an arcuate groove on the back of the lens. In addition to the Quinon, I was fortunate in obtaining the longest optic for this camera—a 135mm f/4 Rodenstock Rotelar, which provides, if nothing else, that more than one major German lens maker got into the Graphic Electric act.

The Graphic is quite nicely finished in too-shiny chrome, its 50mm-base rangefinder is bright, contrasty and quite accurate, and the light-collecting frosting around the round rangefinder aperture serves to illuminate the camera's two projected, non-parallax-compensating viewfinder framelines. This glorious gray beast also sports a mechanical self-timer and coupled f/stops and shutter speeds.

Thankfully, this latter system doesn't pose the usual uncoupling problems since there's no EV scale. If you turn the knurled plastic "ears" on the shutter-speed ring, the aperture ring simply moves along with it, giving you wider aperture as you select faster shutter speeds. And to set apertures alone, you turn a milled dial at the left of and slightly below the PC terminal.

Through-the-finder metering?

This brings us to the Graphic's metering system—which is brilliantly integrated into the camera's overall design concept. To the left of the lens there's an ASA/DIN film-speed dial with settings from ASA 10-5000 (the latter digits being somewhat optimistic in view of the small area of the selenium meter grid). Set the film speed, choose a shutter speed and grab onto the aforementioned aperture-control wheel below the lens. Now guess what happens when you bring the camera to eye level? Yep, just above the projected framelines is a white sector, and as you turn the aperture wheel a white meter needle moves back and forth over the sector. Center it and you've got the proper exposure. Incidentally, there's a duplicate, match-needle index located in an arc-shaped window atop the camera.

Now, a match-needle, non-through-lens metering system—even one with a scale projected above the finder area—may not sound too spiffy by today's standards. But combine it with electric film wind and interchangeable lenses and you have a formidable picture-taking machine—particularly when you consider the Graphic's 1959 manufacture date. Regrettably, the Graphic 35 Electric was not a great sales success despite its fairly reasonable price of $275 with 50mm f/1.9 lens. However, you know what that means—this fairly rare bird now fetches about $150 among collectors.

Incidentally, try as I might I have been unable to determine whether Iloca ever sold the Graphic 35 Electric in Europe under another name. If they didn't, they darn well should have, and if you know what they called it drop me line.

Leicamaniacs on the loose with postwar cameras

Are Leica collectors crazy? Well, I'll show you some postwar cameras that tickle their fancies and then maybe you can tell *me*.

Although I naturally sympathize (and empathize) with practically anybody nutty enough to amass mechanical and optical gadgets, I'm not ashamed to admit that needling Leica collectors is one of my favorite pastimes. After all, how else can you deal with these *enfants terribles* of the camera world who skulk about classifying various "models" of single-stroke M-3 Leicas by counting the number of screws on their fronts. You think I'm being uncharitable? Well, how come practically all the Leica collectors I've run across thumbed their arrogant noses at the "not really Leica" CL when it was in production, but then hot footed it down to the nearest Leica dealer to buy "the last one in mint condition" as soon as it was discontinued? The result of such shenanigans?

This Minolta-produced, compact, meterized Leica is now fetching a bit more than list price if you find one brand new, and a surprising $400-500 used (complete with 40mm f/2 Summicron lens). Not only that but most Leica cognoscenti insist that the CL is destined to be a "rare" Leica that will command, if not astronomical, then merely ridiculous prices in the near future.

Collectors of a less maniacal persuasion (myself included) shake their heads in disbelief. But wait, there's more, and it gets worse. You know the current (in Sept. '79) Leica R3, the first SLR to bear the Leica (as opposed to Leicaflex) nameplate? Well, it's an open secret that it's based on a modified Minolta XE-7 chassis, with most of its normal (50mm f/2 Summicron-R) lenses coming from Leitz Canada, and most of the camera assembly being done in the new Leitz plant in Porto, Portugal. Aha, but the very first production run of this international melange SLR bears the hallowed inscription, "Made in Germany," rather than the more common designation, "Made in Portugal." So what happens? The Leicamaniacs rush in and snap them up, creating the latest in a long line of "instant collector's items" from Leitz. A "Made-in-Germany" R3 is currently worth $1,000—body only—$200-300 more than a "Portuguese" R3 complete with normal lens. I'll bet this makes the folks at Minolta chuckle, but I'll wager that the chaps in Wetzlar aren't laughing.

But perhaps you're wondering how the good people at

A black beauty with original Leitz enamel finish, this "Swedish military" IIIf's worth over five grand with black Elmar!

Why is this M4 special? It's not just the Leitz "50 Jahre" stamp, but it helps. Lens is "standard" dual-range Summicron.

Leitz in Midland, Ontario (Canada) are reacting to all this? I'll tell you how they're reacting—by producing Leica rarities of their own. Now I wouldn't go so far as to suggest that they deliberately attempted to create rare, black, M4 rangefinder Leicas by stamping them Ernst Leitz Canada, Ltd., Midland Canada, but the effect is the same. In fact, this mere label change has produced two different varieties of the rare Canadian Leica M4—the one with the Leitz "50 Jahre" (50th anniversary model) insignia, and the one without. The former one is by far the rarer (about 375 made), and the body alone now fetches about $2,200. The "plain" black Canadian M4 body (about 1000 produced) goes for a paltry $1,000 at present. Incidentally, both models are finished in black chrome like the late, mostly unlamented Leica M5, which is now (you guessed it) discontinued and commanding a premium price (around $1,300 with lens).

Now you might think that the almost philatelic bent of Leica collectors, and their inordinate emphasis on (and willingness to pay exorbitant sums for) mere oddities of surface detail is a relatively recent phenomenon. Well it isn't, and some of the details they look for are not, strictly speaking, on the surface. For example, I may as well let you in on a little secret—you can tell where an M-series

Canadian nationalism? Not really, but Canadian markings make this black M4 pair super rare and headed for stardom.

rangefinder Leica was assembled or last repaired by examining the little seal placed at 12 o'clock on the camera's bayonet mount (after removing the lens, natch). An "L" indicates Leitz in Wetzlar, a "C" denotes Leitz Canada and the letter "Y" stands for Leitz in New York (and, I guess by extension, Leitz U.S.A. in Rockleigh, N.J.). Should your seal bear no letter at all, it may have been touched by (shudder) an independent repairman.

O.K. Now that you are thoroughly imbued with an appreciation for the Leitz mystique (and the incorrigibility of those who seek to immerse themselves in it), let's have a look at a few more postwar Leica rarities currently high on the Leicaphile's heart-throb list. Perhaps you'd better sit down and hold on to your lenscaps friends, for we're going to be talking about the rarest of rare, and the asking and selling prices are truly incredible.

One of the richest sources of these "special" Leicas is, oddly enough, the military, which has a habit of ordering quantities of Leica cameras built to their specifications and marked accordingly. In fact, I've already detailed the Leica KE-7A made for the American military in my May 1974 column. Even more fascinating are two late III-series Leicas made for the Swedish military. First the fabulous "triple crown," a 1960 black-body version of the "last of the classic Leicas," the IIIg. As you can see in its portrait, the IIIg is a knob-advance Leica, and like most of its predecessors it featured baseplate loading, screw-thread lenses and a coupled-but-separate rangefinder (i.e., there are separate rangefinder and viewfinder eyepieces on the back). Unlike its older brethren, the IIIg sports projected parallax-compensating framelines in the finder for 50 and 90mm lenses, a slightly taller body and *geometric* shutter speeds (1/15, 1/30, 1/60 sec., etc.) to 1/1000 sec.

Ever see a black IIIg? Neither had we until Swedish military decommissioned it.

To the Leica collector these bread-and-butter points are not terribly important. What makes this camera a rarity is that it's one of a very few "factory black" IIIg's (from an original batch of around 125) ordered by the Swedish military in 1960. Most went to the tank battalion, some to the coast artillery and all were affixed with the Swedish royal crest consisting of three crowns (see photo). When these cameras were first decommissioned in 1973, they were sold at around $75 each. Soon, word got out about the crowns and the nonstandard paint job, and "triple crown" Leicas started bringing $1,300 at auction. The one pictured (which has a 50mm f/2.8 Elmar lens also adorned with three crowns) is now worth a cool $4,000 even in fair condition. Oh yes, should you stumble across a 35mm f/2.8 screw-thread Leica Summaron with three crowns on the lens-mounting ring, you can probably extract around $1,000 for it from a certifiable Leica nut.

Those minuscule letters under "Germany" mark this as the only "French" Leica.

Crowning achievement of tatty IIIg is Swedish royal crest. Translation: $4,000.

Now as it turns out this Swedish-military bit didn't commence in 1960. Back in '56 the Swedish Air Force and Coast Artillery ordered about 100 black IIIf models (very much like the IIIg but a bit shorter, no framelines in the finder, non-geometric shutter speeds to 1/1000 sec., no self-timer). These are reportedly even rarer than the "triple crown" Leica since only about 50 of the original batch managed to survive the rigors of military service. Also, they were fitted with a factory-black version of the collapsible 50mm f/3.5 Leitz Elmar—very pretty indeed, as you can see from its picture. The black IIIf was also decommissioned around '73, and owner Bob Sperling estimates his near-mint example is worth a staggering $5,000.

Deceptively ordinary Leica IIIa with 50mm f/2 Summitar has unique top plate.

It seems that no matter what era of Leica production you delve into, you invariably come up with a few oddball cameras destined to titillate the jaded palates of the upper-class gents and capitalist parvenues who comprise the bulk of Leica collectors. The unfortuante thing is that they then proceed to sock them away in various safes and bank vaults so none of us plebeian Leica lovers can ever get a glimpse of them. The Leica IIIa pictured is such a case. Fresh from the vault to you it looks suspiciously like any old IIIa in very nice condition, and as such the body might be worth $100-$125. However, once you glance at its top plate you know it's a star. Underneath the common phrase, Wetzlar Germany, is the curious legend "Monte en Sarre" (assembled in the Saar).

The obvious questions: how can a camera marked Wetzlar, Germany be assembled somewhere else, and why would anyone want to do so? Well, the historical reasons are quite interesting. Back in 1952-53, before the Common Market and while feelings of hostility over WW II were still running quite high, the French imposed a very high tariff on German-made goods, including Leicas. So, to get around the tax man, some genius decided to assemble Leicas in the Saar (then French territory, but heavily populated with Germans). About 125 of these flash-synced, vulcanite-covered IIIa's were made, and then the idea was scrapped. The result is an extremely rare, easily identifiable Leica, currently worth about $1,200. Interestingly, the appearance of these cameras (which were assembled of Wetzlar-made parts) is fully up to the Leica standard, but the renowned "Leica feel" suffered a bit in the "French" translation.

Now there are two things you've got to say for Leitz: they make damn fine cameras, and they're not stupid. So, back in '75 they decided to capitalize on some of the Leica-collecting madness by issuing cameras adorned with the 50th Anniversary (50 Jahre) crest alluded to earlier. These included the Leica M4, M5, CL and the Leicaflex SL. Oddly enough, as a marketing strategy, the idea flubbed at the time, but now, years later, the prices of cameras bearing the anniversary escutcheon are beginning to escalate disproportionately. Of course, my spies tell me that lurking somewhere in a locked vault in Rockleigh, New Jersey, there's a special 50 Jahre stamp used to re-engrave new top plates for damaged anniversary-model cameras. Now if we can somehow get our hands on that stamp and remove the original top plate of my 1954 two-stroke Leica M-3.

The Gami:
Italian Rolls-Royce of ultraminiatures

The Gami, Italy's ultraminiature masterpiece. Well, what do you expect; it's named after Galileo!

If Leicas have always elicited the collecting instincts of otherwise normal photographic enthusiasts, there's another entire camera category that's managed to do like-wise—namely, ultraminiatures (sometimes called sub-miniatures by those not attuned to the subtleties of marketing savvy). Now, you might think that folks fell in love with these beautiful, cute, but often impractical little beasties solely because of their jewel-like finish and dainty appearance, or maybe to fulfill their super-spy or sneaky-photojournalist fantasies. However, among hardcore equipment amassers, there are more materialistic reasons for their unceasing popularity—they take up much less room in the closet, display case, bank vault, are few enough in number that one might hope to achieve a complete collection (at least of a given era) and nobody will pester you as to why you're hoarding that Minox IIIS when it really should be in the hands of a deserving photographer.

Do you think the last quip implies that sub—pardon—ultraminiatures are less than serious photographic instruments? Well, to be truthful, a large percentage of them do wind up in top drawers along with the gold-plated letter opener from Kansas City, but you can't accuse their makers of not taking them seriously. Take the Gami, for example, an exquisitely made, satin-finished, alloy-bodied creation of Officine Galileo Di Milano (Italy). Perhaps the greatest compliment you can pay it is to say that in terms of conception, execution and performance it lives up to its maker's famous namesake. Indeed, it is often referred to as the Rolls Royce of ultraminiatures.

Are you suitably impressed? Well let's maintain this level of awe by merely listing the Gami's specifications: closed, it measures 4⅝ x 2⅛ x 1⅛ in., and it weighs in at 10½ oz. In this palm-sized package are a six-element 25mm f/1.9 Esamitar lens that focuses to 20 in., a spring-loaded guillotine-type shutter mounted in front of it that offers speeds of ½ to 1/1000 sec., plus B., a coupled, coincident-type rangefinder with automatic parallax compensation throughout its focusing range, and a three-frame-per-wind spring motor drive. Not bad for a camera that provides a 12 x 17mm format on unperforated 16mm film!

Precursor of 110? Gami's size, shape, format are close; finish is infinitely superior.

Loading's a flip-out: Insert square key on film-wind gear into cartridge end.

O.K., enough fanfare, let's take a few pictures with this Italian marvel. You open the back for loading by turning a coin—(or stout fingernail) operated twist lock from "C" to "O" and swinging up the back. Note the gorgeously smooth, dimpled-stainless-steel pressure plate, and operate the knurled focusing wheel as you observe the beautifully polished die-cast film aperture. That's right, it moves in and out as you focus, while the lens remains fixed—a well-executed example of film-plane focusing. To load the double-ended cartridge you pull upwards on a tab at the bottom left of the film compartment until you see a steel arm with the film-advance gear and square film-advance key affixed to the end of it.

Mount the slotted end of the cartridge over the square key, bring the keyed end of the cartridge into its receptacle and you can now swing the film supply end of the cartridge into its nest atop the film aperture.

Now that the film's loaded, let's set the camera for picture taking. There's no need to set the film counter—it's additive and self-zeroing, so let's direct our attention to the film-speed dial on the Gami's left side. This unlikely looking device has color film settings in red from ASA 20-150, and black-and-white film speeds in black from ASA 12-200. If you set your ASA and turn the outer edge of this milled wheel, you can either set click-stopped apertures from f/1.9 to f/11 using the bottom scale or "weather conditions" (seascape in bright sun, cloudy bright, etc.), using the legend above the wheel. Shutter speeds are set on a circular dial just below the shutter release on the camera's right side, and the geared selector wheel is thoughtfully placed right at the graceful curve of the camera's back edge for convenient thumb manipulation. The focusing wheel just below it is a virtual duplicate of the shutter-speed dial, which means it not only looks jazzy but is extremely functional.

Flip-down grip and thumbwheel focusing facilitate facile picture taking.

All right, let's now wind the film—simple. Just press a button atop the camera and the combined grip handle and lens protector swings out. Pull it down and push it closed and you've just wound the spring motor for three exposures. Since we've just loaded a fresh cartridge we'll bring down the handle again, pop off those three film-positioning exposures (same as 35mm) bringing the film counter to zero. Here you'll find one of the Gami's few foibles. While the shutter-release button is commendably smooth, the shutter is rather noisy and the spring drive imparts a fair amount of camera shake (albeit, after the exposure has been made). However, lovers of fine clockwork mechanisms will drool over the sound of the Gami's fine "bzzzt-click" when it's fired at a half-second, its slowest timed speed.

But wait one little minute—if the Gami is a manual camera—seven-bladed, six aperture diaphragm, nine shutter speeds and all—how come we set the ASA? To find out, let's bring the handle down again and peer through the admirably clear viewfinder. In its center is a large, yellow-tinted, rectangular focusing patch that provides a nice, contrasty focusing image, visible even in dim light. Brace the camera on something solid as you turn the focusing wheel over its full range and you'll notice that the outer finder frame moves vertically for parallax compensation. However, to the right of the finder field comes a real vintage-era surprise—an extinction meter! As you may recall, these blissfully simple but ordinarily imprecise devices incorporated a wedge or strip of varying density behind a series of translucent numbers, and the highest (or lowest) number clearly visible was supposed to give you the correct exposure. While they're generally more accurate than a wild guess, extinction meters are plagued by a physiological phenomenon known as visual brightness accommodation. At any rate, the Gami is one of the very few cameras of its era (born around 1953, deceased approximately 1965) to use this type of metering system, and the ways in which they refined it are remarkable.

Evolution of extinction

To begin with, the position of the variable-density wedge is controlled by the ASA and aperture (or weather condition) you set. This is reflected in the range of white numbers visible along the right edge of the finder. Then, as you turn the shutter-speed dial, a white strip with (egad) more weather symbols numbered one to six (in Roman numerals, natch) moves up and down so you can match the ambient illumination to the highest extinction number you can see. While this elaborate system undoubtedly represents an advance over the traditional "point and pray" extinction meter, I reverted to those old devil shutter-speed and aperture digits for most of my "Gamineering." Oh yes, you say you can't see the digits in the finder too clearly? Well, just remove your bifocals and turn the collar on the adjustable eyepiece.

What else can you possibly say about this incredible camera? That it has a "film loaded" signal behind the shutter release, a built-in slide-up yellow filter controlled by a little metal lever below the lens, that its lens and range/viewfinder are protected by coated optical flats and the PC socket is a screw-in accessory that fits into the European tripod socket below the hinged back? Well, you didn't think that the Gami lacked flash sync did you? As it turns out, these minor points pale into insignificance when you start bringing up the Gami's accessory list, which included an enlarger, a film cutter, spooler, viewer, slide mounters, daylight-loading metal film tanks, beautiful 4X and 8X tele converters that slip over the normal lens, right-angle finders, tripod adapters and myriads of other paraphernalia too numerous to mention.

To answer the obvious remaining questions—yes, the Gami was (and is) a damn fine picture taker for its format size. The camera's prestige probably contributed to the Germans' adoption of the same 12 x 17mm format (but not the Gami cartridge) as the DIN ultraminiature standard around about 1963. Gamis generally sold for approximately $300 to ($297 and $299.50 are two common prices). No, the Gami will not shoot bursts of pictures as some have claimed, but dexterous shutter-button pushers can shoot three frames in under two seconds before having to recock the motor. Today, used Gamis fetch $250 on up depending upon condition, and many accessories (some brand new) are available from Olden Camera, 1265 Broadway, New York, N.Y. 10001, who supplied the camera for this chapter. And while Gami cartridges can be reloaded from 35mm stock using the special film cutter, Edixa Camera Corp., 705 Bronx River Rd., Bronxville, N.Y. 10708 can supply fresh film in Gami cartridges.

Mec 16 SB:
Ultraminiature with TTL meter

Did Leicas get meterized using Black Forest technology? A close look at the Mec 16SB may surprise you!

The moment I started to fondle that luxurious 16mm Gami I knew it was bound to happen—the ultraminiature bug bit me again—right in the pocketbook. What's worse, my irresistible lust for these lilliputian marvels has not only eroded what was left of my "discretionary income," it has also lured me back into the darkroom to do silly things. Yes, like many another "ultraminiaturist" maniac, I rack my enlarger to the top of the column just to see how large an enlargement my newly acquired jewel can eke out of a pinky-print-sized 10 x 14mm negative, and mutter nasties under my breath as I vainly try to stuff 2-ft. lengths of Plus-X #7231 negative film into recalcitrant little cartridges. However, when I started toying with the idea of affixing my wee photographic beasties to a medium-sized tripod in search of optimal image quality, I knew I had gone bananas.

What manner of tiny camera can inspire such fits of frenzy in an otherwise hard-nosed camera fancier, you ask? Well, take the Mec 16 SB, for example. Its picture turned up unexpectedly in Modern's miscellaneous camera portrait file, and it sure looked intriguing with its hanging wrist chain and flip-out wind lever. Closer inspection of the shot revealed its aperture scale is set at f/2 and its shutter dial indicates 1/500 sec. with a 1/1000 sec. setting barely visible above it. Next to the shutter-speed dial (lower right end) is a film-speed dial with settings of ASA 10-100 and what looks like a meter needle in a crescent-shaped window. Hmmm. A 16mm pocket camera

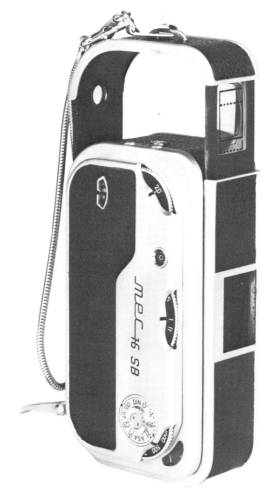

Outwardly unpretentious, Mec 16 SB had six-element f/2 lens, incredible meter.

with an f/2 lens, shutter speeds to 1/1000 sec. and a built-in meter. Pretty jazzy—the only Mec I had ever played with was the plain "16" with f/2.8 lens and no meter.

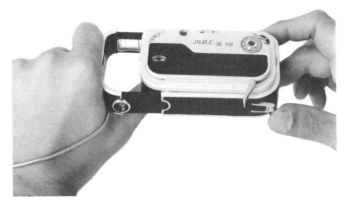

Handy shutter button's on Mec's backside.

Well, to make a brief story even shorter, I called a few of my fellow ultraminiature nuts about this German-made gem and they referred me to one Jules Swirdlin of Exakta Camera Co. (705 Bronx River Rd., Bronxville, N.Y. 10708), the last known supplier of Mec cameras to an unsuspecting America. Did Mr. Swirdlin have a Mec 16 SB to sell? How many would I like in the original unopened boxes at $50 apiece, he asked, and how many reloaded cartridges of fresh film? Incredible. These cameras were made in the early 60's and he had bunches of new ones complete with leather cases at under $60.

When my Mec arrived sealed in its little white hinged box I cautiously lifted the lid only to find a layer of semi-decomposed foam rubber partially adhered to the camera's surface. Moments later, after a thorough cleaning with a soft brush and compressed air, a brand new satin-chrome-finished 4 x 2¼ x 1⅜ in. camera emerged from the yellowish dust. Following the instructions (in English for a change), I pulled up on the chain and the inverted Galilean finder slid open—a satisfactorily clear but not overly large device complete with fixed black parallax compensation framelines. This simultaneously uncovered a lens-protecting cover, and when I peered in at the coated optic itself the identification ring proved it was a 22mm f/2 Rodenstock Heligon, a fine quality six-element lens similar in design to the Schneider Xenon. Impressive. Equally pleasing was the conveniently placed milled focusing wheel (to the left of the lens port) which is calibrated in feet (1 ft. to infinity) including a fixed focus setting labelled "S"), has click-stops at all settings, and features unit focusing of the lens.

Other pleasantries are also in evidence. The SB's overhanging milled aperture wheel below the finder includes a full range of apertures down to f/16, and the aforementioned shutter-speed dial has geometric speeds from 1/30-1/1000 sec. plus B. The hinged film-advance lever advances the film in a smooth 90° wind, and the shutter button is handily placed on the back of the camera. It's threaded for a cable release and operates very smoothly and predictably, though you can feel a small

amount of shutter-induced shake when you press it. On the Mec's bottom is a standard American ¼ in. tripod socket and there's the accursed (but standard) PC connection on top. You may think these latter items are no big deal, but it's surprising how many sub-35mm cameras lack them.

I then aimlessly glanced at the ASA dial bemoaning its lack of faster film speeds when all of a sudden it hit me like a ton of bricks—that little meter needle was responding to the change in light as I passed my hand over the lens port. This could mean only one thing—it must be a selenium meter. If it were a CdS meter the battery would surely have popped out after 15 years or so in storage. Fine, so it was a selenium meter, but then where was the telltale "honeycomb" diffusion grid? Back to the instruction book. There it was on page 13—a diagram of the Mec's metering system. It has—are you ready for this—a behind-the-lens selenium meter placed in front of the metal focal-plane shutter! To answer the obvious question, no, it wasn't the world's first behind-the-lens meter—Topcon perfected one a few years earlier in 1959. However, the Mec's horizontally hinged selenium meter cell does flip out of the light path before the shutter is released, (it has to—otherwise no picture). Ironically, this concept was hailed by many as a world's first when Leitz introduced a similar system on the CdS-metering Leica M5 more than a decade later. Just for laughs, we checked the Mec's Gossen meter on Modern's test instruments, and guess what—it's pretty damn accurate (though admittedly it's not super-sensitive in low light and you have to line the needle and index mark very precisely to get the right exposure).

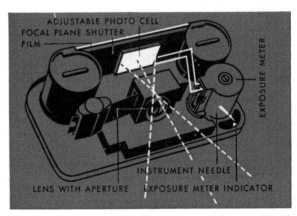

Meter is by Gossen and it's one of the only selenium types ever placed behind lens.

At this point, you're probably wondering just what group of geniuses fabricated this unlikely creation. Well, not surprisingly it was made in Germany's Black Forest; no, not by elves in a cuckoo clock factory—by Feinwerktechnik in Lahr. As you might suspect, the SB's jazzy meter is coupled to both the aperture and shutter-speed controls—a true match-needle system. Rounding out the niceties on the Mec's other side are a filter slot with a spring-loaded cover, a film-type reminder window, and a "film-is-loaded" verification window.

O.K., now that you're suitably impressed, let's take some pictures. To load one of the little almost cylindrical film cartridges you press a chrome button atop the Mec's main camera body (it's in between the front and rear viewfinder glasses) and lift out the main body section. Film is loaded straight across by inserting the fresh film leader on the left into the empty cartridge on the right and dropping each cartridge into its respective receptacle while sliding the film under the spring-retained pressure

No rewind is needed with dual cartridges.

plate. The dual-claw advance system is designed for use with double-perforated 16mm film. If you've loaded the camera properly (it's easy) a black rather than a red signal is visible in the film-load window—a good feature. To complete the loading process, you click off three blank exposures and set the exposure counter to the number of frames on the roll (it's substractive and locks the shutter release automatically when it reaches zero).

Featurewise, the Mec 16SB is certainly impressive, but it's not without its foibles. It's body is made of relatively thin pressed metal. While this material is commendably light (the camera weighs in at 9½ oz.), it's somewhat delicate and the main body-retaining catch borders on flimsy. The lens diaphragm consists of two V-shaped metal strips which provide a diamond-shaped aperture. This isn't as crude as it sounds, and it should certainly be durable, but a more nearly round diaphragm is optically preferable, particularly at small apertures. And what kind of picture taker is this marvelous Mec? Quite good, actually—much better than most ultraminiatures I've used if my satisfactory 11 x 14 enlargements are a reliable indication.

Oh yes, I almost forgot—the Mec 16 SB originally sold at $99.50 and a clean, functional model presently fetches about $100-150.

Rollei 16S:
Ultraminiature that was too good?

The redoutable Rollei 16S: Brilliantly designed, exquisitely constructed, and destined to be inadvertently killed by its own maker!

So, you thought that my brief excursion into the mad, mad world of Leicas meant that my current ultraminiature passion had died down eh? Well, unfortunately for my wallet, it hasn't quite, and my latest acquisition was my most expensive purchase to date. Of course, in many ways, the Rollei 16S is the nicest rangefinderless 16mm still camera ever made, so I'm not exactly crying in my beard over the whole thing.

I suppose, as an old hand, I should have known better than to peer too closely into the "classic camera showcase" at a leading New York camera emporium, but there it sat, resplendent in satin chrome, highlighted by the funky looking Futura S residing next to it (an oddball interchangeable-lens leaf-shutter 35mm made in Germany in the late 50s). At any rate I had to have it, so I wound up paying just a little less than the store's $149.50 asking price for this near mint condition example. And what manner of semi-practical lilliputian marvel can make this jaded camera collector part with so much bread, you ask? Well,

Posh and pocketable, the Rollei 16S was also pricey, but a fine, flexible picture taker.

as it turns out, the 16S is not only a marvelously aesthetic little beast and a fine picture-taker for its size, it also has an impeccable pedigree.

It's seems that back in '63 the Rollei folks in Braunschweig, Germany, noticed that their magnificant twin-lens reflex roll film cameras were not exactly setting the world on fire, sales-wise. Rather than go up against such stalwarts as Leitz and Zeiss (not to mention the Japanese) in the 35mm arena, they decided to field a deluxe, auto exposure ultraminiature—the original Rollei 16. Its place in history is assured as Rollei's first postwar non-TLR.

Does this idea seem dumb in retrospect? Consider the times. Kodak had not yet unleashed its 126 Instamatic avalanche in the shapshot field. Minox had not progressed beyond the match-needle model B and was committed to 8 x 11mm on 9.5mm film, and the Germans (of all people) had finally gotten around to agreeing on a standard 16mm film format and cartridge. The time seemed ripe, and Rollei plunged in.

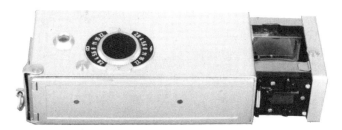

Rollei's bottom had dual aperture scales set by single knurled control (see text).

Now this is the place where I really ought to tell you all about the original Rollei 16 and its distinctive features, but since my diligent research department has been unable to unearth either the camera in the flesh or its instruction manual. I'll do it the other way around.

Refinements built into the 16S of 1965 that were lacking on the 16 include a modified double-claw film-transport mechanism, a new back lock (in front of the pop-up finder eyepiece), a simplified aperture lock, softer-action shutter-release button, and (of all things) a relocated red "universal focus" mark on the focusing scale (I guess they got it wrong the first time!). As you can see, these changes certainly justified a new model designation, but the plain Jane Rollei 16 was basically the same camera as its successor. I was also mildly annoyed to learn that the 16S was also produced in various jazzy coverings, including forest green, desert tan and snakeskin. Mine, of course, is done up in "ordinary" black, but its texture sure looks repitilian.

Getting down to the camera itself, slide the 16S out of its zippered pouch case and you're greeted by an elegant-looking, nicely satin chrome finished elongated box which measures a mere 4¼ x1⅝ x 1¼ in. Pull out on a striated grip atop the camera's left-hand edge (in shooting position) and the camera grows an inch in width as the inverse Galilean-type viewfinder erects into the viewing position and the chrome lens-protecting cover moves to the left, uncovering the coated 25mm f/2.8 Zeiss Tessar lens. One peek through the finder and you know you're dealing with a thoroughbred camera—the view is remarkably bright and clear, and free of distortion, and even the two pairs of projected white framelines (which remain visible in all but the dimmest shooting conditions) don't seem to intrude.

But wait just a darn minute—how come there are two pairs of framelines in this fixed-lens camera? Easy, the outer one covers the field of the 25mm normal lens, and the inner frame and entire visible viewing field corre-

spond to those of the tele and wide-angle attachments that bayonet over the four-lobed mounting ring located directly in front of the Tessar. If you think that these auxiliary lenses are the typical chintzy affairs beloved by off-brand accessory makers in the 50s and 60s, perish the thought. These, friends, are Rollei Mutars by Carl Zeiss, which certainly qualified as the best of their day and are remarkably good even by current standards. Specifically the pair consists of a 1.7X tele and a 0.6X wide-angle lens. These provided a 27° and 65° shooting angles, respectively, roughly equivalent to 90mm and 35mm lenses on 35mm.

Deluxe Mutars were super quality wide-angle and tele attachments, but too big.

And that's not all. Unlike many optical attachments the Mutars have virtually no effect on the effective f/stop set. Of course, this entailed using large-diameter glass elements, so neither one is exactly petite compared to the rest of the camera as you can see. Also, you have to do a bit of extra calculation to focus them, which goes like this—estimate your shooting distance, read it off the frontmost scale engraved onto the Mutar, then read the focusing distance you actually use to get this setting with the Mutar in place off the rear scale, and set this number in the focusing-scale window, atop the camera. Oh well, as usual it's easier to do than to tell about, and the little milled focusing wheel placed in the middle of the camera's leading top edge works very smoothly. The Mutars even have a dual scale for focusing in meters or feet, depending on how you mount them on the camera.

Fine and dandy, but aren't you going to get too much parallax? After all, the 25mm Tessar itself focuses down to 1.3 ft., and this corresponds to just under 3.5 ft. with the 1.7X Mutar. Not on your life! And here, I guess, is the Rollei's *piece de resistance*—its finder is fully parallax-compensated throughout its focusing range. Here's how it works. As you turn the focusing wheel, the front part of the Tessar lens turns in its helical and moves inward or outward from the film plane. This is par for the course for an interlens-shutter camera. But if you now direct your attention to the mirrored front viewfinder glass and watch it closely as you turn the focusing wheel, something really marvelous happens—it seesaws around a central pivot point in a clockwise direction (with the camera in hori-

57

zontal shooting position) as you focus the camera closer. If you now look through the finder as you focus, you'll see the framelines (which are reflected into the viewing area by the partially silvered front mirror using the von Albada system) move toward the right. Incredible—all the more so since it's accomplished with such elegant simplicity.

Inside the 16S you'll find gorgeous guide rails, room for one rewindable cartridge.

O.K., now that we've all finished oohing and aahing, let's get down to business and take some pictures with the thing. As long as the finder's erected, let's pop an index finger in front of the right edge of the eyepiece and pull the little button outwards until the hinged back pops open. Drop a little round-bodied cartridge into the receptacle on the left, pull the film leader in between the guide rails until a bit hangs into the film take-up chamber, and close the back. The frame counter on the bottom of the camera is self-zeroing and additive. Now we'll set the pain-in-the-finger, press-and-turn film speed scale (ASA 12-200) atop the camera, and make sure the bottom-mounted manual-or-auto exposure dial is on "A." Do these things, and advance the film to "0" by means of push-pull action on the slide-in finder, and you're ready to go. Incidentally, unlike some other push-pull film-advance cameras, the Rollei 16S will not advance either the film or its exposure counter until you click the shutter—no wasted exposures.

To take a picture, hold the 16S in your hands "hamburger style" (for horizontals) and press downward on the very smooth, threaded shutter-release button, conveniently placed near the center of the camera top. While the release is very smooth, you *can* feel a slight judder as the camera goes click—it's hard to eliminate it with the hefty springs required in a double-bladed "guillotine type" shutter. However, judging by the really fine quality pictures the Rollei delivered from its almost-110-sized 12 x 17mm format, shutter-induced camera shake is minimal. Moreover, this shutter is in a sense, doubly programmed—by varying the distance between its paired V-shaped blade ends, you can get apertures from f/2.8 to f/22 and, depending on the speed with which the blades move across the optical path, you can get timed shutter speeds from 1/30-1/500 sec. Both functions are set automatically by a Gossen selenium meter with its honeycombed face on the front of the camera.

How do you know you've got enough light to shoot? Simple. To the right of the finder image, in between the front and rear finder glasses, is a little prism which presents a little round, green signal if the light's O.K. If it's not, no green. Light to make this signal visible is furnished by a tiny frosted window on the front of the camera next to the lens. And what if you need flash? Or want to make time exposures? Just unlock the aperture dial and turn it to the aperture scale opposite the "blitz" mark (1/30 sec.) for flash or the second aperture scale next to the "B" mark for time exposures. You needn't worry about running out of film and not knowing it either—when you've reached the last (18th) exposure, the shutter won't click.

Once you've finished shooting a cartridge, you lift the rewind crank into position and turn it counterclockwise in the direction of the arrow until the film's rewound—a rewind button is neither present nor required. As we open the camera back to retrieve our film, let's take one last fond look at the nicely finished 2¼ in. long pressure plate (we knew Rollei would have to get that dimension someplace) and notice the two-pronged sliding film-advance bar which moves in a little slot cut into the bottom film guide rail. Oh yes, don't forget to hinge over the rewind knob with the back open so you can see how the little take-up pins emerge from its underside (they fit into slots on the outside of the cartridge that rotate the film spool inside).

And why did it go kaput?

Do you now wonder, as I did, why this regal mini bit the dust so soon after the 16S model was introduced, or why it was never anything more than a slow-but-steady seller in this country? Well, first of all, it wasn't cheap (the 16 listed at $189.50 and the 16S last retailed at $233). Then, of course, Rollei could never get certain key film manufacturers to supply 16mm emulsion in Rollei cartridges.

But there was more to it than that, according to Charlie Pelish of New York's Fotoshop. "No—Rollei 16's were never exactly hot items," said Charlie, "but they generated a fair amount of interest and sales until Rollei killed it for themselves," How? Easy—they brought out the Rollei 35, a camera that still fits in your pocket and that takes full-frame 35mm film to boot. Once they did that, you practically couldn't give a Rollei 16 away. Of course, now they're collectors' items that bring pretty fancy prices.) "Pretty fancy prices? Just how much are we talking about, Charlie?" "Well, just last week I sold a complete Rollei 16S outfit, complete with both Mutar lenses, special slide-on flash, in a nice presentation case, for just under a hundred fifty bucks." Oh well, I mused, as I kicked myself around the block, I didn't really need those blankety-blank Mutars anyway.

Minicord:
World's finest ultraminiature TLR?

So you think the name C. P. Goerz is only found on large-format lenses and ancient cameras, eh? Well, you're in for a Viennese surprise!

Since I am apparently unable to assuage my current passion for ultaminiature cameras merely by deflating my wallet of inflated dollars, I'm going to do the next best thing and raid someone else's 16mm collection. True, the joy of fondling and making pictures with these enchanting little creatures doesn't begin to equal the smug satisfactions of actual ownership. But if this non-acquisitive approach enables me to present a few of the unpurchased heartthrobs of my youth, to evaluate them rationally instead of nostalgically, and to get them out of my system, I will consider it time well spent.

The first entry in this category is a camera I've lusted after for so long that I'd still like to own one (at a reasonable price) even though I've discovered its tragic deficiencies first hand. No matter. The concept of the Austrian-made Minicord is so overwhelmingly functional and elegant it's hard not to love the camera at first sight. While hardly the smallest of ultraminiatures (it's a cigarette-pack-sized 4⅛ x 2¾ x 1⅛ in.) the camera is as gorgeously finished and styled as any of its species.

Although it may not resemble one at first glance, the Minicord is actually a full-focusing twin-lens reflex. The taking lens is a 2.5cm f/2 Goerz Helgor (not too surprising since the whole camera was produced in Vienna by C. P. Goerz), a very fine six-element optic with focusing down to 15 in. The finder is equally impressive. As you turn the knurled focusing collar and peer through the angled eyepiece atop the camera, you see a large, reasonably bright

The magnificent Minicord: the world's finest ultraminiature TLR, it had excellent lens, finder, quite shutter, trigger wind and a single, fatal flaw.

viewing image that snaps into focus with remarkable precision (especially when you consider the Minicord's tiny 10 x 10mm format on 16mm film). And mind you this is not the laterally reversed viewing image you get with a waist-level TLR. The Mini's top cover houses a roof prism that provides a laterally correct viewing (and action following ability) just like an SLR. Furthermore, the "1.2 power telescopic" viewing lens projects the viewing image onto a ground glass area that's correspondingly larger than the picture format. This clever idea is not unique to the Mini, but it accomplishes three things: it provides a larger viewing image without the problems encountered with high magnification eyepieces, it assures that the viewing area accurately corresponds with the picture area at all but very close focusing distances, and it reduces the observed depth-of-field of the focusing image, aiding focusing precision considerably.

You might think that incorporating such brilliant performance into such a compact viewing and focusing system is enough of an accomplishment, but Goerz put some icing on its little cupcake. In the center of the square finder image there's a finely engraved black circle to enable you to adjust the eyepiece for your own eyesight, and there are manual parallax compensation arrows about seven-eighths of the way up the left and right boundaries of the viewing image (to enable reasonably accurate framing at close shooting distances). Finally, while the viewing lens revolves in a single helical as you focus, and is connected to the taking lens by means of the latter's geared focusing collar (much in the manner of a Kodak reflex or a Richoflex VII) you can't see where these external gears mate—they're fashionably concealed (and protected from dirt) by the "shroud" that overhangs the taking lens.

Of course an exemplary lens and focusing system isn't much good if the shutter's a dud, but here too, the Minicord is outstanding. Near the top of the camera's left side is a knurled wheel with a concave depression for convenient finger manipulation in front of it. Turn this wheel and you can select shutter speeds of 1/10, 1/25, 1/50, 1/100, 1/200 and 1/400 sec. plus B in a little window. If you lift out the removable film chamber section and look inside the rear of the main camera body, you can get an excellent view of the shutter's operation.

To cock the shutter (and wind the film) just pull the trigger—literally. This striated metal device is conveniently placed on the right side of the camera in a hemi-cylindrical channel, and it operates in one smooth, short stroke, just like a pistol. Nice. O.K., let's set the shutter at 1/10 sec. so we can observe its action, cock it and fire it. The curiously shaped threaded shutter-release button is located only ¼ in. to the right of the film-wind (see photo) so rapid sequence shooting is a real possibility (the manufacturer's claim was 15 shots in 10 sec.). As you press the shutter button, the metal focal-plane shutter moves downwards at a leisurely pace, and makes almost no noise whatsoever. If you think this is merely due to the slow speed we've selected, guess again—even with the shutter set at 1/25 to 1/50 sec., you can't hear it operating unless you put the camera up to your ear. Indeed, the Minicord's shutter only begins to "click" audibly at 1/100 sec. on up, qualifying it as the quietest metal focal-plane shutter I have ever encountered.

Icing on the cupcake

Of course, the Minicord sports many other niceties, such as a ¾-in.-long flip-down grip on its bottom next to the tripod socket that facilitates one-handed operation, a depth-of-field scale on its left side (see photo), and our model III of 1958 even has a PC flash outlet. Atop the camera's left side is a manually-zeroed, additive type exposure counter that tops out at 42 (standard Minicord cartridges provided an impressive 40 exposures each). Of yes, I almost forgot, the 25mm f/2 Helgor lens has a front-mounted non-click stopped aperture control with stops to f/11 set via a six-bladed iris diaphragm.

Since it is clear by now that the Minicord is an amazing machine by anybody's standards, perhaps you're wondering why I began on such a note of impending doom. Sour grapes at not having snared this increasingly rare beast? Unfortunately not. To find the Achilles' heel of this Viennese pastry (the one pictured is enamelled and leathered in chocolate brown, others came with these areas done in black) take a close look at the open-back photo.

The first thing that is immediately apparent is that the Minicord (like the Mec 16 and the Rollei 16S) does not have a take-up spool. Film is advanced by claws on either side of the film aperture which fit into sprocket holes on either side of the double-perforated 16mm film. And since the Mini lacks a rewind, it employs the time-honored system of cartridge to cartridge feed—the film supply cartridge occupying the bottom receptacle in the removable back, the take-up cartridge going on top.

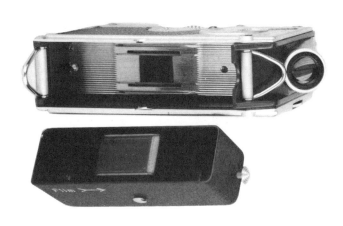

Mini's downfall was sprocketless film advance, limply sprung pressure plate.

This film-advance system, though tempting in its simplicity, is a known troublemaker. Even the Mec 16 and the Rollei 16S had occasional problems with film buckling in the film plane or not advancing properly in conditions of high humidity. Alas, on the Minicord, these problems were aggravated by a relatively short, softly sprung pressure plate and a film supply that was forced to run emulsion side out, against the natural curve of the film. The Minicord's technical nemesis manifested itself in a particularly maddening fashion—one exposure might be superbly sharp, while the next shot, taken under identical conditions, would be fuzzy. The damnable thing is that there is nothing the manufacturer could possibly have done to completely cure this fatal ailment within the confines of the Minicord's established body and cartridge configuration.

I have no proof of this, but it's possible (and ironic) that the Minicord's removable back with its attendant disasters may have inadvertently been created to accommodate another of its designer's wild brainstorms—to wit, the Minicord enlarger. This is probably the simplest, most elegant, and most technically dubious enlarger ever to grace (afflict?) an ultraminiature camera. It consisted of—ready for this?—a copy stand and a lamphouse. What about the rest? Just screw your Minicord onto the copying stand arm, snap off the film back and snap the film-holder-cum-lamphouse in its place and your Minicord is now the world's only enlarger with a 1/400 sec. top speed. How good was the 25mm f/2 taking lens as an enlarging lens? I leave it to your imagination, but it was probably adequate for small blow-ups if you stopped it down to f/8 or smaller.

I hate to leave such a glorious and really brilliant camera on this dour note, so let's put it back together and take some pictures. Pull down the grip, and grab it with your right middle finger. With your right index finger poised on the trigger, and your eye up at the finder, focus the lens by turning the focusing collar with thumb and index finger of your left hand, and take a few pictures. Even after half a dozen practice shots, you'll start to smirk as it becomes devastatingly clear that this little Mini, semi-

Hand-holdability was Minicord's forte, and hinged pull-down handle helped.

tele "normal" lens and all, is one of the most ergonomic and functional ultraminiature designs of all time. Furthermore, as a result Minicord owners in the audience needn't lament over the vagaries of their camera's actual performance. In short, if you have a Minicord in very nice to mint condition (preferably with case and instructions) just send it along to your old uncle Jason who'll promptly send you a cashier's check for $75, approximately half of what it's worth on today's collectors' market. Many thanks to S. F. Spira of Spiratone for furnishing the Minicord pictured and described herein.

German ultraminiatures, big and little

Which German ultraminiature would you prefer: a big one with a limitless lens supply or a tiny, fixed-lens job with an ingenious, add-on meter?

To all the loyal readers who've been patiently (or impatiently) following the progress of my "ultraminiature malaise" these past several chapters, I am happy to report that the latest bout of this recurrent affliction has finally subsided. As proof of my regained sanity, I'm beginning to turn my attention to medium-format cameras of the 50's and have even relegated my white gloves, tweezers and 16mm developing reels to temporary limbo. However, as punctilious proofreaders may recall, when I last mentioned raiding a fellow cameraphile's collection, I also implied there would be a sequel to the glorious Minicord. And so without further ado, here it is—the last pair of 16mm still cameras I'll be presenting for a while (I hope).

Let's commence with the Goldeck 16, a late 50's product from Gerhard Goldhammer of Frankfurt, Germany. This chrome-and-leatherette-clad creation is surely one of the largest 10 × 14mm format (on 16mm film) cameras ever produced, measuring in at a half-frame-35ish 4¼ × 1⅜ × 2⅝ in. Tempted to snicker? Well, the Goldeck's high, wide, and reasonably handsome design has several not-too-obvious advantages.

Biggest ultramini? Nope, but its maker took full advantage of its ample size.

As 110 pocket camera producers of a later generation discovered, a camera doesn't have to have three super-petite dimensions in order to be pocketable—two narrow measurements, or even one, will do quite nicely. In keeping with this philosophy, you'll note that the Goldeck is quite thin (1⅜ in. counting the lens), and it therefore slides into a trousers pocket comfortably with room to spare (though you probably won't forget it's there since it weighs a bit over 12½ oz.). The Goldeck's large body has additional bonuses—it permits the manufacturer to incorporate a proprietary leaf shutter and, more importantly, allows the photographer to mount any standard D-mount 16mm movie lens (they're readily available in a wide variety of focal lengths and are often quite cheap). To prove this to your satisfaction, just unscrew the Goldeck's normal 20mm f/2.8 Color-Ennit lens and, lo and behold, you'll see a standard five-bladed Vario (or Prontor) shutter with a coarse-threaded 25mm diameter D-mount right in front of it. True, the camera's two-format etched-frame viewfinder accommodates only two focal lengths—the viewing field of the normal 20mm lens (with parallax compensation markings) plus the field of view of the only official accessory lens I've seen listed, a 75mm f/3.5 Schneider Xenar.

O.K., enough mental fascination—let's load 'er up and take some pictures. To open the back, push two spring-loaded buttons on the 16's side toward each other (with the camera back pointing downwards) and the camera back will swing open. Knowledgeable ultraminiaturists who examine the Goldeck cartridge closely before inserting it are likely to smile—it's a dead ringer for the so-called "standard DIN 16mm still cartridge" promoted by Rollei and other German camera manufacturers in 1963. At any rate, to load the Goldeck, you pull down the spring-loaded rewind knob on the left side of the camera bottom, pop the cartridge in, and attach the film leader to the take-up spool. There are no sprockets to move the film along, but the take-up spool itself is positively advanced by a geared mechanism. The 1¾-in.-long pressure plate is also cleverly designed—its raised upper and lower edges fit snugly into the recessed film track, maintaining the film plane very accurately yet allowing the film to travel easily.

Once you've loaded the film, press down on the big, chrome, contoured film advance/shutter wind button atop the camera and then fire the shutter by pressing the rectangular button next to it. Do this a few times to position the film at the first exposure and set the subtractive film counter on the camera back to 20. As you might expect, setting the exposure is also a manual affair. Just select apertures f/2.8 to f/16 on the front-mounted click-stopped aperture ring on the front of the lens, choose a shutter speed (1/25 to 1/200 sec. plus B with the Vario shutter on our model, 1-1/300 sec. on models equipped with the Prontor shutter) and you're in business. With the normal lens in place the Goldeck is a fixed-focus camera, but this isn't as much of a limitation as it sounds. According to the depth-of-field scale on the outer flange of the lens, even at maximum aperture you're in focus from about 9 ft. to infinity, and at f/8 it's 5 ft. to infinity. Obviously, with other lenses (whether movie lenses or the standard tele lens mentioned earlier) you get a genuine focusing helical. (Indeed, the optical possibilities are staggering—for example I could've nabbed a 25mm f/1.5 Wollensak Cine Raptar with apertures to f/16 and focusing to 2 ft. for under 20 bucks!) 35mm fans needn't feel out of place either—once you've finished the roll, press the rewind button on the 16's front and turn the rewind crank on its bottom to get the film back into the cartridge.

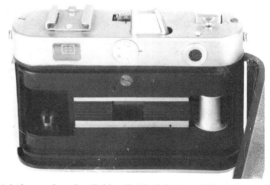

Straightforward and reliable, Goldeck had rapid wind, positive film advance.

As you can now appreciate, the Goldeck 16 is not so much a gadgeteer's delight as a straightforward, usable piece of equipment that takes advantage of "available materials." Rounding out its minor niceties are a standard ¼-in. tripod socket on its bottom, a shutter-release lock (to prevent it from firing in your pocket), a cable release socket, and an accessory shoe for those accessory viewfinders. But perhaps the nicest things about this decently finished, pleasant looking beast with the so-so viewfinder can be boiled down to "feel" and handling. Like a Leica, its rounded ends nestle comfortably in your hands, and, using two judiciously placed index fingers, you can fire the thing at close to two frames per sec. And so you see, dear friends, the world's biggest (almost) ultraminiature is not as silly as it sounds—in fact it's one of the few of its breed that didn't give me a single blurry close-up of my finger on the very first roll I shot! Goldecks are quite rare these days; but are often reasonably priced ($65-85) when you find them.

And now, a teeny mini

Turning to a more traditionally dimensioned miniature marvel, we hereby present the Edixa 16MB, a product of the ever-fascinating Edixa camera factory of Wiesbaden, Germany. Ours is the deluxe meter-coupled model of around 1966 (as opposed to earlier "16" and "16S" models having the same basic body configuration) and you've got to admit it's really tiny—3¼ × 1½ × 1¼ in. sans meter. Packed into this minuscule package are a four-element 25mm f/2.8 Schneider Xenar lens which unit focuses to just under 16 in. and has non-click-stopped aperture settings to f/16, a four-bladed, in-front-of-the-lens leaf shutter with speeds of 1/30-1/150 sec. plus B and full flash sync, and a very nice, large, etched frame viewfinder with parallax compensation markings.

As pictured here, the Edixa's milled focusing wheel is located to the left of the smooth-but-high pressure shutter release button and the exposure dial is on the right. This latter device has an ASA dial (with settings from 6-100) in the middle, a red dot orientation mark on its flat (unmilled) edge, and a most curious two-banded scale arrayed

Elegantly petite Edixa MB sported good finder, fine lens, many clever tricks.

beneath it. Turn the wheel clockwise and you can select B, 1/30, and 1/60 sec. If you turn it further you can set the dot opposite aperture settings from f/2.8 to f/16, all of which appear adjacent to a black band marked "150." Lacking an instruction sheet, my first reaction was, "What the blazes is this—combined aperture and shutter speed settings?"

To find out I turned the lever on the back of the camera from Z (Zu, or shut) to A (Auf, or open) and lifted off the combined camera back and bottom. Peering through the film aperture while I turned the exposure control dial, I noticed that nothing happened as I turned the dial from B to "60," and then to the f/2.8 aperture mark opposite the "150" band. However, as I turned the dial further, I observed a cute little six-bladed iris diaphragm (placed directly in front of the rear lens element) stopping the lens down all the way to a pinpoint f/16. Obviously, then, the Edixa's shutter speeds and lens openings are set separately all right, but why design a camera so you can only get slow speeds (1/30 and 1/60) when shooting wide open?

Add a mini meter? Easy—screw it onto camera and it couples automatically.

As I delved deeper into the Edixa's mysteries, I discovered, to my delight, that there is not only a logical reason for this strangely calibrated dial but a way to override it to get the full range of manual exposure settings. The explanation centers around the MB's most significant accessory, an itsy-bitsy coupled selenium meter measuring in at a nougat-sized 1 × 1⅜ × ⅞ in. If you examine the meter when it's off the camera you'll see a scale with a white moving needle on top that responds to light changes. Press in the spring-loaded coupling shaft emerging from the meter's left side and you'll observe a red meter-index arrow move across the bottom of the scale. There are no other calibration marks in sight. O.K., slide the flat shaft into a receptacle on the camera's right side, orient the two aligning pins, screw in the slotted retaining screw, and the meter is now coupled to the camera. As you turn the exposure control dial, the red index arrow moves from side to side, and you align it with the meter needle to get the proper exposure for the ASA you've set. Since the coupling shaft moves linearly, the exposure control dial must also operate linearly through its entire range, and that's exactly what it does—each successive setting halves or doubles the exposure. In short, the Edixa's oddly calibrated exposure dial enables the simplest possible form of meter coupling, and therefore represents a brilliantly simple solution to the sticky problem of mating a match-needle meter to an existing camera design.

On the Edixa's upper right-hand corner is the gizmo that lets you override the meter coupling to obtain 1/30 or 1/60 sec. at any aperture. Turn it off the meter-coupling setting marked "LW" to "30" or "60" and that's the speed you'll get at any f/stop you select. At the LW setting, you'll get the full range of apertures, but only at 1/150 sec. Of course, once you set the shutter speed manually, you have to set the exposure manually—if you line up the dials and shoot at a slower "override" speed setting, you'll get over-exposures.

Yep, you can even get film

As you might suspect, the Edixa abounds in all sorts of other fascinating details. Film is advanced with a single-stroke wind lever on the bottom (the stroke required is a bit too long for really rapid-fire sequences), the exposure counter adjacent to it is self-zeroing and additive, and you rewind the film back into the standard DIN cartridge after the last (20th or 21st) 12 × 17mm frame is shot. Like the Goldeck, film is advanced and positioned in the MB by a geared mechanism attached to the take-up spool, but the Edixa's spool is removable. The pressure plate and film rails certainly seem well designed and the Edixa had a reputation as a very good picture taker. (It takes the same cartridges as the Rollei 16S and these are available from Exakta Camera Co., 705 Bronx River Rd., Bronxville, N.Y.) Potential Edixa fanciers may discover that the Edixa 16MB is an elusive beast, but if you nail one in the flesh they can often be had for around $75, approximately 75 percent of their last list price.

Incidentally, the Edixa film supply folks mentioned above also have a distinctly odd collection of German lenses that they're presently unloading pretty cheaply. They include old favorites like Steinheil Quinons. Zeiss Jena Flextogons, so-so lenses like the unlamented Steinheil Cassarits and those eternal but lovable (to some) bombs, the Isco Westromats and Westrogons. The catch? Many of the nicer optics only come in relatively unpopular mounts like Exakta (which also fits Topcon) and Praktina bayonet, though there are a number available in Praktica-Pentax screw-thread mount. Or who knows—maybe you'd like a new focusing screen for your Praktisix I—(heaven forfend).

Bertram: Press camera with view camera pretensions

The big, beautiful Bertram was a brilliantly designed press camera with view camera pretensions—so how come it bombed in '52?

Having concluded the ultraminiature festivities with a pair of pocketable German lightweights, let's turn our attention to something more Teutonically substantial—one of Germany's last great attempts at building an all-purpose, medium-format press and view camera. No, I speak not of the Linhofs and Plaubels which might fit this description, but of the bountiful Bertram of 1952—almost 5 lbs. of gorgeously finished camera that does just about everything but stand on its head and whistle Bach's toccata and fugue in C major. A product of E. and W. Bertram of Munchen (Munich), this multi-format, multi-lens, mult-back beast is a magnificent example of fine mechanical engineering. As a matter of fact, by the time we're finished going over its features you'll probably wonder how any 1950's vintage American press photog in his right mind could've toted anything as pedestrian as a Speed Graphic or a (fixed-lens) Kodak Medalist instead. However, since the answer to that question makes such a fitting conclusion, we'll save it for the end.

To begin at the beginning, the Bertram is basically a 2¼ × 3¼-in. roll and sheet film camera with a coupled rangefinder, separate optical viewfinder and bayonet-mount interchangeable lenses. Like many of its breed, it's got a ground-glass back with a flip-up viewing hood, and it can be adapted to make 2¼ × 2¼-in. negs. Nice, you say, but not too exciting? Well, the easiest way for a Bertram owner to set cameraphiles aflutter is to slide out the grip and flash brackets a bit and undo three little knobs on the sides of the camera. All three have flip-up, D-shaped, chrome handles, and there are two on the right side and one on the left side (in shooting position). Once they're loose, you can pull out the camera back about an inch away from the main body. In front of the extended back you'll see a bellows, and there's a sliding strut affixed to each side of the back and its bottom as well (it figures—one screw lock controls each strut). Since each strut is attached to the back with a pivoted fitting, guess what you can do? That's right, you can tilt the back obliquely and lock it in place in any single direction or pair of directions to correct for linear distortion! True, the Bertram's inge-

Ahead of it's time? Yep, this camera's price and technical prowess probably did it in.

tion is close to life-size, it should be mighty accurate—it has to be because the Bertram's front bellows permits rangefinder focusing to about 32 in. with the 105mm lens.

To set shutter speeds (1-1/400 sec. plus B and T) you turn the large, knurled ring around the lens and read the appropriate digits in a little window directly above the lens. All shutter-speed numbers appear upside-down when viewed from the front of the camera so you can read them properly from behind, with the camera at chest level. You set f/stops (f/3.5-22 on the standard lens) by turning the frontmost ring on the lens itself—they're also visible at chest level. To fire the shutter, you first cock it by pushing down on a semicircular knurled tab visible on the left side of the lens (which causes a tiny shutter-cocking-indication pin to emerge from it), and press it a second time to fire the shutter. Although the cocking action requires relatively high finger pressure, the tab's firing action is commendably smooth and predictable.

As you might expect, the Bertram's front is literally festooned with all sorts of interesting doodads. Directly above the shutter cocking/firing tab is a smaller tab that

nious back doesn't afford quite the flexibility of a full-fledged view camera, and the rangefinder won't couple properly if the back is swung, but it's nevertheless an act that few dual-purpose, medium-format cameras can match.

And that's not all the Bertram's back will do. Push it back and lock it in "range-finder-focusing" position and push a knurled tab atop the ground-glass section to the left, and the entire ground-glass section hinges downward and can be easily removed by pushing it toward the right and lifting it off. If you push in a chrome button to the left of the film aperture, locking tabs above and below it move out of the way, allowing you to remove a roll film holder once you've slid it in. Directly in front of the bellows, you can see a large, five-bladed Synchro-Compur leaf shutter.

O.K., let's slide in a roll film adapter and take some shots using the rangefinder and viewfinder. To activate the former with the 105mm lens in place, you grab onto two metal "ears" adjacent to the lens and pull out the lensboard about ⅝ in. until it stops. You now focus by turning the large knurled wheel on the Bertram's right side (in shooting position). Flip up the viewfinder cover and the 2¼ × 2¼ in. (6 × 6 cm) mask (since we're taking full-format pictures) and you're ready to go.

The first thing you'll notice when you bring the Bertram to eye level (aside from its weight) is that the optical viewfinder is usable, but not overly large by modern standards. At any rate, it's tinted blue and afflicted with an obtrusive crosshair pattern that only an aerial lensman could love. A full 1½ in. to its left is the typical dinky rangefinder of the era, with its salmon-colored focusing image. Oh well—at least it's reasonably contrasty, and the smooth focusing mechanism makes it pleasant to use despite its "squinty" dimensions. And since the rangefinder's base is every bit of 3⅛ in. in length and its magnifica-

A swinging press camera, Bertram combined close focusing with multi-tilt back.

opens the (cocked) shutter for ground-glass viewing when you push it up. To the left of the lens is a small window which usually has a "V" displayed in it, but when you cock the shutter *and* push down on the little tab at the upper right-hand corner of the lensboard, it turns red, indicating that the self-timer has been activated. Directly below this latter tab is a knurled knob which locks the lensboard in position, and on the bottom of the lensboard's right side is the sync.-selector lever which sets either M or X in a small window to the right of the lens. Finally, inset in the left-hand end of the chrome bezel surrounding the lensboard are two rectangular windows which indicate which lens (65mm, 75mm, or either the 105 or 180mm lenses) is coupled to the rangefinder.

As usual, I've saved what I regard as the Bertram's piece de resistance for last—although you've probably guessed by now that it concerns the interchangeable lenses. If you bayonet in the 65mm f/6.8 Schneider Angluon wide-angle, make sure you don't pull the front standard out at all —just insert the lens, twist, check that the red needle in the window atop the lensboard reads 65 (which it will do automatically as long as you insert the lens properly) and examine the focusing scale to the right of the viewfinder on the Bertram's back. You will find that, miraculously, the little red number in the window has changed to 65, and you'll see the appropriate focusing scale and red needle point at its right. With the other three lenses (75mm f/3.5 Schneider Xenar, the aforementioned 105mm Xenar, and the 180mm f/4.5 Schneider Tele-Xenar), the procedure is identical except that you've got to pull the front standard out to the detent for proper rangefinder coupling. Unlike other medium-format, interchangeable lenses, the Bertram has no clumsy removable rangefinder-coupling cams—the whole coupling business is accomplished automatically for all four lenses by means of a special coupling lever inboard of the topmost bayonet recess of the camera's lens mount. Channels cut into the rear-most mounting surface on each lens have arcuate slots of different angles cut into them, so the coupling lever moves by a different amount depending on which lens you insert. This simultaneously sets the rangefinder cam profile and reads the proper focal length and focusing scale out at the back of the camera. Ingenious.

Bayonet with a twist: Mount any lens and it couples to rangefinder automatically.

So there you have it, an extraordinarily complex, brilliantly engineered 2¼ X 3¼ package with some of the most beautiful chrome and morocco leather ever to grace a camera. And while the Bertram's overall appearance is undeniably hefty and Germanic, its contours are actually rather stylishly wrought, given the nature of the beast. But wait —we're not quite finished with the technical tour de force department. No, I'm not talking about the clever snap-in strap fittings, or the combined bubble level and film-type reminder dial on top, or even the fact that the Bertram will get you down to 1:1 at maximum bellows extension with the 65mm wide-angle lens. What I'm driving at is the accessory shoe, of all things.

Slide in your handy accessory Bertram sports finder (a non-optical peep-sight-cum-frame device) and, wonder of wonders, it'll automatically adjust the rear sight vertically

How many feet? Check focus distance on auto-indexing scales to right of finder.

as you focus. How? Easy. In back of the shoe's side rails is a little, black spring-loaded cover. Directly under it is a cam that's connected to the focusing mechanism. So, when you push down the rear section of the sports finder to contact the cam, voila—auto parallax compensation with 75, 105 and 180mm lenses.

So getting back to our original question—how come this fabulous camera wasn't a great sales success in the U.S. and slowly faded out of production by the early 60's? Well, according to Charlie Pelish of New York's Fotoshop, there are several resons. "First of all, it cost a bundle— about $700-800 with the lenses. But most of all it was just too complex for its day. Remember, you're talking about the early 50's before photographers—especially press photographers—were used to such complex cameras. And interchangeable lenses weren't considered such a big deal back then. Talk about complicated, even *I* had to read the instruction book to learn how to operate the damn thing. Of course there's no denying that the Bertram was a really beautiful piece of machinery, and it worked very well in practice. Those Schneider lenses were gorgeous. I guess, to sum it up, the Bertram was about 20 years ahead of its time." Too bad. And how much is a Bertram outfit worth today? "I had a pretty complete outfit a while back and I think I unloaded it too cheaply at $650. Current value: about $1,000."

Omega 120: Brilliant American roll-film press camera

Which American roll-film press camera died young, then arose phoenixlike in the land of the rising sun? Hint: It's a native New Yorker.

Judging by the recent deluge of flag-waving mail I've been receiving lately, it's about time I got off my European kick and began extolling the virtues of a couple of ingenious American-made rangefinder roll-film classics of the 1950's. Sad to say, the one illustrious camera I'll be featuring wasn't a great sales success, and it went belly up only a few years after it was introduced. But while this is regrettable for its own sake, and boded ill for the future production of professional-level cameras in this country, it is a tale that has, for the collector at least, a silver lining. In short, when a unique, technically sophisticated camera isn't too popular and isn't manufactured for very long, it eventually becomes rare, sought after and, by the laws of supply and demand, worth a fair amount of dough.

Elegant it ain't, but the Omega 120 of 1954 embodied such sound engineering concepts, it sired its own breed.

The rare bird we'll be detailing is the amazing Omega 120 of 1954, sometimes known as the ugly American. Ap-

pearance aside, it is a camera so replete with worthwhile mechanical innovations and offbeat features, it's hard to know where to begin. To start with, it's one of the very first cameras to embody the so-called "ideal format" on 120 roll film—namely 2¼ × 2¾ in., sometimes known as 6 × 7 cm. In actual fact, the Omega's film aperture measures 55 × 67.3 mm, a frame size which substantiates its maker's claims by enlarging to almost precisely 4 × 5 (or 8 × 10) dimensions with virtually no negative area being wasted.

An exotic body

Does its portrait look ungainly? It is, to be charitable, on the homely side as cameras go, but it also features a well-designed anatomical grip on its right side, an oversized knurled focusing knob on its left; its body is fabricated of (ready for this) cast magnesium. While the use of this exotic and highly flammable material posed undoubted manufacturing risks, Simmon Bros. of Long Island City, N.Y. (makers of the famous Simmon Omega enlargers) thought that the risk was worth it—after all, it kept the camera's weight down to a then-unheard-of 2½ lb. or just a smidgeon over that figure.

Undoubtedly, the easiest way to highlight the Omega's operations in all their fascinating detail is to run a practice roll of 120 film through the beast, so let's do it. You begin

Informative back? You bet. All controls and functions are clearly labelled in military style—which is hardly surprising.

by directing your attention to the back, where there's a geared "pull-push" film advance knob sprouting from the lower right-hand corner that's thoughtfully labeled "Auto-film Transport." Before you lift off the back to load up, you've got to pull and push on this grabbable Bakelite knob as many times as is necessary to get the automatic exposure counter (thoughtfully labeled "Automatic Exposure Counter") to read "Open." You now turn the large knurled knob in the center of the back counterclockwise (in the direction of the arrow thoughtfully labeled "Open"), and lift the back off starting at the left side.

The Omega's insides are unremarkable, with left-to-right film travel, and spring-loaded film-retaining shafts atop each film chamber. However, it's clear that there's something unusual afoot. Why is the perforated aluminum pressure plate held in position by two spring-loaded studs? Why are its top and bottom left-hand corners notched to clear a pair of steel film-guide tabs? And what the heck is that shiny, parallelogram-shaped protrusion emerging from underneath the pressure plate's upper right-hand corner?

To put an end to your puzzlement, just hold the pressure plate lightly by its sides and press in the aforementioned protrusion with a handy pencil. Lo and behold, the pressure plate moves forward about ⅛ in.! This is because the protrusion we've been chatting about is actually one end of a "see-saw" lever affixed behind the pressure plate. Its other end contacts a steel bar attached horizontally along the entire middle of the pressure plate's backside. If you now examine the open back of the camera body as

Revolutionary pressure plate, one of first to really keep roll film flat, employed a brilliantly simple mechanism.

you press in on the shutter-release lever, the whole diabolically clever plot becomes clear—as you squeeze the shutter release, just before the shutter fires, a pin emerges near the upper left-hand corner of the film aperture. And

when this pin contacts the shiny protrusion, the pressure plate is pressed up against the film aperture! Yep, the Omega thus qualifies as one of the first, if not *the* first roll-film camera to forthrightly attack the age-old bugaboo of paper-backed roll film—namely the problem of keeping the film flat. As you can see, the mechanism used is extremely simple, straightforward, and durable. The only penalty incurred is a slightly-higher-than-average shutter-release pressure. (No, the long travel shutter-release action's not really bad on our early model Omega, and its action was actually improved somewhat on later production runs.)

An advanced film advance

O.K., as long as we've got the back off, let's load 'er up. To switch or insert spools, you pull up on one of the spring-loaded aluminum buttons atop the camera (to the right or left of the viewfinder), place the fresh film in the left-hand chamber, the empty spool on the right. After you thread the film, turn the knob on the bottom of the camera clockwise a couple of turns and close the back. Finally, wind the film with this knob until number one appears in the starting window to the left of the back-lock knob, give the auto film transport one "pull-push," and you're in business. The start-window's cover will automatically close, the exposure counter will read "1," and the shutter will be cocked for the first exposure. (To indicate this last fact a red signal will appear in a little window below the lens.) Incidentally, unlike present day "ideal-format" cameras, the Omega only delivers nine shots per 120 roll. This is due to the fact that the frames are spaced slightly wider with each subsequent shot. However, this is a minor price to pay for an efficient automatic frame counter and a really rapid film-advance system which are paragons of elegant simplicity and bug-free ruggedness.

Optical quality control

It's about time we got to the Omega's optical components, so let's start with the lens. It's a 90mm f/3.5 Omicron, a four-element Tessar-type made by Wollensak. This lens not only bears the Simmon Bros. trademark, it was actually subjected to strict quality control procedures at the Omega factory, and I have it on good authority that there was a substantial rejection rate among the lenses received. At any rate, the lens has whole-aperture click-stops down to f/32 and is mounted in a Wollensak flash sync shutter with speeds of 1-1/400 sec. plus B (later models had a sync-mode selector—our model's shutter does not). And as long as we're ogling at the lens, I may as well point out that the Omega has a clever, built-in, hinged Bakelite lens cap which flips up to protect the lens.

While many have said it before, it bears repeating that the Omega is a real photographer's camera—the real joy comes not in examining it feature-by-feature, but in actually using it. Bring the camera up to your eye and look through the bottom window, and you'll see a beautifully contrasty, round rangefinder patch in the center of a circular field. Turn the incredibly smooth, backlash-free focusing knob appropriately and the larger-than-life-size rangefinder images will coincide very precisely and visibly even in poor light. When you combine these agreeable characteristics with a 2¾-in. rangefinder base length, you can appreciate why the Omega's focusing system has long been regarded as a benchmark in American camera design.

Of course, there's more to an excellent focusing system than an accurately aligned, amply dimensioned rangefinder or even a film-flattening pressure plate—the Omega's front standard is a commendably rigid affair held in precise alignment by spring-loaded struts top and bottom, and moved fore and aft by a substantial rack-and-pinion mechanism. To sum up, where the Omega can be light, it's extremely light, and where it needs heavier materials, it's got 'em. This is sometimes known in the trade as intelligent engineering.

All right, we're now confident that our subject is in focus and that our film is as flat as a pancake, so let's take the picture. About an inch above the rangefinder window, there's a nice, bright, clear, two-thirds-life-size inverse Galilean finder to compose with. But wait a minute—How come its front is hinged to the top of the camera? That's right—as you focus the Omega from infinity to its closest distance of 3 ft., the viewfinder tilts forward to accurately compensate for parallax throughout its entire focusing range!

Once you appreciate the superb design and brilliant engineering that went into this camera, and how usable a machine it must have been in practice, you can only shake your head and wonder how it could have died only four years after it was born. Well, as it turns out, there's a rather strange denouement to this tale—perhaps even stranger than the camera itself. And to enable you to fully understand it, here's a bit of potted Omega history.

Potted Omega history

The Omega 120 was originally designed under government contract as a field camera, probably mostly for military use. This project was spearheaded by Alfred Simmon, one of the Simmon brothers, and was largely engineered by a chap named Lou Weissglass. Well, the government contract eventually fell through, and Simmon decided to market the camera on the civilian market in 1954. (At the time Simmon was operating very much in the tradition of a family firm—production people had an input into design changes, and 100 percent of all camera production was tested on film.) As you might imagine, the Omega received an enthusiastic reception in the photographic press, but the press photogs and advanced amateurs for which it was intended didn't exactly line up to buy it. Perhaps its relatively high price (at the time) of $239.50, or its odd appearance, had something to do with it. Ironically, soon after the Omega was discontinued, the very press people who deserted it began to appreciate what a really marvelous machine it was, and proceeded to create a hot (and high-priced) market in used Omega 120s. And, as most of you know, the basic concept of the Omega 120 lurks, in much modified form, in today's Rapid Omega (and the Koni-Omegas that preceded it).

Of course, today's Rapid Omegas bristle with such modern features as interchangeable backs, interchangeable lenses, parallax-compensating viewfinder framelines, etc., etc. As for me, give me the smaller, lighter, spartan beast of yore, the camera that started a revolution in roll-film press cameras with a total production run of only a few thousand. Oh well (sigh), you know what that means. My near-mint condition Omega 120 cost me $275 and is currently worth about $200 more than that. Many thanks to Pete Daidone of Omega for his historical insights, and to Ken Hansen Photographic, Inc. of Manhattan for unearthing one of the nicest Omegas I've run across in years.

Kodak Chevron: Technical success, marketplace flop

Kodak took a good lens, fine shutter, excellent rangefinder, and put them in a practical medium-format package. It didn't sell!

As I implied in the introduction to the last chapter, my appetite for American-made, medium-format classics has not abated quite yet, and I am about to regale you with the tale of another. This one is the 1953 product of a little firm up in Rochester, New York, known as the Eastman Kodak Co., and while this hefty beast has its foibles, it's a pity

that the folks with the yellow box haven't produced a camera this enterprising (or professional) in many a moon. And so, without further fanfare, we present the Kodak Chevron, certainly one of the most fascinating 2¼-square (inch) format coupled rangefinder cameras the world has ever seen.

Now the first thing you notice when confronting a Chevron is its distinctive appearance—which one might describe as last-gasp art deco. And then, when you admire that expanse of beautifully polished metal, a more sobering thought occurs to you: "That thing must weigh a ton."

Well, friends, I'm happy to say that, unlike the Kodak Medalist of the same period, the Chevron is not all that ponderous. It's no lightweight to be sure, but its die-cast aluminum body keeps the poundage down to a reasonable 2 lb. 9 oz. And by the way, that "morocco leather" covering is really made of Kodadur (horrible word), its man-made equivalent.

O.K., so much for outward appearances, what about the tech data? Well, we've already revealed the Chevron's basic category, but to elaborate, its rangefinder is a beaut—one of Kodak's typical long-base (about 2½ in.), split-image jobs of the era, which is conveniently placed just below the parallax-compensating viewfinder at the viewing end. True, both the viewfinder and rangefinder windows are on the "squinty" side by modern standards; but at least there's a choice of two finder eyepiece frame sizes to accommodate eyeglass wearers. Slide the little chrome button on the right of the finder eyepiece to the right, and the larger mask moves into position.

The nicest thing about the separate rangefinder and viewfinder arrangement is that the two windows are so close together that you can literally focus and view at the same time. At most it takes only a slight upward glance to see the subject you've just focused on. And while the approximately half-life-size viewfinder is adequate but unimpressive, the rangefinder is beautifully precise and quite contrasty. It's aided considerably by an extremely smooth (if somewhat "slow") focusing helical, which unit focuses the coated 78mm f/3.5 Ektar lens to its minimum distance of 3.5 ft. in an approximately 300° turn of the heavily knurled ½-in.-wide focusing ring. Come to think of it, most photographers would gladly exchange a good, fixed viewfinder for a mediocre parallax-compensating one, and you can't fail to be impressed when you observe the Chevron's front viewfinder frame move down slightly as you focus closer.

As long as we've got our eyes fixed on the front of the camera, let's take a closer look at some additional mechanical details. Below the lens itself is the aperture control—a hefty bar you can set at apertures from f/3.5 to f/32. If you're wondering what makes the apertures click in at whole-stop intervals, shift your view to the bar's other end atop the lens, where a red delta-shaped tab actually clicks in at the detents, and there's a second aperture scale that's more convenient to use when shooting. (Curiously, it lacks the f/32 setting.) Just above the front lens ring, and facing forward, is a shutter speed scale bearing the legend Kodak Synchro Rapid 800 Shutter, and sure enough, the marked speeds go from 1-1/800 sec. plus B. But how can a medium-format leaf shutter achieve such heights when the vaunted Synchro-Compur in, say, a Rolleiflex TLR, has trouble delivering a true 1/500 sec.? That's an interesting story.

Since Chevron features manual shutter cocking, let's cock the shutter with the little lever atop the lens and see how it works. If you do so while looking through the front of the lens when it's set at f/3.5, you'll notice that, unlike other multi-blade leaf shutters, the Chevron's front blades first open and then shut as you tension them. You notice I said "front blades," for in back of the front five blades is something that looks suspiciously like the two-bladed "everset" shutters found on simple folding and box cameras. Why this strange arrangement? Simple. To obtain super-high speeds (for a leaf shutter) like 1/800 sec., the Synchro-Rapid 800 uses double-ended blades, each shaped like the business end of a vegetable chopper. When the shutter fires, they turn counterclockwise only, and thus are capable of achieving higher speeds than reciprocating blades. The only problem is they're not self-capping—that is, the shutter would open completely, fogging the next frame of film as you cocked the shutter were it not for that second set of capping blades behind them. At any rate, Kodak's brilliant shutter design was a technical success, but whether its complex design succeeded in selling more cameras (it debuted on a scale-focusing 2¼ × 3¼ folder, the Kodak Tourist II) is open to conjecture.

Art deco? Not quite, but Chevron's cast alloy body was stylish and functional.

Chevron's backside has spring-loaded red window cover, concentric film-type dial. Note hinges on either side of back.

All right, enough technical chit-chat. Let's load this impressive piece of machinery and actually take some pictures with it. If you've just decided to unearth a Chevron because it sounds like one of the more practical picture-taking classics, get a load of this. First the good news—the Chevron accepts two different film sizes, including a slide film. Now the bad news: Its 2¼ roll film is 620 and its slide film is 828, both Kodak-only sizes that are fading fast despite EK's solicitude. Oh well, let's just pop in a roll of Kodacolor II anyway.

To open the camera back, you push in a little spring lock and pull down a sliding metal bar. There's one of these on each side of the back, qualifying the Chevron as one of the few cameras with a back that swings out to either the left or to the right. Naturally you can lift the back off completely by opening both sides and, as we'll see, this makes loading 828 a bit easier.

With the back open, you insert an empty spool in the

Fancy film plane accepts slip-in 828 mask. Auto film-stop shaft's on right but mechanism works only when 620 film is used.

left-hand chamber, operate the film-advance lever on at the camera's upper left-hand corner a few times until the film-advance shaft engages the spool properly, insert a fresh roll of film in the right-hand chamber, thread the paper leader straight across, operate the film-wind lever a few times to make sure the paper's traveling correctly, and close the back. Since the Chevron's automatic film counter does not have automatic first-frame positioning, you now have to set it. First you push in a funny little lever under the right-hand rangefinder window very slightly and turn the (hard-to-grab) knurled film-counter dial atop the camera to "N." You now flip up the spring-loaded red window cover on the camera back, advance the film with the wind lever until the number "1" appears, turn the counter to "1" and you're all set. It takes a few flicks of the ratcheted wind lever to advance the film a single frame, but the counter works reliably, the lever's action is very smooth, and all is bliss.

A workable classic

Speaking of bliss, the Chevron is anything but a "drawing board" camera—it really works admirably in the field. Its rounded ends nestle comfortably in your hands, all controls (except for the shutter-speed scale, which isn't visible from shooting position) are well laid out, and even the peculiarly shaped, striated shutter-release bar on the front of the camera works with commendable smoothness. In addition, unlike so many medium-format cameras of its era, the Chevron is really well balanced and easily hand-holdable. Finally, the Ektar lens is a very nice Tessar-type which is a fine all-around picture taker, and the flash sync arrangements on the shutter are very comprehensive, not only covering the usual F and X, but including sync for class M bulbs at different average shutter speeds (1/25 sec. or less up to 1/800 sec.).

But wait a minute—I promised to tell you about the 828 film business. For the benefit of readers under the age of 28 or so, 828 film, sometimes known as "Kodak's folly" was simply "35mm paper-backed roll film"—that is, the overall width of the film was the same as 35mm, it had smaller, sparser sprocket holes on the topside only, and it provided only eight exposures per roll, with negs and slides measuring 28 × 40mm. At any rate, it *was* a clever idea in terms of "mass market 35mm" at the time, and the Chevron accepted it with a special adapter kit. If you've ever used one of those abominable 35mm adapter kits on a 2¼ twin-lens reflex, you've pretty much got the whole plot, but here goes anyway.

The 828 kit consists of a film mask, two 828 spool holders, and an 828 film spool. You insert the spool holder marked "take-up" under the film-advance lever, the one marked "supply" on the opposite end of the camera, pop the mask over the film aperture, and load a roll of 828 in the usual manner. However, the automatic film counter won't work with 828 film, so you set the counter to "N" as previously described and use ye olde red window. Of course, the 78mm lens gives you a moderate telephoto effect on the smaller roll film format.

Well, that's about it. Although 828 was less convenient and the camera has a few other quirks, it is basically a straightforward machine—practical, well thought out, and competent. Tragically, the public didn't seem to agree, and the beautiful Chevron—which was expensive ($225), not professional enough for the pros, nor simple enough for the amateurs—died a sudden (and mostly unlamented) death about two years after it was introduced. Needless to say, you know what that means. Kodak made only a couple of thousand Chevrons at most, and today they qualify as genuinely rare birds, which usually fetch a fairly steep (but not unreasonable) price. For example, the near-mint-condition Chevron pictured herein was nabbed at Ken Hansen Photographic in Manhattan and was sold out from under me for the asking price of $200.

Curious trio: Voigtländer Vito II, Kristall, and Nikette

One elegant folding rangefinder 35, one Italian "Leica Standard," and one Depression cheapie from Berlin make a motley melange.

Most of the time I luck out and stumble across interesting cameras in neat little bunches, like a quartet of British roll-film folders or a brace of Japanese TLRs. At other times, a single camera turns out to be so fascinating and complicated that I ramble on about it for an entire chapter. This time neither of these fortuitous situations prevailed so I'm going to regale you with a tantalizing triumvirate of quaint and curious picture-making machines from hither and thither.

Let's commence with one of my all time favorite folding rangefinder 35s—the Voigtlander Vito III of 1951-54. This beautifully finished German classic bears a striking resemblance to its posh, non-folding, rangefinder-focusing stablemate, the interchangeable lens Voigtlander Prominent. In fact, the Vito III's entire rear body section, including the film chambers, could have been lifted directly from its better-known cousin (but probably wasn't). Apparently, Voigtlander was very much concerned with endowing their cameras with an identifiable outer appearance.

To open the Vito for shooting, you press a little button on its bottom, and the front of the camera pops open, revealing a 50mm f/2 Ultron lens nestled in its pivoted front standard. To lock the bed and front standard into shooting position you pull the latter down until it locks in place with a decisive click. Behind the lens/shutter unit is nothing more remarkable than an ordinary bellows—the fun comes when you focus this intriguing beast.

Bring the Vito to eye level and you're greeted by the typical "squinty" range/viewfinder found on most German classics of the era. Oh well, at least the viewing image is clear and the rangefinder's pinkish focusing patch contrasts nicely with the green tinted viewing image. To focus, you grab hold of the finely knurled collar around the rewind knob and turn it with the thumb and index finger of your left hand. Does this sound strange? It's the very same system used on the aforementioned Voigtlander Prominent.

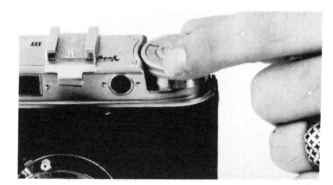
Focusing with a twist of the "rewind knob" was lifted from Voigtlander Prominent 35.

Perhaps you're now wondering how you actually rewind the film. It's easy—atop the focusing control is a little button. Push it to the left (as the arrow points) and a D-shaped handle flips up, which you turn clockwise to rewind the film. Naturally, you also have to press the rewind button to release the sprocket shaft. It's located about a half inch to the rear of the shutter release, and it's deeply engraved with a cross. Why? So when you press it continuously (as you must while rewinding the film) you can feel it turning. When it stops, you can open the back of the camera (by pressing in two spring-loaded latches on the camera's left side and swinging the hinged back to the right), confident in the knowledge that your film will be completely rewound except for a short leader—a thought-

Posh but conservative, Vito III was Voigtlander's last and finest folding rangefinder 35.

ful little touch.

Another bit of elegance is found up front in the focusing mechanism. As you turn the focusing knob, the entire lens/shutter unit and front standard move in and out on two hefty steel bars affixed inside the curved camera bed. The action is extremely smooth and in keeping with company tradition—the glorious 2¼ × 3¼ in. Voigtlander Bessa II used a very similar system. While this is the optically correct way to go, and its execution is a model of mechanical precision, it has been criticized as being relatively delicate and intolerant of abuse. However, the camera can be folded irrespective of the focusing distance you've set.

While the Vito III is up-to-date in featuring double and blank exposure prevention, you do have to cock the Synchro-Compur (1-1/500 sec. plus B) shutter separately with the conventional lever placed atop the lens. Also run-of-the-mill are the non-click-stopped aperture-setting tab (which provides settings to f/16) and the knurled shutter-speed-setting ring directly in front of it, both of which are located in the same convenient place.

Well, that's about it—the Vito III was highly regarded and expensive in its day ($157.50) and it was (and is) a fine picture taker by anyone's standards, comparing favorably with the Kodak Retina IIIc. In keeping with Voigtlander's ultra-conservatism, it is perhaps a bit more spartan than Kodak's best, but it is as finely executed a piece of machinery as you're likely to find. When you consider the camera's comparative rarity and the fact that it's a usable classic, we find the $150 price asked by Ken Hansen Photographic of Manhattan to be quite reasonable.

To go from the almost sublime to the nearly ridiculous, how about an Italian "Leica Standard"? You don't believe it? Well what would you call a Leica-screw-threaded, interchangeable-lens 35 with a viewfinder but no rangefinder? This flashy little abomination is a blood relation to the infamous Kristall 35 with built-in coupled rangefinder, and it is scarcely any better. Its horizontal focal-plane shutter is noisily low pitched and vibrates at high speeds, and its chrome plating is second rate. However, its viewfinder and shutter release are acceptable, and the film wind knob works with reasonable smoothness. Considering its modest specifications, it performs reasonably well.

Poor man's Leica? Hardly, but Kristall would accept Leica lenses.

Lift off the Leica-style bottom plate and peek inside the film cartridge chamber and you'll see the prongs of the rewind shaft, which are so crudely finished they look as though they were hand filed out of a solid billet of metal. By contrast, the brass film advance and shutter-wind gears look reasonably well executed. The final folly of this modest design becomes apparent when you want to set the flash sync for E (electric) or V (vacuum bulbs). To do so, you first wind the shutter and then stick a pencil point into a little slot cut into the camera's *inside* bottom plate (lots of luck if you had film in the camera!). This cumbersome procedure lets you switch a little indented tab to the proper setting.

Actually, I suppose we shouldn't be so hard on the little Kristall, one of the few cameras for which I am utterly unable to locate an original price. Shortly after World War II, European photographers in search of a body for their Leica lenses could do a lot worse than this. As to the value of this curious beast, your guess is as good as mine, but balancing its status as a genuinely rare Leica copy with its lackluster specifications, I'd peg it at $60-75.

Nikette? Sounds like a little old Nikon, but works very much like a Plaubel Makina.

Finally, how about a Nikette? An early Nikon product, perhaps, or a prewar cheapie from Zeiss Ikon? No, not a bit of it. This plastic-bodied, scale-focusing folder bears the legend M.C.W. Fritz L. Lucht, Berlin, and its lens is a 50mm f/3.5 Luxar. So it's a 35mm camera, then? No, it provides 16 1⅝ × 1⅛ in. images per roll of 127 film, and you place each number in the right-hand red window and then the left-hand red window on the camera back to achieve this.

The Nikette has a tab-in-slot type aperature scale beneath the lens with apertures to f/22, and the interlens leaf shutter (which you set with a little wheel above the lens) has speeds of 1/25, 1/50, and 1/100 sec. plus T and B. More interesting is the camera's focusing mechanism. Turn the metal-topped focusing wheel atop the camera's right-hand side and you can set focusing distances from 1 m to infinity. As you focus closer, the included angle between the upper and lower sets of scissors-type struts becomes narrower, the entire lensboard moves forward, and the bellows extends—just like a Plaubel Makina.

The remainder of the Nikette's specs are pretty pedestrian. The flip-up optical finder is decent, the film-wind knob works smoothly, and the entire back section removes for loading just like some old folding Kodaks I know and love. Considering its mid-30's production date,

this modest little camera qualifies as a competent (and typical) amateur camera of the era, and Ken Hansen's asking price of $45 (which is a bit more than the camera sold for new) is about right.

Incidentally, if you're wondering where I obtained the little Kristall, it was loaned to me by Charlie Pelish of Manhattan's Fotoshop, one of the few people I know who can remember selling almost all the cameras I write about when they were brand new! The reason I've saved mentioning him for last is that he has just celebrated his 50th anniversary as a retail photographic salesman. How time flies—I can remember when Charlie could read the serial number off the front ring of a 50mm Leitz Elmar without glasses!

Which camera holds the longest-in-production record? Plus a historical Hasselblad

Which camera holds the world's longest in-production record? I dunno, but here's one from '48 that almost looks brand new.

"Aren't you the guy who writes about old cameras?" Not waiting for a reply, my pudgy, middle-aged interroga-

Appearances are deceiving: This Hasselblad 1600F of 1948 looks almost identical to mid-60's 500C, but it's got metal focal-plane shutter, pre-set lens.

tor smirked as he waved a clean Argus C-3 aloft to punctuate his remarks. "Well, I read your column about these jobs a while back, and as an Argus collector I can tell you —you left one thing out." Only one thing? I thought to myself, perhaps my scholarship is improving. He continued, "You forgot to mention that the C-3 was in production longer than any other 35mm camera!" Hmmm. As a matter of fact, I'd seriously considered saying something as emphatic as that and I told him so. The reason I didn't is that I wasn't sure it was true (I'm still not), and I have no way of checking—even the *Guinness Book of World Records* is silent on the subject.

As it turns out, the fascinating question of which camera holds the world's longevity of production record isn't as straightforward as it seems. For example, take classic rangefinder Leicas. The first one was the Leica II (known as the model D in the U.S.) of 1932, which bears a striking resemblance to the last model of the Leica IIIf of 1954. Does this mean that one can say that the classic rangefinder Leica was manufactured for 22 years running? Or must you count each different model as a different camera even if the only essential difference between, say, a Leica III and a IIIa is the latter's 1/1000-sec. top shutter speed? Even if you decide to go with the manufacturer's model designations you're not out of the woods entirely. While a pre-W.W. II Argus C-3 with slightly different trim and an uncoated lens may be substantially the same as a postwar C-3, where does this leave the C-33 Match-Matic of the mid-60's which is precisely the same animal, but with EV numbers used instead of conventional aperture and shutter-speed settings and a ghastly gray leatherette covering in lieu of black? Suffice it to say that I will cheerfully award one of my glorious filmless folders, a Kodak 3-A

Autographic in nice condition, to the first reader to convincingly identify a *specific model* of 35mm camera that is or was in production longer than the Argus C-3.

Victor victorious

Now that I've revealed my abysmal ignorance, perhaps you're wondering whither this is leading. Well, surprisingly, it's not leading in the direction of ever-more-obscure 35mm cameras at all, but rather in the direction of a very well-known 2¼-square (6 × 6 cm) single-lens reflex that's been magnificently crafted by the same Swedish company for 30 years. I speak, of course, of the redoubtable Hasselblad, a camera so brilliantly conceived at the outset that (aside from the perennial argument over which kind of shutter to use) it has endured with few really major technical changes since its inception. Does the 'Blad thereby qualify as the longest-lived camera in current production? I leave that up to you, dear reader, but after we're through examining the contours and features of the original model—the Hasselblad 1600F of 1948—you'll probably have to ponder a while before offering your opinion.

As most Hasselblad fans are already aware, the camera is named after Victor Hasselblad, under whose personal direction the 6 × 6 cm SLR development project took place shortly after World War II. Mr. Hasselblad himself was not a machinist or a technician—his genius lay in having a clear conception of what kind of camera he wanted to produce and in his ability to organize a brilliant group of mechanical designers and fabricators to achieve his precise goals. In addition to being an avid photographer himself, Victor Hasselblad had considerable first-hand experience with the aerial cameras used by the Swedish Royal Air Force during the war. This provided him with a sound basis for engineering a camera that was, above all, sturdy, durable, and mechanically reliable. It is likewise hardly surprising that lightness, compactness and good handling characteristics were also design objectives that Victor Hasselblad pursued with what might be termed a passionate and supercritical involvement.

So much for my lengthy and oblique introduction—what is this legendary beast actually like in the flesh? Well, my first reaction upon seeing the pictured 1600F from afar was, "Gee, a Hasselblad with a funny lens." Its outer body contours so closely resemble the modern "500" series that you've got to do a close-up double take to be sure of what you're ogling at.

Beginning at the 1600F's back, you'll find one of the Hasselblad's most renowned and distinctive features, the snap-on, interchangeable film magazine. Since 120 roll film has always been a mild pain-in-the-fingers to load, and it provides only 12 exposures per roll, it's hardly surprising that this sensible concept has endured. And while a 1600F magazine will not fit a modern Hasselblad, its basic design and dimensions are amazingly similar to those of the current product.

For example, the mounting procedure (hook magazine onto bottom of camera body, swing it forward until latches engage) hasn't changed one iota—only the slight

Family resemblance? You bet. Latest Hasselblad film magazine on right functions almost identically to 1948 model on left.

difference in the height of the top latches prevents 1600F and 1000F magazines from fitting current cameras. The 1600F's removable film holders load in the time-honored manner by curling the film in a double, reverse S-shaped path, and the ever-present film clamp on the left side of the pressure plate (which clamps the paper leader in place when you unload and helps keep the film positioned as it's advanced) is already fully developed. Indeed, even the magazine-removal catch, the stainless steel dark slide (which covers a shutter-release-actuation pin when in place, preventing you from making blank exposures) and the hinged, D-shaped, film-insert-removal handle remained identically proportioned over the years (except that late model handles included a small, arc-shaped film-advance verification window).

Of course, there *are* other differences. The latest Hasselblad 500 C/M magazine has a hinged film-box-end clip with built-in film speed reminder dial, whereas the 1600F's magazine has a Kodak-only film-type reminder dial on its back which lists such all-time favorites as Super-XX plus the admonition "Use Kodak Film 120." And while you now turn the film crank until on the magazine the counter reads "1," the original magazine has no crank—you flip up the D-shaped film advance handle on the right side, flip down the hinged film-type reminder revealing a conically shaped port, and turn the handle clockwise until you can read the number "1" off the paper backing. You then flip up the reminder dial and turn the film-advance handle *counterclockwise* so the film counter on the right side of the magazine reads "1." From then on, frame counting is automatic.

As long as we're directing our attention to the right side of the magazine, let's take a look at another standard Hasselblad feature that made an early appearance on the 1600F—those cute little film-advance and shutter-cocking signal windows. These are absolutely necessary to avoid double and blank exposures with a camera equipped with interchangeable film magazines. Briefly, there's one tiny window on the lower right side of the main body and another similiar window on the (mounted) magazine about a half inch to the rear. A red signal in the former means the shutter isn't cocked, a red signal on the magazine means the film hasn't been advanced, while a white circle in either window means the respective operation *has* been performed. The proper procedure is simple—just make sure that the color of the signal on the camera body matches the one on the magazine you're about to mount. If it doesn't, either cock or fire the shutter as required.

How far did they go? In '57, the 'Blad got Synchro-Compur leaf shutters in each auto-diaphragm lens, but cast alloy body with steel inner chassis has endured.

Having dissected the 1600F's film magazine, what about the rest of the camera? Well, here's where things start getting interesting—and different. To begin with, the 1600F has a metal-bladed, focal-plane shutter that travels horizontally. It's fabricated of corrugated (and apparently lacquered) stainless steel .015 in. thick, and it closely resembles the rear shutter in (egad!) the very latest dual-shutter Hasselblad 2000 FC. It's not quite as fast at the upper end, topping out at a mere 1/1600 sec., but its nice semi-geometric array of speeds almost makes up for it. Markings on the combined film-wind knob and non-rotating shutter dial (which you pull out and turn to set) are: 1600, 800, 400, 200, 100, 50, 25, 10, 5, 2, 1, and B. Incidentally, the shutter on my near-mint 1600F functions flawlessly, generating an average amount of noise for its type, and the shutter release is quite smooth. However, Hasselblad's second model, the nearly identical 1000F, had its top shutter speed lowered to 1/1000 sec. in the interest of improved reliability.

The chest-level viewing system hasn't changed all that much since the first Hasselblad either, except that the flip-up magnifier now incorporates a light-excluding frame, and the viewing screens are interchangeable. In fact the

1600F's viewing brightness compares favorably with the 500 C/M's—it ought to since the screen consists of a modern ground-glass and plastic Fresnel pattern "sandwich" and the mirror is a large, well silvered, single surface type. In line with standard Hasselblad practice (until the 2000FC), the 1600F's mirror returns only when you advance the film to the next exposure.

Remember way back at the beginning of this chapter I said the lens on the 1600F looked funny? Well here's why: It's a coated 80mm f/2.8 Kodak Ektar made in good old Rochester, N.Y. Why? Because the Hasselblads were the sole Swedish Kodak importers and distributors for many years, so the association was logical—and besides back in '48 the German photo industry was too busy getting on its feet to supply new lens lines. O.K., first the good news: The 80 focused smoothly down to 20 in. from the film plane in an approximately 325° turn of the heavily knurled focusing ring. Now the bad news—it was (like all lenses for the Hasselblad 1600F and 1000F) a pre-set lens, so you had to set the aperture and focus and, just before you fired, manually flick a little lever counterclockwise to stop the lens down to the pre-set shooting aperture. Naturally, you also had to flick it back manually to view at full aperture. Of course, this wasn't Kodak's fault—the first two Hasselblad models had no built-in auto-diaphragm control mechanism. The first Hasselblad to be so blessed was the original 500C of 1957 (pictured). For the record, the additional lenses Kodak supplied for the 1600F were a 55mm f/6.3 Wide Field Ektar, a 135mm f/3.5 Ektar and a 254mm F/5.6 Ektar—all of them "Lumenized" (that is, coated on all air-glass surfaces). All but the 135 are quite rare and virtually unobtainable.

Put it all together and you have a pretty fantastic machine for its day, and one that's managed to endure and

Flash gadgetry: To convert slide-on Hasselblad contact to PC you had to slide in this gizmo. Numbers on circular dial set flash delay for various bulbs and strobe.

prosper as a professional instrument with remarkably few changes in the original design. Modern Hasselblad SLRs have automatic diaphragms, to be sure, and the focal-plane vs. leaf shutter argument has finally been settled by building both shutter capabilites into the 2000FC. But despite the many small and few major innovations that have crept in over the years, this small and meticulous company, to their credit, has never lost sight of Victor Hasselblad's vision—the concept of a small, light, convenient,

flexible, and, above all, reliable tool for making professional quality pictures in the 6 × 6 cm format. Oh yes, I almost forgot—the 1600F was manufactured from 1948 to 1952 and its high price of $389.50 made it a low production camera. Today a clean 1600F in perfect operating condition is a rare find, and the one pictured herein was furnished by Ken Hansen Photographic in New York. It's priced (fairly, I believe) at $700 complete with 135mm lens, original case and snap-on neckstrap.

A fine pair of Leica-inspired rangefinder 35s

Announcing two of my favorite, unsung, rangefinder 35s—one from Germany, one from Japan, both Leica-inspired.

Yep, it's true—Schneider is finally off his medium-format horse and back onto the 35mm bandwagon with a pair of fine quality, interchangeable-lens rangefinder cameras from different ends of the globe. Curiously, each is the product of a famous maker. I've lusted after these cameras for many a year but never happened to have the cash in my pocket at the right time. Now, thanks to the miracle of camera collecting, they're both mine—for two weeks—through the courtesy of veteran camera fancier and promoter extraordinaire Nat Kameny, in whose glass cases they normally reside. Out of deference to age, let's begin with the older (by one year) model.

Did you know that way back in '55 Minolta made a "Canon"? Well, I suppose in retrospect Chiyoda Kogaku (Minolta) would probably prefer it if people referred to their hefty (1 lb. 14 oz.), focal-plane-shuttered creation as a Leica copy—that's at least respectable. However, we all know that screw-thread Leicas of the era had separate

rangefinder and viewfinder windows on the back, while the Minolta 35, Model II has a combined range/viewfinder with a green-tinted viewing area and a contrasting pinkish, circular focusing patch in the center—just like you know who. And, of course, both Japanese 35s had a 39mm screw-thread mount identical to (and compatible with) the classic Leica's.

Once I unscrewed the nicely finished 50mm f/2 Super Rokkor C (coated) lens from the Minolta, I noticed three things: its 9 oz. weight proved it is a brass mounted optic; its spring-loaded infinity catch is a dead ringer for those on Leitz lenses; and its 10-bladed iris diaphragm was an indication (but not proof) that the manufacturer was striving to produce a quality product. Just for laughs, I put this seven-element lens on Modern's optical bench to see what manner of beast it might prove to be. Guess what? It's perfectly centered, delivers a very compact image with some reddish fringing at maximum aperture, gives a good account of itself off axis (toward the edges of the 35mm frame), and is diffraction limited (i.e., reproduces a perfect image of the pinpoint light source) on axis at f/5.6. Needless to say, this lens is very good by modern standards and amazingly good for its day—who knows, maybe those wily Rokkor designers copied the Leitz Summicron!

The remainder of the Minolta 35 is very nice, but mostly rather conventional. The horizontal, cloth, focal-plane shutter has speeds of 1-1/25 sec. plus T and X sync on its front-mounted slow shutter-speed dial. The rotating top dial has speeds from 1/25-1/500 sec. plus B, including the rather odd setting of 1/35 sec. The shutter is reasonably quiet, the shutter-release button is smooth, and the 0.8X magnification range/viewfinder is fairly bright, very contrasty, and a bit "squinty." Oh well, at least the rear eyepiece is conveniently adjustable to your individual eyesight.

The Minolta 35's distinctive features include a hinged, cast alloy back with dimpled pressure plate, and a large, knurled back lock on the bottom of the camera labeled

A competent "tank," Minolta's prestige 35 of '55 was heavy but had a great lens.

"Open" and "Shut." There's also a front-mounted self-timer lever with three labeled delay positions (1,2, and 3) and a self-timer actuation button hiding beneath it. Finally, the rewind button is actually a lever placed rather unconventionally in a little channel to the left of the Leica style film-wind knob.

Leica-like controls, old Minolta logo.

In sum, Minolta's first "Leica" is a very pleasant little "tank" whose only real deficiencies are its ample weight and the so-so satin chrome finish on its body. It's nicely balanced, its rounded ends nestle comfortably in your hands, and its optical performance qualifies it as one of my few photographic heartthrobs that turned out to be better in reality than it was in my fantasies. You may rest assured that a Minolta 35 Model II is a rare bird on these shores, though it's not fantastically expensive if you stumble across one (about $150). It was never officially imported into the U.S., though the hundreds of Korean Conflict veterans that returned via Japan with Minolta 35s over their shoulders must have been mighty pleased with them.

Turning to the European theater, we hereby present a cleverly wrought 35mm creation from Germany—the Agfa Ambi Silette, also known as the poor man's Leica M-2. Your paucity of funds got you a nicely finished, stylish-looking interchangeable-lens Synchro-Compur MXV shutter (1-1/500 sec. plus B) instead of a focal-plane unit. And where do I get the nerve to compare the more modest beast with Wetzlar's best? Easy—lurking beneath that funny flip-up viewfinder cover on the front is a system of true, projected, parallax-compensating framelines for 35mm, 50mm, and 90mm lenses.

Here's how it all works. You begin by bayonetting in a 35mm f/4 Color-Ambion, 50mm f/2.8 Color-Solinar (normal), or 90mm f/4 Color-Telinear lens, and then setting the viewfinder selector switch atop the camera to the same focal-length setting as the lens you've mounted. When you push the spring-loaded finder cover to the left it flips upwards about 100° and you see a beautifully clear, approximately ⅔ life-size finder image with the frame you've selected appearing in bright green. Actually, only the 35mm and 90mm frames appear singly—if you push

the selector switch all the way to the left (50mm setting), both the 35mm and 50mm framelines are visible. The circular rangefinder patch in the center of the finder appears in a matching shade of light green, and as you focus the lens closer, all finder frames move downward and to the right to compensate for parallax.

Now the rest of the Ambi Silette is very straightforward, with body contours closely resembling numerous other 35mm Silettes of yore. True, the smooth, single-stroke film-wind lever is pretty spiffy for a German camera made in '56, the shutter release is commendably smooth, and the rangefinder reasonably good. However none of these features can be called strange. Why, then, did the Ambi's designers take this classically proportioned

Flip up finder cover and what do you see? Frosted window with three framelines, circular rangefinder window.

—even elegant—machine and tack on that dumb looking range/viewfinder cover? I can think of only two explanations, neither of which pleases me much. First, there's the possibility that the camera's designers winced at the sight of the odd-looking, frosted, frameline-illuminating window and decided to cover it up; or, more likely, they felt that the overhanging "peak" (which is lined with black flocking) shielded the frameline-illuminating system from bright overhead light, rendering the frames more visible. Since other 35s with similar finder systems work quite well without a flip-up cover (and don't give me that baloney about protecting the finder-glass) it seems rather frivolous.

Fortunately, the same designer probably wasn't responsible for the Ambi Silette's lens mount system, and it is a gem. To remove a lens you push inward on a ridged tab at the bottom of the camera's front panel, turn the lens barely 10° counterclockwise, and lift it out. You can now get a good look at the lens orientation tab at about 2 o'clock (it mates with a slot cut into the rear-most metal ring of each lens mount) and the very cute rangefinder-coupling shaft, which terminates in a ball bearing that rides on the rangefinder-coupling cam on the back of all Ambi Silette lenses. Both the tab in the camera and the slots on the lenses are keyed with red dots, and remounting optics is commendably swift and sure, with an audible click once the lens is seated.

Quick-flick bayonet's a gem. The Ambi Silette only had three lenses, but they were good ones.

If you're wondering how all this worked in practice, the answer is very well indeed. The Ambi's optics have a reputation as being very good picture takers and the camera was reliable for a machine of its type. Of course, it has its little foibles—the 90mm lens only focuses to a 6 ft. minimum distance (though close-focusing accessories were available) and the film-type reminder dial built into the rewind knob is hard to set. There were also a few corresponding niceties, like very smooth-focusing lenses with apertures to f/22 (f/32 on the 90), and a built-in, slide-out camera stand below the lens-release tab. Although accessory lenses were expensive, the Ambi Silette itself was something of a bargain in its day—$109 with 50mm f/2.8 lens. Presently a clean Ambi fetches about the same, and if you want to sell a complete AS outfit in nice shape, please drop me a line—I'm still lusting.

Zeiss Contaflex 126 did everything but sell

Zeiss's last gasp: The heart-rending tale of an elegant, auto-exposure SLR that did everything but sell.

If the name Contaflex conjures up the image of a rather dated if nicely made leaf-shutter SLR with component interchangeable (rather than fully interchangeable) lenses, you can't entirely blame Zeiss. They tried to give us an incredibly complicated, super expensive, and not altogether functional 35mm twin-lens reflex before the Great Hostilities of the early 40's, and it had fully interchangeable, bayonet mount lenses and a Contax-style vertical focal plane shutter with settings up to 1/250 sec. Unbeknownst to many Americans, Zeiss also managed to market a much more straightforward, pleasant, and usable focal-plane shutter Contaflex with fully interchangeable lenses back

in 1968. And it promptly fell flat on its focusing mount—saleswise at least.

I speak, of course, of the fabled Contaflex 126, a camera whose designers assumed that at least a reasonable number of middling-to-advanced amateurs would be attracted to Kodak's original, easy-loading, pre-pocket, Instamatic cartridge. In general, they weren't, and so the very last all new Contaflex design to be produced went down the tubes in short order. More's the pity, for in its own unpretentious way, the Contaflex 126 is one of the nicest cameras Zeiss ever made.

In terms of its basic identity, the 126 belongs to that most popular of current "serious" camera breeds a behind-lens-metering, auto-exposure SLR. Its CdS metering system takes readings off the focusing screen, is powered by a single, flat PX-13 cell stored in a little compartment on the left side of the bottom plate, and a needle to the left of the finder area reads out camera selected apertures (f/2.8 to f/22) along a vertical scale, with red high light and low light warning areas above and below it. To select shutter speeds (1/30-1/500 sec.) you turn a large, knurled dial to the right of the prism housing, which is adorned with weather and speeding car symbols (1/500 sec.) for the uninitiated, as well as the usual shutter-speed numbers. There is no "B" setting permitting time exposures, and that is probably the camera's worst design feature.

Push downwards on a little button on the left end of the Contaflex and the back pops open, revealing a very cute, square, cloth focal-plane shutter smack in the middle between the plastic chambers that accommodate the 126 cartridge's bulging ends. Below the shutter is the usual

Impressive Zeiss lens lineup was fully interchangeable on the Contaflex 126. See text.

79

spring-loaded finger that engages the edge perforations to stop the film in the right place as it's being advanced, and below that is the automatic ASA-keying tab which rides in a horizontal slot. If all this seems just a bit too pedestrian, cock the shutter by winding the striated plastic film-advance "tab" on the upper part of the camera back, and fire the shutter by pressing on the conventional, threaded shutter button smack in the middle of the shutter dial. Yep, that's right, you can now see that it's a downward-firing, vertical focal-plane shutter, and a pretty quiet one at that. Though the shutter button's not one of the lightest in creation, it's reasonably smooth and predictable.

Perhaps the nicest experience you get when using the Contaflex 126 comes when you lift the camera to eye level and peer through the viewfinder. For a camera with a 45mm f/2.8 Tessar normal lens, the view is surprisingly bright and very clear. As with most Contaflex cameras, the outer viewing area (which has a very coarse Fresnel pattern) is not intended for focusing—that's taken care of by a central, split-image rangefinder surrounded by a nice, fat, fine ground-glass donut. While grabbing the two textured plastic knobs on the 126's permanently affixed focusing ring is a bit of a nuisance, focusing smoothness is good and precision is excellent.

As long as we've got our digits up near the lens, let's take a gander at this Contaflex's most incredible feature—its lens switching system. To remove the normal lens (or any other lens, for that matter), you push in on a spring-loaded chrome tab (it's located at about 5:30 o'clock just behind the lens's knurled front ring) and, at the same time, grab onto the front ring and turn it about 50° counterclockwise until the raised, red orientation dot points straight upwards. You can now lift the lens out to get a close look at the beautiful, three-lobed external bayonet mount which all lenses bayonet onto, rather than into.

If you now glance inside the mirror box with the shutter cocked you can't fail to notice a large, crescent-shaped lever with a hefty bar near its right-hand end and, just behind it, a very small, squarish reflex mirror. The purpose of the bar and lever is to transfer the camera-selected aperture determined by the trapped-needle-type auto-exposure system to the lens itself. Unlike most auto-exposure SLRs, the Contaflex's lenses are held at minimum aperture (by spring tension) when you take them off the camera, so the aforementioned lever is, in effect, an aperture opening lever rather than a stop-down lever.

And just what sort of lenses do you think Zeiss supplied for this "amateur" camera? Well, the Tessar's certainly no slouch, but would you believe a 32mm f/2.8 Distagon, 85mm f/2.8 Sonnar, and a 135mm f/4 Tele-Tessar? Oh well, if you were a skinflint, you could've purchased your Contaflex with a three-element 45mm f/2.8 Color-Pantar. As excellent as these lenses were (except for the last, which was only fair), focusing all of them with the same permanently affixed, double helical focusing tube had some drawbacks. While the 32mm Distagon would get you down to a nice, cozy 12 in., and the 45mm Tessar provided a reasonable 20 in. minimum focusing distance, the 85 and 135mm teles would only focus to 5½ and 13 ft., respectively—not too swift. Perhaps the handsome design and gorgeous finish of these optics helped to make up for it.

If the Contaflex 126 can be faulted for providing a nice, centrally placed tripod socket and a threaded shutter release but no "B" setting, its autoflash system is very clever and beyond reproach. Here's how it works. First set the flash guide number dial to the left of the prism housing opposite the "32" or "45" index marks (depending on the focal length of the lens you're using). Now focus on your subject in the usual manner, and before you fire the shutter to make your flash exposure, push what looks like a left-handed film-wind lever forward as far as it will go and hold it there (against spring tension) as you take the picture. A wacky way to set autoflash apertures to be sure, but it works without a hitch and is actually—believe it or not—convenient. And just to remind you that you've disengaged the CdS auto-exposure system, when you press

Film's eye view of the 126's focal-plane shutter shows film-stop finger below.

Beautiful bayonet mount is affixed to front of double-helical focusing tube. All lenses bayonet onto it swiftly, focus smoothly, but teles can't focus close as a result.

the autoflash lever (marked *Leitzahl*), a little "blitz" mark emerges from the right-hand side of the finder screen. Overkill? Most assuredly.

And just how does the Contaflex 126 compare to some of the more illustrious Zeiss cameras like the Contax in terms of aesthetics and finish? Quite well, I think. Its lines are chunky but quite pleasing to the eye; its main body shell is tastefully done, especially when you consider it's made of leather-textured black plastic; and, while shiny chrome would not be my choice for a camera top, it is certainly nicely proportioned and beautifully crafted.

Post-mortem

So how come this lovely machine died such a horrible death, and was less than a smashing success even in its native Deutschland? It was, as they say, a combination of factors. American enthusiasts regarded 126 as an amateur format and opted for 35mm cameras instead. And while the Contaflex 126 had many advanced features, it lacked slow shutter speeds, a self-timer, and "B". Finally, as you might expect, the camera was pretty high-priced compared to its feature laden 35mm competitors ($175 with Tessar lens) and its lenses were downright expensive ($129.95 for the 32mm Distagon, for example). It was, to coin a phrase, a great idea whose time never came. The best proof of this is the equal lack of success suffered by other "high-class" 126 SLRs like the lovely Rollei SL26 and the decent, competent, and cheaper Ricoh 126 C-flex.

And just how much is this ill-fated jewel worth today, you ask? Well Ken Hansen Photographic, Inc. of Manhattan, which furnished the very complete, near-mint-condition, four-lens outfit pictured in this column, has it priced at a reasonable $175. And this includes not only the original Zeiss Ikon compartment case but also the original Zeiss-Ikon-Voigtlander chamois that came with it! Current value: about $350.

Kodak Medalist:
A professional "tank"

The Magnificent Medalist: The world's first and last professional-level, medium-format camera that took (heaven forfend) 620 film.

Don't worry folks, I'm really not back on my medium-format kick, but a package arrived the other day containing something too good to pass up. In fact, I was rather astounded, when going over rafts of previous columns, to discover that I'd never given this glorious beast more than a passing mention. I speak, of course, of the Kodak Medalist II of fabled memory—the 2¼ × 3¼ roll-film press camera affectionately known among collectors as "the tank" due to its massive, chunky appearance and general air of indestructibility.

Now while the Medalist is anything but flimsy, impressions can be misleading. Far from weighing "a ton" as many conjecture when first eyeballing it, the Medalist weighs in at a hefty but respectable 2 lb. 15 oz., sans film —not bad for a camera measuring about 5⅜ in. wide, 3¾ in. deep, and 4⅜ in. high. The secret lies in the liberal use of aluminum body castings, cover plates, and—tragically —a huge, anodized aluminum, double focusing helical to get the 100mm f/3.5 coated Ektar lens down to 3½ ft.

But let's commence on a more positive note. The original Medalist I was designed at the end of the 30's by a team including Joseph Mihalyi (of Ektra 35 fame) and Chester Crumrine. The man responsible for the camera's "mechanical rhapsody" styling, including all those monumental knurled rings and knobs and gracefully curved body contours was none other than Walter Teague, the same chap who designed scads of "art deco" Kodak box and folding cameras in the early and mid-30's. The postwar Medalist II was basically the same machine except that the next-to-useless "focusing" knob below and to the left of the lens was removed in favor of a recessed ASA-type flash contact. Incidentally, the presence of a flash sync (settable to M or F by a diabolical little lift-and-set pin to the left of the lens) isn't the only way to tell a Medalist II from a model I—atop the former's reasonably

"Tank" for the military? Probably not, but rumors persist that original Medalist I (not this model II) was designed for combat.

large, commendably clear viewfinder is the legend "Kodak Medalist II."

No matter where you turn on this camera, you're greeted by amiable little peculiarities. For example, the back is hinged on both sides and can be swung to the left, to the right, or removed entirely. To release either side, you pinch together two striated, spring-loaded bars, which causes small "fingers" top and bottom to retract within the central tube of a three-part cylindrical hinge. With the back open you can get a good look at the two film chambers, with a pair of film-guide rollers next to the right-hand one, a single, fatter, toothed roller on the left, with the succinct admonition, "DO NOT TURN THIS ROLLER," emblazoned next to it on the side of the film aperture. In front of the top edge of the film aperture you can see the Medalist's elaborate shutter cocking and firing linkage which terminates in a large, pivoted, metal finger connected to the metal ring around the lens which actually activates the interlens Flash Supermatic Shutter.

O.K., as long as the back is open, let's load up. Surprise number one is the film size—yep it's good old 620. Kodak's "narrow spool" version of 120 that's currently available in only two types, Kodacolor II and Verichrome Pan. Oh well, the loading procedure is straightforward—just thread the film right to left, attach it firmly to the spool by turning the nice big film-wind knob a couple of times, snap the back shut, open the spring-loaded red window cover on the back and wind the film until you can just about see the number one. You now turn the little film counter knob (next to the film-wind knob) until it reads "1," turn the film-wind knob clockwise a smidgeon until it "clicks in," and you're in business. The shutter will be cocked as you wind the film; accidental double exposures are impossible; and the counter will count off succeeding frames automatically. The only way to louse up this glorious system is to manually turn that toothed film-counter roller—the one you're not *supposed* to turn!

Once you've loaded your Medalist, glance wistfully at the film-type reminder dial to the left of the finder, which lists such departed favorites (in 620) as Panatomic-X, Plus-X, and Super-XX. Now comes the fun—actually taking pictures. To get the lens from partially collapsed to focusing position (this also unlocks the shutter release), grab hold of the biggest, fattest, knurled ring behind the lens and turn it clockwise about 120⁰ (from shooting position) until the rotary focusing scale to the right of the finder reads infinity. Now, when you bring the beast to eye level and glance at the lower window, you'll see Kodak's superb split-image rangefinder, which presents the focusing images to the eye at about 1½ times life-size and has a huge base length measuring roughly 2½ in. Like the slightly later Chevron, the vertically arrayed rangefinder (lower) and viewfinder (upper) windows are so close together it's almost possible to view and focus at the same time. This is not the usual case with dual window systems, and it certainly helps to speed things up.

The Achilles' heel of the Medalist is its system of massive telescoping double-helical focusing tubes, which are made of anodized aluminum. While the structural rigidity and accuracy of lens-to-film-plane alignment possible with this design are beyond belief, smooth focusing is not its forte. Yes, it can be made to function reasonably well if properly cleaned and lubricated, but the average Medalist you see today is a stiff, recalcitrant focuser at best due to breakdown of the lubricant and dirt (which can enter easily) in the helix.

Probably the finest feature of the camera is its lens, a five-element 100mm f/3.5 Kodak Ektar designed under the direction of Dr. Rudolph Kingslake. It's essentially a Taylor triplet with both its front and rear elements made into achromatic doublets, and it's characterized by an extraordinarily sharp, flat image field, and excellent color correction even by modern standards. Also nice is the fact that the aperture ring (the frontmost knurled ring) pro-

Lensman's view of Medalist shows vertically arrayed viewfinder (top) and rangefinder windows, auxiliary shutter-cocking lever under eyepiece, small frame counter knob, big film-wind knob at left.

Collapse the lens, open the back and here's what you see. Elaborate spring-loaded linkage below film aperture top moves laterally to cock and fire the inter-lens leaf shutter.

vides click-stops down to f/32. The shutter, a Kodak-made Flash Supermatic with speeds of 1-1/400 sec. plus B, was known for its reasonably good speed accuracy and durability under hard use. However, it was never quite as good as the best Compurs in these respects. Shutter speeds are set according to a dual scale atop the lens, with speeds of 1-1/10 sec. plus B set by aligning a red arrow opposite red numerals, and fast speeds 1/25-1/400 sec. by placing a black arrow opposite black numerals. In keeping with flash sync arrangements of the era, either sync setting had to be manually cocked before each flash exposure for the flash to go off.

Rounding out the Medalist's idiosyncracies are two obliquely arrayed tripod sockets on its bottom, a pair of "grab rail" type neckstrap lugs on its front, and a manual shutter-cocking lever (for double exposures or when using sheet film) under the finder eyepiece, of all places. Wait a moment—did I say sheet film? Yep, the Medalist was conceived as a professional "system" camera (some even say interchangeable lenses were planned), and its accessories include cut film backs, extension backs for close-ups, all sorts of flash guns and brackets and a ground-glass back which automatically shifted gears in the rangefinder so it could be used to focus at the altered lens-to-sheet-film distance which resulted.

Finally, I couldn't bear to leave all you Medalist fans without letting you in on its military nickname—"The Flying Cobblestone," a less than complimentary reference to its bulky shape.

Actually the Medalist handles reasonably well once you get used to it. It fits the digital anatomy quite nicely thank you, and if its focusing ring isn't perfectly situated, its shutter release is—and it's fairly smooth and predictable. Some say the Medalist was conceived as an all-around military camera despite the fact that its design was finalized well before World War II. In any event, it served the American military admirably, and I'm quite sure that few of the photographers lucky enough to use it complained about unsharp pictures—even though they probably griped about some aspects of the camera itself.

Mammoth focusing helical is beautifully made, super-rigid, and a magnet for dirt. It must be cleaned and lubed regularly to avoid infamous "stiff focus" disease.

Insofar as the Medalist II's vital statistics are concerned, it was born in March 1946, was officially deceased as of April 1953, and originally sold for $215.25—except that you couldn't get your hands on one until about 1948 (due to military priorities). The Medalist enjoyed a fine reputation among professional photographers and was considered a serious photographic instrument for well over a decade after its timely demise. Today, with the rotten 620 situation and spare parts very thin on the ground, it has been relegated to the category of a glorious American collectors' item which presently fetches about 200 inflation-ridden bucks. Actually, you can live quite nicely with Verichrome (a much underrated film) and Kodacolor if you prefer to actually use one of these impressive looking machines, rather than letting it languish on your display shelf. You can also re-roll 120 onto 620 spools. But whatever you do *don't* try to adapt it for 120 film, and *don't* turn the accursed film-counter shaft if you know what's good for you.

Strange triad spotted in London: RAF Aerial camera, Wrayflex SLR, and Le Furet

A triad of strange cameras recently spotted in London, including an R.A.F. aerial monster, a prismless eye-level SLR and a French mini 35 from the 20's.

I have often toyed with the idea of quitting my job to become the world's leading international camera wheeler-dealer. Aside from the obvious benefits of free travel on the "corporation" expense account, I'm sure I could make a bundle selling Leicas in Japan and rangefinder Nikons and stereo 35s in England at inflated prices. Profitability would be even more pronounced in Germany, where almost *all* camera prices are beyond the pale.

Surprisingly, things sometimes work the other way

'round as well. I managed to locate a brace of fascinating cameras in London that would cost the average Yank about twice as much in his native land. Take my lovable aerial beast pictured here, which set me back about £40 (just under 80 bucks) and would probably fetch more than twice as much in the Big Apple. Why? According to Bob Nicklin of Morgan Camera Co. (London), this R.A.F. camera of the 50's and early 60's was unloaded as war surplus on the British market and is fairly common across the pond.

Even as I attempted to sneak this camera through U.S. Customs by carrying it nonchalantly over my shoulder, a

Magnificent monster? Yep, British airmen needed a stiff upper lip to tote this!

savvy inspector remarked, "Oh, a panoramic camera, eh? How wide a picture does it take?" Got the same response from Modern's staff, oddly enough. Well, despite its semi-trapezoidal shape and gargantuan 8¾-in. width, the format measures a mere 2¼ in. square, which figures since the lens is a 75mm f/3.5 Xpres made by Ross of London (it's a very nice Tessar derivative). As long as I've let this fat cat out of the bag, I may as well tell you that it's 4¾ in. high (with frame finder collapsed), 4¼ in. deep, and weighs a whopping 5 lb. 4 oz. sans film.

British airmen being what they are, I'm certain they came up with some choice nicknames for this tank of a camera, but in the interest of historical accuracy and jolly good fun let's reveal its real name. It is (are you ready for this) a Komlosy, Dunstable No. 147 and it takes (according to the nice, knurled 1½-in.-diameter film counter on its top) somewhere between 40 and 42 pictures per roll. On 120 or 220? Don't be silly—on spooled, double-perforated 70mm! Its body *feels* as though it's made of cast iron, but it's actually very thick, crinkle-finished alloy. For the record, the lens front-element focuses to a minimum marked distance of 5 ft. (not bad for an aerial camera); the heavily knurled front ring on the lens sets apertures from f/3.5 to f/22; and the larger ring toward the rear of the lens controls a 1-1/500 sec. plus B interlens leaf shutter of unknown manufacture.

So what is the logic of this rather big Bertha with the medium-sized format, you ask? Well, the removable back is held in place by screw-adjusted spring tabs above and below it, and the body would probably survive a plane

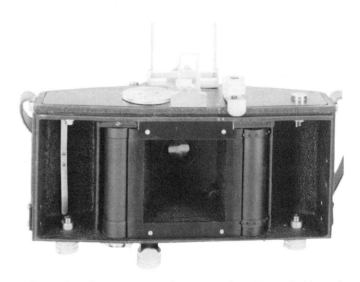

Backless view shows super-sturdy construction, 70mm double-perf sprockets.

crash or a hand grenade blast intact. Film advance and shutter cocking are accomplished by pulling a huge aluminum grip with your left hand, and you fire the shutter by pulling on what looks like a cylindrical solenoid with your right. In short, the whole rig is designed to be held and operated by heavily gloved hands, to damp out camera shake and to excel under combat conditions. It is indeed a well-designed machine that is quite nicely made considering its role in life, and my only regret is that the rear eyepiece of the folding frame finder lacks parallax adjustment, which is, of course, unnecessary on an aerial camera.

Another rare bird I managed to nab in the flesh is the remarkable Wrayflex, which also proved to be much cheaper at Morgan's than it would have been state-side. This gorgeously finished SLR is as elegantly simple in concept as its streamlined shape would indicate, and while its operational convenience and viewfinder are hardly up to modern standards, it's no less ingenious for all that.

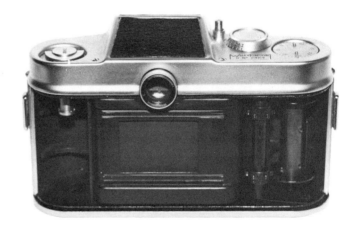

Funny format? You bet. Original Wrayflex of 1950 took 24 × 32mm shots on 35mm.

The original Wrayflex of circa 1950 was reportedly designed by an ex-R.A.F. officer whose name escapes me, and its format was a non-standard 24 × 32mm. Mine is a later model, also made by Wray Optical Works, Ltd., Bromley, Kent, England, which dates from around 1955. Like all Wrayflexes but the last models (which featured conventional pentaprisms) my bargain reflects the image off the focusing screen and into the finder eyepiece by means of an angled mirror instead of a prism. And while the focusing image is right-side-up, it's laterally reversed. Turn the camera 90° for verticals and the focusing image is upside down! To complicate matters, the focusing image is downright dim even by 30-years-ago standards, although models like the one pictured, with the 50mm f/2 Unilite lens (mine has a 50mm f/2.8 Wray Unilus), are a bit brighter.

Shiny lens quartet includes (left to right) 35, 50, 90, and 135mm Wray lenses.

One clever but disconcerting feature of the Wrayflex finder is the magnified focusing dot in the center. Given the dismal finder, it undoubtedly increases focusing accuracy while rendering picture composition a bit dodgy if you've got something important in the center of the frame. How does this "rangefinder" work? Easy, there's a small convex lens cemented (with balsam, natch) onto the ground-glass focusing screen. Equally straightforward are the D-shaped film-wind key on the bottom of the camera (which is reasonably rapid once you get the hang of it), the manually reset film counter, and the D-shaped rewind key.

Have I turned you off by telling you all this? Well, the facts remain that the Wrayflex's cast alloy body is very light and its shape is handy, the removable back is held very rigidly in place with a sliding tab on each side, and the ½ to 1/1000 sec. cloth focal-plane shutter is quiet and reliable (even though the B setting is unaccountably placed in between the 1/250 and 1/500 sec. settings). The shutter-release button is also commendably smooth and predictable.

Other peculiarities? Sure, the reflex mirror and focusing screen are held at a rigid 45° angle by hefty side braces, and the entire mirror/screen unit pivots upward into the

empty "prism" housing before the shutter fires. Remarkably, "mirror bounce" is still present only in average amounts. Once you get past its focusing system and manual diaphragm (to f/16) lens, the Wrayflex is actually quite pleasant to use and it certainly qualifies as a good picture taker.

I consider the 40 quid (just under 80 bucks) I peeled off to obtain my Wrayflex eminently fair. It's really a very pretty, cleverly wrought machine. My only regrets are that it doesn't focus closer than 3 ft. and its 40mm screw-thread mount is just a tad too big to accept my (39mm) Leica lenses. Current value: $125.

Let's conclude with another camera I unearthed in London which proved to be so sufficiently tantalizing (and confusing) that I obtained a second sample from a New York collector just so I could ogle at and marvel over the thing at greater length. You think the Minox 35 EL is a trend-setter? How about a French 35 from about 1923 that measure 3½ × 2 × 1⅞ in. and weighs under 10 oz. despite its thick metal castings.

But wait a minute—did I say 1923? That's about two years before the introduction of the Leica, so this little jewel of a Le Furet #209 qualifies as a member of that most illustrious of camera categories, a pre-Leica 35! Like most of its ilk, even its bare specs are incredible. To get the "ordinary" features out of the way, the format is (egad!) 24 × 36 minus a couple of tenths of a millimeter; its lens is a

Petit et magnifique: Le Furet of 1923.

tiny f/4.5 Berthiot Flor of unspecified focal length with stops of f/4.5, 6, 9, 12, 18; and its shutter is a simple, ever-set, behind-lens leaf type with speeds of instantaneous (marked "I") and B (marked "P" for Pause). The shutter is fired by a lever to the right of the lens (in shooting position) and both speeds are set with a sticky, knurled knob below it. The viewfinder is of the flip-up inverse Galilean type with crosshairs on the front glass. For the record, the manufacturer of this unlikely jewel is E, Guerin C. Pingault & Cie. of Paris, France.

Now for the more salient details of this bench-assembled classic. It apparently takes standard double-perforated 35mm film or non-perf film, because the geared film counter on the bottom of the camera *does not* come in contact with the film or sprocket holes. Both film chambers have slotted inserts reminiscent of Leica cassettes which slide in from the top and are properly oriented by screws in the camera top which fit into notches on the insert tops. The film-advance side (on the right) contains a gear and pawl which may have served as a primitive "count the clicks" film counter, and the number of exposures taken was set by the user manually by pushing in a spring-loaded plunger on the left side of the camera which advanced a counter on the camera bottom. I found it hard to believe, but evidently the film plane frame itself

is removable (there's no other way to get the exposed film out since there's no rewind knob!). At any rate, the two removable "film inserts" are held in place by tabs overhanging the top of the removable back when it's set in place and locked with a little lever on the camera back. Not surprisingly, there is no tripod socket, and the take-up spool is marked "Pathe'," the renowned French movie equipment and film company.

Frankly, I don't know exactly what to make of this remarkable lilliputian creation except to remark that it's a very cleverly integrated design, and beautifully hand-crafted despite its primitive specs. I'm willing to wager that it's worth a bundle on either side of the Atlantic and I'll start the bidding at a thousand devalued dollars.

Wide-angle mania, including a Russian "swinger" and the German Hologon

Wide, wide world of cameras: Some are "swingers" and some ain't; some scale focus and others don't focus at all!

Although persistent and consistent "Camera Collector" readers know in their hearts that I'm a certifiable eccentric, I'm pleased to inform you all that I'm normal in at least one respect—my choice of lenses. And so, while hordes of photographers relegate so-called "normal" 50mm lenses to the status of glorified paperweights, I am content to use same for at least 75 percent of my 35mm shooting. Why? I'm really not sure, but maybe Fuji's Jim-

my Chung is right—that I'm the only columnist at Modern that's 50 years behind the times. Or perhaps it's just a nasty habit, engendered by the poverty of youth and nurtured by years spent making pictures with fixed-lens, roll-film folders and twin-lens reflexes. Lately, however, a new acquisitive affliction has visited itself upon me—one that's aptly described as "wide-angle mania."

Now you might presume that I would broaden my photographic perspective and diminish my wallet in the usual fashion—by scouring the countryside for wide, ultra-wide, and super-wide lenses and popping them onto my shiny, new, current production SLR. Alas, I never do things in the usual fashion, and my yearning to capture the world's wide sweep has (as usual) resulted in a (mostly) unfulfilled lust for additional cameras, mostly with non-interchangeable lenses. These fascinating machines fall into two distinct categories, swingers and non-swingers, so let's take it from the top in Glenn Miller style and commence with the former.

Our first camera is one I always meant to buy when it was new but never did. The Panox, also known as Panon, is an imposing looking beast produced by the Panon Camera Co. Ltd. of Japan, maker of the current Widelux F7. Originally designed in the early 50's for (would you believe) newspaper reporters and the Japanese Coast Guard, it is a swinging-lens, roll-film camera *par excellence*. And just in case you forgot its angular coverage or format, both are conveniently engraved atop the camera. Near the rounded front section of the top are two arrows with the legend "Covering Angle 140°" in between. The top of the film-wind knob is even more informative—it says "120 Film, 6 Ex. 5×11 cm." In other words, you get a half dozen images per roll, each measuring about 2 × 4¼ in.

Caught in mid-swing, Panox's lens, focus knob are seen through front slit.

Curved film insert (top) slides into body and bottom cover holds it in place.

The name Panox itself raises some interesting questions, since the manufacturer is Panon, and most of its 120-format panoramic cameras bear the Panon trademark. A bit of digging revealed the fact that our featured Panox was introduced in 1958, sold at the hefty price of $495, and featured such startling innovations on the previous Panon line as an "automatic" exposure counter, "sturdier" frame finder, simplified lens setting controls, improved take-up spool clip and last but not least, an engraved depth-of-field table affixed to its back.

For the record, both Panons and Panoxes have a knurled shutter-speed knob near the left side of the flip-up finder frame, providing settings of 1/2, 1/50, and 1/200 sec.—take your pick. You cock the shutter (actually a self-capping vertical slit located at the back end of a spring-loaded revolving drum) by grabbing hold of a tab on the right side of the drum's lens aperture, on the front of the camera, and manually revolving the drum all the way to the right against spring pressure until it clicks into "cocked" position at the extreme right. When you press the nice, smooth shutter release on the top, the drum revolves clockwise and the shutter slit inside the camera opens, thus scanning the film.

Lenses by Konica?

Apertures on the 50mm f/2.8 Panox lens (earlier models had Hexar and Hexanon lenses made by Konishiroku) are set by poking an index finger into the front lens port and turning a sharply knurled, arc-shaped control until the f/stop you want (to f/16) is opposite a white index mark. Focusing is accomplished by turning a little knurled knob near the top of the lens port marked "focus" until the desired distance (3 ft. to infinity) appears next to another index mark. The fact that the Panox's focusing scale is calibrated in feet leads me to believe that the Panox was an export version of the Panon AIII, which had nearly identical features.

Loading the Panox is straightforward. You remove the bottom plate after turning two twist locks to "open," and slide out the beautifully made, cast alloy film insert. This holds the film in an arc that matches the shutter drum, and it incorporates two rollers for smooth film transport and two flat springs to hold film on the roll. These are especially necessary in the Panox, which has an automatic film counter as mentioned, but no automatic film stop. Before loading the insert into the camera you set the film counter to "S," and then wind the film until the line under the "1" mark is aligned with a red index mark—crude but effective.

In terms of performance, the Panox (or Panon) has a very good reputation for imaging and mechanical reliability. It's one of the few cameras with a finder frame that doubles as a carrying handle, has two bubble levels on its top, produces a very discrete buzz when fired at the 1/2-sec. setting, and an alarming "bzzzt" at 1/200. I only wish that Panon would produce this gloriously spartan machine once again now that I have the dough to buy one. The one pictured is in very good condition, and presently resides under a $2,000 price tag.

Another swinging-lens panoramic to capture my fancy is the USSR-made Horizont (which means horizon, I guess), a 35mm camera that's got a somewhat crude and tacky finish, but is nevertheless a very effective picture taker. Unlike the Panox, there's no film insert—just an arcuate film plane inside the camera. A roller to the left of the curved film plane holds the film against it on one side, and the sprocket shaft performs similar duty on the right. In case you get confused there's a nice little loading diagram inside the hinged back, which also sports a cartridge-orienting spring.

One of the Horizont's nicest features is its removable optical finder with bubble level that slides into a vertical "accessory shoe" on the front of the camera. It provides a very clear, almost undistorted super-wide view, and the

Horizontally, USSR-made Horizont covers 120° on standard 35mm film cartridges.

87

bubble level is reflected into an area below the viewing image by means of an internal mirror—an excellent idea. To the right of the finder is the combined aperture, shutter-speed, and the film speed reminder dial. Its outer milled ring controls shutter speeds of 1/30, 1/60, 1/125, and 1/250 sec., the second is used to set click-stopped apertures from f/2.8 to f/16, and the innermost ring has an ASA/DIN scale with ASAs from 20-650. To the right of the "control center" is the shutter release, and a nice big film-wind knob with built-in film counter.

Since the Horizont produces 24 × 58mm images, the film counter only goes up to 21 (for use with 36-exposure cartridges), and you set it by pulling up the outer dial and turning a knurled ring inside until the number you want appears in a little window. Unlike the Panox, the Horizont has automatic film stop and true double exposure prevention—the shutter drum is wound as you wind the film. The one feature the Horizont lacks is focusing—the 28mm F/2.8 OF-28P lens is fixed at infinity, but depth-of-field will carry you through at medium or small apertures and/or medium shooting distances. Incidentally, shutter speeds are varied by changing the width of the scanning slit, not by altering the speed of the rotating drum as in the Panox.

In general, the Horizont is a good performer. It's optically competent and does not tend to break down. Its aperture *and* shutter-speed setting rings rotate as you wind the film and (in the opposite direction) as you take the picture, which is a bit disconcerting and some panoramists have reported less than smooth shutter firing in cold weather, leading to a vertical "venetian blind" effect. Still, I wish some enterprising American company would once again import this interesting beast which, to the best of my knowledge, is still in production. It would sure beat paying the $350 asked for the used model pictured herein.

non-swinging-lens, standard 24×36mm format, 35mm machine known as the Zeiss-Ikon Hologon. This beautifully made (and expensive) 1966 camera has a fixed-focus 15mm f/8 Carl Zeiss Hologon lens, described as a three-element design with a second element shaped like a dumbbell. Its shutter is an ordinary horizontal cloth focal plane type with speeds of 1-1/500 sec. plus B and T. Like the Horizont, its optical finder has a bubble level on top of it which is reflected into a "patch" below the viewing area, but its excellent finder is permanently mounted and the bubble appears on a translucent yellow field.

The Hologon (which most assuredly has nothing to do with holograms) is such a straightforward device, there's really not much else one can say about it. Its back comes off with two bottom-mounted twist locks in time-honored Contax fashion, its picture-taking angle is approximately 110°, its smooth-operating shutter release sits atop a concentric control cluster that includes a manually zeroed film counter and the shutter-speed setting ring, and the 180° stroke film-wind lever is ratcheted. Hologons have proved to be exceptionally fine picture takers (that lens may be slow but it's optically superb) and, like most discontinued cameras, are appreciated more now than when they were made. Think you can't live with a fixed focus camera? This one's in focus from 20 in. to infinity! Worst thing about it is the $1,500 asking price. It makes me want to kick myself around the block—I sold mine for a paltry $135.

Finally, I'm determined to squeeze in one last wide-angle camera that never really got off the ground—the fabled Horseman Convertible of 1970. Basically, it's a modular concept camera consisting of three components—a helically focusing lens on a lensboard, a 120 roll film holder, and a very thin "body" section that holds the first two parts together. Indeed, the "camera" part of this camera is

Fixed focus? Who cares! Zeiss-Ikon Hologon's 15mm f/8 lens is sharp from 20 in. to infinity.

One super-wide camera I actually had sense enough to buy, but then proceeded to sell like a fool was the elegant,

Some lens! Horseman Convertible plus 47mm Schneider Super Angulon's a formidable hand-holdable combo.

so simple, it can be described as a spacer containing such pedestrian stuff as a 6×7 cm film aperture, dark slide, accessory shoe, and a tripod socket. In fact the only clue that it's part of a camera are its channel for the lensboard, and a film-holder locking system consisting of two fixed tabs and two retractable ones, controlled by a sliding switch marked "on" and "off."

The standard lens supplied with the Horseman Convertible was a 62mm f/5.6 Horseman (made by Topcon) which provides a 70⁰ angle of view and stops down to f/32. It's got an interlens Copal shutter with speeds from 1-1/500 sec. plus B, and focuses down 1 m. You cock the shutter by pressing down on a knurled tab adjacent to the lens with your left thumb, and you fire the very quiet shutter by pressing an identical tab with your right thumb. The "viewfinder" for this standard optic is very simple—just pull up a wire-and-plastic frame nestled in the 62mm's lensboard and center your eye behind it as best you can—there's no rear peep sight!

As nice as the 62mm lens is (it scored excellent at all apertures center and edge in Modern's tests) the real *raison d'etre* for this camera is the incredible 47mm f/5.6 Schneider Super-Angluon (pictured), which was evidently supplied on a special lensboard by Horseman to a handful of lucky photographers. As you might expect, it's furnished in Synchro-Compur 1-1/500 sec. (plus B) shutter and double helical focuses down to 0.5m. This lens also came with a "real" viewfinder that slides into the centrally placed accessory shoe and provides an extremely bright, undistorted super-wide view.

One can but speculate on the level of photographic performance this cleverly designed camera is capable of de-livering with fine optics, extremely rigid, hand-holdable camera body, and a better than average film holder with automatic film stop and wind-lever advance. When you consider these things and factor in its extreme rarity, the asking price of $900 with both superb lenses seems reasonable indeed.

Modular magic: Lens units slide into groove on front, film holder snaps onto back.

Many thanks to Ken Hansen Photographic, Inc. of New York for supplying the quartet of wide wonders pictured herein.

Quartet of curious cameras: Kodak 3-A Special, Contessa-Nettel, Plaubel Roll-Op, and the Kamra

Once more into the potpourri, with a quartet of disparate picture takers having virtually nothing in common but film.

As my closest friends and associates would be only too happy to attest, I am basically a disorganized person: And while I occasionally play the gadfly, my method of collecting cameras and their attendant historical data is more akin to the housefly, who flits about from pillar to post catching a choice morsel when and where he can. In contrast to this haphazard, eclectic approach, the cameras presented in these columns often fall into neat little categories, giving a false impression of orderliness and planning. But this month I've decided to abandon all pretense and to simply relate the disjointed tale of four utterly un-related cameras that have been cluttering my desk top for the past three months.

The first and largest photographic instrument is one of my all-time favorites, the grand and glorious Kodak 3-A Special, Model A of 1910-14, a member of the renowned "Postcard Kodak" series that produced six 3¼ × 5½-in. images per roll of (discontinued in '70) #122 roll film. Unlike later versions of the 3-A Special, this one lacks the split-image rangefinder built into the base of the front standard, and its removable, die-cast aluminum back is too early to be fitted with a covered "Autographic" slot for inscribing picture data on pressure-sensitive film. But, in lieu of a rangefinder, this early "Special" incorporates lateral as well as vertical adjustment of the front standard, and there's a knurled focusing knob which pulls out to

Special? What else can you call a 3A Kodak worth two months' pay in 1910! Reflex finder has engraved cover, bubble level.

engage a rack-and-pinion focusing mechanism. This works smoothly only if you grab the spring-loaded focus-lock tabs before trying to focus.

High class lens and shutter

Perhaps the most impressive features of this imposing beast, aside from its beautifully tooled morocco leather covering, are its lens and shutter—they are, respectively, an f/6.3 Baush & Lomb Tessar Series IIb, which stops down to an unmarked f/45, and an Autotime Compound (based on the famous German Compound shutter by Deckel) with separate cocking lever, marked speeds from 1-1/200 sec. and separate B and T setting control in a slot below the lens. As was common in those days, the format (3¼ × 5½ in.) is indicated on the lens identification ring instead of the focal length, and both aperture and shutter-speed scales are adorned with verbal pleasantries such as "Shadow, Distant View, and Marine Clouds Snow" and "Very Dull, Brilliant, and Moving Objects, Slow." If this strikes you as less than helpful, even with no meter and super-slow black-and-white film, shutter speeds below 1/25 sec. are thoughtfully bracketed with the admonition, "Tripod."

One caution: If, when closely examining one of these magnificent monuments to a bygone era, you're taken with the high-quality nickel plate, gorgeous engraving, and general aura of quality, please refrain from blubbering such platitudes as "They don't make 'em like they used to." Remember, this model in particular was hardly

intended for the masses, since its original selling price of $80.50 represents roughly two month's salary for the average Joe of the day, and translates into a current retail price of close to $750. Amazingly, its current collectors' value is a piddling $75-100 despite this model's relative rarity.

Remaining in the realm of scale-focusing folders of the World War I era, we now present Contessa-Nettel's answer to the Vest Pocket Kodak (or was it the other way around), a neat little machine with nickel-plated "lazy tongs" struts, pull-out lensboard and everset Derval shutter with speeds of 1/25, 1/50, and 1/100 sec. plus T and B. As usual, the tiny reflex finder behind the front plate rotates 90° for verticals and horizontals and the tiny 7.5 cm f/6.3 lens is calibrated in the Continental aperture system with stops of f/6.3, 9, 12.5, 18, 25, and 36 set with a little pointer running in an arcuate slot below it. For a little lens it's got a pretty impressive moniker, Contessa-Nettel Nettar-Anastigmat, and it reportedly did a decent job of covering the camera's 1⅝ × 2½-in. format on 127 film.

Vest Pocket Kodak? Nope, this look-alike was made by Contessa-Nettel, its lens and shutter are adjustable, but when it comes to focusing....

Surprisingly, this enterprising entry lacks focusing of any kind—not even the front-component type featured on deluxe Vest Pocket Kodak cameras of the era. However, its slide-out film holder frame with spring-loaded spool retainers is a masterpiece of functional simplicity that almost makes up for it. Finally two stumpers—my Diligent Research Department has, as yet, failed to unearth the official name of this jewel, and its got a removable circular plate smack in the center of its leather-clad back which contains the red window. A free roll of 122 film to the first reader who can correctly identify the function of this odd and seemingly unnecessary contraption. Oh, yes—I almost forgot—I'd peg the present value of this pocketable curiosity at about $50-60.

Moving ahead about 20 years (1934 to be exact) but remaining in the Contessa-Nettel's home country of Germany, we hereby present the lovely Plaubel Roll-Op (not to be confused with the German twin-lens reflex of the 50's which has the same name lacking the hyphen). The Roll-Op is one of the neatest roll-film format rangefinder folders I've run across, and it makes 16 pictures in the currently fashionable 4.5 × 6-cm (1⅝ × 2¼-in.) size on 120 film. Like its more famous cousin, the Zeiss Super Ikonta A, the Roll-Op is a beautiful example of the leather-clad, nickel-plated school of German camera design, and its double-braced folding mechanism is commendably rigid. Unlike the Super-Ikontas, this Plaubel features unit focusing of its 7.5 cm f/2.8 Anticomar lens, yet it *will* get you down to 1 m. Although this focusing arrangement is regarded as optically superior, it's got one mechanical disadvantage— you have to rack the knurled focusing tab back to the infinity setting before you can close the beast. To open the Roll-Op you press a little button nestled in between the rangefinder and viewfinder windows on top of the camera, and the front swings open and locks in place instantly. Separate rangefinder and viewfinder windows were

Ingenious exposure counter (left) is based on differentially notched cam.

counter must be manually released by moving a small lever to the left before you can advance the film to the next frame, but at least you have the luxury of automatic film stop and film counting (with even spacing of the frames!) by virtue of an external wheel with smaller and smaller spacings between its external notches as you move further along the roll. This ingenious arrangement compensates for the increasing width of the take-up spool as you wind on the film. For the record, the Plaubel 1 Roll-Op is not only durable and competent, but rather rare. It currently fetches about $150 among knowledgeable collectors.

Let's end these festivities with a whimper instead of a bang in the form of an American curiosity of the 1920's known as a Kamra. This squarish mostly Bakelite creation was a product of the M. Ellison Co. of Hollywood, California, and is something of a phony even though it incorporates several clever features. As you might guess from its early date and "shoebox" appearance, this is one of those machines designed to produce a huge number of pictures of 35mm "movie" film, and its format is approximately 24 × 32mm. Frankly, I surmise that Mr. Ellison's intention was to produce a cheapo version of some of the super-deluxe pre-Leica 35s like the Tourist Multiple and the Simplex, which were strictly for the upper crust. Do I sound unsympathetic? Well, photographically speaking, some of the Kamra's features are even funkier than its name and logo. To being with, the Wollensak f/5 Ellison-Hollywood lens is of fixed aperture and has no focusing mount. And while the handle on the side of the camera both winds the film (if you turn it clockwise) and fires the shutter (when you turn it counterclockwise), the double-metal-bladed shutter behind the lens evidently provided but one shutter speed (probably 1/25 or 1/50 sec.). Now I have nothing against box cameras, but the Kamra is most assuredly one of the most pretentious box cameras ever de-

Roll-Op?: It's Plaubel's tag for a super-deluxe roll film folder with rangefinder labelled Tellemeter, unit-focusing lens.

the order of the day, and while the little optical viewfinder on the carrying strap end of the beast is dinky by modern standards, the rangefinder is quite good—hardly surprising considering its over-2-in. base length. Curiously, the central focusing image is clear, while the background image is tinted a deep yellow. The aperture scale below the lens is calibrated in the aforementioned Continental f/stop system to f/25, and the shutter is the excellent Compur-Rapid with speeds from 1-1/400 sec. plus T and B and built-in self timer.

The remainder of the Roll-Op is, for the most part, unremarkable. It's got a spring-loaded back catch, dual red windows on the back (with sliding cover) typical of "split-frame" formats and, of course, a European tripod socket on its bottom. And although it lacks double-exposure prevention, you *can* dispense with ye olde red windows once you've positioned the first frame. True, the Roll-Op's film

Posh-looking Kamra had big capacity 35mm cartridges, box camera specs. Was it a cheap knock-off of deluxe pre-Leica 35s? You be the judge.

which can probably accommodate 50 ft. of film in a pinch. The take-up cartridge is positioned on the right, the film-supply cartridge is on the left, and the sprocket wheel to the right of the film aperture looks familiar to 35mm fans. Decidedly unusual is the method by which the film is actually taken up on the take-up spool. Attached to the bottom end of the sprocket shaft is a geared wheel with a pulley underneath it. And hanging from the pulley is (would you believe) a metal spring belt of the type often found on old movie projectors. So, once you load and attach the felt-lipped cartridges and orient them properly in their receptacles, you simply pull the belt over a pulley attached to the film-take-up shaft in the right-hand cartridge and you're ready to fly. What about the film counter, you ask? Don't be silly—when you get tired of snapping away, you just open the camera, sever the film connecting the cartridges and process the film you've shot. Incidentally, both cartridges are identical so they'll work for either take-up or film feed.

A caustic evaluation

By now you're probably tempted to say that this spartan beast is cute. Well that's because you never had to make pictures with the silly thing. The Kamra's reflex viewfinder is so small as to be practically useless, the Bakelite body is extremely brittle (ours is chipped in several places), and you had to affix the film to the supply spool to avoid the dreaded "no more film and I don't know it" syndrome. "Try to be more understanding and less caustic," cautioned my buddy. "Perhaps the Kamra was intended for shooting location stills on the movie set under more-or-less fixed lighting conditions." Maybe he's right, but I still think it's a shuck, with its box camera specs and 'Hollywood" marked lens. Oh well, at least this flapper-era flimflam has finally earned its unjust rewards—I understand that Kamras in good nick have brought over a hundred bucks apiece from desperate American camera fanciers. Many thanks to Adolph Knott of Flint, Michigan, for supplying our first three cameras, and to Mark Mikolas of B & H/Mamaya Co. for letting us excoriate his Kamra.

signed because it appears to be so much more than it is.

And now the good news

Actually, my affection for the circa-1928 Kamra increases considerably once I slide over two metal "buttons" on its removable back to the left and lift off its back. Inside are two brass screws which serve as back-mounting lugs, a burnt-orange colored film aperture cum film plane plate, and two commodious mahogany-colored film cartridges

Collectors:
Do they really deprive photographers of the tools of their trade?

Camera collector's complaint—or why are all those non-collector photographers saying all those horrible things about me?

Now that camera collecting is clearly flourishing, can the decline and fall of Western culture be far behind? You may snicker, but there are hordes of somber sociologists

and philosophers out there firmly convinced that the current worldwide collecting craze is symptomatic of some deep-seated social malaise. In the past, I have summarily dismissed such doomsayers as puritanical spoil-sports whose only desiccated pleasure in life is to make us feel guilty (or at least uneasy) about our acquisitive little fun and games. But I have seriously begun to wonder—are we really nothing more than a pernicious new breed of materialists grasping at the discarded remains of The Great Industrial-Mechanical Age?

Unobtainable dream? Hardly, but a really clean, single-stroke Leica M3 with old-style selenium Leica meter, rigid 50mm f/2 Summicron will set you back about $500.

Now this may well be a profound question, but, I regret, it is not one to which I can provide profound answers. What I can do, albeit on a more modest scale, is to air some of the arguments of camera collecting's chief critics and to make a sincere effort to see whether they have any merit.

Let's set the stage for this soul searching exercise with a few stanzas of instant nostalgia commemorating the good old days that ended about 10-15 years ago. Friends, do you remember when camera stores consigned oddball cameras to the assorted junk pile rather than the "collector's corner"? Can you recall when antique shops relegated those creaky old wooden view cameras to the basement, and hadn't yet coined the phrase "photographica" to inflate the prices of everything even remotely connected with making pictures?

Well, it's *still* possible to unearth the occasional "great buy" out there in the boondocks, but as collectors we've got to own up to the fact that the prices of the most *desirable* picture-making machines have gone clear out of sight. And where does this leave us, once the anguished cries of peculiar-camera fanciers have died down? Basically, in a rather unfavorable situation, with farsighted and/or well-heeled collectors having grabbed up the most interesting pieces and the mere mortals among us being forced to hunt elsewhere.

Ah, yes, but do any fertile hunting grounds yet remain in a field plucked bare by the super-rich and super-savvy? Fortunately, the answer is a qualified yes. You say you have a penchant for interchangeable-lens rangefinder 35s? Well, Contax IIs and IIIs are easy to find, and you might even nab a clean, functional one with an uncoated 50mm f/2 Sonnar lens for under a hundred bucks if you're lucky. Ditto for old rangefinder Canons, though admittedly some

Pauper's posh 35? Yep, pre-war Contax III is dirt cheap—a C-note with 50mm f/2 lens—but meter, shutter are hard to fix.

of the juicier items such as VTs VI-Ts, VT DeLuxe models and even IV-S2s with rapid winders are becoming scarce and/or expensive. And while most Leicas fetch prices beyond or bordering on the exorbitant, you can still buy a workable "classic" Leica IIIe or IIIf with a 50mm f/2 Summitar or 50mm f/3.5 Elmar for less than the price of the mythical "average" modern SLR. And for equipment nuts in search of new, uncharted realms, I unhesitatingly recommend 8 and 16mm movie cameras and projectors. Those cinematic items not literally cast into the dustbin can presently be found littering dealers' shelves and junk bins, and many truly high quality items (all but the very earliest machines by Edison, Lumiere, Kodak, etc.) can be had for almost a song.

But enough of greener pastures yet to conquer—what about all those nasty epithets that have recently been hurled at us camera collectors? Is all this nastiness based on fact or mere jealousy? Let's attempt to answer this by focusing on the two chief gripes against camera collectors voiced by the non-collecting photographic public, namely that we deprive them of unique and usable cameras by snapping them up and putting them in our collections, and that once we have snared these delectably proficient picture takers, we simply polish them up and put them on sterile display in locked showcases.

Collectors' casualty? Maybe, but you don't have to shell out $600 for a clean Leica IIIg with f/2.8 Elmar—buy a IIIf with f/3.5!

Forgetting for the moment that only a small percentage of camera collectors have, or can afford, the room to display cameras in showcases, locked or otherwise, I'm forced to concede that the opposition has a good point about the disuse which once-glorious photographic machines suffer once we get our grubby mitts on them. For all one may say decrying the excesses of automobile- and motorcycle-collecting buffs, it is considered poor form among them to retain and restore a vehicle and then to simply display it as a pristine but nonfunctional artifact. To get the mechanical juices flowing, there are rallies, shows, and even vintage races—not to mention gently running one's pride and joy down the road on a sunny Sunday afternoon. And when, pray tell, was the last time you saw one of us antique camera chaps shooting pictures with his superannuated marvel? No, I don't expect photo-historical boffins to go to such lengths as rolling their own 118/124/122 roll film or cutting glass plates to odd European sizes, but what about the myriad unfolded roll-film cameras taking 127, 116, 616, and 620 film that merely languish in dark closets? Here the films are readily available, often in both color and black-and-white, and when Kodak discontinues these sundry emulsions because of *our* lack of interest, who will be first on line to bitch and moan?

This situation is all the more pitiful because many old cameras, folders in particular, are blessed with both portability *and* a nice big format. For example; if you take a roll-film folder as pedestrian as a 2¼ × 3¼ Kodak Vigilant of the late 30's, stick it on a tripod, stop the Kodak Anastigmat lens down to f/8 and set the distance with a modicum of care, you can obtain color or black-and-white negatives that will produce grainless 11 × 14 in. and larger prints that are noticeably superior to what you can get with your fancy 35. Indeed, the very lack of automation and dinky viewfinders characteristic of many classic cameras forces you to take pictures more carefully and concentrate on lighting, composition, and subtleties of expression. I hate to conclude with a harangue on this point but for Pete's sake get out there and take some pictures with your collectible cameras—that's what they were made for!

Nefarious collectors?

Let's now address the most common potshot leveled at us camera collectors—that we're depriving honest non-collecting photographers of worthwhile cameras by hoarding them and/or driving prices up. I am frankly less than sympathetic to this argument for one simple reason—what I call the Camera Condition Corollary. To explain what I mean, let's take the worst possible case against collectors, also known as the M-series Leica Debacle.

Yes, 'tis sad but true—in response to collectors and investors (who are often—but not necessarily—the same people) prices paid for Leica M3s, M2s and M4s (not to mention genuinely rare models like the MP and M2R) have undeniably taken off for the wild blue yonder. For example, a clean M3 that I could've nabbed for around 200 bucks with 50mm f/3.5 Elmar lens a decade ago, now fetches $350 *without lens,* and I'd be lucky to find a *really*

mint model on the open market at any price. Since the M3 is, without doubt, a photographer's camera with unique and useful characteristics (i.e., whisper quietness and a rangefinder that can accurately focus on a black cat in a coal bin at midnight), isn't this proof positive that collectors are a culpable bunch of nogoodniks insofar as the "advancement of photography" is concerned?

I don't think so. After all, if the performance and characteristics of the Leica M3 are what a photographer requires, he/she can easily locate a perfectly functional mod-

Premium priced? Sorta, but the Canon 7S offers the luxury of a built-in coupled CdS meter, so it's worth $275 with f/1.4 lens.

el thereof (with the few external battle scars or brassing of the chrome or black finish) with lens, for less than the price of a top-drawer SLR. Think of it—for less than the cost of your buddy's Nikon, you too can resemble a combat photojournalist. Where I am forced to concede that collectors have done the budding photojournalists of the world no good at all is in the area of lenses for interchangeable-lens rangefinder cameras. Bayonet mount Leica lenses, screw-thread Leica lenses, screw-thread Canon lenses, and even bayonet mount lenses for rangefinder Contaxes and Nikons are hard to find in the focal lengths you prefer, and are generally too damned expensive if and when you're fortunate enough to stumble upon them.

Come to think of it, there's one aspect of the "them vs. us" controversy that nobody I've spoken with has put his finger on, and that's the underlying similarity between photographers determined to use "outmoded" equipment and collectors determined to hoard it. Both groups are clearly technological romanticists of the first order, and this goes a long way toward explaining the ongoing antipathy. As soon as we collectors start to take pictures with our collectibles, we will do much to defuse our detractors' arguments. And as for photographers convinced that the only possible 35 worthy of the name must have a rangefinder sitting serenely above the lens, I hereby commend to them a device known as the single-lens reflex. Hell, it even has a built-in meter that you don't have to remove (to fit a finder) when you're shooting with a 21 or 200mm lens!

The Contarex legend, part 1

The Contarex legend, Part 1. In which a fine German camera and lens maker's brilliant mechanical engineering produces too much camera for too much money.

Just received an informative little epistle from friend and fellow collector Wolf Wehran, Public Relations Counsel for a fairly well-known German optical outfit named Zeiss. Funny, I always thought its official moniker was *Carl* Zeiss and that they were located in Oberkochen, so I guess the Stuttgart address on the stationery indicates that Wolf has set up a factory branch in his basement. At any rate, after effusively praising my previous scribblings, he regales us with some fascinating figures in three interrelated units—dollars, Deutschmarks, and camera production numbers. To quote, "(with respect to your) comments on the Hologon Ultra-wide. My advice: get another one for $475 and keep it. The going price over here is DM 2200 or about $1,100. Only 1400 were made, and their value is bound to go up! By the way, all Contarex models are rapidly becoming collectors' items in Europe. Only 32,000 were made of the first model, 5,000 of the Special, 1,500 of the Professional, 13,400 of the Super, and 3,100 of the Super Electronic; all in all 55,000." Very odd—on this side of the pond Contarexes were, until quite recently, regarded by most photo dealers as unsalable turkeys, so perhaps it's time to see precisely what sort of *rarae aves* they are.

To get straight to the point for a change, the Contarex was undoubtedly Zeiss's first and last attempt to build a world-beating "system" SLR in the 35mm format. When you consider the prestige and product diversity of this ancient and noble firm, that somehow sounds wrong, but unfortunately, it is not. The gloriously complex prewar Contaflex was, as you may recall, a member of that strange species known as a focal-plane-shutter *twin-lens* reflex. And however nice, tidy and well integrated the various postwar Contaflex models may be (and they are indeed underrated in both prestige and monetary value at present), few would claim that these leaf-shutter SLRs with (or without) front-component interchangeable optics qualify as either world beaters or truly "system concept" cameras, despite their nifty interchangeable film backs, copying accessories and monocular adapters. Of course there was an earlier landmark 35mm SLR introduced under the venerable Zeiss banner back in '49, but the poor little Contax D had the misfortune of being born in Dresden, in the Eastern Zone, on the wrong side of the politi-

Beautifully finished, posh and sophisticated, this original Contarex of 1958 currently fetches about $300 among dealers.

cal railroad tracks. And so, despite its clever pentaprism, sound basic design, decent 58mm f/2 Biotar lens and "universal" Praktica-type screw-thread lens mount, it never really developed into the high class SLR system it might have been. Indeed, it was always afflicted with a dim viewfinder, had preset-diaphragm lenses, and by the time it was brought over here in sufficient numbers as a cheapie SLR under Hexacon and Pentacon nameplates (in the mid-50's to early 60's), its quality level had dropped a couple of notches and it had shutter trouble as well.

Okay, enough post-mortem lamentations; suffice it to say that by the mid-50's, the West German heirs of the Zeiss trademark, who were much better equipped to build cameras in the glorious Zeiss tradition, had embarked upon a project to design the greatest, most comprehensive SLR the world had ever seen. A few years later (1958 to be exact), Zeiss brought forth the fruit of their labors—the original Contarex. Rarely in the course of photographic history has a camera been so blessed with mechanical ingenuity and finesse, and at the same time, beset with such complexities and contradictions, both internal and external. It is, at once, brilliantly finished and ungainly looking —the latter attribute earning it the nickname "cyclops" by virtue of its round selenium meter cell affixed to the front of the prism housing.

In terms of its operation, the original Contarex is a match-needle-metering SLR—which may not sound too spiffy by today's standards, but was par for the course (if not quite state-of-the-art) 20 years ago. It was also, to state it kindly, a substantial and hefty machine, measuring just under 6 in. long, 4 in. high, and 3¼ in. deep (with the standard 50mm f/2 Carl Zeiss Planar lens set at infinity) and weighing in at almost precisely 3 lbs. Among its many deluxe features were fully interchangeable film magazines, focusing to just under 12 in. with the normal lens and the ability to accept a superb range of Zeiss lenses (including wide-angle Biogons and Distagons, normal focal length Planars, and Sonnar teles) via a beautifully machined three-lobed external bayonet mount reminiscent of the one used to mount tele lenses on rangefinder Contaxes. It was also up-to-date in featuring an instant-return mirror, and the aforementioned Zeiss lenses were mounted in some of the smoothest-focusing helicals ever to grace a modern SLR.

Wind the non-ratcheted but comfortably contoured single-stroke film-advance lever and bring the Contarex up to eye level and you're greeted by a nice, bright, contrasty viewing image. The outer, full-focusing area of the screen exhibits a moderately coarse Fresnel pattern, and in the center there's a split-image rangefinder surrounded by a very fine textured microprism collar. The combination of an extremely smooth and decisive focusing mechanism and these very well engineered focusing aids made focusing and viewing a real pleasure. Indeed, my only criticism is a minor and somewhat personal one—I've never been enamored of finder fields with rounded corners.

Fine Zeiss lenses bayoneted into Contarex with a smooth twist, but rear of satin chrome barrel was hard to grab. Aperture scale is atop round meter cell housing.

Improved version of original Contarex featured interchangeable focusing screens; data recording strips are shown inserted in back.

To the right of the viewing area is a vertically arrayed white band (which is illuminated by a small frosted window adjacent to the Zeiss-Ikon logo on the front of the camera) with a V-shaped metering-notch-index in its mid-

section. To set the metering system you lift the shutter-speed-setting ring mounted concentrically under the wind-lever pivot, set a black delta opposite one of the film speeds in the ring below it (ASA 5-1300 on export models), choose a shutter speed (1-1/1000 sec. plus B) by turning the knurled shutter-speed dial until the setting you want clicks in opposite a large black delta (with a "pinpoint" sticking out of it!) on the back of the wind lever, and you're ready to go. To actually meter, you turn a convenient knurled dial on the front of the camera (which resembles a Contax or rangefinder Nikon focusing wheel) with your right index finger until the meter needle is centered in the aforementioned notch. Apertures appear in a little window atop the meter cell housing. This system is anatomically well thought out (your shutter finger is not forced to stray far from the shutter button) and the metering system proved to be quite accurate (well within a half stop in most cases), though the needle action is a bit sluggish by modern standards. Is this beginning to sound like a rave review?

All right, let's take some pictures—we'll presume for the moment that the camera has been loaded, the subtractive, manual film counters atop the film-wind lever *and* on the bottom of the film magazine have been appropriately set, and that we've metered the correct exposure, say 1/125 sec. at f/11. Press the not-too-smooth but reasonably predictable shutter release perched in the middle of the main frame counter downwards and something unnerving occurs. The shutter and instant-return mirror are released to the accompaniment of a fairly noisy and rather prolonged mechanical clatter, and when the viewing image returns, lo and behold, the central focusing aids are almost completely blacked out. As you may have guessed, this "brown-out" is caused by a curious omission in the Contarex's otherwise thoughtful design—it has an instant-return mirror all right, but the lens diaphram doesn't return to maximum aperture until you wind the film-advance lever! Oh well, at least the outer viewing image isn't noticeably affected thanks to the Fresnel lens, and the center only gets really dismal at apertures of f/8 and smaller. Almost nitpicking by comparison is my criticism of the huge 1⅜-in. diameter knurled rewind knob which slightly overhangs both the front and rear edges of the camera top. As you advance the film, this big, fat knob turns counter-clockwise, and it can snag some folks' foreheads or eyebrows. Why, I wonder, did they bother to build a flip-out crank into the center of it?

Interchanging lenses on the Contarex is a very pleasant experience because the bayonet mount operates with such luxurious smoothness. It's a good thing, too, since the rear part of Contarex lens barrels is smooth satin chrome—there's no knurled or textured mounting ring provided. To remove a lens, you press in a chrome button positioned at about 2:30 o'clock just outside the external bayonet, turn the rear part of the lens barrel about 90⁰ counterclockwise, and lift the lens out. To mount a lens, you line up two red dots and simply bayonet the lens in.

Internal complexities

As long as we've removed the normal optic, let's take a gander at the inside of the camera's mirror box. The first thing you notice when peering at the Contarex's innards is that the mirror itself is quite narrow by modern standards, and that its sides slant inwards toward the front forming a trapezoid. If you look closer, you'll note something even more curious (and mechanically complex to achieve)—the mirror does not pivot conventionally at its back edge, but it's suspended by a hinge placed a few millimeters toward the front. Also, as the main mirror-driving spring is released to flip the mirror up, this action tensions a second spring which drives the mirror down. Without going into a lot of complicated explanations, suffice it to say that the hinge and rotary actuating arm of the mirror-flipping mechanism form a unique system that's been praised as very durable and condemned as relatively slow operating and too expensive to manufacture.

Further complications in the Contarex's design can be found in the film-wind and shutter mechanisms which incorporate such exotica as numerous bevel gears running at right angles to each other and cam axles that resemble the camshafts on overhead-cam automotive engines! These parts are (mostly) superbly crafted and brilliantly designed, but one wonders, to what justifiable end? The Contarex shutter was extremely expensive to produce, and those who know how to repair it assert that it's easier to repair than most once you know how. Unfortunately, relatively few people do know how and Zeiss never furnished a clear instruction manual to train the uninitiated. Furthermore, whatever its theoretical superiority, it is not demonstrably superior to more pedestrian types of horizontal cloth focal-plane shutters in actual use.

Finally, there's that beautiful system of interchangeable film magazines. To begin with, there's a funny fact about interchangeable film magazines in general—line up a group of professional photographers who shoot 35mm almost exclusively and ask them what feature they'd like to see on a camera designed for them and they'll shout, practically in unison, "Interchangeable film magazines!" Now show me a 35mm camera incorporating this feature that has actually been successfully *sold* to large numbers of such pros and I'll cheerfully eat it for breakfast! With that somber bit of levity out of the way, let's examine the Contarex magazine, which is actually one of the better ones.

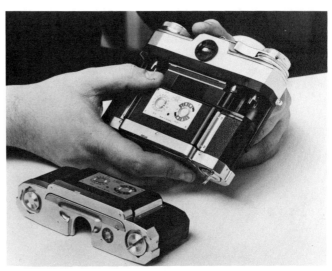

Interchangeable Contarex magazines were one of camera's best features but heaven help you if you goofed!

Before you detach the film mag from the back of your Contarex you've got to do two things—cock the shutter and insert the convex, stainless-steel dark slide in a similarly shaped slot on the camera bottom. Now just turn the two Contax-style key-type locks on the bottom in clockwise and counterclockwise directions respectively (there are no arrows to show you how) and the back comes off easily. Loading the magazine has been condemned by some as overly tricky, but I think it's pretty straightforward (if not super-slick) once you get the hang of it. First you push up and remove the cartridge cover on the right-hand side, push in a spring-loaded safety catch on the back, and slide the dark slide down past the spring-loaded pressure plate but not all the way out. Then pull the film leader across to the permanently mounted take-up spool, insert the end in the slit with the white mark (which is, admittedly, a bit difficult to get in precisely the right place every time), insert the film leader, and turn the milled bottom edge of the take-up spool a couple of times to fasten it securely. Now slide the cover over the cartridge, slide the dark slide fully home, mount the magazine and lock the locks. Of course you must now remember to set the film counter on the magazine *and* the one atop the film-wind lever, to remove the dark slide before trying to fire, and to check that the rewind knob is turning appropriately as you wind the film. In my opinion, most of the bad reputation that Contarex magazines have in this country is attributable to jamming caused by inadvertently winding the film off the cartridge spool or sundry jamming caused by improper loading, etc. Naturally, once you jam film in a Contarex magazine, getting the magazine off the camera and the film out of the magazine is a real challenge!

A successful failure?

Now that we've delved into some (but not all) of the Contarex's complexities, the 6400 Deutschmark question still remains—namely why did such a superbly constructed, eccentric but usable machine fall pretty much flat on its face in the marketplace? Sure it was big, but it was well balanced and designed to fit human hands, and surely there were pros in the world who appreciated its Zeiss optics. The underlying reasons? Well, to coin a phrase, it

was simultaneously too much and too little. Its internal and external complexities (and the fact that it was made in West Germany by skilled, highly paid personnel) raised its price to unacceptable levels. It debuted at $449.50 with 50mm f/2 Planar and sold for nearly $500 shortly afterwards, and if that sounds cheap, multiply it by a factor of about 3 for comparison with today's prices. Prophetically, only one year after the Contarex was introduced, Nikon came out with a camera known as the Nikon F, with a fully removable CdS meter prism that was swiftly converted to through-lens metering, a full line of fine lenses—a sturdy, reliable, mechanically sound system for fewer greenbacks. Amateurs could even obtain cheaper independently made lenses for far less money than Nikkors—a luxury not possible with the Contarex's limited production status and hard-to-produce lens mounts. Of course, the Contarex legend doesn't end here—not by a long shot. Next, we'll see just how Zeiss decided to update its "flagship."

The Contarex legend, part 2

The Contarex saga, Part 2. Wherein the Olympian leitmotif develops along Wagnerian lines, culminating in futuristic visions and ending in tragedy.

Last time we left Zeiss-Ikon in the awkward position of having developed a magnificent 35mm anachronism of heroic proportions only to be assaulted in the marketplace by hordes of Japanese SLRs that were inevitably cheaper and occasionally better thought out. And how did the colossus of West German optical technology respond to this unprovoked attack? In the only way it knew how—by bringing out a series of ever more intriguing Contarexes, all in the same grandly Teutonic mold.

The first model to make its debut after the original selenium-metered "cyclops" (reported in excruciating detail in the last opus) was the Contarex Special of 1960. What was so special about it? Well, to be succinct, it had an interchangeable pentaprism, switchable viewing screens, and no meter. Granted, it would have been nice to have one's built-in meter and screen interchangeability too, but this was a mechanical impossibility given the limitations of the original Contarex design, which had much of its complex metering mechanism protruding from the front of the prism housing! Besides, the Special had considerable merit as an element in the Contarex system even though its bare specifications seem pretty pedestrian.

In terms of control placement, the Special is virtually identical to the original model, retaining such distinctive

Magnificent but meterless, this Contarex Special is fitted with (collapsed) waist-level finder, fetches $375 with 50mm f/2.

Contarex characteristics as finger-wheel aperture adjustment, shutter-speed dial concentrically under the manual exposure counter, shutter-release button atop the wind-lever pivot, and removable back or (optionally) interchangeable film magazine. Happily, its interchangeable-prism-and-screen system is executed with characteristic Zeiss finesse. To remove the prism, you push down on the ridged tab located about half an inch below the eyepiece bezel, and the entire prism housing springs back a bit so you can slide it backward and lift it off. You can't mistakenly push the prism-removal button either, since it's protected by a tablike metal guard directly above it. With the prism off the camera, screen removal is exquisitely simple —just hook finger under a tab at the rear of the screen unit (there's a spring-loaded locking catch built into it), hinge the screen up and forward on its front locating rod, and lift it out. In addition to being operationally and mechanically superb, the Special's screen changing system approaches optical perfection as well. The screen itself is precisely located at three points (two small "claws" at the front of the screen frame grab onto the aforementioned locating rod), and the prism-mounting system is equally robust—there's a single pin at the front of the prism housing and two more pins under its rear section that slide into slots to hold the prism in precise parallel alignment to the screen. Overkill? Perhaps, but it's a far superior arrangement to the "tweeze out" and "drop out" screens that grace many a modern SLR. Oh yes, I almost forgot, there's one tiny snag. Since the screen unit incorporates a thick condenser glass atop the actual screen, it's quite tall, and to keep prism height reasonable, the prism itself has been made somewhat smaller than the one found in other Contarex models. The result? The finder only shows about 83 percent of what you get on film.

In 1967, Zeiss finally got their behind-lens metering act together and brought out a substantially revised Contarex, the Super. This open-aperture-metering SLR had its CdS cell placed at the bottom of the mirror box and took *direct* readings of light passing through the lens (not off the viewing screen) via a beam-splitter and semi-silvered spot in the center of the mirror (Leicaflex SLRs employ a similar system for "limited area" readings). To meter with the

Built like the Brooklyn Bridge, Contarex's prism removal system is operationally simple and optically beyond reproach.

Super, you first set your ASA (6-1600) on a scale located concentrically around the rewind crank, turn the meter on with a lockable switch under the left side of the pentaprism (later Supers had the switch placed under the wind lever), select a speed by lifting and turning the shutter-speed dial under the wind lever, and match-needle meter by turning the usual "focusing-wheel-type" aperture selector dial. You even have your choice of metering indices—there's one atop the camera to the right of the rewind knob which you set by placing a notched green circle over the meter needle, and another along the right side of the finder, which is illuminated by a frosted window adjacent to the top metering index. The metering index in the finder works similarly except that a green band is placed over the meter needle to obtain the correct exposure. All things considered, the Contarex Super's metering system was well thought out and quite convenient—the "external" metering index is not the most legible I've encountered, but the one in the finder is very easy to see, and is one of the few of its era to display set shutter speeds (in white-on-black numerals) in a little window below the aperture scale.

Changing the meter battery (one PX-13 or PX-625) on this camera is a fascinating (not to say unique) experience, since the little devil resides in a compartment under the mirror. Here's the procedure—cock the shutter, push a small button next to the wind lever forward to lock up the mirror, lift a small hinged plate (it's easy), and fish the battery out with your digits. It's a better engineered system than similar below-mirror battery compartments in modern SLRs (you know who we mean). The Super's viewing image, incidentally, is reasonably bright, quite contrasty, still has rounded corners and is, of course, still afflicted with the infamous Contarex brown-out syndrome. That's right folks—with all that technological legerdemain, the machine still lacks an instant-return diaphragm (i.e., you have to wind the shutter for the diaphragm to open to full aperture for viewing).

Of course Zeiss would not want to alienate professional photographers who might be attracted to the Contarex because of its superb line of Zeiss lenses, so a year before the Super was introduced, the world was blessed with yet another Contarex—the Professional. What made it so? Well you are undoubtedly familiar with the fact that professional photographers hate anything as mundane as built-in exposure meters, so the Contarex Professional had none. How about a removable prism like the Special? Nope. However, as with all but the earliest Contarexes you can switch screens via a hinged frame atop the mirror box *a la* Contax RTS. Like the Super it has a hot shoe, and our particular example has a shutter dial you don't have to lift before you turn (many Contarex fans complained about this inconvenient setup and it was changed to a more facile turn-and-click dial on later models).

What else can you say about the Pro? Not much. Ours is fitted with a Fresnel screen much like the Super's except that instead of a microprism collar surrounding a central split-image rangefinder there's a diagonally-split central

Sophisticated behind-lens meter and finder readouts mark the Contarex Super. Lens is rare 35mm f/4 PA Curtagon. Outfit currently brings about $850.

A demeterized Super? Yep, but this Professional's 135mm f/4 brings price to $450.

microprism separated by a thin bar which is actually a cylinder. This system, which also found its way into some Icarex and Rollei SLR models, creates an area of oblique distortion in subjects that are out of focus and is an effective focusing aid.

Another system common to the Super and Pro was the "Blitz-matic" flash system, which worked in conjunction with two "blitz" lenses—a Distagon wide-angle and 50mm f/2 Planar. Normally these lenses were used in non-blitz mode and two yellow deltas at the rear of the lens barrel at about 10 o'clock were aligned. For autoflash photography, you pressed a small button under the rear of the lens and rotated the rear-most part of the lens barrel about 180° clockwise until the appropriate flash guide number appeared opposite the yellow delta at the rear. Yes, this was one of those conventional mechanical auto-flash systems that selected different lens apertures depending on the focusing distance set. Not only that—if you attempted to focus too close for even the smallest lens

aperture to provide the correct exposure, you'd find you couldn't turn the focusing ring past a certain point. Indeed, if you select a guide number of 260, you can't focus closer than about 11 ft. The real beauty of the blitz-matic came when you used it with the Super—as soon as you set a guide number, the camera's metering system would immediately turn off to conserve battery power. Neat.

The works. Contarex SE's shown with Tele-Sensor providing exposure automation, plug-in shutter-speed-readout meter, motor drive less battery pack. Price: $1,300.

And what is the culmination of the saga—to what Olympian heights did Contarex development proceed before its timely demise? Well, there was the last, and in many ways the greatest Contarex—the SE (for Super Electronic), a machine which indicated Zeiss's *thinking* at least was headed in the right direction. Had this camera benefited from today's sophisticated electronics and micro-circuitry, it could have been a winner. As it was, it was a great idea whose time hadn't yet arrived.

Basically, the Contarex SE represented the logical extension of the Contarex system concept. Although operationally and cosmetically very similar to the last version of the Super (it had exactly the same type of through-lens metering system), the SE had three additional features that really pointed the way toward the future—its horizontal cloth focal-plane shutter was electronically timed by a solenoid, its bottom incorporated a keyway to provide the mechanical linkage for a motor drive, and a covered 5-contact socket to the left of the mirror box allowed you to plug in a remote-shutter-control device known as a Tele-Sensor (see photo).

Add-on automation?

This unlikely looking gadget is basically an external, limited area, metering system that transforms the Contarex SE into an aperture-preferred automatic SLR. Plug the Tele-Sensor into the aforementioned socket, slide the unit into the accessory shoe (or mount it remotely on a tripod using the standard ¼ in. socket), set the ASA on the sensor's dial and you're ready to go. Once you match the aperture on the sensor's aperture dial with the one you've previously set on the lens, the Tele-Sensor will automatically set the camera's shutter speed to provide the correct exposure. To check what that shutter-speed will be before you fire, press in a little red button at the back of the sensor's readout-meter section and the needle will point to the camera-selected speed—8 full seconds to 1/1000 sec.

Ungainly looking it may well have been, but the Tele-Sensor was certainly one of the first aperture-preferred, fully automatic metering systems in existence, predating the 1971 Pentax ES by more than three years. Without submerging the reader in yet more details, suffice it to say that the SE's bottom-mounted paraphernalia was equally extensive and inventive, including such accessories as a "real" motor drive with separate exposure counter, single and continuous speeds up to about 2 fps, intervalometer, and various remote-firing widgets. The batteries to power the shutter are contained in a hinged-cover compartment at the back of the prism housing, and there's a spring-loaded meter-shutoff button that you must push down before pushing the wind lever flush with the camera. Many Americans forgot to follow this last procedure, and as a result, the SE has a (mostly) undeserved reputation as a battery eater.

Where does this leave us? Well, considering the variety of Contarex models, their prestigious maker, and their extremely low production figures, it leaves us with some eminently usable collectors' items with a superb (and expensive and difficult to find) line of lenses to fit them. In a way it's too bad that these beautifully crafted, somewhat ungainly looking "Panzer tanks" of SLR-dom represent Zeiss's final attempt to compete head to head with Japan's best. They may not be as usable or up-to-date as today's Nikons and Canons but, if treated with respect and reasonable care, they may very well click and rasp their way into the 21st century.

Profuse thanks to Ken Hansen of Ken Hansen Photographic, 19 W. 34th St., New York, N.Y., for lending us his incredible collection of Contarexes (which are all for sale, by the way), and special thanks to Erwin Stoerrle of Z-V Service Corp., 333 W. Merrick Rd., Valley Stream, N.Y. 11580, who told me more about Contarexes than any single person has a right to know. Any errors appearing herein are mine, I assure you, not his, and anyone wanting a Zeiss or Voigtlander camera of any vintage properly repaired should contact Z-V.

Super Ikonta saga, part 1

The Super Ikonta Saga, Part 1. Wherein Zeiss-Ikon debuts a deluxe rangefinder roll-film series in the depths of the Depression.

Having heavily laced my two previous columns with the agonies and ecstasies of Zeiss-Ikon (in Stuttgart) and Carl Zeiss (in Oberkochen), as they labored to produce and refine the Contarex system, I think it's about time to assuage the world's Zeiss-niks with an unabashedly complimentary tale of what is arguably the most successful medium format rangefinder dynasty in history—the Zeiss Super Ikontas. Since I have long been a personal admirer of these handsome, beautifully crafted, and eminently functional beasts, I was amazed to discover that my previous coverage of them amounts to virtually nil—a passing reference to the "A" and "C" models, but nothing comprehensive. And so, to make double amends, as it were, let's slide back into the Great Depression of the 30's, where necessity, combined with the technical brilliance of Zeiss engineering, produced an ingenious invention destined to

Earliest of "Super As," this c. 1935 Super Ikomat sports 7cm (rather than later 7.5cm) f/3.5 Tessar lens, no body shutter release or Albada finder.

transform their admirable pocketable folding roll-film cameras into more precise yet equally rugged picture-taking instruments.

Actually, when you think about it, there are few cameras more deserving of a competent coupled rangefinder than medium-to-largish-format, roll-film types. With negative sizes ranging from 1⅝ × 2¼ in. to 3¼ × 5½ in. and lens focal lengths running from about 70-170mm, the ability to focus precisely and swiftly without having to guesstimate camera-to-subject distances is an obvious asset —especially when shooting portraits in the 5-10 ft. range. However, coupling a rangefinder mechanism to a lens which is located some 3-6 in. in front of the rangefinder's viewing window is hardly an easy or straightforward task —particularly when the coupling mechanism itself must be able to disengage and/or move discreetly out of the

Early postwar Super Ikonta A, c. 1953, had rare deep-set f/3.5 Xenar lens, double exposure prevention, Albada finder, no sync.

way when the camera is folded. Various spring-loaded coupling arms and shafts have been tried (which usually increase mechanical complexity and cost), and Kodak pioneered a split-image optical rangefinder (no moving parts) built into the base of the front standard supporting the lens of some of their larger folders (notably the 3A Special). Unfortunately, Kodak's "coupled rangefinder" was rather slow and cumbersome to use in any but a tripod mounted shooting situation, and being a waist-level rather than a magnified eye-level device, was no paragon of focusing accuracy.

At this point it would be tempting to say that Zeiss-Ikon launched into a sea of blur with a clever and unprecedented solution to the world's focusing ills. Regrettably, this is not the case—workable designs for coupled rangefinders were produced in Germany, England, and France well in advance of the great Zeiss-Ikon merger of Ica, Ernemann, Contessa-Nettel, Zeiss *et al* in 1926. The genius of Zeiss's design is that it completely eliminated the necessity of any mechanical lens-to-rangefinder coupling system and provided a beautifully clear and contrasty superimposed-image rangefinder system that was applicable to a

wide variety of lens, focal lengths and format sizes. Wisely, the Zeiss designers sacrificed the minor optical advantages accruing to unit-focusing lenses and opted instead for a proven front-cell-focusing design that made it much easier to achieve the Super Ikonta's renowned mechanical rigidity and accurate lens-to-film-plane alignment.

Largest of super Ikomats, this "D," c. 1934, had 12cm f/4.5 Zeiss Tessar lens, Compur-Rapid 1-1/250 sec. (plus T and B) shutter. Format is 2½×4¼ in.

Okay, enough of post-mortem panegyrics—let's delve into the origins of these aesthetic machines that spanned over two decades with only the most minor modifications. It seems that back in the early 30's, Zeiss-Ikon produced a spartan but very capable line of scale-focusing folding cameras known as Ikomats. These invariably featured front cell focusing, f/3.5 to f/6.3 Zeiss Tessar lenses and (usually) early examples of the famed Compur-Rapid rim-set leaf shutter. Around about 1934-35 it was decided that the picture-taking abilities (and sales appeal) of the Ikomat line could be considerably enhanced by the inclusion of coupled rangefinders—and so it came to pass that Zeiss-Ikon brought forth a series of Super Ikomats in the "16 on 120" (4.5 × 6 cm) 2¼ square (6 × 6 cm), 2¼ by 3¼ in. (6 × 9 cm), and "116" (2¼ × 4¼ in.) sizes. Members of this illustrious Super Ikomat quartet were known in Europe by the code numbers 530, 530/16, 530/2, and 530/15, respectively, but we brash Americans persisted in calling them "A," "B," "C," and "D"—a system which stuck and still adheres to full-fledged Super Ikontas on this side of the pond.

Ironically, some of the finest mechanical designs in many diverse fields have resulted not from giving some brilliant engineer a clean slate and a straightforward goal, but by saddling a talented engineer (or engineering group) with the unenviable task of modifying an existing product to provide capabilities never foreseen in its origi-

Classic Super Ikonta C of 1936-38 incorporates all the renowned features of its breed except for flash sync, coated f/3.5 Tessar. Format is 2¼×3¼ in.

central, round, pinkish rangefinder patch will move side to side in the prescribed manner and both images will coincide only when the subject you're viewing is in focus!

By what minor miracle has the little round window at the end of the front "rangefinder" arm transformed this physically unconnected assemblage of parts into a "real" rangefinder? You won't believe this (unless you already know the secret), but if you look closely at the front of this window while you turn the front lens ring or focusing wheel, you'll notice that it turns in the opposite direction from the lens—clockwise as you focus closer. But if you now turn your attention to the rear part of the rangefinder arm window and examine it in detail you'll see that it turns in the *opposite* direction from the front part of the window (it helps to mark it with a thin-tipped marking pen) as you focus. Indeed, if you position your eye directly behind the entire "rangefinder arm" window, you can easily see that whatever you can see through it moves from side to side as you focus back and forth. In short, as you've probably figured out by now, the mysterious little round window actually consists of two contra-rotating prism wedges that act in much the same way as the rotating prism wedge or mirror in a conventional rangefinder. Connected to the lens's focusing mount by a train of reduction gears, they impart a linear motion to the focusing image that coincides with the set focusing distance of the lens. With an effective base length determined by the distance between the fixed "rangefinder" windows (it's just over 1½ in. on the Super Ikonta A) and a life-size (1:1) image magnification, these rangefinders were quite accurate, and the knurled wheel focusing system was and is a paragon of smoothness.

What made the Ikontas Super?

At this point, you're probably wondering what great technological *tour de force* transformed the initial run of rangefinder focusing Super Ikomats into the renowned (and much more euphonious) Super Ikontas. Well, to be truthful, the differences were relatively minor and come under the general heading of refinements. For example, the aperture-setting tab below the Zeiss Tessar lenses on Super Ikomats A, C, and D was changed to a more convenient knurled ring at the rear of the lens with a aperture scale viewable from the top or side. The conventional flip-up optical finders on these models became von Albada finders, in which a white frame around the edge of the rear eyepiece glass is reflected back by a one-way mirror on the front eyepiece glass so that a white finder frame appears to float in the air when you look through the finder. In addition, this rectangular-format triumvirate acquired true body shutter releases (incorporating a simple double-exposure prevention lockout) in place of the peculiar ring-like release on the lower right-hand side of Super Ikomat lenses. You still had to wind the film with reference to ye olde red window lurking beneath a sliding cover, but you couldn't press the shutter release after cocking the shutter a second time without at least *starting* to wind the film to the next frame.

nal concept. Such was the case with the Super Ikomats, which were later to blossom into Super Ikontas. The spartan, scale-focusing Ikomats had a number of features that worked too well to simply be discarded—especially during the Depression, when development costs had to be pared to the bare minimum. These included a very rigid side-bracing system consisting of two hefty hinge struts reinforced by snap-in locking bars when the cameras were unfolded, an existing line of very fine lens/shutter units and, of course, the basic body stampings, including the hinged back, film chambers and film aperture. But how can one possibly add a *coupled* rangefinder to a lens whose front ring turns about 270° and moves forward only a few millimeters to get from infinity to the closest focusing distance?

Zeiss did it in one brilliant stroke by building what is, in effect, a two-piece, optically-coupled rangefinder system. Affixed to the main body section of the camera is a fixed-distance "rangefinder" complete with viewing and focusing image but no moving parts—if you move the camera back and forth (on a Super Ikonta A) both images will coincide at a distance of roughly 6 ft. But attached to the lens/shutter unit is a hinged metal arm with a knurled focusing wheel at the front end of its pivot point. Lift the arm into focusing position and a small circular window at the upper end of the arm will be situated directly in front of the right-hand rangefinder window ("B" models have shorter, fixed vertical arms). If you now look through the small, round rangefinder window on the back of the camera while you turn the focusing wheel, the image in the

You may have noticed that many of the comments above do not apply to the 2¼-square Super Ikonta B or its Super Ikomat predecessor. This is because the "B" was really a slightly different animal at the outset—it already began life with a body shutter release, double exposure prevention with automatic film stop (after manual first-frame positioning), and an 80mm f/2.8 Zeiss Tessar lens. We'll detail its separate lines of development, and those of the magnificent range of postwar Zeiss Super Ikontas in Part 2 of this saga.

Hoist by our own petard...again!

For the time being, suffice it to say that, in addition to their technical prowess, the rectangular format Super Ikontas A, C and D were facile picture takers (if a bit slow operating by modern standards) capable of turning out really first-class results. They were comparatively light and portable yet provided big negative performance—and the uncoated four-element Zeiss Tessar and Schneider Xe-nar lenses found on pre-WW II models were not overly afflicted with flare. They were, as we said, beautifully finished—many metal parts were nickel plated and the body was covered in genuine morocco leather—and even the big C and D fit nicely in your hands by virtue of their angled sides. Finally—and I'm almost ashamed to admit it—Super Ikontas of any vintage are rather hard to find on the open market these days since they're overly prized by "closet" collectors, a rare but valid case of "us" depriving "them" of unique and useful picture-taking machines. And so, as I hang here hoist by my own petard, it is my sad duty to inform you that Super Ikonta As (my personal favorites) now fetch over $200 apiece (more for postwar models with coated lenses), and Cs and (rather rare) Ds can cost even more if and when you can find them. Super Ikonta Bs are a bit more common but still bring a stiff price ($150 and up) depending on age and condition. And you thought camera collecting was a great hedge against inflation, eh?

Super Ikonta saga, part 2

The Super Ikonta saga, Part 2. The birth, transformation, and death of Zeiss's great 2¼-square format rangefinder folders.

Before I launch into a delectable assortment of (mostly) post-World War II Zeiss Super Ikontas, I must confess to a (non-optical) aberration of mine which will explain, in part, why I gave the redoubtable Super Ikonta Bs such short shrift before. The bald fact is I've never been much enamored of 6 × 6cm (2¼ in. square) rangefinder folders—it doesn't matter whose—because this format seems more suited to waist-level twin-lens reflexes and SLRs, which employ this viable, croppable format out of necessity. (Parenthetically, I'm quite certain that the term "waist-level" was popularized out of deference to the world's Graflexes and other large-format SLRs, whereas "chest-level" is a more appropriate description of how the smaller beasts are viewed and focused.) Having leveled in getting that off my chest, let's take up where we left off and say a few words about my least favorite (but still beautifully functional) Super Ikonta.

Like all of its ilk save one (which we'll get to later) the "B" began life as the Super Ikomat B (*aka* No. 530/16) in the mid 1930's, and it was always a slightly different breed of cat than its rectangular format cousins. While Ikomats "A," "C," and "D" had swing-out external rangefinder prisms (their intricacies were discussed in the last column), the "B" sported a shorter, rotating-prism "tower"

Match-needle metering in '38? Sort of, but you had to transfer settings, apply "fudge factor" if light was too low.

permanently affixed to the right side of the front standard. This eliminated the need for erecting and collapsing the arm, as it folded neatly within the "B's" commodious body. Also, "B" series Super Ikomats and Super Ikontas incorporated their viewfinders within the contours of the top plate, unlike the other models which had pop-up optical finders atop their rangefinder housings. Finally, and perhaps most significant, all Super "Bs" from first to last featured an automatic film-stop mechanism and a nice, big, circular (1-in. diameter) automatic frame counter atop the camera next to the film-wind knob. True, when loading a fresh roll you had to wind the film manually until "1" appeared in the red window (under the sliding cover) since there was no automatic first-frame positioning, but automatic framing and film counting by itself was pretty spiffy for a 1935 roll-film camera.

Separate but coupled rfdr. marks early Super Ikomat B. 11-shot counter was automatic but had to be set for first shot.

As was the case with most Super Ikomats, the transition to Super Ikonta status (which occurred in 1936) was evolutionary. In place of the separate rangefinder and viewfinder windows found on the back of the Super Ikomat "B," the Super Ikonta featured a combined range/viewfinder. To accommodate this change, the second small rangefinder window in the rangefinder housing atop the rear of the bellows was eliminated—only the window directly behind the rotating-prism arm remained. More noticeable is the enlarged viewfinder section with its ⅝-in. square window that protrudes about 3/16 in. from the top plate. This provides a reasonably large, green-tinted viewing image with the small, circular rangefinder patch appearing in a contrasting pinkish shade. Mind you the Super Ikomat's separate viewfinder was adequate, but the combined range/viewfinder transformed the Super Ikonta B into one of the fastest focusing (and most desirable) rangefinder folders of its day.

Frame-spacing woes

Interestingly, this major refinement was not accompanied by any significant revisions in the rest of the camera. The shutter was still the redoubtable rim-set Compur-Rapid with timed speeds from 1-1/400 sec. The lens was an extremely fast (for its format) 80mm f/2.8 Tessar, a creditable performer except wide open at the edges, and the S.I.B. still provided 11 2¼-square negs per roll of 120 film. Why

only 11 when most other 6×6 cm folders gave you 12? To find out, pull up the back lock on the right side of a "B" and swing the back open toward the left. Do you see any friction rollers to monitor the film travel as found in, say, a Kodak Monitor? Nope—the proper spacing of consecutive frames as they're wound onto the roll is accomplished by differential gearing between the wind knob and frame counter, a satisfactory but less precise method. Best proof of this is the fact that the meterized Super Ikonta BX of 1938 went to a 12-exposure counter, but this was later dropped in favor of the 11-shot counter in most postwar models. Aside from their faster lenses, and generally swifter operation, "B" series Super Ikontas were the only members of their illustrious family designed to be focused left-handed, with a small knurled wheel directly in front of the shutter speed and aperture scales. This left the right index finger free to cock as well as fire the shutter—a separation of function that contributed no small part to the "B's" rapid-fire capabilities.

An Ikonta like a Contax III?

Although I already blew the surprise element by revealing the existence of the delicious Super Ikonta BX of 1938, let's just give it credit for being the first Super Ikonta to sport an exposure meter of any kind. As you'd expect, this moderately sensitive selenium cell device was perched atop the camera body (there was even an accessory shoe on top of it), and it featured a hinged protective cover. Like the meter in the Contax III (or indeed virtually any built-in meter of the prewar era) the BX's meter was fairly convenient but none too reliable—which is to say it wasn't very durable.

As expected (and fondly hoped by many) the hefty (2 lb., 2 oz.), beautifully finished Super Ikonta B made a reappearance after World War II in only superficially revised form. As you'd expect, its 80mm f/2.8 Zeiss Tessar lens (dubbed Zeiss-Opton in the early 50's) was now coated, its Synchro-Compur 1-1/500 plus B shutter had MX sync, and (like the BX of '38) the black enamel on its front was replaced by chrome. Fortunately, the nickel-plated side struts were as commendably rigid as ever, genuine morocco leather still adorned the body, and, if anything, the superb

A "real" Super Ikonta? Yes, but model III of '54 had stamped top, used rivets.

range/viewfinder was even brighter and contrastier than before (did I say my enthusiasm for this machine was lukewarm?). Along about 1952, the world was treated to its second meterized Super Ikonta BX. This featured (glory be) a shorter but more sensitive selenium cell meter which featured the same direct reading system as before but had improved legibility. Other features remained the same as the postwar Super Ikonta B. Unfortunately, this top-of-the-line model was discontinued only 5 years after its inception, in 1957—which is probably why a late "BX" in fine shape now fetches about $250-275.

So ends the production run (or is it reign) of one of the very few 6×6 cm rangefinder folders I would deign to own, but this doesn't conclude Zeiss-Ikon's infatuation with this square-format breed by any means. A half dozen years before that fateful day when all Super Ikontas bit the dust in 1960, a new, more conventional 2¼ × 2¼-in. rangefinder folder made an appearance. This lighter, less audacious machine had a conventional range/viewfinder (no exotic rotating prism wedge on the end of an external arm) which was coupled to the front-cell focusing, coated 75mm f/3.5 Tessar lens by an ingenious system of cams and levers that provided a reasonably precise lens-to-rangefinder connection but was nevertheless able to fold out of the way as required. Incidentally, the shutter used was still the Synchro-Compur with speeds from 1-1/500 sec. plus B. Egad, in the midst of all this tech talk I forgot to tell you its name—it was called the Zeiss Super Ikonta III.

Although the S.I. III was and is a nicely made camera that's considerably lighter than any "B," and though it incorporates a body shutter release, blank and double exposure prevention, and an automatic film counter of the more reliable friction-roller type, few collectors would put it in the same class as the more expensive "A,B,C,D" Super Ikontas—it just doesn't have the unparalleled ruggedness and precision feel of the 1930's-based models. Now this doesn't mean that the Super Ikonta III and the later meterized model IV weren't fine cameras capable of first-class performance. It's just that the overwhelming mechanical solidity was lacking. This is a hard thing to put your finger on, since the "traditional" Zeiss side-struts on both models were as rigid as ever, and the IV's meter, with its cell placed in between the rangefinder and viewfinder win-

The last Super Ikonta, meterized model IV shared model III's basic body.

dows, was actually better integrated into the body than the one in the BX.

Apparently Super Ikonta fanciers felt the same way because many model IIIs were sold with three-element Novar lenses at $89 (the 1952 Super Ikonta BX listed for $163) and neither model had a production run much over four years (the III was born in '54, discontinued in '58; the IV lived from 1956-60). Indeed, the very last camera to bear the fabled Super Ikonta name, the poor little model IV, proved that it outlived the popularity of the folding roll-film era by having a last list price of only $79, even though it had the built-in meter and the then-popular LVS (combined f/stops and shutter speed) scale. Of course, as with most erstwhile marketing woes, Tessar-lensed versions of the Super Ikonta III and IV now fetch upwards of $175, and while this hardly compares to the $200-275 being charged for mint condition "real" Super Ikontas with letter designations, it ain't hay. Finally, to keep things reasonably tidy (for a change) and square (format), I've decided to save some really rare birds for the conclusion of our Zeiss-fest next time.

Super Ikonta saga, part 3

The Super Ikonta saga, Part 3 (conclusion). Including the grandiose model "D," a strange Russian copy of the "C" plus a few seldom seen tidbits.

Since the square-format Super-Ikontamania concluded with a promise to unveil oddball examples of this magnificent breed, what better way to begin than by unfolding the Super Ikonta D, a camera few Americans have ever seen. True, I did touch upon its tech specs in the first part of this tantalizing trilogy, but surely the biggest and rarest of Super Ikontas merits longer shrift than this.

"D's" 1/250 sec.) and was capable of producing enlargements indistinguishable from those made with the larger negative, it's hardly surprising that the "C," with its more readily available film size, was considerably more popular. Lest my case prove too convincing, let me quickly add that the "D" offered one major advantage over smaller Ikontas that shouldn't be underestimated, especially in the 30's—its bigger neg provided much nicer contact prints which were cheaper and/or easier to make than enlargements.

Rarest Super Ikonta model? Probably, and this "D" of 1939 was last of its breed.

The original "116 format" Super Ikomat D of mid-30's had frameless viewfinder.

The reason for the noble "D's" relative unpopularity and consequent scarcity is not too difficult to fathom. It is the only Super Ikonta model not designed to take 120 film, and while its 2½ × 4¼-in. format on 116 roll film combined with a very good 12 cm f/4.5 Zeiss Tessar lens, can certainly provide superb quality enlargements, the camera is definitely more ponderous and bulky than its close cousin, the Super Ikonta C. When you consider that the "C" had a faster lens (f/3.5), higher top shutter speed (1/400 or 1/500 sec. depending on vintage, instead of the

The transition from the Super Ikomat 530/15 of 1934 to the Super Ikonta D of 1936 entailed the usual refinements —the shutter-release "plunger" next to the former's lens gave way to the true body shutter release to the left of the range-and-viewfinder windows; its plain pop-up finder metamorphosed into an Albada type complete with reflected frameline; and chrome trim adorned the rangefinder housing of later models. Aside from other even more nitpicky differences, the only other notable change took place in the last Super Ikonta D made just before World

War II. In an apparent concession to American tastes and recognition of the dominance of our film market by the Folks Up In Rochester, this "D" produced 2½ × 4¼-in. negatives on 616 film instead of 116, its thicker-spooled European equivalent. Since 616 was a Kodak-only film size that was never too popular in Deutschland, Zeiss's move may indicate that the "D" sold better over here. At any rate, it remained an expensive ($94 in '39), limited-production camera—so any "D" is therefore considered a true collectors' prize, presently fetching $150-200.

Let us now bid farewell to the posh, elegant world of Super-Ikontadom and turn our attentions to a Super Ikonta "C" look-alike of dubious repute, the Russian "Moskva." Now I know there are collectors out there who are going to write me nasty letters asserting that the Soviet Union was not capable of producing a camera of this caliber in the early to mid 60's—that they must have appropriated the entire remains of the prewar Zeiss factory in Jena and shipped it—lock, stock, technicians, machinists and barrel—to Siberia. Well, I am here to proclaim without the slightest equivocation that I'm not sure what the hell happened to sire this unlikely beast, but the world's Zeiss-niks should certainly get a chuckle out of it. I will, however, admit to two tentative opinions. First, many of

It looks like a Super Ikonta C all right, but it's really a Russian Moskva!

the Moskva's details (such as the focusing wheel next to the lens, body-opening and shutter-release buttons, and back-locking catch, among many others) bear such a striking resemblance to the Zeiss-Ikon originals that they must have been made with the same tools and/or from the same dies. Secondly, I am inclined to believe the legend stamped into the spring-loaded pressure plate that says (in

108

Russian and English) "MADE IN USSR"—in other words, I doubt whether this particular beast was actually assembled in Germany's Eastern Zone as some have asserted.

Actually, it's not that outlandish that the Russians would want to produce their version of the S-I "C" a decade after the West German original was discontinued, or that they would be capable of doing so. As a design, the camera has obvious merits; and the Eastern bloc market, such as it was, had few other choices in a high-grade 6 × 9 cm camera. Certainly if, as I surmise, they used the original drawings and some original parts and dies to create it, design and tooling costs would be virtually nil. And what sort of a copy did they create, lacking Zeiss-Ikon's expertise, not to mention the superb metallurgy and finishing materials available to the Germans in the late 30's? A serviceable-but-mediocre copy, as it turns out.

In terms of features, the Moskva (which, by the way, means Moscow) mostly resembles a postwar Super Ikonta "C" with a few prewar Super Ikomat touches. Its lens is an 11-cm f/4.5 Moskva Industar-23 (the numerical suffix may indicate it's a triplet) which focuses to 1.5 m (about 5 ft.) in precisely the same way as the German original. In fact, the focusing mechanism is commendably smooth, and its coupled rangefinder provides a nice, contrasty green-tinted focusing spot with the surrounding circular field having a pinkish hue. However, Super Ikonta fans will miss the Albada viewfinder—the Moskva has a plain, frameless pop-up optical finder similar in design and details to the one found on the old Super Ikomats. The shutter is a three-bladed, non-flash-synced "Moment-1" with speeds of 1-1/250 sec. plus B, and apertures from f/4.5 to f/32 which are set on a non-click-stopped scale below the lens.

Incidentally, the "C's" blank and double-exposure prevention system survived the Russian translation intact—a little red dot appears next to the film-wind knob to warn you that the film has been wound, and you can't press the shutter release until you have at least *started* to wind the film to the next exposure. As before, the film will stop in the right place only if you see to it that consecutive numbers on the paper film backing wind up sequentially in ye olde red window on the back.

A strange mixture

The most disappointing feature of this otherwise admirable Slavic effort is undoubtedly its finish and feel, which are both several notches below the "real" Super Ikonta. The Moskva's covering is genuine leather all right, but it's a far cry from morocco; the black enamel is lackluster, and many chrome bits and stampings are crude compared to Zeiss Ikon's best. Incredibly, the chrome side struts, film-spool retainers, tripod socket, and focusing wheel are chromed very nicely—which is what leads suspicious types to conclude that they must have been swiped from the Germans. Frankly, I'm not so sure—Russian cameras have always presented a strange mixture of crudeness and class, and I don't see why the Moskva should be an exception. Final bit of intrigue: The pressure plate also bears the phrase "Model 2" (in Russian), raising the heart-stopping possibility that the same crew "knocked off" one of the other Super Ikonta models! At any rate, Spiratone's Bernie Danis values his redoubtable Russian at about $200, about four times what he paid for it at one of the semi-annual PHSNY (Photographic Historical Society of New York) Photographic Fairs.

Lord only knows the official model designation of this "16 on 120" rangefinder camera with clever collapsible lens.

Not content to regale you with Russian rarities, let's briefly turn to two cameras about which I know sufficient facts to whet my appetite, but not quite enough to satisfy it. The first might be described as an early Japanese answer to the Super Ikonta A, a 4½ × 6-cm rangefinder folder that makes up in elegant execution what it lacks in sophisticated features. The name engraved on the front of its top-mounted range-viewfinder unit is "Lord," a brand associated with small 35mm rangefinder cameras made by Okaya Optical Co. in the late 50's and, oddly enough, with an unrelated line of interchangeable-lens, leaf shutter 35s made by Liedolf in Wetzlar, Germany, home of you know who. Since it lacks flash sync and appears to have an *uncoated* 7.5 cm f/3.5 Simlar lens made by Tokyo Optical Co. (of Topcon fame), this spartan beast probably dates from just before or (more likely) just after World War II.

The "Semi-Lord" (for lack of a better model designation) sports a couple of nice technical features in addition to its stylish rounded ends. For one thing, it is a collapsible camera sans bellows—the lens pulls out to shooting position by pulling it straight out on a two-piece telescoping tube. Also, the lens features a helical focusing placed at its *back* section next to the camera body, all the easier for coupling the combined range/viewfinder. For the record, the Lord focuses down to 1 m, and the front-mounted Seikosha shutter has speeds of 1-1/250 sec. plus T and B, and there's a curious "joy stick" in lieu of a body shutter release. The film-advance system is pretty cute also—once you position the arrows on the paper backing and set the counter atop the film-wind knob to "S," you wind one full turn and come back to each successive number until you reach "F" (finish?) after the 16th exposure. Presumably the knob was ratcheted so it would stay in place once you stopped winding. Regrettably, all I have of this beautifully simple camera is its portrait supplied to me by an unknown benefactor at Tokyo Optical Co. in Japan. I'll bet it's a decent performer and is most assuredly rare, but more than this I cannot say.

A glorious "no show," this prototype from Leitz would surely set Leicaphiles' wallets aflutter, but don't hold your breath.

Finally, herewith, a little item guaranteed to make Leica nuts eat their hearts out. Yes, it's the prototype Leica 110 camera that *almost* made an appearance at Photokina 1976 but was represented only by super-sharp 110 slides projected at the Leitz booth. Why Leitz decided not to go ahead with it is anybody's guess, but its specs (if not its appearance) are mouthwatering. The lens is a 26mm f/2 Summicron, on the bottom in the photo are the focusing dial on the left (0.5 m to infinity), the aperture dial next to it (f/2-f/16), and a ridged film-advance tab on the right. A small tab at the edge of the left-hand circular port controls an ND filter for one-stop exposure override, the circular windows just above the rectangular lens port contains a CdS cell, and there appears to be a sliding lens-protecting cover. I wouldn't even venture to guess what some Leica-maniacs might be willing to pay for a one-off Leica 110, but bidding starts at $5,000.

Gamma Duflex from Budapest: First eye-level SLR?

What better way of celebrating the Camera Collector's 10th Anniversary than by unveiling a Hungarian masterpiece that should have set the world on its ear?

Although I am hardly humble or self-effacing by nature, I have at least managed to refrain from calling myself a "camera expert" or even an "old-camera expert," despite the fact that these monthly diversions have now been appearing for precisely one decade. This does not mean to suggest that I find myself utterly lacking in expertise, only that the subject of the world's picture-taking mechanisms is so vast, profoundly complex, and extensive in scope that one brain simply can't contain all the major and minor

A mysterious beast from Budapest, the Gamma Duflex of '49 was probably the first eye-level SLR and much, much more.

lines of development (including the many *cul-de-sacs*), much less the myriad minutiae. But however thinly spread the veneer of one's intellect may be in certain areas, certain unalterable facts are well known among photo-equipment *cognoscenti*, to wit: The world's first eye-level single-lens reflex 35 was the Contax S (the original model of 1949 with the flash sync contact in the tripod socket); the world's first instant-return mirror appeared on the Asahiflex IIa in 1954; and the first *fully* automatic *internally* actuated auto-diaphragm mechanism graced the Asahi Pentax S3, or was it the Japanese Zunow Reflex?

As it turns out, there is one minor problem with all these painfully acquired facts—every single one of them is absolutely wrong, only because a Hungarian by the name of Jeno Dulovits, the chief camera designer for the Gamma

Works of Budapest, was persuaded to design a 35mm pentaprism SLR despite his initial objections. Rather than prolonging the suspense, herewith the technical scoop in one fell swoop. The Gamma Duflex, which undoubtedly existed in prototype form well before the Contax S, is a 35mm single-lens reflex with eye-level focusing and viewing, an instant-return mirror, and a bayonet-mount, internal auto-diaphragm lens. In addition, the Duflex incorporated such modern features as a non-rotating shutter-speed dial, settable either before or after winding the film, with marked speeds of 1-1/1000 sec. plus B, a thin metal focal-plane shutter that moves horizontally, a separate optical viewfinder with true projected framelines for 35, 50, and 90mm lenses and an intentional double-exposure button to override the built-in double-exposure prevention (it also zeroes the film counter when pressed with the camera

Why two eyepieces? One at left is for through-lens focusing, but optical finder (center) is brighter, shows more (see text).

back removed). To say these specifications are advanced for a late 40's camera is a monumental understatement. Indeed, the only reasons the Duflex hasn't achieved the notoriety of lesser machines with fewer outstanding features is that only a few hundred of these futuristic SLRs were made—and most of them remained in eastern Europe.

Let's now back up a bit and let you in on some of the unlikely details of the Gamma Duflex's creation, which were first revealed to an unsuspecting western world in the April 1970 edition of the Hungarian magazine FOTO. (My compliments to the Japanese photo magazine CAMERART for relating the salient details in English in their March, 1978 edition.) It seems that way back in 1943 during the Second Great Unpleasantness, one Dr. Nandor

Barany, a technical advisor to the Gamma factory, urged the company to produce cameras with viewfinders having "correct image prisms" which had already been used in conjunction with telescopes for quite a while. An associated chap named Jozsef Nemeth designed just such a correct image prism, and Janos Barabas, Gamma's chief optical designer, experimentally confirmed the photographic advantages of a camera incorporating such a prism. Meanwhile, the aforementioned Jeno Dulovits (who had designed the famous Duto soft-focus attachment lens popular in the 30's and still produced under other names by many optical companies today) first objected to the prism, then relented and designed the prototype Duflex System Reflex S (which evidently had a true pentaprism) and the Gamma Duflex, a porro-prism single-lens reflex camera which was "discontinued after only several hundred units were made." Why Dulovits opposed the correct image pentaprism design has never been made clear, but perhaps it had something to do with his concern with keeping the camera compact and lightweight. The fact that the Duflex sported a non-standard 24×32mm format (same as the original rangefinder Nikon M and the Czech Opema 35) is one indication that Dulovits was determined to keep the prism and flipping mirror as small as possible.

Functionality with style. Matched knurled wheels at Duflex's upper ends control film winding (right), rewinding (left). Button near rewind allows double exposures.

Okay, enough historical palaver—let's take a close look at the magnificent Magyar beast itself. The first thing that strikes you when hefting the Duflex is that it feels solid, but not overly heavy—just under 1 lb., 12 oz.—and its rounded ends nestle comfortably in your hands. With lens, it measures 6 in. wide, 3½ in. high, and 2¾ in. deep, and it balances quite nicely. In terms of appearance, the Duflex is a pleasant-looking, rather streamlined machine with bottom and top places finished in very good quality laquered chrome (reminiscent of certain Alpas) and various other bits (such as the edging on the removable back) in lovely shiny chrome. If the leather trim isn't genuine morocco leather, it sure is one hell of a fine imitation.

Once the initial "feature shock" has worn off slightly, you remember that the hallmark of virtually every SLR worthy of the name is absent: There's no telltale angular pentaprism housing. The porro-prism consisting of abut-

ting mirrors is under the flat part of the top plate which sports the beautifully engraved "Gamma, Hungary" logo. Also stylish are the knurled inset knobs on the camera's upper sides. Atop the right-handed film-wind knob is the turn-and-set shutter-speed dial, which looks quite contemporary except for the uneven spacing of the shutter-speed markings, which are arranged in the old, non-geometric sequence—1, 2, 5, 10, 25, etc. The corresponding control on the left-hand side is the rewind knob, which is surmounted by an elegant rounded "handle" for pulling up the rewind shaft when loading and unloading film. Attention to sculptural details and symmetry is everywhere evident—in the striated handles atop the two aforementioned controls, in the almost-art-deco horizontal bands that divide the camera body into well-proportioned segments—even in the rounded, contoured lens-release lock which resembles that on early M-series Leicas.

First internal auto-diaphragm? Yep. As you fire, pin at right of lens lock pops out to actuate spring-loaded mechanism in lens.

As long as we've brought up the subject, however obliquely, let's take a gander at that lens—a 50mm (5cm) f/3.5 Gamma Budapest Artar which appears to be uncoated. Aside from swiping the name from a fine, old Goerz process lens, it is an unremarkable design—probably a Tessar formula optic—but its physical features indicate that Gamma was going all out to endow it with as much pizzazz as possible under the circumstances. For example, it's one of the few standard 50s I've ever seen that stops down to f/32 (the two knurled ears on the aperture ring resemble those on the 50mm f/2.8 Leitz Elmar, but the Artar lacks click stops). The focusing control resembles the one on 50mm f/3.5 Leitz Elmars except that it's designed to be operated with the left hand, and it lacks an infinity catch. However, the Artar will get you down to an amazingly close 0.5m (about 20 in.) taking full advantage of the reflex focusing system.

Push in the locking button and turn the lens about 75° counterclockwise and you can lift the lens off its three-lobed external bayonet mount, giving you a good look at the mirror box. Aside from the small, trapezoidal mirror found in many early SLRs, the Duflex's mirror box is unremarkable, but next to the red dot on the lens-mount plate is something prophetic indeed—a small metal shaft which pops out as you press the shutter release, stopping the lens down to the f/stop set on the aperture ring. This shaft presses against a spring-loaded "button" inside the lens mount (see photo) and when the shaft pops back as the mirror returns, the lens automatically returns to maximum aperture—just like most of the SLRs now rolling off the Japanese production line. All right, we'll now, with trepidation, approach the moment of truth. First, let's align the red dot on the lens with the one adjacent to the external lens mount, seat the lens, and give it a smooth 1/5 turn until it locks in place. Now we'll turn the camera around and peek through the reflex finder on the left-hand side.

A 50mm Hungarian Artar? They filched the name from Goerz, but at least gave you f/32 and focusing down to half a meter.

The viewing image is, to coin a phrase, pretty damn dim, partly because the mirror on our sample Duflex has seen better days, partly because porro-prisms constructed of mirrors never transmit as much light as solid glass pentaprisms and partly because the mirrors available in Hungary in the late 40's were obviously none too terrific—particularly when used in conjunction with a fairly slow lens. Withal, the image is usable in reasonably bright light and the lens can be focused with adequate precision, particularly at close distances. However, it is apparent that the Duflex's reflex finder shows considerably less than you'll actually get on film—about 80 percent according to our measurements. While this may prove workable at times, it seems clear that the Duflex's reflex viewing system, brilliantly advanced though it may be, was designed and conceived of primarily as a *focusing* system and not as a combined viewing and focusing system of the modern type.

And how, pray tell, were you supposed to view your subject? Well, you may remember that, back at the beginning when I was rattling off the camera's features, I mentioned the multi-frame viewfinder with true projected frames for 35mm, 50mm, and 90mm lenses. The eyepiece for this admirable device is also located on the back of the

camera (natch) and it provides a nice, bright view at about half-life-size magnification, and it's afflicted with only a moderate amount of barrel distortion. Although the three framelines make it a bit cluttered, it isn't all that confusing once you get the hang of it, and the framelines, though not provided with parallax correction markings, do indicate almost the entire picture fields at medium-to-far distances.

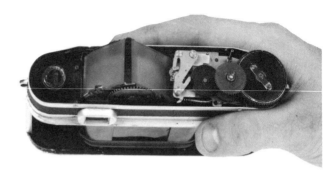

Commendably simple but somewhat crude, Duflex's insides don't match its posh exterior. Note abutting mirrors of porro-prism.

What's it like to take pictures with the world's most unsung photographic landmark, you ask? Well, regrettably, the metal focal plane shutter on our model was not working properly and, as you've probably guessed, spare parts are rather thin on the ground. We *were* able to get it working for a few test firings, though, and can report that it makes an average amount of noise; the instant-return mirror still works flawlessly, and the shutter release itself is reasonably smooth but requires fairly high finger pressure. Regrettable, too, is that the Gamma Duflex's internal mechanisms, though commendably simple in basic design, are not executed with the same fine precision as the camera's elegant exterior would indicate. The shutter, in particular, was a simple design of somewhat delicate construction similar to that found on the 6 × 6-cm Reflex Korelle of the mid-1930's. It is our judgment, therefore, that the shutter speeds could not be considered accurate by modern standards. But compared to the farsighted engineering genius that flows from every nook and cranny of this incredible machine, this is piddling criticism indeed.

My sincere thanks to S.F. Spira of New York's Spiratone, Inc. for making his super-rare Gamma Duflex available for our delectation, and for doing much of the initial research necessary in the preparation of this column. Oh, yes, I almost forgot. Although Mr. Spira's modesty prevents him from revealing the purchase price of this superb and important instrument, I do know that it took a few years hunting among European dealers and auction houses in order to find it. I therefore doubt there are any Gamma Duflexes presently loose in this land—or even in the Hungarian countryside. But if you find one in nice shape, offer its owner $500 for it. You can't possibly go wrong.

Exakta saga, part 1

The Exakta saga, Part 1. Wherein a humble trapezoidal beast from Dresden becomes the world's first 35mm SLR system.

My detractors, many of whom have the nasty habit of writing me impassioned and articulate letters, are forever accusing me of conniving to inflate used camera prices. Presumably, my prime motivations in this nefarious undertaking are both straightforward (i.e., to increase the value of my own collection and to reward the cohorts who supply me with delectable equipment) and devious (to render good, used cameras as such scarce and sought-after commodities that photographers will be driven into the—shudder—new camera market). My response to such calumnies is the same one offered by reporters and royal messengers down through the millennia—I raise my arms in the air, palms pointed beseechingly upward, and lament, "Please don't condemn the bearer of bad news. I am only reporting the situation as it exists."

Now, if you think this is nothing more than a sly cop-out, ponder this. After finally deciding to give in to the sundry pesterings of colleagues, publisher and friends and do "something on Exaktas," I chuckled to myself, "This is going to be a piece of cake—I'll just meander down to my usual used-camera haunts and dredge up bunches of these neglected, dust-covered waifs of cameradom." You can imagine my amazement when the sixth dealer I questioned said precisely the same thing as the previous five: "Old Exaktas? Nothing right now. I get 'em in from time to time, but they move pretty fast. Funny, though—only a few years ago I wouldn't even take 'em in trade. Now they've become collectors' items!" So, feel free to tar me with any brush you like, friends; you can't honestly blame me for the current "Exakta situation."

Actually, when you think about it, it's sort of surprising that "Exaktamania" is such a recent development, since these machines possess all the earmarks of other successful "classics." First and foremost, all but the last 35mm Exaktas have the look of fine European machinery, with lots of cute little dials with knurled edges, external shutter-release couplings and whatnots, and what must be regarded as a classic trapezoidal body shape accented with (usually) good-quality chrome. They evolved with typical (and excruciating) German slowness over a period of nearly 40 years, mostly by agglomerating seemingly picayune little features onto this basic body shell. And when this sound basic design could no longer accommodate the fea-

The original Exakta 35? Not quite, but this early postwar Exakta I is substantially the same. Flip-down focusing magnifier is at front of focusing hood; plug-in adapter allows use of PC-contact flash. Early, coated 58mm f/2 Biotar provided life-size viewing image. Current value with lens: $100-125.

tures required in a modern SLR, they finally changed it—most people would say for the worse. In that sense, a 35mm Exakta collection (minus the last two or three models) would resemble a Leica collection or a Zeiss Contax collection (albeit on a somewhat lower level of exterior finish and ultimate mechanical quality), with the strong family resemblance among individual models depicting rational development along systematic lines. Indeed, although the original Kine Exakta of 1936 cannot claim to be the world's first 35mm SLR (that honor apparently belongs to the Russian Sport of 1935—sorry no portrait), it is most assuredly the progenitor of the world's first 35mm system.

The first Kine Exakta—so called to differentiate it from earlier roll-film Exaktas produced by the Ihagee Kamerawerk, AG of Dresden—was a very basic, but extremely well-thought-out little machine. (The "Kine" part refers to the cinematic origins of 35mm film.) This is understandable since Ihagee was well known before the war as a manufacturer of high-quality (and always mechanically fascinating) cameras, running the gamut from roll-film folders with unit-focusing lenses to the Vest Pocket Exakta, a very pleasant SLR which made 4.5 × 6 cm negatives on 127 film. Indeed, the V.P. Exakta, its larger, much rarer

113

Spelling error? Not really. This early postwar model I sports "Exacta" nameplate also found on some Exakta IIs of same vintage. Finish was usually second-rate; value (body only) about $70.

stablemate, the "Square" (6 × 6 cm) Exakta, which used 120 film, and the 35mm version are all cast in the same trapezoidal body mold, and all were fitted with horizontal-motion, cloth focal-plane shutters. Aside from its smaller size, the Kine Exakta differs mainly in having an internal sprocket wheel, a friction-type (non-ratcheted) 36-frame film counter on top, and no red window on the back.

Since a surprising number of features found on this original model "Exakta I" endured until the last trapezoidal-bodied VX 1000 was produced more than 35 years later, let's run down the list. First are the left-handed, long-throw film-advance lever and front-mounted left-hand-operated shutter release, two "controversial" features lifted directly from the earlier V.P. Exakta. The logic of their placement? Well, the front-mounted shutter release did permit the later use of external auto-diaphragm lenses, and besides, any fool knows you're supposed to focus a camera with your right hand, and this leaves your left hand free to wind and shoot! Actually, it's not a bad system once you get used to it, but Exakta wind levers—even the late model "shorter throw" type—can hardly be called *rapid* wind levers. The Exakta, like the Alpa (which also traces its origins to the deep, dark 30's), is designed for a slow, deliberate frame of mind, and speedy operation is not its forte.

Remove the Exakta I's back and you're greeted by a nicely finished interior with cartridge compartment on the right, sprocket wheel and removable take-up spool on the left. At the bottom of each end is a pivoted handle—the right-hand one for rewinding the film, the other to pull a spring-loaded locating pin downward, enabling the take-up spool to be removed. Over the years, the rewind evolved into a knurled knob and finally a folded crank, but the basic bottom layout remained the same, including a heftily mounted tripod socket in the middle, up towards the lens mount. Speaking of the lens mount, this deep,

three-lug bayonet mount, with the external, spring-loaded locking catch, is yet another hallmark of all "classic" Exaktas, and lenses are, with few exceptions, fully interchangeable from first model to last. Before we close the back, we can't fail to mention what is perhaps the most peculiar feature found on all classic Exakta 35s but the VX 500—a film-cutting knife! This unlikely device is basically a shaft with a tiny blade affixed to its top, and it's found on the left side of the film aperture. To cut the film while it's still in the camera, you undo a tiny knurled knob next to the rewind from its threaded shaft and pull the knob downwards, neatly slicing the film perpendicularly to its direction of travel. Who needs such a knife, you ask? Well, it's handy for impoverished scientists who want to quickly develop, say, a half-dozen photomicrographs without running through the entire roll, and if you remove the take-up spool and substitute a special or standard cartridge, you don't even have to unload those six frames in the darkroom.

O.K., let's close the back and direct our attention to the original Exakta's top once again, where the distinctive but clumsy shutter-speed setting controls are located. To the left of the chest-level finder is the "fast" shutter dial, controlling speeds of 1/25-1/1000 sec. plus T and B. In keeping with its era, it's a "lift and turn to set" affair which rotates in a clockwise direction as the exposure is made. The spacing between successive settings is uneven, but at least you can cock the shutter manually for intentional double exposures by rotating the knurled dial counter-clockwise until it clicks in place.

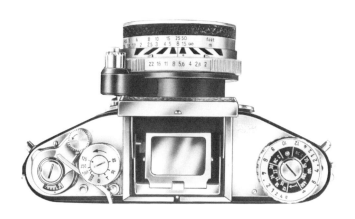

Atop an old Exakta? Nope, but this top view of early-60's VX IIb shows the "classic" layout, with fast and slow shutter-speed dials, long-throw wind lever, manual exposure counter settable by turning knurled knob.

Setting slow shutter speeds and/or using the Exakta's self-timer are a unique experience. You begin by setting the fast shutter dial to T or B, and then direct your attention to the slow-speed control to the right of the chest-level finder. This knurled, lift-and-set dial has 13 numbers in black (1/10 sec. to 12 sec. with no 1/5 sec. setting on the Exakta I, 1/5 sec. to 12 sec. with no 1/10 sec. setting on most other models). To obtain this impressive range of slow speeds, you have to wind the film, thereby cocking the shutter, set the desired speed opposite an index dot, wind the spring-loaded slow shutter control as far as it'll go in a clockwise direction, and press the shutter release —not exactly a convenient procedure. Setting the self-timer is equally amusing, except you set the index mark opposite one of the red digits. These cover a slow speed range down to 6 sec., usable in conjunction with the self-timer, and it matters little which one you use if you want to use the self-timer in conjunction with *fast* shutter speeds—the shutter will still click about 12 sec. later as long as you cock the shutter, set a red number, and wind the slow-speed dial before firing. Yes, as you've probably guessed, this comprehensive but pesky system is found on all classic Exaktas with provision for slow speeds.

How to spot an Exakta II? Best way is to look for Roman II under nameplate. Aside from modern flip-up magnifier with protective front cover, features are almost identical to Exakta I. With black 58mm f/2 Biotar, this one will fetch about $150.

The time has now come to take a peek through this early 35mm SLR to see what we can see. We'll mount our early postwar 58mm f/2 Carl Zeiss Jena Biotar, set its manual (not pre-set—manual!) aperture ring to f/2 for maximum brightness, press the button on the back of the folded chest-level finder so it springs into viewing position, gaze downwards and—nothing! Forgot to wind the film,

eh? Well, what do you expect—an instant-return mirror? All right, wind the film and there it is—a rather bright viewing image on the screen. How did they do it? Easy. The Exakta is blessed with a good-quality single-surface mirror, and its plain ground-glass focusing screen is surmounted with a big, fat condenser lens which serves the same basic function as the modern Fresnel lens in evening out the illumination. Oh, there's a bit of barrel distortion, but, by and large, it's a surprisingly satisfactory view, even by modern standards.

Of course, with its non-removable chest-level finder, the Exakta I is not ideally suited to following action, since the viewing image is reversed left to right. An even more serious shortcoming is the lack of a modern-type focusing magnifier. There's a 2X focusing magnifier all right (a round one on really early model Is), but to position it, you've got to push in the front part of the erected viewing hood until it clicks into place about ⅛ in. above the condenser lens. So, you can either focus with relative precision on the central part of the viewing image *or* see the entire frame, but not both at once. Indeed, the original directions advise you to compose your shot by gazing at the screen at a distance of 6-8 in. as though it were nothing more than a tiny reflex finder affixed to the front standard of an old folding camera. As if to make up for these shortcomings, the focusing hood incorporates a number of clever tricks—an interlock prevents you from firing the camera unless it's open for viewing; when the magnifier is positioned for "critical focusing," its front and rear sections constitute a non-optical frame-type viewfinder; and the magnifier springs back to normal viewing position at the touch of a cute little button on its rear flap.

Despite its strange combination of fascinating capabilities and curious drawbacks—the original Biotar lens focused down to a blistering 3 ft.—the Exakta I was clearly destined to have a long and profitable future. Perhaps no other camera had as many thing going for it, and so many obvious things that needed improvement. And so it came to pass that, after a production run of nearly 10 years (until 1946), in the face of monumental production difficulties resulting from World War II, and the fact that Dresden was on the wrong side of the political railroad tracks (East Germany), Ihagee finally brought forth the Exakta II in 1949. It had a modern-type flip-up finder magnifier with protective cover, a flip-up rewind "button" next to the frame counter instead of a knurled lever, a slightly revised frame counter with a cutout window, and a Roman II under the Exakta nameplate. Don't be disappointed. As we'll see next time, the "big change" took place in 1951, with the Exakta V, which had a removable reflex finder hood replaceable with a pentaprism.

Many thanks to Earl Seymour of Seymour's Camera in Manhattan, Jules Swirdlin of Exakta Camera Co. of Bronxville, N.Y., and Ken Hansen of Ken Hansen Photographic of Manhattan for their generous assistance in the preparation of this column.

Exakta saga, part 2

The Exakta Saga, Part 2. How a simple, unassuming waist-level SLR acquired interchangeable finders and became the darling of the scientific set.

Last time, we bid adieu to the poor, prismless little Exakta II with promises of interchangeable finders to come. But before we tackle the modern Exaktas' ingenious top-mounted accessories, let's say a few words about the incredibly vast assortment of optics that were produced for the trapezoidal beasts from Dresden. Indeed, with the possible exception of the now-waning 42mm screw-thread mount originated by Praktica and nurtured for nearly two decades by Pentax *et al*, it's safe to say that more lenses from a greater assortment of optical houses were offered for the Exakta than for any other 35mm SLR before or since.

Best normal lens for Exakta VX? Hard to say, but 50mm f/1.9 Schneider Xenon shown is certainly one of the most prestigious. This competent combo presently fetches $150 or so.

How many lenses are we talking about? Well, the Exakta Collectors' Club's list numbers roughly 1400 distinct entries, and the roster of optical firms involved reads like a European "Who's Who in Optical Manufacture." Among German companies alone (in no particular order) are: Steinheil of Munich, Schneider-Kreuznach, Carl Zeiss Jena of East Germany (later ignominiously shortened to "aus Jena" in the U.S. after protracted legal hassles), Enna, Schact, Kilfitt, Novoflex, and naturally, Meyer (from Gor-

litz, also on the "wrong" side of the political railroad tracks). Of course we mustn't forget Angeniuex of Paris, Kern of Switzerland, or the virtually endless list of Japanese manufacturers (including such old friends as Soligor, Vivitar and Tamron to name just a few) who also supplied lenses for the once-very-popular Exakta line. The obvious question in all of this is what about the Ihagee factory, the Exakta's daddy?

Well, I wouldn't be prepared to go out on a 800mm lens barrel and say that Ihagee never ground a lens. And the company most assuredly labeled lenses for some of its folders and SLRs of the mid-30's "Ihagee Anastigmat."

A scientific setup? You bet! This lucky Exakta VX IIa sports Ihagee's Magnear close-focusing finder and "Cobra" device to couple shutter, auto-diaphragm on lens.

However, Ihagee made damn few, if any, picture-taking lenses for the 35mm Exakta, and even those second-rate normal lenses labeled "Exaktar" were not made at the Exakta factory (some originated in Japan). If you're tempted to berate the company as "parasitic" on that account, don't. Unlike, for example, Plaubel—which produced its fair share of optical "bombs" because its management insisted on making its own lenses, come what may—Ihagee had the good sense to realize that its expertise and excellence lay in the mechanical arena. Besides, given the political climate in postwar East Germany, any enterprise which succeeded in not only producing, but also developing a viable SLR system and successfully selling it on the world market, is deserving of our commendation.

All right, enough optical palaver, let's take a gander at what is probably the most significantly updated Exakta 35 ever—the Exakta V of 1951. Outwardly, this machine is differentiated from Exaktas I and II by having two sets of push-in (*not* PC) flash contacts on either side of the lens, and a cute, striated finder-release button placed in between the "Ihagee" and "Dresden," just below the Exakta nameplate. Press the button downwards and you can lift off the prism (or waist-level finder) and get a good look at the cleverly simple and secure finder locking system. At first glance, it appears that the spring-loaded bar directly behind the Exakta nameplate holds finders in place by means of a pin emerging from its center, but as it turns out, said pin merely affixes the lock button to the bar. What actually holds the finders in place and in proper alignment are two pivoted arms on the sides of the finder housing, each of which terminates in a protruding triangular "ear." Insert a finder and press it downwards and each of these ears engages a pin on each side of the body of the finder, locking it in place with an audible click.

But surely this VX IIa is meterized? Well, sort of. Its genuine Ihagee "meter prism" sports an uncoupled selenium meter and auxiliary optical finder. Price with 58mm f/2 C.Z. Jena Biotar, about $125.

A meterized Exakta? Not quite. It's a standard VX IIa with Schneider's selenium-metered f/1.9 Xenon. Shutter settings on side-mounted scale had to be transferred to shutter dials on body.

Clearly, the main reason for having such an interchangeable finder system is that it permitted Ihagee to equip the Exakta with a pentaprism while retaining the advantages of alternative waist-level viewing for scientific and nature photography, among other things. In addition, it enabled Ihagee to offer specialized finders of various sorts, which is one reason that, in the 50's and 60's, scads of labs, individual scientists and medical folks adopted the Exakta system. Eventually, the camera's "top door" even saw such startling appendages as through-lens meter prisms, but these tall, ungainly affairs were never very popular for reasons we'll get to later. For the moment it suffices to say that the Exakta V (please don't ask what happened to models III and IV), when fitted with its elegant-but-fragile chrome topped "pointy" pentaprism, was nothing short of a revelation. Eye-level viewing was rea-

sonably bright even by modern standards, focusing was quick and precise, and with a right-side-up, laterally unreversed viewing image, you could actually follow moving subjects and photograph them at the same time! Think I'm losing my marbles? Well, folks, you've got to remember that this is back in 1951 and the only other camera capable of performing such shenanigans was the Contax SLR, which was often hard to find and sold for 475 bananas.

Actually, the Exakta V, for all its sophistication, is a rather rare bird, since it was manufactured for only about a year. Hot on its heels was the much more common Exakta VX, which sprouted such startling improvements as a film-transport warning signal (a series of red lines, visible in a tiny window to the right of the slow-speed dial which rotate only when the film is advancing properly), a *hinged* removable back, and a built-in film-speed reminder dial to the left of the slow-speed dial. More importantly, the VX's film aperture and main body were manufactured in a single, rigid casting (as opposed to having the film plane established by a screwed-on metal, film aperture plate) which did wonders for lens-to-film alignment. Last but far from least, the VX sported a very nice "pull-down-and-turn" back lock on its bottom, consisting of a knurled knob attached to a spring-loaded shaft. Like most Exakta features, it is unusual, a mechanic's delight, and you either love it or hate it. I like it and was sad to see it go on the last two "classic" Exaktas, the VX 1000 and VX 500.

As if the Exakta epic isn't confusing enough, there were, in fact, two distinct Exakta VXs—the first one (the original) was introduced in 1952 and discontinued in '54. The second or "automatic" VX debuted in '54 and was phased out in '57. As you might expect, both models are practically identical except that the later version had sprouted a few minor improvements. These include a ratcheted exposure counter (instead of the former "friction" type) that's set by turning (what else?) a small knurled wheel adjacent to the film-wind pivot; a hinged shutter-release lock, which is essentially a chrome collar which physically prevents you from pressing the shutter button when it's in the down position; an improved rewind mechanism (if you can consider a spring-loaded button you must keep depressed during rewinding an improvement over a pivoted knob which you don't); and finally, an improved shutter mechanism which allows you to fire the shutter with the waist-level finder folded. You think that's amusing? How about a list price of $392 from 58mm f/2 Biotar? (Don't panic, a similarly-equipped VX today fetches about $125-140.)

And what better way to conclude the festivities than by extolling the virtues of my favorite 35mm Exakta of all time, the VX IIa, introduced in 1958 and discontinued in 1963. Featurewise, the VX IIa (inquire not about the fate of the VX Ia) hardly broke any new ground to speak of, but, largely for aesthetic reasons, it remains the most sought-after of classic Exaktas. Aside from all the aforementioned little doodads that found their way into late VXs, the IIa sports regular PC outlets thoughtfully labeled X, M and F (for long peak focal-plane bulbs), and on the inside you'll find a stippled, rather than flat pressure plate (please don't ask me why). Operationally, the VX IIa's most noteworthy advance concerns the slow speed/self-timer mechanism, which is virtually noiseless in contrast to the rasping, high-pitched cacaphony of previous Exaktas' slow-speed gear trains. In terms of appearance, to get nitpicky, the IIa's alternately knurled slow-speed knob is prettier (and easier to grasp) than the continuously knurled control on older models, and the round film-speed reminder dial directly below it is nicer looking, too.

Basically, the VX IIa is admired because it represents the pinnacle of Ihagee's 35mm achievement. It is well-finished throughout, unlike most subsequent models, incorporates every little nicety the company ever devised (unlike previous models which lacked or later models which deleted this or that), and it has the reputation (whether deserved or not, I'm not sure) of being the best assembled and most reliable of 35mm Exaktas.

Not content with resting on their laurels (and to the utter confusion of Exakta collectors and users alike), Ihagee then sprung upon the world a second version of the VX IIa, which was not as nice as the first. I haven't been able to snare one of these curious animals in the flesh, but it has an "ugly modern" silver-on-black nameplate with "EXAKTA" appearing in upper-case print characters instead of elegant script, and the chrome finish was reportedly down a notch on the "early" VX IIa. Why didn't they leave well enough alone? Frankly, I wonder the same thing—even the flattened-out pentaprism looks out of place on the late model VX IIa. I guess they were preparing us for the slightly less magnificent delights of the VX IIb, but that, friends, will have to wait for the next episode, "The Day the Exakta Lost Its Button." Many thanks to Cambridge Camera and Seymour's Camera of New York City, Exakta Camera Co. of Bronxville, NY, and Brooks Cameras of San Francisco for supplying the Exakta equipment.

This is an VX IIa? Yep, that's what it says in chrome under inelegant Exakta nameplate, but it isn't nearly as nice as the '58 original.

Exakta saga, part 3

The Exakta Saga, Part 3. The slow, excruciating demise, complete with lost buttons, cruder chrome, and an attempted "heirlift" from Berlin.

As I expected, it didn't take the Exaktamaniacs and nit-pickers long to begin excoriating me for any misplaced minutiae or lapses of logic contained in the last Exakta installment. All right, I do apologize for the upside-down photo of the renowned Exakta film-cutting knife in use, which is being pulled up rather than down as stated in the caption, but to call me to task on my procedure for setting the slow-speed dial is really a bit much! In short, anyone using these scribblings in lieu of an instruction manual had best beware.

Second-most-desirable Exakta 35? I'd say this VX IIb with early 50mm f/2 Pancolar qualifies, and it's certainly a usable bargain at $125 or thereabouts.

Actually, the nameless nitpicker is technically correct—to set slow speeds on any classic Exakta you're supposed to cock the shutter, set the fast-speed dial to B or T, wind the slow-speed dial, set the desired slow speed (red numbers for 12-13 sec. delay *plus* slow speed), and *gently* press the shutter release. I advised the hapless multitudes to do all of the above, but to set the slow speed first and *then* wind the slow-speed dial—a method which usually works as well but isn't always possible if the spring-powered slow-speed mechanism is completely, or almost completely, wound down. And so, friends, in the interest of consistency and adhering to the official instruction manual (two things which are of paramount importance in operating

German machinery), I stand corrected. I will not, however, accede to said nitpicker's description of my mistake as an "egregious error"—anyone who didn't realize that you had to wind the damn thing first if the number couldn't be set probably thought the problem was a dead battery.

Okay, enough sackcloth and ashes department, let's get back to the glacier-slow downhill trek of the trapezoidal beast from Dresden on its way to ultimate oblivion. You'll doubtlessly recall that at the end of the last installment, we detailed what mechanical mavens and technological aesthetes regard as the pinnacle of Ihagee's 35mm achievements, the magnificently snazzy VX IIa. This model was replete with every precious doodad and thingamabob the factory could muster, and the surprising thing is, despite the agglomerative nature of its evolution, the whole thing hung together remarkably well in terms of function as well as appearance. Alas, the handwriting was already on the Berlin Wall—as already mentioned late model VX IIa's began to lose some of their aesthetic pizzazz, and so, in 1963, enter the VX IIb.

Last "real" Exakta? Just about. VX 500 has no slow speeds, brings about $100 with 50mm f/2.8 aus Jena Tessar.

As expected, the changes incorporated therein were hardly earthshaking, but virtually all of them had one aim in mind—to reduce production costs. You would have thought that, tools and dies having long since been amortized, the company could have rested on their laurels or even (shudder) redesigned the Exakta to accept a coupled,

119

through-lens metering system and/or internal auto-diaphragm lenses, but no. What we got was geometric shutter speeds (¼,⅛—no 1/15—1/30, 1/60, etc.), a revised slow-speed dial with broader, uniform knurling, a film-speed reminder dial built into its top, and, incredibly, no finger-locking button under the nameplate! True, the finder was still held in the proper orientation by spring-loaded hooks which engaged pins on either side of the finder housings, and VX IIb's as a rule don't suffer from finder falloff, but the change was universally decried. Equally unappreciated was the glued on nameplate above the "shield shaped" front plate, and the fact that the satin chrome finish on top and front plates had deteriorated from good to mediocre and coarse grained. Withal, the VX IIb performs quite well, has a quiet slow-speed gear train like its immediate predecessor, and mine has a convenient accessory shoe affixed to its pentaprism. (That makes sense, you skimp on the prism-retaining mechanism so you add a shoe to mount accessories onto it!) I know that Exakta fanatics will want to hang me from the nearest yardarm for the statement I'm about to make, but in spite of its minor flaws, I'd still be forced to nominate the VX IIb as the second most desirable Exakta 35 in terms of actual picture taking.

Through-lens metering VX 1000? Yep, but Examat prism shown is of the infamous transfer-the-setting variety.

The last models that can accurately be termed classic Exaktas were the VX 1000 and its stripped down stablemate the VX 500, which was actually the last Exakta to be fully assembled in the Ihagee factory (the last East German Exakta, the 1971 to 1974 Exakta RTL 1000, was actually produced in the Pentacon factory). The VX 1000 featured (what else?) revised knurling on the slow-speed dial, ASA settings up to 3200 but no film-type indicator in the film-speed index (the film-type reminder migrated to the back-opening lug on the bottom), a black fast-speed dial with numerals in silver, and a more modern-looking, shorter-throw (hooray, only 200⁰ or so) film-wind lever with coaxial frame counter sans spring-loaded, geared setting knob. Also lost in the shuffle were the Exakta's unique back-locking arrangement (the VX 1000 and VX 500 have a con-

ventional spring loaded, pull-down catch). Perhaps the most amazing thing about these last two "genuine" Exaktas was the re-emergence of the finder locking catch beneath the nameplate. Evidently so many Exakta owners bitched and moaned about its absence on the VX IIb that it was eventually reinstated.

Now if this were any other camera but the Exakta, that would be the end of the tale—birth, procreation, and death—but this Volkswagen of SLR-dom was destined to act out a lingering demise that is, to some, almost as fascinating as its golden age. Frankly, I must admit that the Exakta RTL 1000 for all its internal auto-diaphragm action and semi-coupled through-lens CdS metering turns me off sufficiently that I can't bear writing about it even if you could bear reading about it. Exaktas in name only were Ihagee West's Exakta Twin TL (which is really a Japanese Cosina down to its Copal Square shutter and Exaktar lenses) and the "Petri-fied" Exakta FE 2000 (whose 55mm f/1.7 Exaktar lens screwed into a Praktica-type 42mm screw-thread mount).

A real Real down to its 50mm f/2.8 Schact Travenar lens, this is rarest Exakta model.

But, to conclude these festivities on an equally quixotic and infinitely more Germanic note, here, in brief, is the story of the rarest of all 35mm Exaktas, the Exakta Real (which monicker probably was intended to denote "genuine" rather than "royal" as in Spanish). Apparently none too pleased at the course of the Exakta's development on the wrong side of the Iron Curtain and determined to make a couple of Deutschmarks in the process, one Johan Steenbergen, a Dutchman who was one of the principal founders of the original Ihagee factory in Dresden before the war, bought up the essentially worthless shares of a group of the original stockholders in that company with the notion of wresting the proud Exakta name from these bolshevik upstarts. That was back in 1959, and for four years the new—er, old—company produced nothing but fancy lawsuits on both sides of the Atlantic, which demanded financial compensation from the Exakta factory as well as Exakta importers, for use of the name. After protracted litigation, the East German Ihagee Factory retained most international rights and were able to label their cameras Exaktas in all countries except West Germany, where they lost the case in what has been called a "rigged tribunal." Dresden Exaktas destined for the Bundesrepublik were henceforth dubbed Elbaflexes (after the Elbe river, I presume) while in the U.S., the courts decided the issue along Solomonic lines, with both Ihagee, Dresden and Ihagee West (Berlin) obtaining equal rights to the name. Considering the diminishing luster of the Exakta moniker, one wonders whether these battles were worth the trouble.

Real's top deck: conventional layout.

Then, at the Photokina exposition of 1963, something remarkable happened. Ihagee West showed an honest-to-gosh working model of the new Exakta Real, a hefty machine that is said to bear the unmistakable stamp of the Edixa factory's design staff. Although superficially resembling a classic Exakta in its trapezoidal body contours, this slightly larger (5⅞ × 3⅞ × 3¼ in. with 50 mm f/1.9 Schneider Xenon lens), heavier (2 lb. 6 oz. with same optic) beast was brand new from the ground up, and sported a host of desirable mechanical features representing a valid and worthwhile evolution of the basic Exakta concept. It had, alas, no meter, but its right-hand-operated, single (200°)-stroke wind lever, and conventional top-mounted rewind crank certainly made life easier. Its most obvious departure from standard Exakta practice is the presence of two cable-release-threaded shutter-release buttons, which work with commendable smoothness, and permit facile right- or left-handed operation. Its internally-flanged lens mount is considerably wider than the standard Exaktas (46mm to be exact), to improve the lot of optical designers and to allow sufficient space for an internal-auto-diaphragm-actuating "roller pin" (it's located directly below the enlarged, 29mm-deep mirror). But an adapter was available to let you mount virtually any Dresden Exakta lens on the Real, and, of course, the left-hand shutter release was properly positioned to engage with the Dresden model's external auto-diaphragm lenses. Directly in front of the Real's film-wind lever (which has a coaxial, but non-self-zeroing frame counter that slowly turns from

a green to a red background as you near the 36th frame!) there's a large knurled knob which is the shutter-speed dial. Settings from 2 sec. to 1/1000 sec. are read out in a little arcuate window behind this knob, and the dial has the advantage of being non-rotating so settings can be made before or after winding the film. However, the numerals are not evenly spaced, B and T are mysteriously placed in between 1/15 and 1/30 sec., and the last three numerals, 250, 500, and 1000 are too bunched together to be legible.

Quality on the inside

To open the Real's back you pull up on the top-mounted rewind crank and then turn the outer ring of the film-speed reminder dial below it (shades of the Nikon FM). Inside, you'll find an interior that's very well finished—perhaps a notch or two above the East German Exaktas—with a cloth focal-plane shutter in the middle. Unlike the "classic" Exaktas, the Real loads on the left, takes up on the right, has a large, flat pressure plate with a film tension roller to its left, and double light baffles on its hinged cast alloy back plate. On the front, aside from the aforementioned shutter buttons, you'll find a small shutter-lock lever which locks both releases simultaneously, a left-handed self-timer lever, and a small black button to activate it. The small lens-release lever works in a similar manner to the Dresden models, but its mechanism is internal. Finally, surmounting the Real is a removable pentaprism with a permanently affixed accessory shoe that is held in place by two hefty flat springs and slides off the back. And you purists in the audience would appreciate the Real's viewing screen—an utterly unadorned slice of ground glass surmounted by the condenser lens, just like the ones from the Eastern Zone.

How did this all work out in practice, you ask? Very well and not very well at all. The camera itself had a few foibles, like a delicate frame counter mechanism and a guaranteed-to-peel-off leatherlike covering, but by and large it was a very nicely executed, eminently workable design. Regrettably, by the time the original heirs to the Exakta mystique got the camera into production (four years later in 1967!) much of the glamour was gone from the name and production costs had escalated. Indeed, the Real would have had to sell for about twice the price of the East German model, putting it into head-to-head competition with the Japanese SLR onslaught. True, the Real had an instant-return mirror but by then so did the Exakta VX 1000 and Nikon, Topcon, Pentax *et al* had behind-lens CdS metering built in, and numerous other amenities. Of course, when it comes to being a super-rare production SLR, few can hold a candle to the evanescent Real—precisely how many were made is something of a mystery, but the number was assuredly in the upper hundreds or lower thousands. Number 00948 pictured herein is the property of Modern's publisher who was lucky enough to be in the right place (Cologne, Germany) at the right time with the right number of D-marks. Today I'd peg this jewel at around $1,000, but this is just a ballpark guesstimate.

SLRs from Dresden: Square, Exakta, Korelle, Praktisix, Pentacon Six

I left my heart in Dresden—or, if you can't stop writing about Exaktas, how about spicing things up with a few other distinctive SLRs from the same city.

Well, I've almost gotten those damned Exaktas out of my system in the course of researching the last three chapters—but not quite. Indeed, there's one machine of the mid-to-late 30's that, with the possible exception of the Berlin-made Exakta Real covered in the last installment, is the rarest of all Exaktas. Aesthetically and functionally, it's also one of the nicest, and it set me to thinking about roll-film cameras of similar design, which constituted one of the most sensible approaches in constructing a 2¼ SLR, but which are now virtually extinct except for the Pentax 6×7.

First modern SLR? In terms of fast optics, features, well-integrated design, this late 30's Square Exakta probably was.

The camera to which I refer is the renowned Square Exakta of 1937, a cleverly conceived beast that probably ranks as the first thoroughly modern roll-film SLR. Do I hear any complaints? Then take a gander at the elegant

machine pictured. You can see that it's blessed (afflicted?) with the traditional Exakta accoutrements of the era—a pop-up chest-level viewing hood with built-in magnifier (it flips up from the top of the back section), a fast-shutter-speed dial with speeds up to 1/1000 sec. above the left-handed shutter release button on the front, and the large, knurled show-speed/self-timer dial adjacent to the hinge for the back. Yes, both dials rotate when they're in use, and those cute little round sockets on both sides of the huge 80mm f/1.9 Meyer Primoplan bayonet-mount lens are indeed the precursors of the notorious PC flash sync cord outlets. Not too visible are the frame counter (atop the camera next to the back-opening catch) and the huge film-wind lever on the bottom, pivoting on the right.

A Depression favorite, the spartan Korelle was a Kamera Werkstatten creation.

What makes it so special? Well, the Square Exakta had automatic film stop, bayonet-mount, fast lenses and reasonably bright viewing nearly 25 years before any other 2¼ SLR with lateral (side-to-side) film transport. It was beautifully made and finished and convenient to use. What did it in was a combination of high price (about $300 in 1937) and focal-plane shutter/film-wind problems—a disease that has plagued many of its successors. Unfortunately, I was unable to snare one of these rare birds in time for a complete dissection herein, but you've got to admit, even its formal portrait bears witness to its well-integrated design. Oh, yes, for you inflation-hedging investors out there, I'd presently peg a clean, functioning machine as pictured at a cool $650.

Delving into the origins of such a nice, handy, medium-format SLR, I began to cudgel my brain to come up with its antecedents. By golly, there was an American-made 2¼ SLR with lateral film transport—a two model "series" in fact. And while the model II offered only a limited array of screw-thread interchangeable lenses, these focal-plane shutter 2¼ × 2½-in.-format SLRs were pretty advanced for their day. These were, of course, the National Graflexes which debuted way back in 1933. Yet, despite their basic specs—which included automatic film spacing, the Nationals, with their deep, leather-sided chest-level-viewing "chimneys" somehow seem to date from an earlier era (this despite the fact that the Model II was produced up until World War II).

I hate to give products of native Yankee ingenuity such short shrift, and I promise to devote a future column to the entire National Graflex saga as it deserves. Nevertheless, there *is* a lineal descendant of the aforementioned Square Exakta that more closely parallels its design, albeit on a simpler, less sophisticated level. I speak, of course, of the Reflex-Korelle, heartthrob of so many Depression-era photo-cognoscenti which was introduced back in 1936. The model I, which I haven't a picture of, was basically quite similar to the model II I fondled in preparation of this column, except that it lacked slow shutter speeds and had no self-timer—which brings us to the more comprehensive model II.

Convenient Korelle control array with shutter dials on right, film wind on left.

The first thing one notices in picking up a Korelle II is its relative lightness compared to contemporary 2¼ SLRs—it weighs almost precisely 2 lbs. complete with 75mm f/2.8 Schneider Xenar lens. It fits nicely in the hands—a characteristic of the breed—and is also well balanced. Like most classic Exaktas, the Korelle has separate fast (1/25-1/500 sec.) and slow (2-1/10 sec.) shutter-speed dials atop the camera which rotate as the shutter fires, but they're placed next to each other, to the right of the finder hood. To its left is a beautifully chromed flip-up film-wind

crank of distinctively bulbous design, with a built-in automatic frame counter directly in front of it. Like most cameras of its era, the Korelle lacks automatic first-frame positioning—you've got to line up the first frame manually in ye olde red window on the back, and set the counter to number 1 using a tiny button just above the left-hand neckstrap lug. Press the back-opening catch on the camera's left-hand side and swing the back open toward the right and you're greeted with a spartan interior, with a thin film roller on either side of the film aperture and a cloth focal-plane shutter in the middle. The 120 rolls are held in place at the bottom by spring-loaded lugs that can be pulled out and locked in the out position (to facilitate loading) by pulling and turning a pair of knurled knobs on the bottom. Erect the viewing/focusing hood by lifting the front section in place, and the three other sides automatically spring into proper position. Lift the magnifier in place and peer down into the unadorned ground-glass viewing screen, and even with the lens wide open you'll see what many have acclaimed as the original "dims-o-flex" viewing image—the center is none too bright or contrasty, and it gets considerably worse at the edges. Considering the abysmal finder, the Korelle actually is fairly easy to focus accurately, but you'd better be composing your shots outdoors if you hope to see the corners of the screen. For the record, the Xenar lens on our Korelle focuses smoothly down to 1 m in a 240° turn of its very thin, knurled focusing ring, has non-click-stopped apertures to f/16, and if you unscrew this optic from its 42mm (!) mount, you'll notice that the entire top edge of the rear of the lens mount has been bevelled away to clear the flipping mirror.

Almost instant-return mirror

Speaking of flipping mirrors, the Korelle's deep, trapezoidal-mirror mechanism incorporates what might be termed a primitive version of "almost-instant" return. As you relax your finger pressure on the shutter release (please wait until after the shutter completes its travel—there's no mechanical interlock), the mirror will simply fall by gravity back to the proper viewing position. In other words, the mirror's flipping motion—whether up or down—is controlled by a simple pivoted arm arrangement with only a very weak spring on its flip-down end to keep the mirror from flopping around if the camera is shaken.

Fine, simple, and functional, but what if you want to make a long time exposure—on a tripod, for instance. Easy, just slide a little button on the side of the squarish shutter-button housing on the camera's right side from "A" to "E" (sorry, no English translation) and the mirror will lock in position as soon as it reaches the top of its travel. In front of the aforementioned mirror-lock button there's a threaded cable-release socket, and just below it is a mechanical self-timer. The mirror-lock button doubles as a self-timer actuator so the mirror will automatically lock up when the self-timer is used—ingenious. Incidentally, while the self-timer and slow-speed-gear train emit the typical rasping sounds while in operation, at fast speeds the shutter is extremely quiet—quieter in fact, than most modern SLRs.

Despite its foibles, the Dresden-made Reflex-Korelle qualifies as a genuine landmark among 2¼ SLRs and in fact was in production in its various German guises until at least 1959 (the year of the demise of the Master Reflex). The Master has features similar to the Korelle II but had a larger lens mount to alleviate optical design problems, and one takeoff on the Master—the Reflex 66, was produced in Japan up until the mid-60's. In the 30's many pros mounted the then-superfast f/2 Ernostar lenses (lifted from Ermanoxes and other Ernemann cameras) and mounted them on Korelles, and back in the World War II era Consumer's Union (of all people) chose the Korelle as a more convenient and better performing-alternative to the Primar (Kurt Bentzin) Reflex. Alas, some poor Korelles lived

This one's a trouble-maker. Original Praktisix had great potential, but was plagued with film-wind, focal-plane-shutter woes.

out their lives behind pretty miserable 75mm f/3.5 Victar lenses, but these simple, manual diaphragm SLRs nevertheless endeared themselves to many photographers, which is probably why these nicely finished (but not breathtakingly so) machines have finally earned their place in the sun. As recently as 10-15 years ago you couldn't give 'em away, but this star presently resides under a $200 price tag at Ken Hansen Photographic in New York City.

Having devoted so much space to the Korelle's history, I can do no more than adumbrate subsequent efforts at constructing a lateral-film-transport (as opposed to vertical-film transport a la Hasselblad) 2¼ SLR, except to say that both East German and Japanese efforts in this direction took the logical step of providing pentaprism finders atop their easily hand-holdable bodies.

First, there's the Pentacon Six nee Praktisix, by VEB Pentacon of Dresden (now in the German Democratic Republic). Though considerably larger and heavier than the almost petite Korelle, the Praktisix introduced in 1956, made up for it by incorporating numerous refinements in a still comparatively handy package. To begin with, the

Praktisix has its Korelle-inspired film-wind crank on the right like a proper 35, and it is coupled to an automatic frame counter with semi-auto first-frame positioning (you have to line up the arrows on the paper backing with an orientation dot below the film aperture). There's no instant-return mirror—it flips up when you press the shutter release and stays there until you wind the film, which also opens the lens to maximum aperture—but at least all shutter speeds (1-1/1000 sec. plus B) are set with a single large (1¼-in.-diameter), knurled dial to the left of the finder housing. The prism (or chest-level finder) is held in place by four sturdy lugs which mate with holes at corners of the finder bottoms, and the holes are firmly secured onto the lugs by spring-loaded bars controlled by buttons on the side of the finders.

Operationally, the Praktisix's prism finder image is yellowish, fairly dim, but with reasonable contrast. The very

Pentacon Six had fewer troubles than its predecessors, but its "transfer-the-setting," through-lens meter is slow to operate.

good quality, five-element 80mm f/2.8 Carl Zeiss Biometar lens (dubbed Aus Jena B on many Praktisix/Pentacon Six models imported into the U.S.), focuses smoothly down to 1 meter, and, in terms of control placement and overall design concept, the fairly well-finished Praktisix is a competent and interesting machine. Unfortunately, the film-spacing and shutter-wind mechanisms cannot rate similar kudos, which is why there were subsequent Praktisix II and Pentacon Six models. When Modern tested the latter some years ago, we still encountered occasional frame-spacing problems, and film "unflatness"—the perennial bugaboo of roll-film cameras in general—reared its curly head. Still, in all, the current Pentacon Six with its through-lens, CdS, uncoupled (transfer the setting) meter prism is a seviceable beast capable of quite good results but isn't currently imported into the U.S. I had hoped to be able to sneak in the last of the breed in terms of its date of introduction—the Japanese Norita—but don't despair medium-format reflex fans. I'll cover it (them?) eventually.

Oh, by the way, to avoid letters from outraged Pentax 6 × 7 aficionados—yes, I must admit the SLR of your dreams also fits this category, but it was really conceived as a scaled-up 35 rather than as a scaled sideways Korelle, and besides, it's sold here and in current production.

Cautionary words on buying "collector's item" cameras

A cautionary tale concerning collectible cameras, or how to avoid donning the financial dunce cap when accosted by bogus ads.

While amassing piles of quaint and curious information on obscure Japanese roll-film SLRs, I happened to take a 10-minute break to peruse the latest depressing news in my local quasi-suburban daily known as the *Middletown (New York) Record.* While searching for the comics and astrology page, which has been reduced in size in keeping with its frivolity, I stumbled upon a tiny advert in the Merchandise for Sale Section that at once aroused my curiosity and incited my ire: "Attention camera collectors," it began, "Polaroid J66 camera with case in excellent condition, $85." Now I don't know how many of you remember the J66, or were lucky enough to avoid buying one, but it certainly qualifies as one of Polaroid's true duds, a gray plastic, selenium metered disaster that was a so-so picture taker in the best of times and had to have a special kit installed to take 3000-speed, Type 47 film (presumably it didn't leak enough light to affect the ASA 400 Type 42

film). How do I happen to know these things off the top of my head? Well, as it happens, I was managing a camera department in a second-rate department store at the time Polaroid unleashed this bomb, and I tried it and hated it.

Now it goes without saying that just because a camera happens to be ugly and functionally mediocre doesn't mean it's not a collectors' item. The Fotron certainly was both, yet it's collected with some interest, not to say avidity. But the J66, or its unfortunate smaller sister, the J33 (which took Polaroid Type 32 or 37 roll film)? Maybe 50 years from now they'll be considered collectors' items, but certainly not now. Both were produced in the hundreds of thousands, and if you can get as much as $15 for yours, I suggest you take the money and run. In deference to Polaroid Corp., let me quickly add that many of its cameras were quite lovely and several of them (notably the 110A, 110B, 150, 180, and 700 models) *are* collectors' items *and* good picture takers. The snare and delusion I am attempting to steer my loyal readers around is the self-proclaimed "collectors' item" that's in overabundant supply and for which there is little, if any, demand.

Collectors' item? Hardly, but that didn't prevent some cagey chap from advertising it as such! Its true I.D.'s outlined in text.

Rare Miranda D? It's a model D all right, but it isn't all that rare, nor is it worth the $160 asked. Would you believe $75?

Of course, private individuals advertising in the local rag are the least likely offenders. With the current respectability that camera collecting enjoys come hordes of entrepreneurs anxious to convert their dusty junk piles into instant cash, and what better way to capitalize on the shopworn waifs of cameradom than to shine 'em up and put 'em in the window as "collectors' specials." As an example of this pernicious trend, I recently spotted a meterless Miranda D (actually a rather nice, "plain Jane" SLR of the late 50's) lurking beside a $160 price tag proclaiming "For the Serious Collector!!" I'd peg this beast at around $75 at the outside, and when I asked the pawnshop owner for the rationale behind this ripoff, he calmly replied in the interrogative, "Don't you know that Miranda is out of business and the original ones are quite rare?" Well, aside from the fact that the model D is hardly "the original Miranda" even on these shores, a defunct camera manufacturer does not necessarily an instant collectors' item make. Granted, there *are* some interesting and admirable Mirandas, Petris et al., but they don't presently command special prices nor are they accurately billed as collectors' pieces any more than, say, an early Pentax Spotmatic or a Canon FT.

In a sense, these two examples of purveyor's perfidy constitute the most straightforward deceptions. More devilish by far is when a bona fide collectors' item is labeled as such, but the price asked for it is exorbitant. Take the little gem pictured, which was found on the shelf on a New York camera emporium priced at $150. It is, as its nameplate suggests, a Taxona, which is basically a mid-50's, Dresden-made takeoff on the pre-war Zeiss Tenax I. And what is a Tenax I, you ask? Basically it's a compact, scale-focusing 35 with a 24 × 24mm format (just like a

leaf shutter instead of a Compur, and a *coated* Carl Zeiss, Jena Tessar lens (of all things a 37.5mm f/3.5 with stops to f/16). Most remarkable of all, from a collector's standpoint, the DDR-made Taxona sports the fabled Zeiss-Ikon logo stamped into the genuine leather covering on its removable back, marking it as creature of the great Zeiss Trademark Litigation period (it also has the Pentacon tower trademark engraved into its front plate).

Now Taxonas aren't exactly as common as blueberries —they border on being rare, at least in the U.S. And while they're nicely made, function quite well, both mechanically and optically, and their satin chrome finish and assorted brightwork are lovely, they don't fetch as much as the "real" Zeiss originals. More to the point, they're not worth $150 per copy except to the most desperate collectors of Eastern European photographica, and, as you may have guessed, this species of collector is rather thin on the ground. What it boils down to is this—the adorable little (and I do mean little; it measures 2¾ × 2⅛ × 4¼ in.) is worth about 75 bucks, or half the asking price. It goes without saying that many stores deliberately inflate the price tags of such items to give themselves some "haggling room," and the message is equally clear—if you have a pretty good idea of the value of a given camera you want to buy, don't be ashamed to bargain; for better or worse it's the name of the game, particularly when dealing with retail outlets other than camera stores.

A true classic of late 30's, Zeiss Tenax I is currently worth around $75 despite its so-so 3.8cm f/3.5 Novar lens.

Rarity isn't enough to inflate value of DDR-made Taxona to match its $150 price tag. Astute collectors will offer $50-60.

Robot Star) and a vertical, lever-type film advance. The signal differences between it and the Taxona are that the latter has its viewfinder housed within the top plate (the Tenax's was a pop-up type), a 1-1/300 sec. plus B Tempor

This brings us to the 64,000-yen question, namely how are you supposed to know how much any camera is really worth? So long as you're not talking about true rarities, where the matter or value is often dependent on the chemistry between buyer and seller, there are several ways to determine whether the photographic gem you're lusting after is worth its weight in dough. First off, you can ask a friendly camera dealer with whom you've done business how much he'd pay for a mint-condition Blatzflex with 50mm f/2 Neo-Fuzztar lens or whatever, and add a percentage to that figure if you're buying it from a retail store. Your local camera (collecting or garden variety) club usually has a few members who are "equipment mavens," and they may be able to provide a sandlot price figure, providing the equipment isn't too exotic. And, of course, you can always shop around (by telephone or on foot) to see if another store features a Blatzflex at a lower price.

Then there are the print media. Many localities have a "seller's newspaper" consisting of nothing but ads for everything from washing machines to cabin cruisers. The asking prices for various items, while usually inflated by about 10-20 percent to allow for "offers," do provide a fairly accurate barometer of current photo equipment prices. Ditto for the "Merchandise for Sale" section of large or local newspaper and photographic magazines, although as the opening tale in this column suggests, *caveat emptor* should always be your password if you want to avoid getting stung. Finally, there's *Shutterbug Ads*, America's largest compendium of advertisements for photographic equipment, which should be on every "serious collector's" subscription list. Over the years I've only purchased a few items from the individuals and firms listed therein (though I've sold about half a dozen cameras to folks advertising in its "Want to Buy" section), but it's proven to be an invaluable source of pricing information. Of course, you can always follow the age-old antique collectors' maxim "If they call it an antique, it's overpriced—if it's sold as used furniture it's probably a steal." The only trouble with that rule of thumb is that it doesn't always work with cameras. The machine of your dreams may indeed reside in the store's "collectors' corner," and if you really want it you should be prepared to pay an equitable price, which is generally not the same as a "steal." However, in these financially uncertain times when people are

What makes Petri Half collectible? Not just the fact that its maker's kaput. Most half-frame 35s are collected with fair avidity these days because they're cute, functional, and comprise a distinct category.

seizing the most diverse and curious objects as "hedges against inflation," you'd better be able to tell the difference between the privets and the crabgrass. Egad, I almost forgot, the address of *Shutterbug Ads* is P.O. Box F, Titusville, FL 32780, and their current subscription rate is $35 per year via first-class mail, $10 per year by third class. Also, many thanks to Metro Outlet Corp., one of the few remaining used merchandise emporia in New York with a good selection of collectible cameras, for supplying the (ugh!) Polaroid J66 pictured.

Contaflex saga, part 1

The Contaflex Saga, Part 1. Can a spartan, leaf-shutter SLR of noble ancestry succeed in the real world without a single interchangeable lens?

I am sorry to disappoint admirers of defunct Japanese 2¼ SLRs for the second time, but the great Norita Narrative awaits the arrival of (would you believe) a photographic likeness of the fabled Rittreck 66, its lineal ancestor. In the meanwhile, considering the epistolary frenzy generated by the recent Exakta series, I have decided to drag yet another admirable but under-appreciated (hence undervalued) German 35mm SLR onto center stage and under Schneider's CC40 Magenta spotlight. I'm fatalistic about letting myself in for it, since recently departed 35s

(especially SLRs) *always* generate mounds of correspondence from Modern's readers. Why? Probably because there are so many of 'em lurking in the top drawers of original owners who refused to accept the pittance offered for them at trade-in time. This ought to make them smile. As for those hapless Contaflexers who unloaded theirs for a song, they'll probably be weeping into their Steinhagers before this segment concludes.

Let's commence the festivities with some miscellaneous musings on the name Contaflex. Hardbitten collectors of Germanic photographica will be well aware that the moniker was applied to the fabulously expensive, super-elite, twin-lens Contaflex (a fully systematized 35mm twin-lens reflex) of 1938. However, the name has its origins in the renowned Contessa-Nettel factory which was subsumed under the Zeiss-Ikon banner in the great Z-I merger of 1926. The "Contessa" half gave us such immortal names as Contessa, Contina, Contarex, Contaflex, and, of course, Contax, while the "Nettel" part engendered such cognates as Nettar, Nettax, and Super-Nettel. This bifurcated nomenclature reflects the fact that "Contessa-Nettel" was itself formed by the merger of these two hyphenated entities. In any event, Zeiss wisely decided to abandon its lavish TLR after World War II, and they were therefore free to use the illustrious Contaflex name to herald the introduction of its brand-new SLR—the original Contaflex I of 1953.

For such a camera bearing the weight of such a patrician heritage, the little (5 × 2½ × 3⅝-in.) Contaflex I is a spartan beast indeed. Its stocky, angular body contours and ample weight (1 lb., 10 oz.) look as though they might be unhandy, but nothing is further from the truth—this beautifully finished machine will nestle comfortably in the smallest hands and its well-centralized weight contributes to a feeling of stability. Technically speaking, the greatest disappointment comes when you discover that the Contaflex I is bereft of lens interchangeability of any kind. True, its 45mm f/2.8 Zeiss Tessar lens offers very good performance even by current standards, but its alternately knurled front-focusing collar will only get you down to just under 3 ft., which isn't quite close enough for close-up portraiture with a semi-wide-angle optic. And while the focusing system is commendably smooth, Zeiss decided to simplify the camera mechanically by using the optically less desirable "front cell" focusing system in which the front optical group moves away from the fixed rear elements behind the shutter to focus the lens closer. Other standard fare to be expected on a '53 vintage SLR is a lightly knurled, large-diameter (almost 1¼ in.) film-wind *knob*, Synchro-Compur interlens leaf shutter with speeds from 1-1/500 sec. plus B, MX sync and built-in self-timer, and, of course, no instant-return mirror—you have to wind the film to the next frame for viewing.

A Zeiss original, the Contaflex I of '53 was clearly an amateur's SLR as indicated by non-interchangeable 50mm f/2.8 Tessar.

Whatever your misgivings at the model I's basic specs, wind the film-wind knob and bring the camera to eye-level and they'll begin to fade away. The Contaflex I (and indeed all of its successors) is blessed with one of the brightest, contrastiest viewfinders in all of SLR-dom. And how, pray tell, did they manage this feat with only an f/2.8 lens? Easy. Glance through the camera and what you see is a coarse Fresnel-pattern focusing screen with central split-image rangefinder surrounded by a distinctly grayish fine ground-glass focusing collar. The horizontally divided rangefinder works quite nicely even in dim light; the collar section snaps in and out of focus as you focus, like a ground-glass should (it works best in bright light), and the outer Fresnel area just sits there, providing a nice, bright viewing image. Now try to focus on a detailed object, at a

Spartan but functional, Contaflex I was blessed with logical controls, fast-focusing lens that went from infinity to 3 ft. in under 90° turn. Accessory shoe was removable.

medium distance, in the outer viewing area. Notice that you can turn the focusing ring as far as you wish in either direction and the object will *still* look sharp—that's right, you simply can't use the entire area for focusing! What hath Zeiss wrought? A focusing screen with "clear Fresnel" outer area, conventional ground-glass collar and "clear" central split-image device. Both "clear" parts are bright as can be because they transmit an *aerial* image (brightness is further aided by a condenser lens over the screen). But unless it's part of a split-image system or viewed in conjunction with a fixed visual reference point (such as crosshair reticle), an aerial image cannot ordinarily be used to focus a camera.

Turning to the mechanical side, the Contaflex I's back is reminiscent of the rangefinder Contaxes—it has two locks, one on either end, that must be turned to unlocked position by means of D-shaped handles before you slide the back off. As you'd expect, the interior is beautifully finished and the back itself incorporates a film-tensioning roller, oversized pressure plate, and black flocking on its bottom inside surface. Once the camera's loaded, you manually set the additive frame counter to zero by turning a top-knurled ring located within the film-wind knob and concentrically around the shutter release. As you wind to frame 1 notice that the inner, numbered section is geared to turn faster than the outer ring because it has to make a complete revolution before it advances to the next number. Complicated, these Germans.

Although the Contaflex's shutter release is very smooth and predictable, requiring moderate finger pressure, the sound that emerges from the beast when you fire at, say 1/60 sec., is curious to say the least—a startlingly loud "chir-rik" on the downstroke and a muted click as you relax your finger pressure. Of course, you've got to bear in mind that there's invariably lots going on inside any leaf-shutter SLR which accounts for the racket. For one thing, as you press the release, the shutter must first close; then the mirror flips up; then the shutter opens and closes to make the exposure as the diaphragm stops down. No wonder Zeiss decided to leave the mirror return and shutter-reopening (for viewing) as separate operations, performed during the film-wind part of the sequence.

Add non-coupled meter to Contaflex I and it becomes a model II. Teleskop 1.7X tele lens screwed over Tessar via adapter.

To round out the mechanical end of things, let's take a peek at the exposure-setting controls. Both the shutter-speed and aperture-setting rings are conveniently located behind the front-most focusing ring, and in front of the mirror box housing. The latter, which provides f/stop settings from f/2.8 to f/22, has a spring-loaded lockout device to the right of the 2.8 which locks in at all whole aperture settings and must be pushed in before you can change 'em.

Concurrently with the Contaflex I, Zeiss-Ikon produced the Contaflex II (introduced in 1954) which was identical in all other respects to the I, but had a built-in uncoupled selenium meter located on the camera's left "shoulder," just below the rewind knob. This device was forward-looking in offering film-speed settings from ASA 5-640, and though it has but one sensitivity range it is quite accurate and fairly sensitive for a meter of its type and size, reading down to about f/2.8 at 1/60 sec. at ASA 400. Both the Contaflex I and II were phased out in 1958 after what must be described as a financially and technically successful production run. Incidentally, Zeiss did offer

screw-in converter lenses for wide and short tele work with these machines, which evidently weren't too popular —judging by their present scarcity.

What can one say about these cameras that isn't already obvious—that they're neat, jewel-like, and stylish, but operationally conservative to the point of being dull? Yeah. What's more, like most leaf-shutter SLRs, they're plagued with complex mechanical connections in the film-wind-to-shutter coupling area (among other places), which is why the early models I've just yakked about are somewhat more reliable than the later ones, a pair of which we'll get to in a bit. But despite the fact that their narrow diameter interlens leaf shutters restrict the light path and undoubtedly gave optical designers fits devising wide-angle and tele lenses for the later "component interchangeable"-lens models, and in spite of their aforementioned inabilities and foibles, these are *nice* cameras that are fine, usable picture takers. And if you latch onto a I or II it won't really

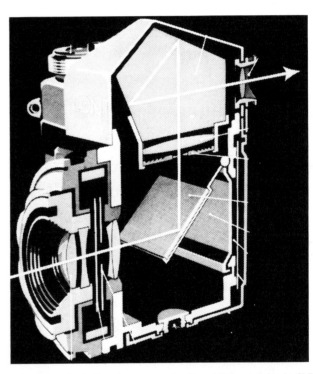

Slice Contaflex in half and you can see (in addition to classic SLR lightpath) interlens shutter and diaphragm, condenser lens over Fresnel-pattern screen.

require any of the numerous accessories that were made for it (except, perhaps an accessory shoe to mount a flashgun) to make it as perfectly functional and complete as it ever was. That's right—here's the kicker; you can get a Contaflex II in clean condition (let collectors have the meterless model I; users should opt for the model II) for 75 bucks or even less! That's not too bad for a product of fine West German craftsmanship, especially when you consider that it sold for a cool $176 back in '58.

Like all wary marketing folks, Zeiss decided to test the waters with two new Contaflex models before discontinuing the old fixed-lens models. And so, in 1957 they introduced the Contaflex III and IV which were basically al-

129

most identical to the I and the II except for having a few additional features. The most important of these was unquestionably lens interchangeability of the removable front-component type. This also brought with it unit focusing via a conventional double-helical system. By pressing a small, spring-loaded tab beneath the "Synchro-Compur" on the front plate and turning the front-most knurled ring on the lens about ⅛ turn counterclockwise, the 45mm f/2.8 Tessar's front component can easily be lifted out. Replacement components that can be bayonetted in include a 35mm f/3.2 wide-angle and 85mm f/3.2 and 115mm f/4 teles, all dubbed Pro-Tessars. While this optical array was and is quite restricted compared to the offerings for fully interchangeable SLRs, the Zeiss components are of high quality.

Another less desirable feature that found its way into the "second generation" Contaflexes was the notorious LVS system of coupled (and hard to uncouple) shutter and aperture settings. At least these had the virtue of working in conjunction with the IV's still uncoupled selenium meter. In terms of handling, the "unit focusing" Contaflexes, with their wide, knurled focusing tabs on the close-to-the-body focusing rings take a bit of getting used to, but (in my opinion) prove to be satisfactory in the end.

Should you therefore opt for a nice Contaflex IV for a piddling C-note or so in preference to the fixed-lens II? Well, if you're really going to haunt the used-camera emporia for the extra lenses (which often fetch as much as the whole camera!), by all means have at it. If not, the

Nope, it's not a IV, but this later-model Contaflex Super has same front-component lens array including (left to right) 85mm f/3.2 Pro-Tessar, 50mm f/2.8 Tessar (on camera), rare Pro-Tessar 1:1 macro, and 115mm f/4 Pro-Tessar.

original models are excellent "second cameras" for everyday shooting and they'll supply mechanical finesse and that indefinable German pizzazz (virtually no plastic y'know) for less money than just about anything else. One final caution, though—make sure the Contaflex of your dreams is mechanically sound and/or guaranteed for long enough so you can check it out. Like other leaf-shutter SLRs, Contaflexes are a bitch to repair, and the hourly rates of people who repair fine German machinery are not to be believed.

Contaflex saga, part 2

The Contaflex SLR Saga, Part 2. Wherein the basic beast acquires film mags and modern metering but remains its lovable, leaf-shuttered little self.

I kinda blew the suspense by revealing a portrait of the Contaflex Super last time, but we'll try to make up for it by lacing this penultimate Contaflex SLR opus with some astounding facts and opinions. Since the previous episode concluded with both praise and condemnation of the Contaflex's front-component lens-interchange system, let's flesh out the Super's fleeting portrait with its technical and aesthetic details.

To begin with, I must confess that the original Super of 1959 is my personal favorite among all the various Contaflex SLR incarnations. Why? Well, it's as beautifully finished and assembled as the very first models, has interchangeable lens components, a 180° rapid-wind lever in place of the film-advance knob, and its "match-needle"

What's so super about this Contaflex? Well, aside from its name (Super), it has match-needle metering, lever advance, and (egad) interchangeable film magazines.

selenium-cell exposure system is as sensitive (as it reads down to about ¼ sec. at f/2.8 with ASA 400 film), accurate, and convenient as any of its type. When you add to this agreeable set of specs the capability of accepting interchangeable film magazines one wonders why these fine, distinguished machines often languish on dealers' shelves for months with under $100 (or so) price tags!

Lamentations aside, the chief distinguishing features of the Contaflex super are its milled-edge ASA/aperture setting wheel on the front of the camera (it's directly forward of the rewind crank), and the enlarged (1-1/16-in. long) selenium-cell grid affixed to the front of the prism housing. Adjacent to the "exposure" wheel is a small, frosted light-collecting window that illuminates the metering index to the right of the finder field. There's also a second external metering index atop the camera to the right of the combined rewind crank/film-type reminder.

compared to their modern, behind-lens couterparts; their acceptance angle is wider (usually about 60°) so they're prone to being overly affected by skylight. Tilt your Contaflex Super slightly downwards when shooting landscapes and take close-up readings of people when possible and you'll seldom experience exposure problems.

Turning to the Super's other end, we have the glorious option of mounting interchangeable film magazines, a system photographers often clamor for, but seldom use. Remove the "regular" back by twisting the time-honored keys and lifting it off and you're confronted with a conventional-looking interior. But, as is often the case, initial appearances are deceiving.

Snap out a simple plastic cartridge retainer from the film-supply channel on the left, remove the take-up spool, wind the film so the magazine's locking-pin can slide into its mating slot above the film-wind shaft, and mount the Contaflex magazine just as you would the back. You *can*

Fully auto exposure is the Contaflex Super B's strong suit. Larger selenium cell adorns front of prism housing; film-speed dial's below rewind crank.

A concave dark slide? Yep, and Contaflex film magazine also has separate frame counter, double-exposure and blank-exposure prevention lockouts.

All right, here's how the whole shebang works. First, set the film speed by turning the inner part of the aforementioned aperture wheel until the appropriate digits are aligned with a black delta. Now grab hold of the black plastic "ears" on the shutter-speed dial and select the speed you want. Finally, wind the single-stroke film-advance lever so you can focus and view (that's right—still no instant-return mirror) and bring the camera to eye level. As expected, the view is exceptionally bright and clear for reasons outlined in the last chapter. If anything, the Super's finder image is a tad brighter and more contrasty than that of previous models. As mentioned, the metering index is on the right—there are no numbers— just a vertical white band with a notch at its midpoint and a black needle. Drape your left index finger over the top part of the aperture wheel and turn it until the needle in the finder coincides with the notch, and voila—the correct exposure. As with all 35mm Contaflex SLRs, both shutter speeds and aperture scales can be read off the lens housing from above.

Of course, selenium meters do have a few disadvantages

fire the shutter once without removing the magazine's dark slide, causing a possible blank exposure, but you won't be able to wind the film until you push in a spring-lock button and slide the slide out from the bottom of the camera—a good safety interlock. Furthermore, the Contaflex magazine is (glory be) easy to load. Cock the shutter, insert the dark slide, and unlock the locks and it lifts off. Pull on a tiny spring lock and the cartridge compartment slides up and off. Simply insert a standard 35mm cassette, pull out the dark slide about 1½ in. so you can thread the film across the pressure plate (which has film-retaining grooves top and bottom), slide open the take-up spool housing, thread the film into the slot marked with the white rectangle, and secure the leader by rotating the spool's knurled bottom collar. Now all you do is mount the magazine (making sure the shutter has been cocked), pull the dark slide, fire off a few film-positioning frames and you're ready to go. Incidentally, on the magazine's back you'll find, in addition to verbal warnings in German and English, separate film speed and film type reminder dials, and on the bottom there's a manually set, subtractive film counter. The latter device matches the Super's film counter-cum-shutter button on the top right deck, which also counts *down* to zero.

Did I forget anything? Nothing major, I'm sure (though I fully expect a few letters from outraged Zeiss fanatics detailing my omissions). In fact, that's just what's so nice about the Super. Zeiss gave you everything you could have asked for and more, given the inherent limitations of the Contaflex design, but the camera's sterling virtues— excellent viewing system, fine balance and handling qualities and full flash snyc at all speeds—were retained. In short, the Super represents a classic case for the advantages of an evolutionary approach applied to a sound basic design.

In the groove: That's where you put Contaflex mag before sliding it up, locking it in place. Note elaborate film-type dials.

Perhaps you're now wondering what additional features could possibly be integrated into what is, after all, an unpretentious leaf shutter SLR with medium-speed lens components. Would you believe autoexposure, autoflash, and full exposure info in the finder? Well, that's precisely what you'll find in the Contaflex Super B of the early to mid 60's.

Outwardly, the Super B differs little from the plain old Super, but the changes are portentous. Gone is the little, round, aperture-setting wheel—pretty much in its place is an enlarged, striated light-collecting window to illuminate the readouts in the finder. The B's ASA scale is now found along the bottom edge of the rewind crank assembly. To set it you press in a little shielded tab and rotate the top (milled) edge of the dial until a delta points to the proper number (ASA 5-800). Grab the dial without pressing in the tab and rotate it clockwise from "sunburst 1" to "cloud 2" and you'll get about 1 stop less exposure—a useful device on an auto-exposure camera.

Since your curiosity has now been sufficiently piqued, let's run through the Super B's operations. Move the plastic tab on the aperture ring to its bottom position and the aperture ring will click in and lock at the "A" setting. (You must push in a little locking tab before you can make manual f/stop settings.) Since we've already set the film

speed, bring the camera to eye level, give the brilliant finder image a passing glance, and direct your attention to the "exposure information center" just outside the right edge of the finder field. The top part of this vertical scale displays apertures from f/2.8 to f/22 in black digits against a white background, and there are red under- and over-exposure areas below and above the digits, and a green "metering range" bar arrayed along their right. As you'd expect, the meter needle floats in the white band to indicate the camera-selected aperture and responds differentially to various lighting conditions.

This is a Contaflex? Yes, but the 126 took 126 cartridges, had focal plane 1/30-1/500 sec. shutter, own lens line.

Should the needle wind up in the red areas, you can switch shutter speeds without removing the camera from your eye—just grab the knurled tabs on the shutter-speed-setting ring (near the front of the lens barrel) and turn it as you glance at the white-on-black numerals appearing in a tiny window just under the aperture scale in the finder. That's right folks, the "B" displays the set shutter speed in the finder—pretty spiffy for an SLR of the early 60's.

Additional revisions? Well, in place of the metering index on the plain Super's left shoulder there's a camera-selected-aperture scale; atop the prism housing in front of the accessory shoe are a pair of "flashmatic" contacts (the left-hand one is ye olde PC tip), and if you turn the aperture ring from "A" in a *clockwise* direction you can set flash guide numbers.

Despite its autoflash, auto-exposure and information-filled finder, I'm not enchanted with the Super B (which is definitely a bargain at its current $150-175 retail price). Perhaps its somewhat shinier, slightly "grainier" chrome finish and plastic (instead of metal) focusing "ears" turn me off. Or maybe it's the fact that those f/stops and shutter speeds in the finder are none too visible in dim light. Probably the real reasons are less romantically nit-pickey though. As it happens, the very last Contaflex 35s, the Super BC and the virtually identical Contaflex S were very similar to the Super B except for one minor detail; they had behind-lens CdS metering! Without going into excruciating detail, let's just say that these models had the entire passle of previously enumerated features, but added a single CdS cell above the finder eyepiece (the eyepiece also acted as a beam splitter) and a small, finger-openable, one-way battery compartment on the front of the camera. (We'll present portraits and full details in the next concluding Contaflex SLR installment.) It is said that early Super BCs were afflicted with poor ground connections in their metering circuits, but that later ones not only worked but worked extremely well. If that doesn't whet your appetite, the very last "Auto S" was also produced in

black finish, adding a touch of sexiness to the ultimate Contaflex SLR's siren charms. Yep, they were the first of their breed to attain collectors' item status so if you're determined to snare one, it'll probably set you back $200-250! Many thanks to Camera Barn and Ken Hansen Photographic, both of New York City, for supplying the equipment featured herein. Finally, if your Contaflex or other Zeiss camera is in need of repair, contact Z.V. Service Corp., 333C West Merrick Rd., Valley Stream, NY 11580.

Contaflex saga, part 3, Exakta TTL meter, Kowa UW

The Contaflex Saga, Part 3. The last of the 35mm breed. Ruminations on the first SLR with behind-lens metering, and more.

This is really the denouement of my Contaflex outpourings, since I wittingly spilled both bags of beans last time.

The first took the form of a portrait of the Contaflex 126, the last camera to bear that illustrious name. The second was a bag of facts lacking a picture, so to make up for it we'll show you two—one of a rare black-finish Contaflex Super BC, and another of the nearly identical Contaflex S,

which is why each sports a battery chamber where focal-plane-shutter SLRs usually have their self-timers, and neither has an external meter grid. Operationally, they're identical to the Super and even include the same distinctive light-collecting grid for the finder readouts to the left of the prism housing front, and (alas) the same non-anatomical, non-ratcheted film-wind lever. Withal, the two pictured are evidently the most desirable models among a burgeoning bunch of Contaflex collectors, and as such they've been known to change hands for about $250 ("plain" chrome Super BCs can occasionally be found for much less since they're much more common). By and large (with exceptions noted last time), late-model auto-exposure Contaflexes are excellent picture takers and quite reliable, but expensive and difficult to repair when they break. Personally, I still prefer the match-needle, selenium-meter Super.

I suppose that in the interest of historical completeness —not to say accuracy—I must mention a few of the Conta-

Last and greatest? In terms of metering, automation, panache, and price, black "S" model is most desirable of Contaflex 35s.

aka Automatic S. To reiterate, the latter was (sob) the last-ever Contaflex 35, a casualty of the Great Japanese Technological Onslaught of the late 60's, and both the BC and the S featured auto exposure, autoflash, and interchangeable front lens components like the plain old Super B. Their distinguishing mark and *raison d'etre*? Behind-lens metering with the cell reading off the focusing screen,

Super rare black BC? Frankly, I'm not sure, but it is the only example of the breed I've seen that sports Zeiss Ikon nameplate.

133

flexes I love to hate, namely the ones with Prontor shutters, three-element normal lenses and front lens components which were interchangeable with those on the non-SLR Contina (but not Tessar-lensed Contaflexes). Why Zeiss would afflict a patrician machine like the Contaflex with such mediocre components just to sell a few more cameras at the "low end" I do not know, but the Contaflex Alpha, Beta, and Prima certainly didn't fare well on the U.S. market and they may have even tarnished the Contaflex's "quality" image. At any rate the Contaflex Alpha of 1958 was similar to the Contaflex III (i.e., round film-wind knob, no meter) and it was fitted with a 45mm f/2.8 Zeiss Pantar lens in Prontor 1-1/300 sec. shutter. The Beta was identical to the Alpha, but sported a built-in, non-coupled, selenium meter like the Contaflex IV. The Prima was the cheapie Pantar-lensed version of the Super, with match-needle selenium metering, a rapid-wind lever, and a Prontor Special Reflex shutter. In answer to the obvious questions, Pantar lenses were so-so at wider apertures, pretty good at f/5.6 on down, and the Prontor shutters were definitely more troublesome than the Compurs fitted on Tessar-lensed Contaflexes. As you might expect, these three less desirable sisters are often sold at bargain prices because nobody loves 'em except Contaflex collectors. (Would you believe $70 for a mint Prima with case?)

Since a study in Contaflex lore can be viewed as a game called "where did they put the meter" let's move sideways a bit and try to answer a persistent query entitled "who was first with the meter" or, more specifically, which SLR had the first behind-lens meter? For a long time I thought that honor belonged to Topcon, whose clever engineers put a CdS cell behind slits in the RE Super's mirror back in '63. Then somebody told me that was wrong—that Asahi showed a Pentax with behind-lens metering at an earlier Photokina exposition. There the matter remained, unsettled in my mind, until I received a note from Norman Rothschild, *Popular Photography*'s editorial doyen and a notorious Exaktaphile. To paraphrase and expurgate his colorful prose, the gist of his remarks was as follows: "Though I took issue with many of your half-baked opinions, I nevertheless followed your recent Exakta scribblings with some interest. But dummkopf, why the hell didn't you point out that the Exakta *was* the first SLR with through-lens metering?" Dumbstruck, I pored over my bulging Exakta file only to discover there was no through-lens metering Exakta until the advent of the unreliable Examat and Schact meter prisms of the late 50's...or was there? Among the close-up accessories folders I unearthed an unlikely-looking gizmo called a Color Meter that debuted back in 1956 and was, like so much other Exakta paraphernalia, a collaboration between Ihagee Dresden (the Exakta's manufacturer) and a West German firm, in this case Gossen.

Basically, the Color Meter is a device designed primarily for close-up use with short-mount lenses on bellows where figuring exposure-increase factors can be quite tedious. The Dresden-made, satin chrome part of the plot is a tall, thin metal housing with a male Exakta mount on its back and a female Exakta mount on its front. Mount it on the camera with the two side-levers in the up position and you can look straight through the front mount and see the mirror box. Slide the levers downward as shown in the picture, and a circular selenium cell is interposed in front of the mirror. Plug a two-prong cord in the receptacle above the lens mount and the old-style Gossen meter attached to the other end of the cord is activated and will read out the amount of light impinging upon the cell. Wunderbar!

First behind-lens meter? Probably, but Ihagee/Gossen Color Meter's brilliance was mostly confined to lab and studio.

Photog's-eye view of "Auto S" shows PC and Flash-matic contacts atop prism, built-in eyepiece blind in up position.

Actually, the Color Meter can be used for taking close-up readings with almost any Exakta-mount lens, but because of the thickness of the "meter box," few will focus to infinity. Metering action shots is obviously out of the question, and the few folks I've chatted with who've actually used one of these contraptions reported that it was fiddly in use and mediocre in terms of metering accuracy. Oh well, there's no denying that it was a brilliant concept for its day, and in its own cockamamie fashion it pointed the way toward the future. So I guess I'll have to amend my future remarks about the Topcon, and describe it with unaccustomed precision as the first *production* SLR with *built-in* through-lens metering.

What's different about this 35mm Kowa SLR? Aside from its 19mm lens and $400 (used) price tag, nothing much.

To conclude with another oddity of SLR-dom, herewith the Kowa UW 190, a leaf-shutter reflex with an important optical difference—a non-interchangeable 19mm f/4 Kowa lens! Long-time Japanese camera aficionadoes will instantly recognize the UW's contours as those of the SETr and SETr2—machines that supplied an incredible number of features for remarkably little money. Unfortunately, despite having good quality 50mm f/1.9 lenses, commendably accurate metering systems, and (on the last model) interchangeable lenses, most Kowa 35mm SLRs were mechanically troublesome and pretty tough to repair in many cases. Does the super-wide-only UW share these lamentable traits? Probably, since it appears to be nothing more than an SETr with a funny lens. For those who don't recall the basic specs, the Kowa SETs had through-lens CdS, match-needle metering—you set the 1-1/500 sec. plus B shutter-speed dial first and align the meter needle in the finder with a pincers by turning the (f/4 to f/16 in this case) aperture dial just in front of it. As far as the UW is concerned, its viewfinder is surprisingly bright considering the 19mm's f/4 aperture, and the super-wide optic focuses down to below 8 in. "Who needs an SLR with an unremovable 19mm lens?" you ask. That's what most marketing honchos said back in 1972 when the thing was introduced. The inevitable results: Few were sold, the UW is super-rare in the U.S. (it was never officially imported), and it's currently priced at $400—about eight times the value of mechanically identical SETr. Yes, the 19mm lens was very good, even by current standards. Many thanks to Ken Hansen Photographic of New York for supplying the equipment pictured in this column.

Folding Pocket Kodaks and basic box Brownies

Turn your folding money into folding pocket Kodaks and basic box Brownies? Why not? Many are usable classics and most can be had for a song or a sawbuck.

I know what you folks out there are thinking—in fact you communicate it so often that I am reduced to scribbling one-sentence replies (if you're lucky) to complex questions on aesthetics, finance, technology and heaven knows what else, drawing upon the meager resources contained within my fallible noggin. And so, in a vain attempt to stem the avalanche of epistles from flea-market scratchers and garage-sale pickers, I must return once again to a subject close to my guts—yes, you guessed it— foldy old molding Kodaks (as you used to be allowed to call them) and box cameras. Assiduous fans of this monthly masterpiece know of course that, despite my flippant remarks and cast aspersions, I'm really not kidding. In fact, cameras in these humble categories constitute 83.7 percent of my modest collection of 250 cameras. (If that figure astounds you, you're obviously not acquainted with your local Photographic Historical Society, many of whose

A good 2¼ × 3¼ camera for $10? This c. 1914 Kodak No. 1 Jr. qualifies, and it takes ubiquitous 120 film.

Ever vigilant for good buys, Schneider nabbed this Kodak Vigilant 620 for a paltry $4.50, about a fifth of its value.

members have collections two and three times that size. There's even one chap in California purported to have amassed 12,000 cameras.)

All right, having established my affection for the kinship with the hollow-eyed haunters of the knick-knack tables, let's say a few words on what you can expect to find out there in bazaar-and-garage land. To lend an air of authenticity to these proceedings, I selflessly devoted my last couple of Sundays to what I euphemistically call field research. Armed with nothing more impressive than a rapidly shrinking sawbuck (that's ten dollars if you're too young to remember when they were worth sawing) I set about to see what manner of ancient picture-taking machines I could find. And after making the rounds of two bona fide flea markets, one Lion's Club bazaar, and a couple of garage sales, herewith the results.

As I've mentioned countless times before, despite my mechanical and/or aesthetic appreciation for cameras and other photographica, just as I am about to plunk down some greenbacks for a superannuated folder, a little voice reminds me, "Cameras are for making pictures!" So, naturally I tend to buy cameras that are conveniently usable as opposed to filmless classics. How does one avoid buying a filmless classic by mistake? Easy. Just remember that you *can* still buy Kodacolor II film in 116 and 616 sizes, and your dealer can special order it in quantities as small as one roll if he's sympathetic. Obviously, these two sizes are in a "shoot it while you can" situation. Among other classic roll-film sizes, 620 and 127 are in better shape with three film types each—both are available in Kodacolor II and Verichrome Pan black-and-white, and 620 also comes in Vericolor II, while 127 Ektachrome is still rolling off Kodak's limited-production line. Needless to say, 120 film is available in almost any emulsion that strikes your fancy, while such glorious sizes as 101, 104, 105, 117, 118, 130, 828, and (sniff) 122 have long since bitten the proverbial dust.

In pursuit of curious Kodaks

With the practical stuff out of the way, let's begin our hunt. First, the Lion's Club bazaar and rummage sale, which was held on a drizzly Sunday afternoon. Actually

the weather was a plus factor for the buyer since it limited the attendance and made sellers particularly anxious to hawk their wares before the great downpour. And while still cameras (as opposed to modern slide projectors, movie cameras and a rusty old Kodak darkroom timer) were to be found at only one table near the parking lot, I was able to snare two delicious (albeit common) specimens for the grand total of $9. Did I mind haggling the price down from $15 even though either one of the cameras alone was easily worth that figure? Not this skinflint—besides, that's part of the sport of such events.

With due deference to its age, the first of this noble pair is a No. 1 Kodak Jr., which commenced production around 1914 and was manufactured well into the 20's. Its Kodak Ball Bearing shutter still functions perfectly—it's an ever-set type with speeds of 1/25, 1/50, B and T. Its lens is a Bausch & Lomb Rapid Rectilinear calibrated in the Uniform System. You focus the thing by placing your thumb and forefinger on the finger rest at the bottom of the front standard (thereby pushing in the focus locking lever), and moving it back and forth until the bottom end of the focus-lock lever engages with one of the notches next to the distance scale—8, 25, or 100 ft., take your pick. Primitive? You bet, but even back then the metric equivalents of 2½, 8, and 30 "metres" were also listed.

When you consider that this No. 1 is in nearly perfect shape and that it makes eight 2¼ × 3¼ images per roll of 120 film (better tape the red window shut when you're not actually winding), you'd have to admit that it qualifies as a good buy for the user-collector. Its sole major defect: The carrying strap is long gone, but the fact that it came with the original stylus attached to the Autographic flap on the back (the old system used for recording data on

Fixed-focus elegance in a weirdly folding package, this ancient 1A's still usable, but only with Kodacolor II in 116 size.

special, discontinued pressure-sensitive film) more than makes up for it. Rare it ain't, but I'd peg the current value of this spartan beast at $15-20, and it still makes nice pictures.

Even more impressive than the No. 1 was the common-but-classic Kodak Vigilant Six-20 that came with it. This is a very sturdy folder fitted with a Flash Kodamatic Shutter with speeds of 1/10-1/200 sec. plus B and T and a 105mm f/4.5 Kodak Anaston lens with front cell focusing to 3½ ft. This lens is a rather good triplet, and the fact that it's blue coated indicates the camera is post-World War II (it was produced from '39 to '49). In addition to the usual two-position reflex finder, the Vigilant sports a flip-up optical finder with manual parallax correction on the eyepiece (a tiny knurled wheel moves the eyepiece up and down as its arrow is set to shooting distances ranging from 4 ft. to infinity). When you figure that this camera alone would fetch $25 or more in most retail establishments, I'd rather rummage for it, thank you.

Moving on to the flea market, here was a much larger event with better weather (bright sunshine) but slimmer pickings. I turned down a majestic but commonplace 2C Pocket Kodak (1926-1932) priced at a reasonable pre-haggle $7.50 because I already have two and besides it takes #130 film (providing a 2⅞ × 4⅞-in. format), which was discontinued in '59. But then my eyes focused on a curious leather-covered, folded object with a curvilinear "door," and, yes it was indeed the self-same old style No. 1A Folding Pocket Kodak so many of you inquire about. This particular version with the metal lensboard and two-position, wood-bodied reflex finder dates from 1909-1915 and (like all 1A Kodaks) it makes eight 2½ × 4¼-in. images per roll of 116 film. (Imagine shooting Kodacolor in this lovely contraption?) Its other chief claim to fame is its dual, opposed, spring-loaded side struts which still provide very

Inside the Bulls-Eye: Pointer shows one of three stops in place behind oval slit in simple rotary shutter. Round finder's on top.

rigid lens-to-film plane alignment. Adjustments are limited, with T, B and I (Instantaneous—about 1/25 sec.) shutter speeds, apertures of 1, 2, 3 and 4 (the sequence begins at f/11 if memory serves), and fixed focus. However, that f/11 lens is an achromat and it performs amazingly well if you don't expect sharp pictures of things closer than 6 ft. Pity this model lacks a tripod socket. Why do I go on like this? Because I blew my entire ten bucks on this one since it was in much better shape than the 1A I already owned—couldn't talk that old codger down any further. Oh well, I've seem similar 1A's exchange hands for more than twice that, so I'm not crying in my carrot juice.

At the first garage sale I couldn't unearth anything more interesting than a Kodak Starmite with chipped back, so I left empty-handed. The second garage, however, was attached to a rambling turn-of-the-century structure sporting a peaked roof and a "tower," and I half expected to discover a Daguerreotype camera for a hundred bucks lurking inside. No such luck, but I did find a really nice box camera that I wish were in better cosmetic shape. As you can see, it's a No. 2 Bulls-Eye Kodak, Model D, which was made from 1905-1913, and it probably got its name from the unabashedly round viewing window atop its built-in reflex finder (which obviously requires a bit of guesstimation in composing your rectangular shot).

Actually, the Bulls-Eye (no apostrophe)—which made six 3½ × 3½-in. images on #101 roll film—is prettier on the inside than it is on the outside; its wooden cabinetry is beautifully crafted. Evident in the inside view are its simple everset shutter with "T" setting override and three Waterhouse-type stops on a pivoting leaf of sheet metal. As with all cameras in this column, film is advanced with a knob using ye olde red window system. Think this basic box isn't worth too much? Actually, it qualifies as the very best buy of this whole project—it's worth about $40-50 and cost me but a deuce. Pity there's no 101 film to shoot in it.

Finally, here are the results of flea market II. Hewing once again to my "conveniently shootable" rule and ten-dollar limit, I found a mate to my No. 1 Kodak Jr., a No. 1 Pocket Kodak, which also takes 120 film and has the same limited range of shutter speeds. Like the 1A, its lens had stops of 1, 2, 3, and 4 (f/11 to f/32), and its focusing system is controlled by a screw mechanism with settings ranging from 6-100 ft. (and 2-30 meters). This cute machine, produced from the late 20's to early 30's, lacks its autographic stylus, but is still well worth the $4.00 it cost. Ditto for the 1933-1941 Kodak Six-20 Brownie which went for half that amount, twin reflex finders, art deco front plate and all. Straightforward in the extreme, it produces eight 2¼ × 3¼-in. images per roll of 620 film, has T and I shutter and two Waterhouse-type stops. Its only wrinkle is a built-in spring loaded "distance lens" providing an infinity position when left in place and a "5-10 ft. distance" when you hold the button under the lens in its right-hand position as you shoot.

As you probably surmised by now, the secret message in all of this is that you don't need to be a hardbitten camera collector or a thousandaire to enjoy a spate of photographic browsing now and then. And while you're unlikely to stumble upon a genuine bonanza, you can sometimes locate some mighty interesting and usable cameras.

Now all you need is an enlarger that accepts some of these wonderfully old-timey roll-film sizes and you're all set. As a matter of fact if you'd like to buy an old 4 × 5 Solar in perfect condition, I'm having a garage sale next week and. . . .Oh yeah, before I forget and Exaktaphiles eat me for breakfast, the official name of that early through-lens metering widget I described last time is the Ihagee Macro-Micro Photometer, not the Color Meter as I implied.

The Praktina Papers: A tale of two brilliant but ill-fated SLRs

The Praktina papers: the sad story of an advanced German SLR system that had everything going for it except the Zeitgeist.

Any mistaken notions I had that Exaktas were the poor homeless waifs of cameradom have certainly been shot to hell by the legions of loyal letters I've received in response to the Exakta saga. Indeed, the manifest shortcomings and inconveniences built into the Beasts of Dresden have apparently been transformed into lovable little quirks in the

Too far advanced? Not really, but mid-50's Praktina FX was probably the first SLR with add-on "winder."

eyes of Exaktaphiles, and such technological non-events as left-handed, 315° film-wind levers, lift-and-set shutter dials, and external auto-diaphragm couplings are praised as signs of "character" in an age of homogeneous Japanese automatons. Alas, it was not ever thus. Unscrew the rose-colored filter from your finder eyepiece and the classic Exakta emerges as a worthy and interesting machine beset with numerous foibles. And who knew them better than VEB Pentacon, their Dresden-based neighbors who brought you cheap and nasty Prakticas (an apt description

of the originals dating from the late 30's to the mid 50's, though later models were considerably improved), and brilliant but soon dated Contax D's and S's later sold under the Pentacon and Hexacon banners?

Now when the Pentacon brigade saw the even-then-old-fashioned Exaktas selling in fantastic numbers in the late 40's and early 50's it must have rankled them, even though they were theoretically socialist comrades in arms and optics. But they were at that point separate companies, if that phrase is appropriate, and Pentacon decided that a little friendly technological competition was in order. Since the Prakticas were the entry-level SLRs of their day with little pretense to great reputation, it's not surprising that Pentacon's new high-tech flagship was launched under a new masthead. But I've always wondered why it wasn't called a Contax. In fact, if Pentacon could have engineered an auto-diaphragm system and removable prism into the svelte body contours of the Contax-Pentacon-Hexacon they might have really had something 20 years ahead of its time. As it was, the new Praktina was hailed, quite justifiably, as a breakthrough since it *was* about a decade ahead of its time in terms of features.

Slide-out meter prism? Yep, but FX's was uncoupled, transfer-the-setting selenium type. Camera shown with 50mm f/2.8 semi-auto Tessar fetches about $100.

The only things that kept it from being a resounding success in this country were distribution problems on the one hand (a Byzantine succession of half-failures and joint ventures which were resolved too late in the camera's history) and an unhealthy dose of cold-war politics on the other. Being made in East Germany—the enemy camp—was bad enough back in '53; being stamped "Germany, USSR Occupied" was the *coup de grace.*

All right, I suppose that I have now painted myself into the dark corner of having to defend Praktinas—a task that's easy enough conceptually, but tougher in terms of the cameras' execution. This is a gentle way of saying that Praktinas, in this country at least, have a lousy reputation for breaking down and not being able to be fixed. Is this reputation justified? I doubt it. In the mid-50's in the U.S., Praktinas were used by the major news services, *Life* magazine, and by numerous sports photographers. And while they *were* somewhat finicky in delivering accurate slow speeds and required knowledgeable repair people to attend to their innards, Praktinas, by and large, were rugged, well-designed machines that established an enviable reputation for reliability. (I now expect to receive a sack of mail from disgruntled Praktina owners who switched to Exaktas.) And why, pray tell, would so many distinguished pros opt for a "communist" camera? Features, man, features.

Now before you start to chuckle about the "primitive" capabilities I'm about to rattle off, please bear in mind that it's 25 years ago, hardly anyone had even heard of a Japanese SLR, and most of the biggies (Nikon, Canon and Minolta, for instance) hadn't yet produced one. Enter (in 1955) the Praktina FX with breech-lock bayonet-mount lenses (with breech lock affixed to the camera rather than on the lens *a la* Canon), single non-rotating shutter-speed dial under the film-wind knob with speeds of 1-1/1000 sec. plus B, internal semi-auto diaphragm coupling, slide-off pentaprism with interchangeable screens, separate secondary optical finder for normal lenses, standard PC flash contacts, and (the *piece de resistance)* a quickly detachable spring motor winder unit! (It was actually called a motor at the time, but since it advances the film one frame at a time it falls into the present winder category.) Feature-wise, pretty impressive you'll admit, and when you add the facts that the FX was well-balanced, contoured to fit human hands and fitted with Carl Zeiss Jena lenses, you've got to admit it was a pretty good buy ($249.50 with non-meter prism and 58mm f/2 Biotar lens). A comparable Exakta listed for nearly twice as much.

Into the breech-lock mount

Operationally, the Praktina was much simpler and more straightforward than most other SLRs of its day. The large milled shutter-speed dial overhangs the front and rear of the camera's top deck, making it easy to set. The breech-lock ring is a reasonably swift and much more secure way of mounting lenses than Practica's screw or Exakta's bayonet mount (providing you don't forget to lock each lens firmly in place once you mount it), and the

semi-auto diaphragm represents a definite advance over the old manually turned preset ring or (heaven forfend) non-preset manual diaphragm of earlier optics. Never used a semi-auto lens, you say? Well, on a semi-auto lens (usually on the bottom of the barrel, so to speak) you'll find a spring-loaded diaphragm lever which returns the lens to maximum aperture when you cock it. Remove the FX's lens and, on the left-hand side of the mirror box is a spring-loaded arm with a little pin on its end. As you press the traditional angled shutter-release button, the arm and pin move forward until the pin contacts a stubby plunger on the rear of a mounted lens. When that happens the lens automatically stops down to the aperture you've set on the f/stop ring, providing you've cocked the lens, natch. By contemporary standards, the requirement that you manually cock the lens for each exposure is a pain in the butt, but it represents a decided advance and ultimately paved the way for the fully-auto diaphragm system we'll get to a bit later. For the record, the Praktina FX's controls (especially the shutter release) operate with commendable smoothness, and the standard unadorned ground-glass focusing screen provides a reasonably contrasty, albeit fairly dim, focusing and viewing image. Since there's no Fresnel lens in, on, or about the focusing screen, this is to be expected, and if you find the reflex viewing system too dim for your taste (as you might in really low light shooting situations), just move your eye about an inch to the left and you'll find a lovely, bright and clear separate optical finder that covers the field of view of a 50mm lens.

Second and last Praktina, the IIA is less common than FX, fetches considerably more dough—about $200.

Does all this strike you as painfully straightforward in these days of analog-to-digital converters, flashing LEDs and dedicated tripod sockets? Well, you can transform it into something incredibly up-to-date by simply mounting the "winder" unit, an admirably petite device that connects to the Praktina with almost breathless simplicity. Merely orient the motor's round keyway underneath a slotted key on the right side of the FX's bottom, wind the camera's film-advance knob until the key and keyway

139

mate, turn the alternately knurled locking knob on the motor's right side until it stops, and screw in a second knob that tightens a screw into the camera's tripod socket. There's nothing to remove. To take rapid-sequence pictures, wind the hefty aluminum spring-wind knob on the motor's bottom until it stops and you can now shoot up to 18 pictures in rapid succession (roughly 2 frames-per-sec. at the beginning and 1 frame-per-sec. at the end of the motor's run). Since the film is advanced only when you relax pressure on the winder's "coupled" shutter-release button, it's possible to cock the semi-auto lens diaphragm before the mirror returns to viewing position. What's more, the motor endows the Praktina with what is, in effect, an instant-return mirror—pretty zippy for a mid-50's SLR, and one of the main reasons Praktinas were so popular with sports and action photographers.

The Praktina's remaining tricks include an unhinged, removable back designed to accommodate a 250-exposure bulk film back, a prism lock curiously located under the lens barrel, and a self-timer. A long accessory list included lenses from 35 to 1250mm, an uncoupled, transfer-the-setting selenium-cell meter prism, electric motor drive, various photomicroscopic, macro and waist-level finder attachments and screens, and, yes, a rapid-wind lever that fitted to the camera body in a location familiar to Kodak Retina fans. All in all, quite a machine.

When is a winder a motor? When it's a screw-on, spring-wound Praktina motor that advances film one frame when you release shutter button. Value: about $100.

First fully auto diaphragm? No, but Praktina IIA was probably first 35mm SLR with internal, *fully auto diaphragm system, breech-lock ring affixed to body.*

In 1957, Pentacon unleashed the second (and sadly, the last) generation of the Praktina in the form of the Praktina IIA. In the lugubrious tradition of German camera development, it was practically identical to the FX except for a few minor details and one major change. The IIA had geometric shutter speeds (1/15, 1/30, 1/60 sec., etc.) in place of the FX's "old style" sequence (1/10, 1/25, 1/50 sec., etc.); it sported a single PC outlet settable for X, F, and FP sync by turning a small tab under the rewind knob to these settings, and its ASA/film-type reminder dial (also under the rewind) covered a wider range of settings.

Naturally I've saved the most momentous alteration for last—the Praktina IIA was one of the first SLRs with full-auto diaphragm action controlled internally using a pin and lever system. Mount a semi-auto lens on the IIA and you won't be able to cock the diaphragm-opening lever—the lens will remain at the f/stop set on the aperture ring. Mount a lens designed for the IIA, however, and the lens will automatically stop down to the aperture you set as you fire the shutter and will return to full aperture as you wind the film to the next exposure. Add the winder to the IIA's bottom (the couplings and motors are the same as the FX's) and (with the exception of built-in metering) it handles like one of the latest SLRs from Japan. Regrettably, the IIA's lenses would not work automatically on the FX.

In any case, whether you love 'em or hate 'em, you've got to admit that mechanically and conceptually Praktinas were exceptionally advanced and well-thought-out for their day. Had they been produced on the right side of the political railroad tracks and marketed properly they would probably have fared much better. As for their present fate, it pretty closely parallels that of the classic Exaktas, which is to say until about three or four years ago you couldn't give 'em away, much less trade or sell them for a reasonable sum. Today they're the darlings of weird photographic machinery collectors such as yours truly and I've seen them exchange hands for figures ranging from about $100-$350 depending upon model, condition and lens fitted. Like their lenses, Praktinas are often available for a song when hawked by unsuspecting owners or stores, so keep your beady, acquisitive eyes peeled.

Profuse thanks to Ken Hansen Photographic of Manhattan and to Jules Swerdlin of Exakta Camera Co., Bronxville, N.Y., for supplying equipment and information for this column. The latter specializes in repairs, lenses and accessories for Praktinas and other DDR-made cameras.

Canon Pellix: Reflections on the fixed-mirror solution

Reflections on the Pellix—a doleful tale of Canon's technically brilliant SLR that created more problems than it solved.

Lest my devoted readers erroneously conclude that the East Germans of the early to mid-50's held a patent on weird and wonderful SLRs that were none too successful in the cold, hard light of the marketplace, herewith a Japanese creation cursed with similar ill fortune. I speak of the legendary Pellix, Canon's ingenious mid-60's answer to a question nobody asked, namely, "Why can't we have a 35mm SLR with a mirror that just serenely sits there and reflects instead of flopping noisily about, causing momentary finder blackout and camera shake at slow shutter speeds?" Pretty sensible for an unuttered query, actually,

A technological tour de force *lurks within the solid but conventional looking Pellix body. Model shown is second and last QL of 1966 with 55mm f/1.2.*

and the answer is all too elementary. If a stationary mirror is fixed at a 45° angle to the lens axis to reflect the viewing image into the pentaprism above it, the accursed thing will prevent any light from reaching the film, no? Aha, but what if said mirror is a pellicle mirror that reflects about 30 percent of the light upwards through the finder eyepiece and allows roughly 70 percent of it to travel straight back to the film—wouldn't that make for a virtually vibrationless SLR without even the split-second finder darkening common to the instant-return majority?

It sure would and it sure did, but it entailed so many niggling problems, design compromises and added costs that this brilliantly executed and conceived machine bombed with such a thud that we'll probably never see its like again.

Radical metering system? You bet. Pellix had pop-up CdS cell behind mirror for semi-spot readings but you had to meter at shooting aperture.

Resembling the beautifully finished, handsome-looking Canon FX and FT of the same era, the Pellix is a more adventurous design in ways unrelated to its unique semi-transparent mirror. For example, its horizontal focal-plane shutter is made of titanium foil instead of the usual cloth, probably to obviate the possibility of direct sunlight burning a hole in the shutter—a distinct possibility due to the light-transmitting mirror. The metering system is equally clever, bearing a distinct similarity to some of the "film plane" metering systems currently in use. As you'd expect for a single-lens reflex 35 of the mid-60's, the Pellix's behind-lens CdS meter was of the stop-down variety giving readings at shooting aperture. However, when you press the combined self-timer/meter-switch lever toward the lens to turn the meter on, something fairly incredible takes place inside, behind the pellicle mirror—a ⅜ × ⅞-in. CdS cell on a hinged frame emerges from its hiding place in the bottom of the mirror box and positions itself just below the center of the film plane, about ¼ in. in front of the film. This system offers two advantages: it measures

141

light coming from (approximately) the central ⅓ of the picture area and (since the only thing cutting down the light reaching the cell is the pellicle mirror itself) it offers enhanced meter sensitivity compared to other systems using beam-splitters. Indeed, the Pellix could read down to f/1.4 at 1 sec. with ASA 400 film—pretty spiffy for 1965.

In addition to its splendid limited-area metering system, the Pellix sported a host of lovable little doodads. Turn a knurled ring around the rewind knob counterclockwise, moving the index dot from "open rectangle" to "black rectangle" settings and a blind slides in place in front of the eyepiece. This seeming frill is anything but—with a pellicle mirror, bright light entering the eyepiece can (and will) fog the film! You say you want to lock the meter on so you can change shutter speeds with your index finger rather than hold in the spring-loaded meter switch? Easy on the Pellix QL—simply push the little chrome lock button under the self-timer lever to its bottom position and *then* push the meter switch on and it'll stay put. Fumble-fingered film threaders found the second (and last) "QL" version of the Pellix a delight for another reason— it featured Canon's quick-loading system. Just pull the film leader out slightly until its end coincides with a red mark and the white sprocket teeth align with the sprocket holes, and as you close the camera back a chrome whatsis with rollers on its underside holds the film in position so it automatically affixes itself to the take-up spool as you wind. Finally, like other mid-60's Canons, the Pellix's back opens not by pulling up the rewind or sliding a catch, but by lifting and turning a D-handled knob on the camera's bottom.

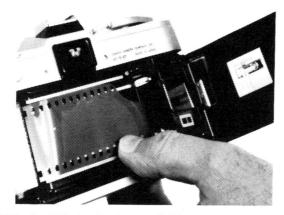

Quick loading? That's what Canon called it, and it worked—just position film carefully, close cover and wind away.

One could go on and on extolling the Pellix's virtues— its extraordinarily solid (1 lb., 10½ oz.) body, silky smooth shutter release, nicely contoured, ratcheted, 174° wind lever, etc., etc., etc., but, sadly, these are not the things that shaped its destiny. Bring the camera up to eye level, and the pedestal I've so carefully constructed begins to crumble. The Pellix's viewing image is noticeably dimmer than that of the conventionally constructed Canon FT when lenses of the same speed are mounted on both. To quote from our August, 1966 report on both models, "The Pellix

delivers approximately ⅓ of a stop less light to the film, and the finder is about ⅓ less brilliant than standard mirror SLR finders even though special care and coatings had been applied to the Pellix prism." What's worse, the out-of-focus areas in the finder have a mushy, flarey appearance with a noticeable lack of contrast. Although the on-film image was affected to a much lesser degree (about one quality grade according to our tests), photographers wondered what the Pellix was doing to their film. Wasn't it logical to assume that the viewfinder told the tale—that sharpness as well as light transmission was going to the dogs? In the end it was probably this insuperable "psychological" obstacle that spelled the camera's demise.

Clean top deck gives little inkling of anything peculiar, but eyepiece blind controlled by knurled ring under rewind knob was a must (see text). Note busy index finger making a stop-down meter reading.

That loss of light to the film played havoc in other ways, too. While the metering system reads the actual light transmission from behind the pellicle mirror and thus automatically compensates for any light lost, the same does not hold true for flash exposures, which depend on accurate f/stop settings. Canon's answer to this dilemma was necessarily imperfect due to the up-to-⅓-stop variation in light transmission from pellicle to pellicle. "Add one full f/stop exposure at any given guide number," said they. In color photography, the pellicle proved to be nearly neutral in its effect, but not quite—it had "a slight tendency toward warmth, like a mild skylight filter." Finally, the pellicle was affected by temperature extremes—in beastly hot weather in the tropics it was known to cause out-of-focus pictures due to focusing errors, and in frigid climes, pellicles occasionally tore. Oh yes, I almost forgot—while the Pellix *was* outstandingly jar-free in operation, it was not as quiet as you might expect—the titanium-bladed shutter produced a moderately loud clatter.

Despite the mounting collection of minor and serious foibles I have listed, the Pellix was undoubtedly a decent performer as well as a marvelous technical achievement. Regrettably, the price of admission ($299.95 with 50mm f/ 1.8 lens) was some $60 more than its robust, sleek and competent stablemate, the Canon FT. Back then, three C-notes was a fair pile of dough and the conventional approach carried the day. Of course, as I never neglect to mention, yesterday's marketing disasters become today's rare and valuable collectors' items. And while the Pellix's price hasn't yet taken off for the wild blue yonder, the mint-condition example pictured, with its 55mm f/1.2 Canon FL lens, is pegged at a healthy $250. Imperfect it may be, but it's a great way to astound your friends and to activate your old Canon FL lenses.

The Combat Graphic:
Oversized "35" goes to war

The Saga of the KE-4(1). Or, what happens when you design a military roll-film camera like a scaled-up rangefinder 35?

Despite their manifest deficiencies and complications, rangefinder cameras, especially those with interchangeable lenses, exude a certain indefinable sexiness. Even when compared with the leanest, most hand-holdable SLRs, a rangefinder Canon, Contax, Nikon or Leica comes off like a Ferrari among downsized Oldsmobiles, a spare, straightforward, no-frills sporting machine with few pretensions at cosseting comforts or electronic reassurances—a sleek, solid, spartan mechanism ready to interact instantly with the well-tuned digits and behind-the-eyes exposure system of the photographic connoisseur.

A technological myth feeding on bogus nostalgia? Partly. And with it the disdain for built-in exposure systems, the contempt for electronic or plastic anything, the brassed Leica hung over one shoulder on a minimal, real leather neckstrap and haunted, searching, committed eyes mimicking Bresson or Brassai. What a pity none of this tangy, gutsy mystique has ever been successfully transferred to medium-format rangefinder cameras. After all, the view-camera brigade is rife with zonal profilers and backpacking poseurs—what's wrong with 2¼ × 3¼ or even 6 × 7?

Why do I pick, of all arcane predilections, rangefinder roll-film cameras? Oh, I don't know—roll-film SLRs are just too damned serious and businesslike and scale-focusers aren't sophisticated enough to be deemed professional. Even bona fide models of the folding persuasion aren't exactly what I have in mind—too effete and delicate. The machine on which to base a viable medium-format myth must be something rugged and substantial —like (wince) a Kodak Medalist. But come to think of it, *they* never had interchangeable lenses, and their leather clad contours were a bit on the squat, dumpy side. But wait a moment, I've got just the camera. And don't snicker just because some lowbrows are wont to dismiss it as the Jolly Green Giant's Leica CL or a pocket 35 made to military specs *and* designed by a committee. The proud machine of which I speak is the Combat Graphic of 1954, also known in G.I. lingo as Camera, Still Picture KE-4 (1) made by Graflex, Inc.

In full battle dress, fearless G.I. photog wields Combat Graphic complete with bayonet-mount flash, carry strap.

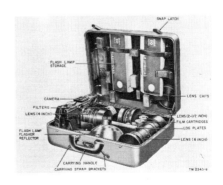

Kit and caboodle, dubbed Camera Set KS-6(1), includes wide, normal, tele lenses, caps, filters and much more.

Now it is hardly the fault of this noble government-issue picture-making creation that it arrived too late to partake in the Korean police action and had been pretty much decommissioned by the time we became ensconced in the Vietnam conflict. The Combat Graphic still has all the technical and aesthetic credentials a medium-format mythologist requires, its relative lack of actual combat service notwithstanding. It is grand, it is gargantuan, it is olive drab accented with black, and it fairly bristles with interesting features that continue to amaze, delight, and confound the enemy. So, let's back up a bit and sketch in a few details of its gestation and birth.

It all began as the brainchild of one John Maurer, an outstanding designer of compact, electric-motor-drive, 70mm aerial cameras for the U.S. Air Force. With memories of the military photographer's plight during the Second Great Unpleasantness still fresh in his mind, he went about designing the ideal combat camera—something substantially more convenient than the 4 × 5 Graphics that were most often toted, yet offering greater flexibility than the Medalist and far better image quality than the various Kodak 35s that were pressed into service. Like the eventual production version of the Combat Graphic, Maurer's elegant prototype of circa 1950 had a combined range/viewfinder and interchangeable lenses, but was more compact than the ultimate version. When this promising design was turned over to Graflex, Inc. for a production feasibility study it came under the purview of Hubert Nerwin, recently of Zeiss-Ikon in Germany and part of the Contax 35mm design team. What finally emerged about two years later was not only a paragon of structural integrity and durability, but also one of the most audacious rangefinder cameras ever produced.

Wide view setup consists of camera, 2½ in. f/4.5 Ektar lens, rear finder frame pushed forward to W.A. position.

The Combat Graphic (aka Graphic 70 in civilian dress) is basically a scaled-up classic 35 (sorta Contax-ish) that takes up to 50 2¼ × 2¾-in. images on double-perforated 70mm roll film—the kind that comes in or is loaded into 70mm Kodak cartridges (which also look like scaled-up versions of you know what). Even its bare dimensions are heroic. Its cast magnesium body is almost exactly 10 in. wide, 5 in. tall and—with the standard bayonet-mount, amber-coated, 4 in. (102mm) f/2.8 Kodak Ektar set at infinity—nearly 5¼ in. deep. All that exotic metal keeps the C.G. reasonably light at 5 lbs. even, sans film.

All controls are where you'd expect them with a few notable exceptions. The knurled, click-stopped aperture ring (with settings to f/22) is at the front of the lens, and ⅜ in. behind it is the 5/16 in.-wide knurled focusing ring which takes the 4-incher down to its 4-ft. minimum distance in a smooth, high force turn of about 330°. The 1⅝-in.-wide shutter-speed dial atop the beast also requires some hefty finger pressure to switch settings, and they're unevenly spaced with T, B, X, 1, ½, 1/5, 1/10, and 1/25 sec. bunched together in white digits and 1/50, 1/100, 1/200, and 1/500 sec. markings strung out along the periphery in red numerals. The threaded shutter release is found on the upper right-hand section of the *back* of the camera, which seems an odd location until you find that it falls nicely under your thumb when your right-hand fingers are curled around the integral finger grip on the front.

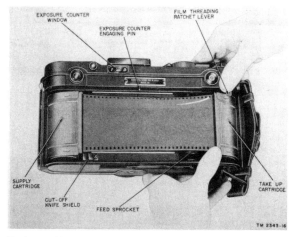

Gee, Dad, just like a 35, but C.G. features 70mm-wide film, cartridge-to-cartridge feed with cutting knife.

Two things you won't find on this military machine are a rewind knob or a film-advance lever. The former isn't required because of the cartridge-to-cartridge feed system, and there's a built-in film knife that emerges to slice off frames in mid-roll when you push a button adjacent to the finder eyepiece. Whither the winder lever? Look on the bottom of the camera and you'll find a 3-in.-long crank nestled in a little recess. Turn it clockwise about nine times and you have stored enough spring power to advance the film about an equal number of frames. Yep, the C.G. is a motor-drive camera all right. True, it won't shoot sequences—you've got to press the release separately for each shot, but the whirring sound of the large horizontal cloth focal-plane shutter firing toward the left and immediately capping itself before the film is wound left to right isn't something you'll soon forget.

Moving slightly to left of center along the camera's backside, you come to a small self-zeroing frame counter. Directly above it, atop the camera, is a flip-up frame finder that looks like something off an aerial gunsight (why not?) and has vertical parallax compensation on its rear section (settings for 4 ft., 8 ft., and infinity—take your pick). To the right of this last device is a little lever settable to "0" or "20" for flash-sync delay with electronic flash or bulbs respectively. Speaking of flash sync, the sync connector is just a tad more secure than the notoriously wimpy detach-o-matic PC socket—it's a huge 1½-in.-diameter, three-lobed bayonet connector with a pair of terminals in its middle that look like something off a heavy-duty washing machine, and it's found on the right-hand end of the camera top. On the opposite end there's a glass-covered port containing a film-wind indicator. It looks for all the world like a red and white version of the international radiation symbol, and it whirls merrily as the film is advanced.

Ready, aim, fire!

We are now set for that most delicious moment— bringing the khaki monster up to eye level. What? You say the entire finder image is a shocking orangey-pink? That's because the camera's not loaded or out of film and a translucent pink mask has come across the finder—something the photographer could not miss even in the heat of battle. Load up as per the illustration and the finder clears (as soon as film pressure turns the supply end shaft), revealing a reasonably bright, clear finder with a pale green vertical stripe down its middle and a round focusing patch in a contrasting shade of yellow smack in the center. Considering the C.G's dimensions, the finder is actually rather small, but the low magnification provides excellent eye relief if you're shooting with goggles or a gas mask. In any event, the rangefinder is very precise—with a base length approaching 4½ in. it ought to be—and the 4-in. Ektar is said by those who know and love it to be extremely sharp, delivering 40 lines-per-millimeter *on film* across the entire field at f/5.6.

Now we've already pointed out that Uncle Sam's oversize Leica had interchangeable lenses, but before we immerse ourselves in optics, let's complete its list of sundry doodads. As you'd expect there are two standard American tripod sockets—one tapped into a strengthened part of the bottom body casting just behind the lens, the second on the right side of the body, right in front of the attachment plate for the removable back. More fascinating is a little round frosted window placed in a triangular section of the front finder window bezel. Since the C.G. lacks finder framelines, what could it be? A frame numbering window, of all things! To quote from the instructions: "The exposure numbering device behind the numbering window is a numbered dial that revolves as the film advances . . . the numbering device is coupled to

a transparent film-marking dial and automatically numbers the film with number shown by the exposure counter." Whoever wrote that number should be numbered among the numbering numbskulls—but at least it's clear. The last clever gadget I'll mention is the flip-up frame finder eyepiece. Push it forward and you uncover a little inscription that says "2½ in. lens position" and it gives a rough indication of what happens when you mount the wide angle.

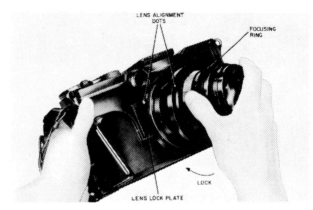

Military mount? A bayonet, natch, but rangefinder coupling is tricky (see text).

O.K., since we're lucky enough to possess the entire KS-6(1) (the Signal Corps designation for the camera, three lenses, flash gun and miscellanea, all in an olive drab Halliburton case) let's look at the lenses. To dismount the normal 4-in. Ektar, just push in the ridged portion of a giant tab next to it, turn the lens about 80° counterclockwise, and lift it out. As you do so, marvel at the three beautifully machined external bayonet lobes upon which the lens fits, and the huge spring-loaded coupling notch that engages a tab just inboard of the mount of the lens to couple the rangefinder. Although commendably positive, this system means you can't remove a lens when it's set to the closest focusing distances, and to be absolutely sure that it's rangefinder coupled when you remount it, you must turn the focusing ring to infinity.

The 7½-in.-long, 8 in. (205mm) f/4 Kodak Ektar is a fittingly monumental hunk of glass, with amber coating, click-stopped apertures to f/22 and focusing down to 8 ft. As you mount it, the Graphic's finder automatically "zooms" to tele position and the size of the viewing field shrinks slightly. Handling for such a high firepower combo can only be described as superb. By comparison the 1¾-in.-long, 2½-in. f/4.5 Ektar wide-angle seems almost petite. It's also click-stopped to f/22, focuses to 4 ft. and doesn't change the range/viewfinder field when you mount it— use the aforementioned flip-up finder method.

Well, that, friends, is the bare bones story of the Combat Graphic, a machine whose prototypes were tested to 30,000 cycles without breakdown and which served the U.S. military if not wisely, then too well. It is reported unreliably that only about 1500 of these magnificent beasties were ever made, that they cost the government about

$1,800 apiece back in the early 50's, and were eventually offered in the mid-50's for about the same price as the civilian Graphic 70—"The Most Accurate Photographic Instrument Of Our Time." G.I. photographers who actually used the thing under field conditions fall into two hostile camps—they either loved it or hated it. Given better luck and half a chance to earn its rep in a popular war, I'm sure the Combat Graphic would not only have earned its stripes, but also spawned a photographic myth to rival

that of the Leica Ms and Nikon Fs. Both as a camera and as a weapon, it could have well been *the* confrontation machine of the 60's and early 70's. But despite the slings and arrows of its outrageous fortune, it's still worth a fair pile of cash. I'd peg the outfit pictured in this column at about a grand. A Distinguished Service Cross to Ken Hansen Photographic of New York for making it available and a Good Conduct Medal to Ed Kaprelian for filling in some of its historical details.

The original Kodak camera of 1888: A test report

MODERN tests The Kodak—from a previously undiscovered manuscript found languishing in our laboratory files.

In honor of the 100th Anniversary of the Eastman Kodak Company, we will dispense with our usual banter and concentrate on a genuine antique that qualifies as one of the most significant cameras of all time—the original Kodak (that's right; no model designation) of 1888. What follows is a complete Modern Tests report as we might have published it had this magazine been in existence way back then.

THE KODAK:
A CAMERA FOR EVERY HAND

MANUFACTURER'S SPECIFICATIONS: The Kodak, fixed-focus "box camera" for 100 circular negatives 2⅝ in. in diameter on factory-loaded, factory-developed 70mm roll film. Body No. 1127. LENS: Rapid rectilinear type of unmarked aperture and focal length (test camera lens was determined to be 2¼-inch [57mm] f/9), permanently mounted in shutter and set for "universal focus." SHUTTER: Spring-loaded, rotating barrel type tensioned by pull string and ratchet mechanism, provides single speed of approximately 1/45 sec. VIEWING: No viewfinder; picture area can be estimated with reference to 60° angle lines inscribed atop camera. OTHER FEATURES: Shutter may be fired several times (six on test camera) when fully tensioned whether film is advanced or not; "open shutter" setting possible for taking interior views, etc., using procedure described in text. Camera may be forwarded to Eastman Dry Plate & Film Co., Rochester, New York for reloading and return, with resulting prints sent under separate cover (see text for details) for total cost of $10.00 pre-paid. Alternatively, film may be unloaded, reloaded and developed by the user, employing Eastman Developing Outfit (see text). PRICE: $25.00. Includes camera loaded with one 100-exposure

roll of Kodak Negative Film, leather case with carrying strap, instructional booklet and lens cover.

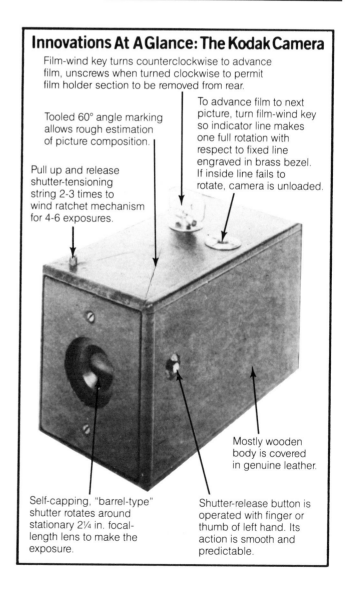

Innovations At A Glance: The Kodak Camera

Film-wind key turns counterclockwise to advance film, unscrews when turned clockwise to permit film holder section to be removed from rear.

Tooled 60° angle marking allows rough estimation of picture composition.

To advance film to next picture, turn film-wind key so indicator line makes one full rotation with respect to fixed line engraved in brass bezel. If inside line fails to rotate, camera is unloaded.

Pull up and release shutter-tensioning string 2-3 times to wind ratchet mechanism for 4-6 exposures.

Mostly wooden body is covered in genuine leather.

Self-capping, "barrel-type" shutter rotates around stationary 2¼ in. focal-length lens to make the exposure.

Shutter-release button is operated with finger or thumb of left hand. Its action is smooth and predictable.

Oftentimes, the true significance of a new invention is to be found not in the application or perfection of radically new concepts of design, but in the amalgamation of existing ideas into a form that is at once unique and more useful than any that preceded it. Such is evidently the case with the Kodak camera produced at Rochester, New York, by the Eastman Dry Plate & Film Co., in brief, an eminently portable, box-like device that bids fair to turn the entire world, and in particular both professional and common folk, into competent amateur photographers, owing to its extreme simplicity of operation. Perhaps even more important in this regard is the complete freedom the Kodak affords those who use it from entering the arcane, ill smelling, and often highly intricate realm of chemical manipulation and dark-room work associated with the photographic process itself. Indeed, to quote from the camera's principal inventor, Mr. George Eastman, in a recent statement enumerating the advantages of factory developing and printing upon which the Kodak is based, "The principle of the Kodak system is the separation of the work that any person whomsoever can do in making a photograph, from the work that only an expert can do. . . . We furnish anybody, man, woman, or child, who has sufficient intelligence to point a box straight and press a button. . . with an instrument which altogether removes from the practice of photography the necessity for exceptional facilities, or in fact, any special knowledge whatsoever."

Before we comment upon the quality of the photographic results obtained or describe the method by which the "exposures" are developed, let us examine the thoughtfully engineered, cleverly conceived mechanism that constitutes the Kodak camera. In both appearance as well as function it could hardly be more straightforward. Its basic form consists of a wooden box measuring but 6½ in. long, 3¼ in. wide, and 3¾ in. high covered in fine-grained leather. In the front is a round aperture containing the lens and shutter, and at the rear is a film magazine which slides out for removing the exposed emulsion and reloading a fresh supply. This last operation may be carried out by the factory, or by the photographer himself at his discretion, by following the clear and concise instructions supplied with the Kodak. Incidentally, the Kodak uses the selfsame Eastman Negative paper packaged in long cylindrical rolls, upon which that company has established an international reputation in conjunction with the well-known Eastman Walker roll-holder. Consequently, the reloading procedure need be carried out only after 100 pictures have been made! (or sooner, if so desired, by cutting off the exposed portion and re-threading the film magazine).

Undoubtedly the capability of making such an extensive number of pictures without refilling the camera will prove a boon to foreign travelers as well as those in diverse scientific and commercial vocations, but what is even more remarkable is the way in which the controls of the Kodak have been conceived to eliminate virtually any possibility of error. To arm the shutter for instanteous exposures one simply pulls a string gently upwards and re-

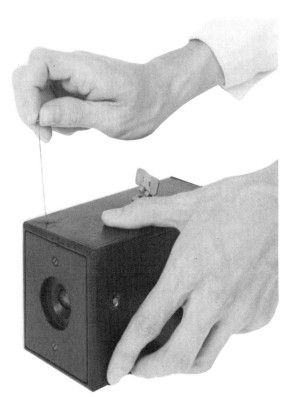

Tensioning the shutter mechanism. Upon pulling and releasing the string a few times, the shutter is set to make approximately five exposures.

leases it, repeating this operation two or three times. The shutter is now set to make five or six exposures before it need be tensioned once again. To make an instantaneous picture in bright sunlight one merely holds the Kodak firmly in both hands, aims it level to the main subject or subjects to be photographed, and gently presses the shutter button with the thumb of the left hand. Once the "click" is heard the exposure has been made and it is imperative to wind a hinged key atop the camera in a counterclockwise direction immediately, so the area of the emulsion that has been exposed to light is moved away from its position directly behind the lens and a fresh (unexposed) section of film takes its place. The precise amount of winding required is easily judged by observing the motion of a line on a circle within a brass bezel adjacent to the winding key. One full rotation of the moving line with respect to a fixed line engraved on the bezel indicates that the sensitized paper film has moved only as much as required to prepare the camera to take the next picture. Even spacing of the pictures on the roll is assured by the fact that the above-mentioned rotating indicator is affixed to a roller in the magazine that makes direct physical contact with the film as it moves through the camera.

In analyzing the elements that make up the Kodak system, it will at once be seen that the entire camera mechanism and each of its component parts has been executed with a commendable single-mindedness of purpose, and this will doubtless prove to be the main reason for its success in the marketplace. While neither the use of paper rolls coated with light-sensitive emulsion nor the idea of building a roll-holder into a camera is entirely new (the latter having been described by Professor E. Stebbing at the Societé Francaise de Photographie some five years ago), the way in which these have been integrated into a fool-proof, compact, rugged design is truly extraordinary.

Various component parts of the Kodak shown after disassembly. (The identity of several of these will already be evident.) At upper right, exposure button; at middle right, shutter spring; in middle foreground, shutter-tensioning cord and pulley; in left foreground, shutter-ratchet pinions.

Actually, the only part of the Kodak camera that can be accurately described as technically unique is its shutter, which consists of a brass cylinder with two opposing rectangular aperatures cut into the center of its curved surface. When the button is pressed to take a picture, this cylinder pivots around the lens affixed within it at 90° to its axis of rotation, so that the two rectangular apertures simultaneously pass by the front and rear portions of the lens respectively, allowing sufficient light through to make the exposure. The escapement mechanism is so arranged that once the exposure has been made, the shutter cylinder continues to revolve further, until its opaque areas cover the front and rear of the lens. In other words, this is a self-capping shutter of the "barrel" type which rotates in a single direction.

Equally ingenious is the simple pawl-and-ratchet mechanism situated on the right side of the shutter which tensions an easily replaceable common watch spring as you operate the string. Lest it be objected that Mr. Eastman's ingenuity neglected to provide an "open-shutter" setting for the recording of interior views or stationary subjects outdoors under unfavorable conditions, this is easily accomplished by pressing the button several times until the shutter runs down (while the front of the camera is held pressed against a dark-colored piece of clothing to prevent light striking the film) then gently flicking open the aperture with a fingernail if required, and immediately covering the lens opening with the circular cap provided. Once the shutter is open, interior views are recorded by placing the camera on a firm support and removing and replacing the "lens cover" in accordance with very com-

prehensive instructions on indoor exposures listed in the Kodak booklet that accompanies each camera.

Yet another vexation that has been lifted from the shoulders of Kodak users by the cleverness of its design is the need to focus the image. The optimum point of sharp focus is precisely set at the factory, then tested as regards

Shutter mechanism in situ with tensioning cord visible. Note ratchet-toothed mechanism affixed to side of shutter "barrel."

actual performance at close, medium and far distances before the camera leaves the works. While knowledgeable photographers may commend such care in preparing so simple a machine for use by the general public, many may protest that the so-called "fixed focus" camera already exists and hardly constitutes anything original, much less particularly desirable. To this we must reply that the elimination of focusing has here been achieved not only in a manner much in keeping with Kodak philosophy, if we may use that exalted term, but also with careful attention to scientific principles. Indeed, the logic followed by Mr. Eastman and his associates in carrying forth the design of the Kodak seems, at least in retrospect, to follow inescapably with syllogistic rigor. If one presumes that the exterior dimensions of the Kodak are limited by practical considerations of portability, then the size of the image, and the emulsion on which to record it have already been largely pre-determined. If one further assumes that the shutter exposes the film in approximately 1/50th part of a second in bright sunlight (this figure having been chosen to eliminate the adverse effects of very slight subject and camera movement while the exposure is being made), one has simultaneously determined the effective aperture of the lens within rather narrow limits. Bearing in mind the sensitivity to light of Eastman Negative Film, the diameter of the lens must therefore be about one-eighth the lens-to-emulsion distance (that is, a value of 4 in the Uniform System, or f/8 in the most common European system). But how is it then possible to achieve a set-focus lens of so wide an aperture that remains capable of providing sharp pictures over the widest possible range of subject distances? The answer lies in keeping the focal length of the lens as small as possible in the interest of maximizing depth-of-focus. The result of these last-mentioned factors combined is that the Kodak tested at our laboratory did indeed provide instantaneous photographs of excellent quality in bright sunlight, with the actual exposure quite close to these nominal values of U.S. 4 at 1/50 sec. In addition, we ascertained that the Kodak was capable of producing well-defined pictures at distances ranging from slightly under 4 ft. to 50 ft. and beyond.

These splendid results have undoubtedly been made possible by the use of a lens of surpassingly short focal length (just over 2¼ in.) which has a 60⁰ angle of view with respect to the subject pictured. Furthermore, this lens is indirectly responsible for endowing the Kodak with a very singular pair of characteristics. Firstly, a camera covering such a wide field scarcely needs a viewfinder if it is aimed with reasonable care and kept level to eliminate perspectival distortions of the subject, and so the Kodak has none, save for a 60⁰ angular marking tooled into the top of the camera, (toward the front) to serve the photographer as a rough guide. Secondly, since the lens is, according to the Eastman Company, of Rapid Rectilinear

The wooden housing which contains the cylindrical metal shutter is clearly visible once the front cover and the mechanism itself have been removed.

design (a pair of symmetrically disposed achromatic lenses with an air space in between them) and the extremely wide imaging angle would ordinarily make for quite poor definition in the extreme corners of the image field, Mr. Eastman decided to get around this dilemma in the simplest, most direct fashion by eliminating the ill-defined corner images entirely, creating a circular picture area just over 2½ in. in diameter on each "negative." This is achieved by the expedient of affixing a circular metal mask to the front of the roll-holder magazine and causing the image-forming negative paper to run under it, thereby causing it to be held reasonably flat.

This brings us to the magazine itself, a fitment based in large measure on the Eastman Company's extensive experience with the highly successful Eastman-Walker roll-

holder for plate cameras. Should the user wish to unload and re-load the Kodak himself, this is easily accomplished by following Part 2 of the Booklet accompanying the camera entitled "Refilling The Kodak." However, this is not ordinarily required owing both to the large number of exposures per roll and to the fact that most users, particularly novices, prefer to return the camera to the works, thus being "relieved of all work connected with the taking of pictures, except merely making the exposure."

The actual re-loading procedure requires, in addition to an extra spool of Kodak Film and an extra reel, an Eastman Orange Candle Lamp (essentially a common candle lamp with a close fitting translucent orange shade) and a dark room having a shelf or table. To explicate its mode of functioning let us proceed with opening the camera. In order that the magazine may be removed one first turns the winding key in a clockwise direction (that is, the opposite direction from film winding) until the key completely unscrews from the camera and may be lifted off. Now the back end of the camera is firmly grasped with one's fingers and the magazine is pulled back away from the main body of the camera. It will now be evident that the wooden magazine incorporates no less than five wooden rollers, all of which revolve on metal shafts. The two smallest rollers are situated on either side of the circular film aperture to ensure that the film winds smoothly as it traverses the image plane. The roller placed farthest from the camera back is the "film supply" roller. It is easily removable by orienting its top-retaining clip so that one of its straight sides is parallel with the camera back, then pulling the clip out and removing the roller. This roller is supplied with a spring-loaded friction-type tensioning device on its lower end to keep the film under tension as it is wound onto the take-up spool, thereby ensuring that it lies flat in the film aperture whence it is exposed. This is of vital concern, for any buckling at this point could easily result in improperly focused pictures.

Once a fresh roll of film is inserted with its emulsion side facing outwards, toward the left side of the magazine, the film is threaded over the film-spacing roller, the (narrow) "film plane" roller, and under the circular film aperture. The film-spacing roller incorporates two sharp pins which notch the film as it passes through the camera (so that individual exposures may later be cut and developed without risk of cutting a picture in the middle!) and atop this roller is the rotating part of the exposure-spacing device previously described in conjunction with film winding. Once the film has passed over the second narrow "film plane" roller, its end is firmly attached to the final or "film take-up" roller by means of an integral bar-type catch. This last roller is connected directly to the winding key when the camera is assembled, and it is ratchetted to rotate only in a counterclockwise direction. Since the film is firmly affixed to the roller on which it is supplied, it is quite easy to know when one has exposed the entire roll of film; the winding key simply cannot be turned. We commend the Kodak magazine to the study of engineers as an example of a mechanism of almost breathtaking sim-

149

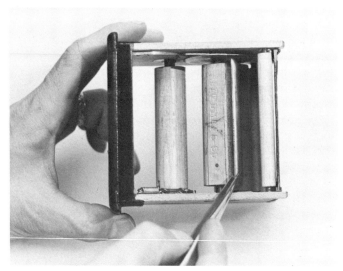

This roller, which incorporates a film-retaining bar, moves the film through the magazine as the key (not shown) is wound.

Detail view of film magazine interior shows that roller which holds the unexposed roll of film in place. The pointer indicates the spring-loaded friction mechanism at the bottom of this roller which assures that proper film tension is maintained.

plicity which nevertheless fulfills a highly complex set of functions.

Frankly we are loath to cast too jaundiced an eye on so intelligently conceived and punctiliously executed a camera as Mr. Eastman's Kodak, lest our carping be taken out of context by others or magnified out of all proportion in subsequent quotation. In general, if we judge it rightly, this humble, simple, picture-taking machine is intended to bring the joys of photography to the multitudes of ordinary citizens throughout the world, and in so doing to shake the very foundations of photographic art and science as we know them. However, in the interest of advancing and perfecting what is acknowledged to be a very great invention, perhaps a few critical remarks here are not out of place. To those experienced in the photographic arts, the absence of a ground-glass or other form of direct vision or optical finder on the Kodak may seem a retrograde step; an over-simplification. However, we must report emphatically that this is not the case. Each of the several members of this publication's staff who used the Kodak quickly accustomed himself to pointing it properly, and the wide viewing angle of the lens fitted allows sufficient latitude in aiming, especially if the angular line engraved upon the camera is used for sighting. However, when taking indoor views we were not always able to find a table, chair, or pedestal of the correct height on which to rest the Kodak and would recommend that a standard American ¼-inch tripod socket be incorporated in the bottom of the camera to afford maximum flexibility in this regard. Then there is the matter of the shutter mechanism. When our Kodak was pointed directly toward the sun (as it might inadvertently be when carried outdoors without its case for example), with direct sunlight impinging upon the shutter "barrel," we found that it was

occasionally possible for enough light to pass around the edges of the closed shutter to fog one or more negatives. We respectfully suggest that the Eastman Company consider fitting the Kodak with a shutter of the self-capping "rotary sector" type presently found on several inexpensive European and American plate cameras. This simple mechanism is not only reliable and perfectly light-tight under all conditions, it also permits the facile incorporation of an "open shutter" setting by the expedient of pulling upwards on a shaft that arrests the blade in the open position, and it is evidently possible to design an "everset" version which is always ready to fire and need not be separately tensioned. Not the least advantage of shutters of the above-mentioned type is their extremely low cost of manufacture.

Finally, if we may be permitted to enlarge upon our comments concerning the optical qualities of the lens fit-

The Kodak lens in its shutter, held in place for viewing on the optical bench. By observing the image of a point light source that has passed through the lens, with a microscope of modest power, certain of its image-forming characteristics may be ascertained.

ted to the Kodak, herewith an amplification of our previous remarks. The inherent image-forming characteristics of this lens are in every way satisfactory, and eminently suited to the task of general picture taking without the burdensome necessity of focusing upon the subject, the most pleasing and lifelike renditions having been obtained when we meticulously followed the maker's instructions to "place the subject such that bright midday sunlight falls upon the most important parts to be recorded with the sun situated behind the photographer's shoulder." As was therefore to be expected, photographs taken *contre-jour* with sunlight falling directly upon the lens and shutter exhibited much inferior tonal qualities and indeed could be described as having a muddy or "lackluster" appearance. Likewise, pictures taken in cloudy or hazy weather with the sun partially or wholly obscured may also be descibed as appearing flat or dull.

As the above descriptions largely apply to the effects wrought by changes in light upon the final "positive" image, the following analysis of the optical properties of the Kodak may also prove useful for those more experienced in the photographic arts in respect to image definition per se or what is termed in the common parlance, "sharpness," the Kodak lens cannot be said to equal the crisp, finely detailed results obtainable with the finest European and American cameras having a full complement of adjustments (such as an iris diaphragm and facility for focusing). Of course this could hardly be expected in a "machine" with so universal an application. In particular, prints of identical size to the negative (produced by main-

Street scene with major subject (pushcart) at 6-ft. distance shows good definition except at the forward edges of the picture. Note moderate perspectival distortion in buildings resulting from pointing the Kodak slightly upwards.

taining direct contact with the emulsion and the positive paper) exhibit quite reasonable definition of all parts of the picture, and even modest enlargements of, say two to three diameters, are in many cases suitable for exhibition.

This New York street scene includes unposed walking subjects "stopped" by Kodak's instantaneous shutter speed of nearly 1/50 sec. Note that the range of clear definition extends from quite near camera all the way to "infinity."

However, attempting to enlarge Kodak negatives to dimensions beyond this may show areas toward the circumference of the picture to become progressively softer looking and may not bear favorable comparison with photographs produced using a higher grade or class of apparatus, or accommodating significantly larger plates

In conclusion, let us leave the subject of the Kodak itself and consider for a moment the Kodak system of which it is so fundamental a part. In consequence of a most prolific and well-executed advertising campaign which has captured the popular imagination to an unprecedented degree, most well-informed Americans are now familiar with the Kodak slogan, "You press the button; we do the rest" and the fact that the Kodak is ordinarily posted directly to the Eastman Company for unloading ahd reloading with fresh film. We are pleased to report that upon dispatching our Kodak to the works via express the freshly loaded and sealed camera was returned to us in only five days by return post, and it being winter, our finished pictures arrived exactly one week later. In consequence of our experimentation with exposures for indoor scenes only 88 of the pictures on the roll were judged to be printable, and we received duplicated prints of others to total a full complement of 100 photographs. While the cost for this prompt service, $10.00 payable in advance, may be judged sufficient to deter poorer elements among the working class from taking up the avocation of photography, it is nonetheless appealing to a very wide segment of the populace at large and compares most favorably with the cost of portraits made by itinerant photographers or those with studio facilities.

Those undertaking their own developing and finishing work will doubtless find Kodak films expedient to work with, as the manipulations required can be easily mastered with some small effort and the Kodak instructional booklet is most lucid in its descriptions of what is required. Indeed, a sample finished film negative accompanies each Developing Outfit so the user thereof may easily judge the success of his efforts. Herewith, a brief description of the developing procedure. Once the film has been removed from the camera in a dark room illuminated solely by an Eastman Orange Candle Lamp, the film roll is cut into individual pictures along every second perforation on the film edge, soaked thoroughly in water and then developed until all action of the developer ceases. Then the "negatives" are transferred to a tray of clean water, and subsequently "fixed" in a solution of hyposulphite of soda which dissolves away that part of the silver where the light of the image has not penetrated, leaving the negative film clear in those portions. The emulsion itself must now be transferred from the more-or-less opaque paper to a perfectly transparent support, a glass plate specifically prepared for this purpose with a solution of liquor ammonia and methylated spirits, and then carefully coated with rubber and collodion. The emulsion is then very gently transferred to the glass, rendered flat with a squeegee, and the paper is stripped off the back of the emulsion after soaking in hot water. Finally, a gelatin skin and a final coat of collodion are applied to protect the delicate emulsion, rendering it suitable for making positive prints. In summary the finished negative "consists of a very thin image-bearing film supported on the gelatin skin and enclosed between two films of collodion varnish, which renders the negatives impervious to changes of the atmosphere."

It will be clear from the above that development of Kodak negatives should not pose an insuperable task for

The Kodak with its accoutrements. On the left, the leather carrying case with strap. In the foreground, the lens cover with its grasping ring. Kindly note that the Kodak shutter is shown here in the open position and that the angular sighting lines atop the camera are clearly visible.

those familiar with such laboratory work and, in fact, the entire process compares quite favorably with present-day dry plates in respect to the total dark-room work required. It will be equally evident to discerning observers of photography's expanding horizons that the true merit and significance of the little Kodak is not to be found in the shrouded obscurity of the dark room, but rather in the brilliant sunshine of the world's streets, fields and byways where multitudes of ordinary persons with no special aptitude or training will set forth to capture and preserve their most cherished memories.

Three British Ensigns and an odd Czech

A salute to three British Ensigns running the technological gamut plus an odd Czech just for fun.

I thought, as long as I was flying to Cologne, Germany, to cover the massive Photokina show, why not first pop over to the land of the rising pound to ogle at some British collectibles? And so, having de-planed at London's Heathrow airport, I took the tube (less bread, no jam said they)straightaway(more or less) for Tottenham Court Rd., home of the world's most expensive YMCA ($42 a day) and Morgan Camera Co., your classically understated olde English camera emporium.

Gorgeous it ain't, but the terribly British Ful-Vue focuses down to 2 ft.!

Having carefully developed a nodding acquaintance with the manager thereof, one Robert Kicklin, hereinafter referred to as Bob, I just breezed into his establishment one morning brash American style, grabbed his hand and exclaimed "Hi, Bob, how're things going in the decrepit—er, classic—camera biz?" After a lengthy, invective-punctuated dissertation on the evils of the Value Added Tax (which sadly, even applies to ancient cameras sold in the U.K. at an inflationary 15 percent rate) Bob admitted that sales of our treasured photographic relics had fallen off noticeably compared to the fever pitch of a couple of years ago. I reminded him that there was indeed a worldwide recession on, and that the situation was pretty much the same on our side of the pond. As usual in these cockeyed times, lower demand has seemingly pushed prices even higher, which would have distressed John Maynard Keynes, not to mention Adam Smith. One example: A clean, functional Komaflex S (a nice Japanese, fixed-lens SLR of the early to mid-60's that took 4 × 4 cm images on 127 film) was being flogged to the tune of £65 or just under $160, about twice the U.S. asking price.

But the purpose of my diversion to London (that's English for detour) wasn't to snipe at Morgan's prices for seedy Leicas and Japanese classics-to-be; I wanted to examine some distinctively English machinery and to detail its delights and follies. I wasn't disappointed, for the place was rife with curious British beasties of every description. This time we'll concentrate on Her majesty's royal roll-film classics, adding, just for fun, one modest but lovable "focusing box camera" from Prague.

Egad! A focusing gap!

Let's commence these festivities with a small, crinkle-finished, 2¼ × 2¼ in.-format, box camera that only an Englishman could love, the very British Ensign Ful-Vue which gets its name from the large, bright reflex finder perched atop its taking lens. While the finder elicits few complaints, this camera's appearance is decidedly dumpy, in the manner of certain British motorcars of the 50's (the Wollesley and Singer Gazelle come to mind) and its pressed sheet metal body is—well—tinny. I don't mean to imply that the Ful-Vue is fragile—far from it—and it certainly focuses closer than most box cameras. Turn the chrome front lens ring and you can select three footage ranges, marked 2, 3-5, and 6∞ respectively. Please don't ask me what to do if your subject is between 5 and 6 ft. away! In any event, the left side of the camera comes off, revealing a well-designed sheet metal film holder insert for 120 film which is a bit fiddly to re-install, and the everset shutter (push upwards to take the shot) offers T (time) and I (instantaneous settings). Simple, sort of crude, but cute. Well, what did you expect for a fiver (£5, that is).

Staying with the same film and the same era of British cameradom, but moving upward umpteen levels in sophistication, we now present the Ensign Commando (nice to have a model name instead of numbers and/or letters), one of the classiest and cleverest rangefinder roll-film cameras ever. To begin with, it offers two formats on 120 film—6 × 6cm (2¼ square) and 6 × 4.5cm (2¼ × 1⅝) and the viewfinder shifts from one format to the other by means of a little sliding control in between the range/viewfinder windows. After you position the first frame (using the ever-popular ruby windows with sliding cover) the film will automatically stop at the next frame as you turn the film-wind knob, and the shutter cannot be fired a second time until the film is wound to the next frame. The first of these useful traits is achieved using a curious looking, external spring-loaded gizmo found at the base of the knurled film-wind knob.

A rugged Commando? You bet, and specs are high-tech, too. Combined range/viewfinder's good; focusing system's odd.

As you can probably judge from its portrait, the Commando is very nicely finished, and I can assure you that it's also extremely rugged (and heavy) for a camera of its type. Particularly commendable is the very rigid front standard, which is after all, easier to attain in a film-plane-focusing folder. That's right chaps, this camera focuses its coated 75mm f/3.5 Ensar Anastigmat lens down to about 5 ft. by rotating the focusing knob on its upper left-hand corner which moves the film plane (and film) closer to or farther away from the stationary lens (shades of the Mamiya Six). Other oddities? The counter counts (alas only to 11 with 2¼-square format) as you press the shutter button, there are bottom rollers *and* rollers at the film plane in each spool cavity, and the British-made Epsilon leaf shutter has speeds of 1-1/300 sec. plus B and is fitted with a PC flash sync outlet. Did I say Morgan's was high-priced? Not on British stuff. This eminently usable collectors' item was tagged at £40 (just under a C-note).

Still sticking with the British Ensign trademark (nautical nation y'know) but moving backwards in time to The Great War (aka WWI), we have here one of the prettiest scale-focusing roll-film folders I've ever seen—the Ensign

Carbine Tropical. For the record, an ensign is more or less the naval equivalent of a second lieutenant and "tropical" describes a species of (usually high class) camera having as little leather trim as possible. Usually this meant substituting teak or other wooden bodies for leather clad ones which rot in tropical heat and humidity (there's not much that could be done about leather bellows since there was no plastic equivalent at the time). However, the Carbine represents the alternative approach—its all-metal body is finished in gloriously rich-looking burnished copper and its bellows is described as "Russian leather."

Spartan elegance personified, this Ensign Carbine of WWI era was designed for duty in the humid tropics.

Both camera and Mulchro leaf shutter (which offers settings of T, B and 1-1/100 sec.) are clearly labelled "Made in England by the Houghton-Butcher Mfg. Co. Ltd., London" and the lens is a 4 in. Aldis Uno Anastigmat with stops down to f/23! To focus (down to 6 ft.) you simply pull out the very rigid front standard to operating position and fine focus by means of geared arm on the right side of the bed. Another indication that this is a top-line model is found in its rising front, operating via another geared arm which must be flipped up before you fold the camera shut. As you can see, the Commando sports two finders—a tiny reflex job above the lens and a wire-frame type with a slide-up rear sight (not shown) just like a bullet-firing carbine.

I almost forgot to tell you—the Carbine shoots eight 2¼ × 3¼-in. negs per roll of 120 film and its performance is said to be very good even by modern standards. Granted

it's not much of a technical tour de force, but each of its details—like the geared lateral movement of the front standard controlled by a small milled wheel—exudes thoughtful craftsmanship. Incidentally, these subtle old world touches (in near-mint condition, I might add) will set you back a cool £65 (about $160)—quite a bit for a scale-focusing folder.

What better way to conclude this sojourn than with a funny Czech. Why do I chuckle? Probably because the

No bum Czech, Prague-made Druex sports streamlined post-art-deco styling reminiscent of 50's Kodaks.

Prague-made Druex resembles so many Kodak cameras of the same era (late 50's?) and its 75mm f/6.3 (to f/22) lens is labelled Druopta Praha Druoptar which sounds like a Latin motto gone wrong. Kidding aside, it's a functional little beast with nicely finished plastic body, front-cell focusing system (1 meter to infinity) and 2¼-square format on 120 roll film. Shutter speeds are 1/25, 1/50 and 1/100 sec. and the everset shutter is called (what else?) a Druo. Its back comes off for film loading, its pop-up optical finder is really quite decent, and it's got a covered red window on its backside. All this and post-art deco styling too for a paltry 17 bucks? Well, there is the little matter of plane fare.

Collecting weird, offbeat cameras: Edinex, Wirgin TLR, Ricohflex, Zorki

How to have fun collecting peculiar, offbeat and even weird cameras without squandering lots of moolah, dough, scratch, etc.

Although I am a non-conformist by temperament and intellectual conviction (my motto is that "fifty million Frenchmen can't be right"), this month I will defer to the publisher's wishes and the none-too-subtle proddings of our staff and write a "how-to" column for this "how-to" issue. Faithful followers of these desultory scribblings already know that my tastes in photographica run from plebeian to posh, so it will come as no surprise that the motley collection of cameras herein have two things—no, actually three things in common now that I think of it— they're all a bit strange, they're all affordable by all but the most impecunious collector, and none of them is likely to appreciate in value rapidly enough to be considered an investment. In short, hedgers against inflation need read no further—this column is for folks who just want to have fun.

as that (unlike leather-clad metal cameras) would resist the ravages of mildew and moisture encountered on sojourns to the tropics. But, snob appeal swiftly transformed these handsome folders into a fashionable (and expensive) bourgeois alternative.

Enter the Wirgins—Joseph, an engineer, Henry, a medical student, "Doc" (nee Max), a chemist, and Wolf, who became the company's accountant. The first pair of Wirgins decided that Ernemann, Contessa-Nettel, Voigtlander et al, had been cashing in on the tropical plate camera craze for long enough—so they founded the Wirgin factory, which turned out tropicals for about 25-35 percent less than the industry giants, buying lenses, shutters, etc., from the then-flourishing independent German camera component manufacturers. "Doc" was a good salesman (he eventually represented the firm in the U.S.), the product was successful, and, following the same "cut-rate" theme, the brothers decided that if Leitz could sell this newfangled miniature known as a Leica for $75-100, they

Poor man's Leica? Sorta. What late-30's Adox lacked was helicoid focusing.

More, but less. Edinex III of mid-50's got features, lost elegant simplicity.

By pure happenstance, three of these "fun machines" happen to be products of the Wirgin factory of Wiesbaden, West Germany, so let's say a few words about the brothers Wirgin and how they got started in the camera biz. It seems that back in 1923 or thereabouts, one of the more popular high-priced camera types was known as the "tropical" plate camera, usually distinguished by having bodies made of teak or other fine-grained hardwoods. The original notion was to furnish the upper crust with camer-

could sell a poor man's version for a sawbuck. Which brings us to the Edinex 35, also successfully marketed under the Adox and Midget Marvel monikers.

Our particular model appears under the Adox banner, dates from about 1937, and qualifies as almost top-of-the-line with its Compur-Rapid 1-1/500 sec. (plus B) shutter and front-cell-focusing 50mm f/2.8 (to f/16) Schneider Xenar lens. The cheapie version, sold at a blistering $9.95, had a three-element, 50mm f/4.5 Wirginar lens with three-speed (1/25-1/100 sec. plus B) Vario shutter; and the super-deluxe model featured a 50mm f/2 Schneider Xenon lens in Compur-Rapid shutter. Regardless of the shutter and optics, the original scale-focusing Edinex did indeed qualify as a proletarian Leica in many of its basic specs— it had a one-piece cast-alloy body shell with removable baseplate, a collapsible lens using a "tube" system like the classic 50mm f/3.5 Elmar, and it was adorned with a small but clear plain optical finder and a receptacle for vertically attaching a non-coupled rangefinder (yes, you can find a similar item on certain early Leicas, notably the "A"). Even the leaf shutter-cum-lens unit mounted on the front end of the collapsible tube was not entirely un-Leicalike —the legendary (and now horrendously overpriced) Compur-shuttered Leica B had a similar arrangement (albeit with helicoid instead of front-cell focusing).

Non-Leitzified features also abound. While the Edinex of the 30's loads in classic Leica fashion, it has a semi-auto rather than fully-auto frame spacing system—you've got to push a milled wheel next to the additive, manually-set frame counter in a clockwise direction (it springs back) before you wind the film to the next frame. Obviously, this means that the shutter cocking and firing are independent of film winding, and there's nothing to prevent forgetful photographers from making blank or double exposures. Curiously, the rewind control (a dial) is located to the left of the finder next to the rewind knob, and there's a slotted, removable screw cap on the camera back, directly in line with the lens axis. Its function? As near as I can tell, it's a "bore sight" enabling you to check the lens for general cleanliness and (using a thin, translucent sheet of paper) its focus as well. Finally, the Edinex features nicely textured "ears" on the sides of the lens to facilitate pulling it out to shooting position and locking it in place, and for your $25 (with Xenar lens, Compur-Rapid shutter) you got rather nicely finished nickel-plated "brightwork." Withal, the original Edinex remains remarkably spartan and doodadless, a major part of its charm. All in all, not bad for 75 inflated bucks, and that uncoated Xenar is a good picture taker even by comtemporary standards.

Everything you always wanted?

Without going into the typically leisurely evolution of the Edinex, let's recap the whole bit by the handy expedient of examining a late postwar model III dating from the mid-50's. As you'll see, it's a classic case of getting everything you asked for but liking it less. True, our Edinex III is fitted with a mediocre 50mm f/2.8 Steinheil Cassar lens (a triplet) in a pedestrian Prontor-S (1-1/300 sec. plus B and self-timer) shutter, but these are the least of its problems. Again, the super-deluxe version sported the infinitely preferable 50mm f/2 Xenon/Synchro-Compur combo.

The major developments incorporated into late model Edinexes are five biggies intended to bring the no-frills beastie into serious contention without sacrificing its svelte charms. The list includes a coupled range/viewfind-er, helicoid focusing, automatic film stop with double- and blank-exposure prevention, flash sync, and a removable back section to facilitate film loading. Unfortunately, while the rangefinder is adequate, with an easy-to-see pinkish circular focusing patch, the viewfinder isn't nearly as bright and clear as the original. The removable back section, while handy, is a tinny-looking sheet-metal plate that fits into a rectangular aperture cut into the die-cast back, and its simple sliding lock is not very confidence-inspiring. I have no quarrel with the other improvements, particularly the very smooth focusing helical which gets the collapsible lens down to its 3 ft. minimum distance in an amazingly long 260° (or so) turn and has a convenient milled focusing ring in addition to a nice big focusing tab.

The price of sophistication

Amazingly, the collapsed depth of the Model III increased by only 3/16 in. but this, alas, along with a 5-oz. weight gain (to just under 20 oz.) is enough to spoil its virtues as a trousers-pocket 35. Incidentally, the III retains the original removable baseplate for loading, its rewind control (clutch) has been moved to a conventional location next to the wind knob, and it provides the choice of two shutter releases—a body shutter release on top (which can't be fired until the film has been advanced) and a funky little auxiliary release on the back, right side of the lens/shutter unit (convenient for intentional double exposures). The shutter, as always, must be manually cocked.

Despite my personal preference for the "purity" of the 30's model, which harkens back to small-as-possible 35s of the 20's, I must concede that the Wirgin design team, whoever they may have been, did a creditable job of bringing the Edinex up to date. In fact, if you can snare one with a better lens (a Schneider Xenar, for example) in good nick, I think a C-note or a bit less is a fair price.

To round out our Wirgin section, herewith a pretty disastrous but entertaining product of the Wiesbaden works, the Wirgin TLR of the mid-1930's. To get some of the evil stuff out of the way first, the taking lens is a 75mm f/4.5 E. Ludwig Victar, one of the least inspired triplets of all time, and the shutter is an everset leaf type with speeds of 1/25, 1/50, 1/75 and 1/100 sec. plus T and B. Focusing is by a curious system of pivots and levers connecting the single-helical taking and viewing (an identical Victar!) lenses and controlled by a lever moving in a vertical channel on the camera's left-hand side. Actually the mechanics of the focusing system are simple and almost elegant, but the focusing image is miserably murky, and that's being charitable.

Granted, the reflex mirror in our particular sample is not in pristine shape, but even so, the finder can never have been better than barely adequate.

Perhaps the most curious feature of this machine is its cute little non-coupled extinction meter just above the taking lens. It's adorned with the Wirgin nameplate and has a small rotating tab on its left side to set it for two different film speeds. As all such devices it uses a step wedge through which you read numbers and set the camera controls accordingly. In this case, the lower the number that is clearly visible, the brighter the light—the exposure conversion table conveniently affixed to the right-hand flap of the focusing hood inexplicably includes f/stops down

Matched lousy lenses? Wirgin TLR's pair of E. Ludwig Victars certainly qualify.

to f/2.8 and shutter speeds to 1/1000 sec. Additional oddities include the removable back and the frame counter. The former slides off by pushing upwards on two tablike locks on the sides of the camera, pulling the film-wind knob out and pulling the back off; the latter consists of a circular set of numbers (1 to 12 as is usual with 12-on-120-film cameras) around the wind knob. There's no red window on the Wirgin's backside, and no geared spacing mechanism on the film wind, but when you peruse the numerical array, the plot becomes clear—the spacing between successive digits decreases progressively to allow for the ever-increasing diameter of the take-up spool as more and more film and paper are wound on, and there's an index dot on the wind knob so you'll know how far you've wound it. Obviously, the potential for disaster is high with this primitive setup, but you've got to give it high marks for ingenuity. How can you be sure that the first frame is properly positioned, you ask? Those clever devils in Wiesbaden put a red window on the camera's bottom, next to the tripod socket! As you can appreciate, I cannot commend the Wirgin TLR to the user-collectors of this world, but if your taste runs to low-buck rarities, you can collar a Wirgin TLR (if you can find one) for approximately $50-60.

To those in search of more common but usable TLRs, such as one for a youngster getting started down the primrose path of manually setting apertures and shutter speeds, let me commend the Ricohflex VIIS of 1955. This pleasantly simple 2¼-square camera from Japan boasts

A pleasant peasant, mid-50's Ricohflex is spartan, decent, very cheap.

externally geared viewing and taking lenses a la Kodak Reflex of the same vintage (the latter is a 75mm f/3.5 Riken—a decent triplet) and an X-sync Riken leaf shutter with speeds of 1/10-1/200 sec. plus B. Film advance is via knob in conjunction with ye olde covered red window and shutter cocking and firing are uncoupled to the film wind, but this modest machine has much clearer, brighter viewing and is a much better picture taker than the previous Wirgin. While it's no match for a Yashica-Mat, Minolta TLR, Rolleiflex or Rolleicord, Ricohflexes are fairly common, quite durable, and often remarkably cheap—prices can run under $40.

Finally we have the Russian Zorki—no, not the competent but uninspired model 4, but the Leica look-alike model III (I think—it's not marked) dating from the late 50's. While no Zorki is even in remotely the same league as the screw-mount Leicas upon which they're based, this one is the best copy of a screw-mount Leica (the IIc?) I've ever seen from the USSR, and its finish, plating, and engraving

Best Russian "Leica"? This 20-year-old Zorki gets my vote on finish alone.

are more than merely workmanlike—they're quite good, particularly the chrome plating on the lens barrel, focusing tab, various knobs, and baseplate lock. Indeed, the focusing mount of the collapsible 50mm f/3.5 Industar lens (a copy of you know whose Elmar) is silky smooth, the rangefinder and viewfinder are definitely above average in brightness and clarity, and even the film-wind knob turns with reasonable smoothness. Flies in the sour cream? Well, like the Leica IIc and IIf, there are no slow speeds (top dial covers a 1/25-1/500 plus B range), the shutter release requires an agricultural touch, and the "leather-grained" body covering is, believe it or not, a textured pattern cast into the metal body shell! Like most Zorkis our featured model is a good picture taker in addition to being a "fun" collectible. As a matter of fact, its lens performs almost as well as the Leitz original. However, user-collectors of Zorkis are cautioned to check and adjust their cameras' shutter speeds if consistent exposures are to be expected—the factory's quality control is a bit lax on this point. I still wonder whether even a nicely made Zorki is worth the $100 price asked by Ken Hansen Photographic of New York City (Ken freely admits he paid too much for it), but it's surely worth buying if only to bring to the next meeting of the Leica Historical Society.

Many thanks to Jules Swerdlin for filling us in on the Wirgin Bros. Camera Works. Some Wirgin products may still be available from his firm, Edixa Camera Corp. of Bronxville, NY.

Folding Vitessas: Voigtländer's ingenious 35s

The folding Vitessas: These venerable Voigtlander 35s of the 50's offered speed, sophistication and elegant complexity.

Over the past few months, my camera consciousness has been continually nibbled at by a small but vocal band of Vitessaniks pleading for expanded coverage of their favorite German rangefinder 35. Before I launch into an exposition of these stylish, mechanically fascinating beasts by Voigtlander of Braunschweig, a mild word of admonition for two of the aforementioned letter writers. In response to your charges that I've never breathed a word about these estimable machines herein, I plead not guilty.

It looks the same as later models, but original '50 Vitessa has unique specs.

Go back to the June, 1974 "CC" column and you will find a rather complete dissertation on the Voigtlander Vitessa T, the one with interchangeable lenses. Nevertheless, I'll freely admit that I have never given the redoubtable folding "barn door" alias "clam shell," models the attention they deserve, so to remedy that situation, here goes.

Way back in the halcyon days of 1950, when the dust had hardly settled from the Second Great Unpleasantness, good old Voigtlander was already up and at 'em with a formidable folding 35 having a fast lens, a unique rapid wind and a readiness to do battle with the likes of the Kodak Retina II and (a year later) the IIa. To emphasize its speedy, rapid-fire image, they dubbed it the Vitessa (*vitesse* means speed in French).

To activate this splendid creation you push lightly on the shutter release button and "clack," the barn doors open and the "combi-plunger" atop the left-hand side of the camera pops up about 1⅜ in. The correct procedure is now to pull gently on one of the barn doors until the front standard containing the lens/shutter unit springs forward and locks into place. True, you can eliminate this second step by simply pointing the barn doors straight down as you press the release, having gravity do the work, but this will eventually bend or break the hardened steel locating tabs which position the lensboard. Obviously, this does little to improve lens/film-plane alignment.

Now that our Vitessa is open for shooting, let's examine its curious array of features, starting with the most obvious one—the vertical plunger. Inside the outer casing of this radio-aerial-like device is a solid spiral rod which rides in a stationary two-sided, slotted insert. As you push the plunger downward, the spiral rod is therefore forced to turn counterclockwise, and a gear affixed to its bottom

Cheapie version? Not really, but model N has slower f/3.5 lens, MX shutter.

Photog's-eye view of "L" shows, from left, eyepiece, focus wheel, film-speed dial.

turns the sprocket wheel and film take-up shafts in a clockwise direction. Simultaneously, an interconnected tooth-and-claw ratchet mechanism advances the geared frame counter (located about an inch below the viewfinder window) one notch. Complicated, but ingenious.

Lest you be tempted to criticize this curious rapid-wind system, bear in mind that top-mounted lever winds were virtually non-existent back in '50, and the Vitessa's plunger is actually a bit quicker (albeit not as comfortable) as top or bottom-mounted levers, yielding only to the Leicavit/Canon-type trigger system in terms of sheer speed of operation. Not only that—Voigtlander's system was commendably compact and neatly concealed within the Vitessa's slightly rounded body contours.

Now let's have a look at those distinctive "barn doors" and the focusing system. Spread the barn doors a bit so you get a clear look at the folding mechanism and you'll appreciate how fiendishly simple it really is. Behind the front standard is a small leather bellows, and on the bottom is a conventional scissors strut, the right front pivot of which slides laterally in a metal channel so the "scissors" can open wider when the lens is collapsed. Four spring-loaded arms (actually two C-shaped brackets) pivot from the inside sides of the doors *and* are connected to four pivot points just inside the corners of the front standard. So as the lensboard is pushed forward, its position is precisely determined by four claw-like pins solidly affixed to the inside of the doors. As you can appreciate, it's rather tricky to do justice to this mechanism with mere words, but it has two noteworthy characteristics. First, providing the camera is handled with reasonable care and not "popped open" as previously described, the Vitessa's folding system offers immense structural rigidity. Second, unlike other systems featuring a scissors strut, the included angle of the strut is not altered to focus the camera. A cam under the focusing knob is attached to a rod which pushes the front standard outward against the spring's tension as the lens is focused closer. Incidentally, folding the Vitessa is quite easy if you do it properly—just open the doors

slightly, position your thumb and forefinger on two red "half moons" on the chrome lens surround, push the lens almost all the way in and close the doors behind it. To nest the plunger, push it gingerly downward until you detect a light detent and let go.

As long as we've mentioned focusing, let's take a gander at the Vitessa's range/viewfinder and the milled knob that controls it. The focusing control is conveniently placed at the upper back portion of the camera, where it falls quite naturally under your right thumb. An approximately 270° turn of the wheel takes you down to roughly 3 ft. (3.5 ft. is the closest marked distance) from infinity, and the round, rotating distance scale surrounded by a depth-of-field scale is engraved atop the camera. With a rangefinder base of nearly 1⅜ in. and 0.6× magnification the Vitessa should and did accurately focus the fastest lens fitted to the fixed-lens folding models, the 50mm f/2 Ultron. However, the range/viewfinder, while reasonably clear and having good separation of the pinkish rangefinder image from the greenish outer viewing area, was none too bright, and not really large enough for comfortable viewing. In other words, you'd probably conclude that it was about average for its era. However, you'd be dead wrong, for the Vitessa is one of the very few pre-Leica M3 rangefinder 35s to provide automatic parallax compensation throughout its focusing range! It's accomplished with a vertically and laterally shifting black mask, coupled to the focusing mechanism, which is situated just behind the front viewfinder glass.

To round out its sundry details, the Vitessa's shutter release is smooth and fairly light in action, while the plunger is a smooth but high-finger-pressure affair. Actually, the former is quite remarkable since the release button (and double-exposure prevention) action must be transferred 90° to the left along the bottom of the camera by a system of levers. The entire back of the camera slides off from the bottom once the bottom-mounted locking catch is turned. On its right-hand bottom section is the nesting rewind crank; on the left the tripod socket.

Now that we (hopefully) have the essentials of the folding Vitessa firmly in mind, it's time to tell all you Vitessa-maniacs which models you've got. Since the folding versions, all manufactured from 1950-1959, are really quite

A conventional interior? Not quite. Main body at left features right-to-left film advance. Pressure plate in back (right) has tab on top to push it forward as camera is closed.

Afflicted with LVS? Yep, but meterized Vitessa L had uncoupled exposure scales.

similar in basic specs, it's the small features that enable you to identify them.

Beginning with the original model of 1950 (the rarest since it was only made for one year): It's most easily identified by the absence of an accessory shoe in the middle of its top plate. If you suspect that somebody has excised the shoe from another model, check the shutter—it should be an X-sync-only Compur-Rapid (speeds of 1-1/500 sec. plus B; no sync-setting lever) and most original Vitessas sport the coated 50mm f/2 Ultron lens. Its current value in excellent condition is about $150.

Actually, a number of more subtle differences distinguish the very first Vitessas from subsequent models. For one thing, parallax compensation is accomplished manually by rotating the rear eyepiece bezel, and the rangefinder focusing patch is diamond-shaped rather than rectangular. Slide down the back section and you'll notice two additional curiosities—the pressure plate is hinged from the top and affixed to the main body casting, and the slide-off back cannot be removed from the body entirely (without

tools, that is) since it's attached with spring clips. Finally, an ingenious mechanism within the camera raises the pressure plate slightly as the film is advanced to prevent film scratching, and the pressure plate moves forward to shooting position after the film is wound—shades of the original Omega 120!

Much more common is the 1951 Vitessa, which enjoyed a longer production run (to 1954). Outwardly similar to the previous model, it featured (you guessed it) an accessory shoe and Synchro-Compur 1-1/500 sec. plus B shutter (but no self-timer) and an MX-sync lever. It currently fetches a bit less than the '50 model—around $125.

In 1955, Voigtlander got around to offering the most deluxe version of the folding Vitessas, the "L," adorned with a direct-reading selenium light meter nestled in around the shutter release and the notoriously fiddly LVS control to go with it (it's on the lower right-hand area of the lens surround). Film speeds from ASA 6-200 correspond to letters A through F, and they're set in a little window next to the meter needle with a small milled wheel on the back of the camera. Once the film speed is set, just read the number the needle points to and set the LVS dial (changing the shutter speed by turning the front-mounted shutter speed ring around the lens if required) to the number indicated. In short, setting the LV number is tantamount to selecting an aperture—both are controlled via what was the aperture-setting tab on pre-LVS Vitessas. The Vitessa L was offered with Synchro-Compur MX shutter with self-timer with either the 50mm f/2 Ultron or 50mm f/2.8 Color-Skopar lenses. The latter is a very good performer, even by current standards, and the whole plot fetches about $150 with either lens.

Finally, we have the 1954-59 Vitessa N which had all the features of the "L" except that it had no light meter and was fitted with a 50mm f/3.5 Color-Skopar lens. Early ones had no LVS and either fetches $100.

Of course no report on the folding Vitessas would be complete without mentioning the really superb finish applied to all these cameras, and the beautifully precise fit of all components. The bodies are finished in satin chrome accented in shiny chrome around the lens finder windows and doors, and the meticulously fitted leather covering is real leather. Inside, the basic body shell is a hefty (and complex) alloy casting with a steel plate affixed to its bottom, and behind the pressure plate (in the removable back of all but the first model) is a tab-actuated control which pushes the pressure plate forward against the film channel as the back is closed for improved film flatness! In short, the folding Voigtlander Vitessas represent a departed era in camera design, an era when mechanical ingenuity was paramount and clever ideas were put forth with a fine disregard for production economies. I shudder to think what it would cost to manufacture a new Vitessa L today, but we shall not see their like again.

Finderless Leicas:
All elegant, some quite rare

You don't have to be a rangefinder fan to love classic Leicas—some of the rarest and most elegant ones had no finder at all!

As many of you are well aware, one of my perverse joys in life is poking fun at the excesses of that lovable bunch of fanatical nit-pickers known as Leica collectors. After all, a well-heeled gent who's willing to shell out untold thousands of bucks for a certain camera merely because it's blessed with a titillating serial number or afflicted with an obsolete screw head pattern makes a tempting target—all the more so when there are sufficient numbers of like-minded maniacs behind him in the queue, so he can actu-

Priceless prototype UR-Leica of 1913 lacked finder, had lose-proof lens cap.

ally profit from his extravagance! But enough of barbs and sarcasm; this time I've decided to relent a bit and confess to having a personal affection for those most serenely spartan of 35mm creations, the finderless Leicas, which have always appealed to me in the manner of true sports (as opposed to sporty) cars—sans radio, sans heater, sans roll-up windows, sans everything but the bare essentials.

Now obviously such a bastion of conservatism (in both positive and negative senses) as E. Leitz, Wetzlar would hardly undertake to produce rangefinderless, viewfinderless camera bodies merely to satisfy the whims of nuts like me who would stalk the world with scale-focusing Leicas sporting accessory finders. They were primarily intended to be used as lower-cost bodies in specific applications where finders, both "range-" and "view-" were unnecessary and might even be a nuisance. In short, these bare-bones machines were and still are most often found attached to Visoflex reflex housings, mounted on

microscopes, telescopes and medical instruments, on reproduction stands and those most glorious of copying devices, the Reprovits, or on the late lamented Focoslide ground-glass focusing gizmo.

As you may already have surmised, the world's scientific establishment—even with all its gadgets and passion for photographic records—generated only a limited market, so finderless Leicas were generally produced in much smaller numbers than their range/view-findered counterparts by the simple expedient of excising those costly components (and often the slow-shutter-speed dial as well) from then-current "standard" cameras. Are they therefore worth less than the corresponding full-featured Leicas? Well, they were at their time of production all right, but today these stripped-down models include some of the lowest-production, rarest Leicas of all—and their prices have escalated accordingly.

First finderless Leica in production, Ic, had no flash sync or slow speeds.

What was the first finderless Leica? Well, I suppose some super-punctilious types might claim that it was the almost mythical UR-Leica, the principle Leica prototype constructed by Oskar Barnack back in 1913. However, I don't think that prototypes—even brilliant and illustrious ones—count, so we are faced with the rather curious historical fact that Leitz didn't get around to making de-viewfindered Leicas until after WW II. While there were many *non-rangefinder* models, beginning with the Leica A of 1924-25 and culminating with the Leica M1 which was discontinued in 1964, those totally devoid of finders comprise a unique breed.

The very first was the Leica Ic, introduced in November 1949 at serial number 455001 and discontinued only two years later in 1951 with serial number 562800. It's basically a Leica IIIc with removable 5¼-in.-long baseplate, 39mm threaded lens mount and all the other classic Leica features too numerous to repeat; but on its top, in place of a rangefinder and viewfinder, are a pair of accessory shoes to accommodate them. Also absent is the front-mounted slow-shutter-speed dial, replaced by a cute round leather-covered blanking plate, and the flash sync socket, which isn't present on unaltered "c" series Leicas, which are all non-sync cameras. Curiously, the early Ic featured herein (serial number 455137) bears the legend D.R.P. (Deutsches Reich Patent), under the "Leica" engraved in its top plate. This is usually a reliable indication that a German camera was made before or during the war (y'all remember the Third Reich) and it suggests that this camera was assembled from prewar parts. Like most immediately postwar Leicas, ours is afflicted with a rough feeling, inelegant-looking artificial leather covering, but is up to the renowned Leica standard in all other respects. For the record, its shutter speeds cover the curious sequence of B, 1/30, 1/40, 1/60, 1/100, 1/200, and 1/500—sorta semi-geometric. Oh yeah, our clean but non-mint body is priced at 5 bucks less than $500.

time the If rolled around it got its original first class leather covering back. If you think the If might be cheaper than the scarcer Ic you're right, but not by much. Our near-mint body's tagged at a hefty $460.

Moving right along, we present the last and reputedly the rarest of screw-mount finderless Leicas, the Ig, which, as you may have guessed, is based on the delectable IIIg. Lacking besides the rangefinder and viewfinder, is the IIIg's beautiful self-timer, but as a consolation you got a present and functioning slow-speed dial which, in conjunction with the geometrically sequenced top dial provided the full range of speeds from 1-1/1000 sec. Cosmetically, the Ig's most curious feature is its semirecessed rewind knob—evidently Leitz found it easier and more aesthetic to provide a flat top deck to accommodate the camera's two accessory shoes and shutter dial. Another identification point is the Ig's round ASA/DIN and film type reminder dial, also lifted from the IIIg. Not wishing to bore you with an "ordinary" Ig, I have managed to unearth a super-rare "Ig Repro" which lacks flash sync and slow speeds. Only about 100 of these were made so these seemingly insignificant omissions will set you back a cool $1,700 or so for the body alone. The Ig Repro, as its title suggests, was designed to be used with the Reprovit II copying device and neither flash sync nor slow speeds was needed.

Finest "normal" finder for finderless Leicas was Leitz 50mm shown here on If.

The next finderless Leica, the If, is a bit more common, but not much. Based on the IIIf/IIf chassis, it began life in '52 at No. 562801 and was terminated in '56 at No. 851000. Like the Ic, it is surmounted by twin accessory shoes and, like the IIIf, it has a film reminder dial built into the film-wind knob, and flash sync delay, controlled by a dial and scale, placed concentrically around the shutter-speed dial. There were two versions (again like the IIIf)—the black dial and the red dial, the color referring to the flash sync delay digits (0 to 20 millisec.). The earlier black dial model had the same shutter-speed sequence as the Ic; the red dial used the slightly more conventional sequence of B, 1/25, 1/50, 1/75, 1/100, 1/200, 1/500 sec. The *coup de grace* is the If's flash sync terminal which sits smack in the middle of the slow-speed dial blanking plate. Oh well, at least by the

Rarest of a rare breed, Leica Ig Repro lacked slow speeds, flash sync.

Naturally, once Leitz embarked upon a policy of offering finderless cameras for scientific work, they couldn't very well stop with the demise of the last of the screw-mount Leicas in 1960, so enter (in 1964 with camera No. 1102501) the Leica MD, just the title to massage the egocentric medical profession. Based on the Leica M2 chassis with frame counter concentrically around the wind-lever axis, it was produced until 1966 (terminating at No. 1660820). Shutter speeds from 1-1/1000 plus B were controlled by a single non-rotating dial on top in classic "M" Leica fashion, and the MD sported but one accessory shoe. Its signal feature was really an accessory—a slotted

Based on M4, MDa looks ordinary . . .

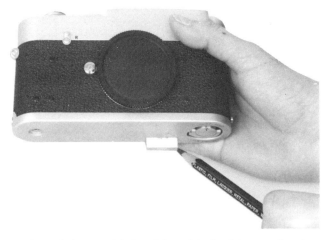

But underneath is a special slotted baseplate for data recording (see text).

Today's finderless Leica? Here's MD-2 shown on Visoflex III. It ain't cheap.

baseplate through which plastic data strips could be inserted to record information directly on the negative. While this reduced the picture area to 24 X 32mm (shades of the original Nikon rangefinder camera), it warmed the hearts of photomicroscopists and other denizens of the lab. Occasionally Leica MDs are seen in gray paint finish, which does nothing for their good looks, but makes them worth even more. Current value of a chrome Leica MD body: around $700.

The penultimate finderless Leica is, appropriately enough, designated the MDa, and, like its predecessor, it's missing a rangefinder, viewfinder, and (it figures) the frame-selector lever and self-timer as well. Like the MD,

it's designed to accept the special slotted baseplate (see photo), and it sports the Leica M4's encased frame counter and distinctive angled rewind crank and (inside) its rapid-loading system sans removable spool. The Leica MDa was first manufactured in 1966 (No. 1159001) up until the late 70's (around 1978), making it the longest running finderless Leica so far. It was replaced by the only finderless Leica in current production, the Leica MD-2 which is a beautiful black chrome M4-2 minus its ogle-through optics and finder frame selector lever, and retaining its flash sync terminals on the back (now conveniently labelled M and X) and do-it-yourself "write on" film reminder. Like all the cameras detailed herein, the MD-2 is a lovely machine that certainly has its uses outside the labs and reflex finders and copying devices that are its natural habitat, but if you think they're gonna sell you a no-frills Leica for a song, think again. The MD-2 body is priced at $872, and the last time I looked I couldn't find too many bargain-priced lenses to fit it. Of course you can always scrounge something cheap and good (like a 50mm f/3.5 screw mount Canon) and M-adapt it!

Many thanks to Ken Hansen Photographic of New York for supplying the cameras and retail prices used in this chapter.

Four cameras in search of a theme: Zeiss Kolibri, Minolta Super A, Topcoflex, Peerflekta II

Four cameras in search of a theme. A mouthwatering melange of formats, features and origins.

Although my personal style of camera appreciation is desultory rather than disciplined, I usually try to codify my ramblings herein by latching onto an easily definable subspecies of photographic beast, and (hopefully) distilling its essence by describing individual examples in detail. But occasionally, despite my best categorizing intentions, I am besieged by fascinating "one off" creations that don't fit neatly into any film, format, or feature slot that's on my mental list. And so, rather than having them languish any longer on my shelves in anticipation of suitable column mates, herewith three nearly flawless gems and one rhinestone in the rough.

Let's lead off with one of my very favorite "vest pocket" roll-film cameras, the exquisitely spartan Zeiss Ikon Kolibri of 1930. The near-mint example pictured below was given as a gift by a friend to Modern's Associate Publisher, Steve Rosenbaum, back in 1970 (I should have such friends).

Basically, the Kolibri is a split-frame-127, scale-focusing camera, with its lens/shutter unit affixed to the front of a pop-out tube. Cameras of this general configuration were quite popular as a "miniature" alternative to 35mm back in the 30's, and the reasons are not hard to fathom. They produced 16 negatives measuring about 1⅝ × 1¼ in. per roll of 127 film and most were fitted with 50mm lenses (usually ranging from f/2.9-f/4.5) so they were relatively easy to scale focus accurately. Another common feature was a *pair* of red windows on their backsides—to get 16 smaller negs you had to place each number on the paper backing (1 through 8) into first one, then the other window before winding to the next digit.

Open and shut case of tooled leather holds Kolibri, filters, screw-in stand.

A non-35 with 50mm normal lens, the Zeiss-Ikon Kolibri has 1⅝ × 1¼-in. format.

The svelte Kolibri was one of the best if not *the* best camera of this type ever made—though fans of the more comprehensive but less pocketable Nagel Pupille might disagree with me. Measuring but 4¾ × 2⅝ × 2 in. folded, its bottom-hinged, cast-alloy body is covered in tooled morocco leather offset by touches of first-class nickel plate on the shutter-control ring, film-wind knob, lens tube, and finger notches (for pulling the lens out to shooting position). As you would expect, the lens is a 50mm f/3.5 Zeiss Tessar which stops down to f/22, and the shutter is a quiet and accurate rim-set Compur with speeds of 1-1/300 sec. plus T and B. Focusing (down to 1 meter) is controlled by a lever tab above the lens and it's of the double helical variety.

To load the Kolibri you push a textured back lock button in the direction of an arrow and it springs open and hinges downwards. The interior is beautifully finished but conventional, with rollers on either side of the film aperture. The only odd features are the pressure plate, which is affixed to the back with flat springs on one side only, and the hollow, spring-loaded roll holders on the bottom of the film chambers, which make film loading a breeze. Once you've loaded up, grab the finger notches, pull the lens out to shooting position, flip up the front and rear sections of the direct optical finder, cock the shutter and you're ready to go. Unlike many split-frame-127 cameras, the Kolibri is normally held and viewed vertically, so you're shooting horizontals rather than verticals. Certainly the controls are arrayed so that horizontals are easiest to shoot, overcoming one of the main objections to cameras using this format.

Where the Kolibri scores most is in performance and aesthetics as opposed to features per se. Even by modern standards its lens and shutter are very good and its film channel (raised edges on the pressure plate, run parallel to the film, coming to rest just outboard of the precision-machined film-guide rails) is engineered to provide good film flatness, the bugaboo of all small roll-film sizes. In short, it is an elegantly simple machine that slides into a pocket and is capable of first-class results. Not surprisingly, the fairly rare Kolibri qualifies as a "primo" collectors' item which currently fetches about $200 among collectors of same. It's such a well-conceived camera I only wish someone made a modern version, though none is likely to be intrepid enough to attempt a single-handed resurrection of the "dying" 127 film size.

Our second typological waif was discovered residing at the bottom of a glass case—the "collectible camera" showcase at Ken Hansen Photographic in New York. As soon as I saw it I smiled, for here was a 35mm camera I had lusted after but lost years back when I opted for a Leica IIIg instead (a wise decision as it turned out). The fabulous Minolta Super A of 1958 was a member of that fascinating but ill-fated class of machinery known as interchangeable lens, leaf-shutter, rangefinder 35s. And at the time, it was a logical extension of the very popular fixed-lens rangefinder Minoltas, the A and A2, which had similarly shaped bodies, the same smooth-but-overly-long-stroke (210°)

A high-tech leaf-shutter 35, the Minolta Super A had super finder, range of lenses.

wind-lever action and similarly top-mounted shutter-speed dials.

What differentiated the Super A from its more pedestrian brethren was primarily its simple but clever system of interchangeable optics, including a faster normal lens, a 50mm f/1.8 Super Rokkor. Visually, the Super is wider and therefore sleeker-looking than the chunky-but-lovable A2, and it sports a sexy, curved-frame illuminating window on its left front corner, just below the folding rewind crank. The backside and interior of the camera offer few surprises, except for the almost invisible black-on-black admonition molded into the eyepiece bezel extension. "Full Frame For 35mm Lens; Lined Bright Frame For 50mm Lens." There's also a funny little pin above the film aperture which mates with a flat affixed to the hinged back to activate the self-zeroing frame counter only after the camera's been closed.

But before we turn to the finder, let's examine the feature-laden front section. The focusing tab on the left side

Portentous backside table indicates depth of field of 35, 85, 100mm lenses.

of the lens barrel looks classic enough and it takes the lens down to its minimum distance of 3.5 ft. in a very smooth, approximately 120° turn. However, when you bring it back to the infinity mark, you'll notice that atop the lens are a red dot, a milled gripping surface, and a clockwise-pointing arrow labelled "Off." Turn the milled ring and the lens comes off, eh? That's what *I* thought, and it took me about 10 frustrating minutes (sans instruction book) to realize that you have to push in the little button in the middle of the focusing tab first. Once you do this, you can remove the lens all right—the knurled lens-removal ring is permanently affixed to the lens, and on its back are bayonet slots that fit over male bayonet lugs on the front of the camera's fixed-focusing mount that's coupled to the rangefinder. This Canonesque breech-lock system means that no lens can focus any closer than 3.5 ft. and that the aperture scale of each rotates as you focus, but Minolta's clever system eliminates the cumbersome (and costly) necessity of precision machining focusing cams for all lenses and coupling them to the rangefinder with a pivoted cam follower. For the record, Minolta offered a reasonably comprehensive optical array for the Super, including a 35mm f/3.5, 85mm f/2.8 and 100mm f/3.8 in addition to the normal lenses (a 50mm f/2 and a 50mm f/1.8 were listed)—not bad for a camera with a list price of $129.50.

Rounding out the minutiae, on the bottom of the Super A's front are a PC connector surrounded by a knurled MX sync selector lever, and two reinforced locating slots designed to accommodate a close-up device. Up on the right side of the lens is another slot, which shows a red dash signal to indicate that the shutter's cocked. (It's more important than you might think because the top speed supplied by the 1-1/400 sec. plus B Seikosha MX shutter must be selected *before* you cock the shutter.) Final piece de resistance was a shutter-coupled, accessory selenium meter which slid into the Super's accessory shoe.

Despite its minor foibles, the Minolta Super A was really quite a grand and competent machine, and its 7-element normal lens was a fine performer according to our now ancient tests. Construction and finish are likewise very good and so is the true projected frameline (but non-parallax-compensating) viewfinder—if you don't mind overall greenish tinges with contrasting pinkish focusing patches, that is. The current price tag on this near-mint beauty is $130, or precisely four bits more than it sold for originally. When you consider what's happened to the dollar over the last 23 years, that qualifies as something of a bargain.

Now, a few concluding words for lovers of weird twin-lens reflexes. The Topcoflex pictured was (as you might expect) produced by Tokyo Optical Co. of Topcon fame about 25 years ago, and in terms of quality, finish and features it sits about halfway between the classic Rolleiflex and the redoubtable Minolta Autocord—mighty prestigious company indeed. With a one-throw hinged crank on the right and knurled focusing wheel and spring-loaded roll-holder knobs on the left, it's certainly "Rollei-er" than the Minolta Autocord. Aside from this (and the fact that the first frame must be positioned manually before the counter takes over) it has few novel features. The taking lens is a very good 75mm f/3.5 Topcor stopping down to

Very Rollei-esque in concept, Topcoflex of 1960 has performance to match, with very bright finder, matched 75mm f/3.5 lenses.

f/22, the shutter is a Seikosha MFX with speeds of 1-1/500 sec. plus B, and the viewing lens is a 75mm f/3.5 Toko. As with Rolleis you set aperture and shutter speeds in a little window atop the lensboard, but it's done by moving levers a la Autocord/Rolleicord. Aside from its robust construction, perhaps the Topcoflex's most important feature is its nonremovable Tokobrite viewing screen, with Fresnel pattern and central fine-focusing spot. It provides a good, bright, contrasty image out to the extreme corners that's rivalled only by the much costlier Rolleiflexes. Current price of this oddball, which was nabbed virtually unused in its original box and case—a paltry $150.

A mid-50's cheapie, the Peerflekta II is uninspired but serviceable.

But perhaps your taste runs to the semi-kitsch, with performance and finder brightness secondary considerations. In that case you could do worse than opting for the Peerflekta II, pictured. Made by the Welta division of the East German Pentacon empire it was imported by Peerless Camera of New York in the mid-50's. Its original name was the Reflekta and its mediocre-but-serviceable components included a 75mm f/3.5 ROW Polylyt lens, 1-1/200 sec. (plus B) Cludor shutter, and helicoid focusing (via knurled lever below taking lens) to a blistering 4 ft. The Peerflekta's hinged back lock (with no safety system) is scandalously chintzy, its film advance and counting system is by ye olde (covered) red window and its finder image is dim and somewhat fuzzy. Is there anything to love? Well, the Peerflekta was reasonably well finished and its weirdly place shutter release (to the right of the nameplate, just below the erected finder hood) was smooth and predictable—but best of all, the Peerflekta sold for under $20, and that enticed many poor souls down the hypo-stained path of photograpic hobbyism. Today, this forlorn beast fetches about $60-70 in clean shape, which is more than it's really worth.

Incidentally, if you're looking for a genuine kitsch bauble at a more agreeable price, Cambridge Camera of New York is currently hawking the lovable Leudi II extinction meters popular in the 30's for a mere $12.50 apiece.

Which rangefinder 35 sired the Contax II? Probably not the Contax I!

Bastard sons of the great Contax II? Actually, one of these vintage Zeiss 35's was legitimate, and the other may have sired the king!

Never let it be said that we quaint-and-curious-camera fanciers can't make distinctions that are infinitely finer than a gnat's eyeball. Last week, while glancing through an ad for some obsolete German delectables, I came across the deliciously precise description of a late 30's Contax II as "mint minus." Ye gods—can you believe that there are cameras out there in better-than-excellent shape that aren't quite "mint," which is to say "as new"? Do you suppose that a "mint minus" camera would be distinguished by an absence of abrasions and scratches, but evidence of infinitesimal wear in the tripod socket threads or inside the neckstrap lugs? And, heaven forfend, when does a "mint minus" camera sink to the lowly depths of mere excellence? When the pressure plate bears witness to more than two rolls of film having traversed its pristine surface? Oh well, since I must plead guilty to at least two separate counts of buying brand-new cameras for the sole purpose of collecting them, I suppose I shouldn't snicker at the excesses of my cohorts in cameramania. Besides, residing right next to my own "mint minus" Contax II with erratic shutter (nabbed for the glorious sum of $60 including very sharp 50mm f/3.5 Zeiss Tessar lens) is its bastard son, a fairly rare Nettax, alias Super Nettel III. Aptly named, this brilliant but silly machine was destined to nettle me to new heights of historical research and a deeper understanding of the exquisite complexities of Zeiss-Ikon geneology.

Having acquired most of my camera smarts in the rough and tumble of the marketplace, I was under the naive impression that the great and glorious Contax II of 1936, surely one of the landmark interchangeable lens rangefinder 35s, sprang from the loins of the ingenious but troublesome Contax I. In other words, the mechanical geniuses at Zeiss-Ikon had de-bugged and modernized the original boxy Contax while retaining its basic features (such as shutter type, lens mount, and removable back). As a corollary to this interpretation, it was equally clear that the magnificent Contax II had sired three lesser-but-fascinating 35mm offspring, the Super Nettels I and II and the aforementioned Nettax. Parenthetically, every one of these mechanical sounding camera names was derived from "Contessa-Nettel," one of the principal corporate components of the great Zeiss-Ikon merger of 1926. Alas, the deeper I delved into this murky business the more

A 35mm Super Ikonta? Sorta, but 1934 Contessa Nettel had Contax-type shutter.

obvious it became that my hunch was wrong, but the truth that emerged is indeed stranger than fiction.

It seems that back in 1934, in the midst of the great Depression, when "unprofitable" camera lines were dropping like flies, the wizards of Zeiss-Ikon brought forth the roll-film Super Ikontas, based on a new coupled rangefinder principle incorporating contra-rotating prism wedges (instead of the pivoting mirror plus fixed, semi-

Poor man's Contax II? That's the slot the Nettax was supposed to fill but didn't.

A super-rigid folder, Contessa-Nettel's front was well-supported and located.

silvered mirror rangefinder as used in the original Contax). For details on this rangefinder see the July, '79 Camera Collector, but suffice it to say that it was not only more precise, but quite a bit more rugged than the rangefinders that preceded it. Then, brainstorm—why not make a 35mm version of the Super Ikonta using the vertical, metal roller-blind Contax shutter and a Contax-style removable back. The result was an ingenious non-interchangeable-lens folding hybrid called the Super Nettel.

Now, like the Super Ikontas, the Super Nettel had its focusing wheel and contra-rotating prism wedges affixed to a corner of the front standard with a separate fixed (mirror plus prism) section behind two square windows just above the top rear section of the leather bellows. But there the similarities end. The folding mechanism is pure vintage Nettel, with pivoted "lazy tongs" struts supporting the front standard on both sides, and bottom alignment of the lensboard assured by pins running in arcuate slots. The bed-erecting system is immensely rigid, ensuring precise lens/film-plane alignment, and to fold the camera, you must press in on two striated metal tabs just outboard of the struts before pushing the hinged bed upwards. The S-N has separate range- and viewfinder windows a la the Super Ikonta, but the finder is a small-but-clear, inverse Galilean type. Also, unlike the front-cell-focusing Ikontas, the S-N features unit focusing of the lens via a single helical, focusing distances being read out somewhat inconveniently on the front of the rotating

focusing wheel (with respect to a fixed index mark with surrounding depth-of-field scale) on the front standard. As long as we've brought up the lens, I may as well mention that the original, black-finished version of the Super Nettel was available with a choice of 50mm optics, an f/3.5 Triotar, an f/3.5 Tessar (the most common lens), and an f/2.8 Tessar.

Naturally, I've saved the more interesting stuff for last, and here is where the Super Nettel's influence on the later Contax II can be shown to be as important as that of its putative daddy, the Contax I. To begin with, the S-N's main body has angled ends, which can almost be called rounded, and its shape is so Contax II-ish that the backs are almost (but not quite) interchangeable. This represents a radical departure from the Contax I's rectilinear contours, though the dual twist locks on the bottom of the removable back remain a standard Contax/Super-Nettel/Nettax feature. Inside the body is an updated and simplified version of the famous (infamous?) metal vertical roller-blind Contax shutter with speeds from 1/5 to 1/1000 sec. plus B. In true Contax fashion, the Super Nettel was designed to accept a Contax cartridge in each film chamber.

But the clincher on the Super Nettel's identity comes when you examine the top deck. Here, miraculously, two years before the Contax II is one of its more renowned features—a combined film-wind and shutter-speed setting knob surmounted by a threaded shutter-release button. As with all subsequent Contax rangefinder 35s until the last one in 1961, you select speeds by lifting the dial and turning its index dot to the speed indicated on the concentric scale below it. True, you can only set speeds *after* you wind the knob and cock the shutter, but at least nothing external moves as the exposure is being made (one of the chief objections to the otherwise superb Leicas of the era), and the wonderfully smooth shutter botton is, as they say, ergonomically located. On the other end of the top is a milled metal rewind knob virtually identical to the one on the subsequent Nettax, and to the left of the film wind/ shutter dial is an external, manual exposure counter that may have been lifted from the Contax I. In the center of the top deck is a housing containing the tiny separate range- and viewfinder windows (unlike the Contax II's exquisite combined range/viewfinder) and an accessory shoe.

A successful hybrid

Despite its hybrid status, perched between the magnificent Super Ikontas and the legendary Contax II, the Super Nettel was quite a nice, competent machine, and it was truly pocketable (preferably in a vest or jacket pocket because of its medium weight). For the record there was a Super Nettel II introduced in 1936, but its chief claims to fame were a natty satin chrome finish on body, brightwork, and folding bed and 50mm f/2.8 Tessar lens. Alas, today Super Nettels border on being rare and are avidly sought by Zeiss fanatics. So, as you'd expect, a Super Nettel I in fair nick currently fetches about $375, while a clean model II could easily bring $500-600.

This brings us to the Nettax, a strange, Contaxy beast if ever there was one. To understand why anyone would build a machine falling in between the Super Nettel and the Contax II, herewith a bit of Depression marketing strategy. First of all, the Contax II was expensive, selling for around $200, and however glorious the Super Nettel was, it was still a folding camera with a fixed lens and therefore not considered to be in quite the same class. But just suppose you knew precisely what kind of photography you were aiming at (say general outdoor work in good light) and you didn't need the Contax's super-speed lenses, slightly higher top shutter speed, etc.? You'd run right out with Reichsmarks in hand and buy the true son of Contax II, a Nettax, or so thought the marketing boffins at Zeiss-Ikon.

A strange design, Nettax had fixed rangefinder elements behind "eyes" in body, moving components grafted onto lens.

So, what then is a Nettax, you ask? Well, you remember the Super Nettel II, the jazzy chrome version. Take the entire rear end of one of these bodies, tidy up and enclose the front part of the main section (since you won't need to collapse the lens into it), and graft on a strange, asymmetrical, three-lobed bayonet mount and there you have it—everything but the lens, that is. The standard Nettax lenses were a 50mm f/3.5 Tessar collapsible or a 50mm f/2.8 ditto with a double-helical focusing mount and Leica-like focusing tab and distance scales on the front (except that the focusing index and depth-of-field scale are on the moving focusing ring and the stationary distance scale is on the front of the lens mount housing). As with the Super Nettel, the fixed optical elements of the rangefinder are on the front of the camera, just below the top deck (the windows are round instead of square), and those contra-rotating prism wedges are found in a curved protrusion at the rear of the lens, giving interchangeable Nettax optics a unique "kidney shaped" appearance. Bayonet in the lens (the spring-loaded release lock resembles those on longer, externally bayonet-mounted Contax optics) and the prism wedge window locks into place in front of the right-hand window in the body, thus "coupling" the rangefinder optically. When you bring the camera to eye level and glance at the small, separate range- and viewfinder windows, you can almost swear you're peering through a Super Nettel.

And why would anyone opt for a Nettax just to save a few measly bucks? Beats me, and apparently few image-oriented Depression scrimpers could see the logic of it either—the result being that today the Nettax qualifies as a genuine rarity. It was ingenious to be sure, but it wasn't really pocketable, lacked the Contax II's range/viewfinder, and fast and slow shutter speeds (shutter speeds were the same as the Super Nettel) and aside from the 50mms, only one interchangeable lens was ever specifically made for it, a 105mm f/5.6 Triotar that's presently regarded as a true collectors' prize ($1000 or thereabouts). Some Zeiss catalogs list a wide-angle for the Nettax—a 28mm f/8 Tessar —but in reality this was a Contax lens that could be Nettax-adapted with a special gizmo that I've never actually seen. Ironically, the most successful of Zeiss's 35mm designs of the 30's, the Contax II itself—is worth roughly $600 less than a clean Nettax (about $140 complete with 50mm F/2 Sonnar) proving, I suppose, that ubiquity breeds contempt.

Many thanks to Olden Camera of New York for supplying the strange and wonderful brace of cameras used in this column.

More cautionary words about buying "rare antique" cameras

"I am prepared to sell this rare and unusual antique camera for the sum of $3,000 in cash or negotiable securities. . ."—from a reader's letter, Quito, Ecuador.

Although it pleases me to think of my readers as aesthetically and technologically motivated admirers of ancient and discontinued cameras, I know better. What you folks are primarily interested in is how much filthy lucre your photographic relics will fetch on the open market, and I have mounds of your correspondence to prove it. In fact, I receive an alarming number of letters asking, in effect, for free appraisals of cameras and even entire collections, all purportedly for insurance purposes. I an-

A rarity for your wrist, Steineck ABC of '49 took 8 pix on circular film disc, had 12mm f/2.5 lens. Value: $300.

swer these politely, sympathizing with far too many victims of various forms of larceny, concluding when possible with ballpark estimates of a few items and words of admonition that "this does not constitute an official appraisal." I also cater to your fiduciary inclinations by furnishing approximate retail prices (valid for at least three months in these inflationary times) of all cameras appearing in this column—if I didn't, the torrent of epistles would be even less manageable than it already is.

Now that you're all suitably irked, I wish to extend sincere apologies to the many faithful readers who never ask for price quotations, who send me their old folders rather than turning them over to inquisitive four-year-olds for demolition, who correct my mistakes without rancor, and whose interest in photographica is genuinely his-

torical, optical and mechanical, rather than financial. As for the rest of us, the epistolary majority (plus, I must confess, yours truly), I propose to tackle one of the most intricate monetary queries arising in this little bailiwick—the ever popular "What makes a camera valuable?" Or, to state it with greater precision and less verve, "What are the various factors that determine the market value of a camera, and how do these interact to produce that much-sought-after (but seldom realized) phenomenon known as the 'rare and valuable collectors' item'?"

Old but not gold, the Kodak #2 Folding Autographic Brownie of c. 1910 takes ubiquitous 120 film, is worth only $25.

Let's begin by disabusing you of the most widespread fallacy—one that occasionally rears its head even among experienced collectors who ought to know better—namely that the older a camera is, the more valuable it's likely to be. As with most great untruths, there are germs of reason behind it. After all, really old equipment like Daguerreotype cameras, of the 1840's-1860's, mid-19th-century novelty and wide-angle cameras, and the original Kodak of 1888 *are* worth a bundle if they're in remotely respectable condition, and, in general cameras of later vintages are more likely to have survived intact. However, there are oodles of 19th-century cameras of no particular distinction, which are not worth a heck of a lot—various Kodak roll-film folders (such as the scale-focusing beast depicted) and box cameras of the 1890's, an assortment of plain-Jane Rochester Optical Company "field" 4 × 5 view cameras of the same era, and myriads of pleasantly grandfatherly postcard-format cameras of the World War I period all come readily to mind, as do their prices. Almost all are contained within the category of "very common machinery" whose value to an interested collector falls into the broad and ignominious $10-$50 range. Does this mean that none of the cameras in this class is worth more? Hardly. After all, the second version of the fabled original Kodak (the 1889 model) falls into the "Kodak box camera of the 1890's" category and it's worth about $1,200. Even a Kodak Bulls Eye #2 folding camera can bring close to a hundred bucks if it's a pristine example. The simple point I'm making is that age alone doesn't tell the tale.

Ah, you're saying to yourself, perhaps it's rarity that makes one camera worth a bundle, while its high-production cousin is worth a pittance. No, not entirely, but here you're on somewhat firmer ground, for there are few super-valuable cameras that can genuinely be described as common. And you can safely predict that most really high-production cameras like the Argus C3 (black version with coated lens), the Box Brownie 2A of the 20's, and the original Kodak Instamatic 100 of 1963 will never be worth a mint, at least not in our lifetimes. Unfortunately for the logical adherents of this "fewer means pricier" philosophy, there are many rare, nearly rare, and downright uncommon cameras which fetch very modest prices and are not at all easy to sell. Innumerable oddball 9× 12 cm German film pack and plate cameras of the 20's and 30's, many of the lesser brands of Japanese fixed-lens rangefinder and scale-focusing 35s of the 50's and 60's, a plethora of cheap and nasty subminiatures made in Occupied Japan in the late 40's and early 50's, and an assortment of unusual but mechanically straightforward twin-lens reflexes from the 30's through the 60's and diverse countries of origin all slither into this category.

Well, if it isn't old age or scarcity per se which are guaranteed to make your light-tight picture-taking boxes a gilt-edged investment and all that rot, must we resign ourselves to shelling out for the one of the dozens of inaccurate camera pricing guides to make any sense of it all? Are we condemned to treat every camera we come across as an individual case, or are there some general patterns that emerge from studying the market?

A rarity? Yep, original Olympus M-1 (before the O was added) fetches $250.

First auto-exposure SLR? Nope, but Konica Autoreflex of '67 was first AE SLR with focal-plane shutter. Value: $275.

Best binocular camera? Probably. German made CamBinox of early 60's had submini format, first-class lens and viewing optics.

Well, I'm sure I won't startle anyone by declaring that the world's most valuable cameras are those in the shortest supply for which there is the greatest demand. Short supply is quite easy to define—the cameras in question must have either been produced in limited numbers to begin with or to have been subsequently decimated by a process of attrition. So much for supply-side economics; clearly the most important variable in the "cash value" equation is *demand*—or to put it another way, what is it that motivates people (particularly well-heeled collectors, museums, and, yes, speculators) to buy certain cameras and eschew others? Well, as you probably figured, there are no ironclad rules that can possibly apply to such ephemeral emotions as technological lust and historical greed, but I'll do my best to classify the noble elements that define a true camera collector's prize:

1. Technological or historical firsts. Most cameras of the 1840-1860 period are quite valuable since all qualify as "pioneer cameras." The Kodak of 1888 was the first commercially successful roll-film box camera, and the Kodak Super Six-20 of 1938-45 was the first autoexposure still camera in series production. Both are worth a bundle—$3,000-$4,000 and $900-$1,000, respectively. A bit closer to home, the original, non-through-lens-metering, Konica Autoreflex of 1967 was the first focal-plane-shutter SLR with automatic exposure (it also had half-frame capability) and it's worth about $275, quite bit more than most other

SLRs of that era. Likewise, the first model of the Leica (Leica A) is worth a fair amount ($425 with 50mm f/3.5 Elmar) despite being relatively numerous, and a clean Contax I can bring as much as $300 from an interested collector. Does this mean that all "firsts" are worth a mint? No indeed. The first Polaroid camera, the model 95 in luxurious brown leather, only brings about $35.

2. Low production models in a famous line. Certainly the various incarnations of the rangefinderless, leaf-shutter, fixed-lens Leica B are high-priced examples (about $3,500) in this category, as are the 35mm interchangeable-lens version of the Zeiss Nettax ($500-$750), the 4.5 × 6 cm box-type Ermanox of the 20's with f/1.8 or f/2 lens (about $1,200, the Kodak Ektra (especially with lenses and accessories), the ill-fated, super-deluxe Konica F (about $350), and the last version of the 4.5 × 6 cm folding roll-film Konica Pearl (the model IV of 1958, $500 or so). However, it all depends on how you define the word "famous." Vest Pocket Kodak cameras are certainly "famous," but many numerically low-production versions aren't worth all that much more than standard issue models, while others (such as the fabled, color-coordinated Vanity Kodak which came complete with mirror, compact, and matching case) can bring a small fortune ($300) from the right buyer.

In short, while there are always exceptions that disprove the rule, "low-volume oddballs by major makers," is indeed a fertile field for cash collectors.

3. Strange, peculiar, and special-purpose cameras. Weird cameras, particularly those that fulfill their intended functions, and are well-made in limited numbers, often fetch high prices among collectors. Various binocular and gun cameras, including the superbly constructed 1960's Cambinox ($400), and the lethal-looking Mamiya Pistol Camera of 1954 ($1,000)—a half-frame terror designed for the Japanese police—are good examples, as are the original Latvian Minox of the late 30's ($400), the multifaceted, supercomplex and intricate Compass of the same era ($1,200), and rafts of stereo cameras (including the prized f/2.8 lens version of the American Stereo Realist, which is currently fetching upwards of $300), "pocket" and "wrist" watch cameras, and cameras disguised as everything from binoculars to books to walking sticks.

In search of values

Now that you have all three of Schneider's Jello-Clad Rules Of Instant Fortune Making, replete with multifarious exceptions, you ought to be less sure than ever whether that mouldering wooden box camera you found in Aunt Martha's attic is worth lots or not. Good, for this salutary uncertainty accurately reflects the fact that, save for a few broad guidelines and lots of specific knowledge on your part, there *is no sure way* of telling whether a given camera is worthless, worth some, or worth a bloody fortune. How, then, can you ascertain its true worth without getting ripped off? I wish I could recommend one of the numerous price guides on the subject, but I cannot in good conscience. You can, of course, contact your local Photographic Historical Society, if any, or you can sub-

First electronically controlled shutter? It's found in Polaroid 900 for only $50.

scribe to *Shutterbug Ads*, P.O. Box F, Titusville, FL. 32780 ($10.00 per year) and assiduously peruse its pages in search of a price range (beware, asking prices are seldom the same as selling prices). Finally, as a matter of last resort, you can write to me and ask—but puh-lease confine your camera price questions to three per letter, don't expect official appraisals, and regard any cash offers I may tender you as being about 50 percent below actual market value!

Gutless wonders:
Dummy Leicas for window display

How much is that Leica in the window? Oh, a few hundred bucks, even if it's a gutless wonder!

On a sweltering summer day, with the Kodak-patented hazy sun streaming down upon the concrete and asphalt contours of midtown Manhattan, my eye gravitates toward the display window of a well-known camera emporium. And there, perched resplendent in the heat and humidity of its transparent torture chamber is a mint Leica M3, its satin chrome tastefully offset with touches of shiny metal, knurled and textured control rings and a meticulously-fitted genuine leather covering. Oh, the agony of it —what a cruel and uncaring thing to do to my favorite rangefinder camera of all time, the mate to one I foolishly sold to buy a (shudder) auto-exposure SLR with digital readouts in the finder. But as I contemplate the fate of the poor Leica's cloth focal-plane shutter, the various lubricants in its gear trains and helicals, and the balsam betwixt the elements of its rigid 50mm f/2 Summicron, my face suddenly brightens as my eyes alight upon the neatly lettered price sign propped up against the finder frame selector lever. Three hundred fifty bucks! It can't be—an M3 in that pristine condition is worth more than twice that amount. Why, that camera looks as though it's never even had a roll of film through it!

Well, it's probably the old "That price is only for the body" trick. And besides, it's probably got a duff shutter or internal damage. Still, this particular store usually labels such merchandise "As is." I'd better have a closer look before barging in there and making an idiot of myself. Fortunately, the M3 is positioned up close to the window so I can get a pretty good look—let's see, the serial number ought to indicate whether it's a single-stroke or double-stroke M3. What's this? Serial number M3-12716A? Must be a special production run to end in a letter. How about the lens—"Summicron 1:2/50 Leitz Wetzlar and *no* serial number! Omigod, one glance through the front finder glass and the ruse is revealed. Like many honest and dishonest folks before me, I've been duped by a Leica dummy!

A real steal at $350, but this Leica M2 has certain built-in shortcomings.

And what is a Leica dummy, you ask incredulously? Quite simply, it's an empty shell of a Leica camera body fitted with a single element lens, both designed to look exactly like the real thing. The basic notion behind these non-cameras was anything but dumb—to furnish storekeepers with relatively inexpensive mock-up Leicas for their store windows, so when a thief decided to bash in said window, he would get something worthy of his nefarious efforts, which is to say nothing much. It is one

Best rangefinder 35 ever? Leica M3's my pick, but this one only shoots blanks!

of the ironic twists of the camera-collecting insanity that today these gutless wonders are often worth considerably more than fully functional models of "lesser"-brand 35s. And in a few peculiar instances, a clean dummy with lens is worth more than the real Leica that inspired it! Such is the topsy-turvy world of Leica collecting that anything limited production and Leitz gathers value exponentially. And when you consider that only a few thousand at most of any model dummy was ever produced, you can see the cockeyed logic of it all.

All right, let's take a closer gander at the glorious M3 that took in this bewhiskered curmudgeon. One glance through its "eyepiece" reveals a complete absence of internal range/viewfinder optics. Pry off the bottom plate (there's no locking baseplate handle on this one) and lift the pressure-plateless hinged back and you're greeted with more nothing—no take-up spool, no shutter, no shutter mechanism; just a beautifully detailed cast-alloy body with receptacles for all the guts. The only gear visible is the frame counter gear, which has been welded in place. Ditto for the rewind knob, frame-selector lever, rewind lever, and shutter release, which can't be budged. Curiously, the spring-loaded wind lever can be wound and it returns to its original position; the self-timer lever can be moved 180° but it doesn't return even when you press the functioning release button above it; and the shutter dial can be set at any non-speed you wish. Finally, the lens-release lock works, the "lens" can be "focused" (albeit with a rough, un-Leitzlike feel) and this particular bogus Summicron optic is set forever between f/8 and f/11. Remove the "lens" and you're greeted with nothing but a gorgeous M-type bayonet. Glance through the back of the lens and you'll notice that the single, curved and coated front element is backed with a blackened disc so as not to give away the plot when it's mounted on a bogus camera.

Now you might think that such an elaborate con game would be impossible to improve upon given its elegant simplicity, but such is not the case. Our slightly later M2 dummy, serial number M2-13066A, is virtually identical to

Last of classic dummies? I'd say so, but collector who nabbed it sure isn't.

the aforementioned M3, but its non-Summicron is locked in at a much more useful f/5.6 and its rewind knob can be made to turn. And the M4, last of the classic dummies, has all of the above plus a fully functional rewind crank, movable field frame selector lever, spring-loaded shutter release (very smooth and utterly silent), an operational film-type reminder on the back of its swing-up back and—wonder of wonders—an honest-to-Pete pressure plate inside. Of course, I'm beset by nagging doubts over this last feature, as it's entirely possible that somebody absconded with the "real fake" hinged back and installed a "fake real" one instead.

Now you mustn't get the idea that this dummy Leica business was all some sort of postwar foolishness associated with M-series models only. Actually, this particular brand of deception began back about 1927 with the very first store window dummy Leica, the redoubtable model A. One of those babies with fixed, fake uncoated 50mm f/3.5 Elmar lens is currently worth about $750 and, like all Leica dummies, is the *sine qua non* of showcase collectors who never use their Leicas for (ugh) picture taking anyway. I was unable to unearth one of those gems, but herewith its close cousin, an early postwar IIIf (black flash sync delay dial) complete with slightly later 50mm f/2.8 Elmar, the one-element version, natch.

A one-element Elmar? This Leica IIIf dummy's got one with slick focusing.

Alas, only the shutter dial works on this model, and the lens is not set on any aperture whatsoever. This is partially offset by the fact that the lens "focuses" with consummate smoothness. The shockers with this beast are two: 1. It's worth about $350, or $75-150 more than a real model IIIf similarly equipped; 2. Remove the baseplate and you're greeted by the ultimate hollow emptiness—no internal chassis whatsoever!

Lest you erroneously conclude that Leitz quit befuddling burglars with the M4, herewith what is purported to be the last of the hollow Leicas, a nice black Leica R3 SLR discontinued only a few years ago. Alas, this particular shell lacks its fake 50mm f/2 Summicron-R so I can't comment upon its non-optical qualities but, as you'd expect, the R3 has more movable parts than its predecessors to deceive the unwary crook. These include the wind lever,

Last Leica dummy was probably the late R3. Splendid, but at $180, too dear.

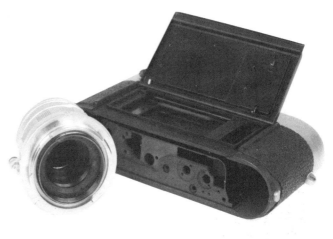

Inside joke: Remove base, lens, and M-series dummy's gutlessness is clear.

ASA dial, rewind crank, eyepiece blind control lever, multiple exposure control, depth-of-field preview lever, and back lock. You can even unscrew the "battery compartment" cover. Despite these obvious non-technical advances, I have it on good authority that the R3 was and will be the last dummy Leica to roll off the production line. Evidently, the Portuguese who assemble the current R4 and the Canadians responsible for the M4-P lack the wry Wetzlarian weltanschauung.

Actually, one cannot conclude a column on so quaint and curious a subject without mentioning a few more funny facts about these non-photographic instruments. First of all, they stand as some kind of monument not only to the unquestioned value of the cameras they represented, but in a strange way they are just as much a part of the Leica legend as the real cameras. Since they employed parts right off the Leica production line (presumably occasionally quality control rejects) they are without exception gorgeously finished and exquisitely detailed. They had to be; otherwise they'd instantly be recognized as fakes. Secondly, these gutless bodies are much, much lighter than the standard bodies, so few thieves would burden themselves with actually stealing these replicas once they hefted them. This was a good thing, since these "display cameras" were fairly expensive (the R3 dummy was listed at $180 dealer price, and the M4 cost a cool $160). Also, in addition to deterring or fooling thieves, these store-window dummies were indeed used by reputable dealers to bear the brunt of exposure to heat and sunlight, and during the Depression they served to fill out expensive Leica inventories at minimal cost. So what was the real reason they were discontinued? Too high a price, and insufficient demand. Besides, in these calamitous times, thieves, camera store owners and manufacturers alike seem to have lost their sense of whimsy if not their sense of humor altogether.

Voigtländer Bessamatics: Best leaf-shutter SLRs?

What's the world's best interchangeable-lens, leaf-shutter 35mm SLR? Hard to say, but this German beastie's a candidate.

I am always suspicious when somebody backs himself into a technological corner before asking a simple question. Take the reader who prefaced his query on leaf-shutter SLRs with a passel of mumbo-jumbo about the alleged difficulty in using focal-plane shutter SLRs with flash fill outdoors. If he wanted to know "the identity of the best all-round leaf-shutter SLR with interchangeable lenses" as he succinctly put it at the end, all he had to do was ask. I am still enough of a hedonist to aver that merely wanting something of a certain type is justification enough in seeking it. Still, it is an interesting question, and I must conclude that opting for an "obsolete" leaf-shutter SLR "system" is definitely a more romantic, elegant, and ultimately more flexible approach to daylight flash fill woes than simply plunking down the bucks for a more powerful flash unit. Besides, shooting at a flash sync speed of 1/500 sec. allows you some control over depth-of-field—something that's rather tough when shooting at ap-

Incredibly advanced for its day, the 36-82mm f/2.8 Voigtlander-Zoomar shown on Bessamatic Deluxe had convenient controls but was front-heavy.

The original Bessamatic of '58. Far from far out, but single-stroke wind lever, coupled meter with needle in the finder were then state-of-the-art features.

ertures such as f/11 and f/16 to eliminate ghost images.

Now taking this guy at face value, I'd likely steer him toward a late model Zeiss Contaflex, not necessarily because it's "the best," but because it's a nice camera, a good performer, and if you're willing to spend a bit more money than you might imagine, you can obtain some of its many accessories and lenses and can even get it repaired. However, if you want to be nit-picky about it, the Contaflex was never an "interchangeable lens" camera, as the rear optical components remain in place behind the shutter. It is usually referred to as a camera with "interchangeable optical components." Well, even hewing to the hardline definition of lens interchangeability, there *were* a handful of leaf-shutter SLRs graced with this feature, to wit, the Topcon Auto 100, Edixa Electronica, Retina Reflexes, Kowa SER and SETR's, and the Voigtlander Bessamatics and Ultramatics. How would I propose to select the "best" from this diverse bunch? Largely on the basis of hearsay and pure emotion. The Kowas are notoriously unreliable and hard to fix; the Topcon Auto 100 is sort of dull, and not beautifully made; the Edixa Electronica is weird and borders on the rare but is impractical; and I hope the world's Retina Reflex fanciers will forgive me, but I feel these solid, well-made cameras lack a certain sex appeal (maybe I'll change my mind when I finally get around to doing a Retina Reflex saga). That leaves the Voigtlanders, and in particular one of my favorites, the noble-looking, nicely finished, unpretentious Bessamatic.

When the Voigtlander Bessamatic made its debut back in late '58 it was almost high tech. Like the Kodak Retina Reflex S brought out about the same time, it was an SLR based on the famed Synchro-Compur 1-1/500 sec. (plus B) leaf shutter, and unlike the Contaflex III and IV introduced a year earlier, it had *full* lens interchangeability, with all optical elements in their double-helicals mounted directly in front of the shutter in a three-lobed bayonet

The ultimate Bessamatic? Final CS of 1967 had through-lens CdS match-needle metering, full finder readouts.

mount. Other "modern" features included a long throw, but single-stroke, rapid-advance lever and a moving meter needle and lollipop-type match-pointer located along the right side of the viewing image. However, one glance at the front of the prism housing reveals the Bessamatic as a creature of its time, for here is where you'll find the camera's selenium meter grid. Actually, there's nothing wrong with a selenium meter providing you don't expect it to provide readings in near darkness and can deal with its rather wide acceptance angle intelligently. The Bessamatic instruction manual cautions the photographer to take close-up readings when photographing backlit subjects, light things against dark backgrounds or vice-versa and this is good advice even if you're shooting with a more modern camera.

Push in a spring-loaded lever under the lens, turn the lens about 25° counterclockwise by its rear-most knurled ring, and lift it off and you'll probably be surprised when you examine the lens. The standard 50mm f/2.8 Color-

Skopar (the alternative lenses were a cheaper 50mm f/2.8 Lanthar or a more expensive 50mm f/2 Septon) is not only surprisingly petite (1¼ in. long, 2 in. maximum diameter), but also lacks any f/stop scale! However it does have a heavily knurled focusing ring toward its front, which takes the lens down to its 3.5 ft. minimum distance in a smooth clockwise turn of about 150°. Mount the lens on camera using the standard "match-the-red-dots, seat, and turn" system and you'll notice that two red index tabs emerging from under the lens-mounting ring will indicate the near and far ranges of depth of field on the focusing scale. Clever.

Here's how the whole plot functions. Press in and/or pull outward with your fingernail on a damnable little button on the ASA dial under the rewind knob and turn the red index line on the outer ring to the appropriate film-speed number (ASA 6 to one line past ASA 1600, whatever that is). Now select your shutter speed using the knurled plastic ears on the shutter-speed dial placed (concentrically) around the shutter, toward the rear of the lens and you're ready to meter. Since you've just mounted the lens, the shutter will have been cocked and the mirror's in viewing position—you can't mount the lens otherwise.

Glance through the Bessamatic's finder and you'll see a very bright viewing image with a coarse Fresnel pattern in the outer areas. Like the Contaflex screen, the Bessamatic's is non-focusing save for the central focusing aids, a central split-image rangefinder surrounded with wide-ish microprism collar. But first let's turn our attention to metering. To match the moving needle with the camera at eye level, grab hold of the outer knurled ring on the ASA dial (which is now locked in at its film speed setting) with your left thumb and forefinger and turn it until the "lollipop" pointer comes to rest over the meter needle. As you do this the aperture ring affixed to the camera turns, contacting a spring-loaded tab on the back of the lens unit, predetermining the actual shooting aperture. The Bessamatic's optics feature true internal diaphragm action and the lens does not stop down until the instant of exposure. However, as with most cameras of its ilk, there's no instant-return mirror—you must wind the film, cocking the shutter before the mirror returns to viewing position. Actually, leaf-shutter SLRs are quite mechanically complicated enough without having instant-return mirrors— the shutter and diaphragm must be open for viewing; then, as the mirror flies up the diaphragm must close down to shooting aperture and the shutter must open and close again to make the exposure. The result is a protracted, but fairly subdued mechanical clatter when you press the release, and a fairly long interval between the time you press the shutter and the exposure is executed. The noise level is not helped one bit by the mechanical racket accompanying film winding, which takes place both on the wind and lever-return actions.

Bright, but not light

Despite our addiction to modern SLRs with their full-focusing screens, we must admit that the Bessamatic's viewing and focusing systems, as well as its match-needle

metering are quite pleasant and efficient. The camera is rather heavy (over 2 lbs. with 50mm f/2.8), but it imparts a solid, well-balanced feel even when some of the longer lenses are used. Curiously, Voigtlander never got around to making a 28mm lens for the Bessamatic (even though Kodak offered the 28mm f/4 Curtagon for the competing Retina reflexes), but the tele end of the spectrum was well-catered for. Interchangeable optics included the 35mm f/3.4 Skoparex, 40mm f/2 Skopagon, 90mm f/3.4 and 100mm f/4.8 Dynarexes, and a 135mm f/4, 200mm f/4, and 350mm f/5.6, all bearing the Super-Dynarex trademark. In addition there was the famous 36-82mm f/2.8 Voigtlander-Zoomar, the first zoom lens for any 35mm SLR offered for sale to the general public.

Aside from its overall attention to detail, the Bessamatic has few frills. In the classic (and questionable) Voigtlander tradition, it lacks even neckstrap lugs. However, there are a few niceties—dual (top and bottom) locks on the hinged back, a baffle behind the mirror that fits into the film aperture to form an efficient light-tight seal, a film-type reminder wheel atop the film-wind lever, and a small foot below the lens-cum-mirror box surround, allowing the camera to stand level on a flat surface for time exposures. Perhaps most curious of all, however, is the clever system used on the film counter. Like many German cameras, the Bessamatic counts down, telling you how many pictures

An elegant touch on Bessamatics with subtractive film counters was knurled midsection of sprocket shaft (see text).

you have left, rather than how many you've taken. But when you push the rewind tab (about a half inch behind the shutter release) forward to "R" and turn the rewind knob, the counter counts up to let you know when to stop rewinding! Not only that—to set the film counter (which is not self-zeroing, obviously) you must manually set the counter to the mark *after* the number of shots on the roll. How? Push the rewind control to "R," open the back of the camera and turn the sprocket wheel until the correct (circle or diamond) symbol appears in a little window on the back. But you wouldn't want to turn that nasty old sprocket wheel with your tender little fingertips would you? No, so Voigtlander has thoughtfully provided a milled gripping surface in the middle of the sprocket shaft. Incredible.

Another typically German feature of the Bessamatic was its relative non-obsolescence, a polite way of saying they hardly ever changed it. In 1965, the company brought forth the Bessamatic M, which was almost identical to the Bessamatic except that it was about $35 cheaper ($185.95 with 50mm f/2.8 Color-Skopar lens) and had no built-in meter. More significant was the earlier (1962) Bessamatic Deluxe, which was virtually identical to the original model (its shutter was a Synchro-Compur X lacking an M-sync setting and the take-up spool and film-type reminder dial were slightly altered). The big difference was that it had a downward pointing prism affixed to the front of the prism housing, which reflected the set shutter speed and aperture up into a little "T-shaped" window above the viewing screen. This was pretty spiffy back in '62 and I don't believe I'm mistaken in stating that the Bessamatic Deluxe thereby qualifies as the first SLR with what has come to be known as a "full information" finder.

The final Bessamatic was the model CS of 1967, which was basically a Bessamatic Deluxe with through-lens CdS metering. In place of the meter grid above the lens was a bottom-hinged cover concealing a button battery and battery check button. Minor revisions included a self-zeroing, additive film counter, film-loaded signal on back, and the absence of filter factors next to the metering knob.

An optical bombshell

Now, turning back to that great hulking Voigtlander-Zoomar lens, we have a curious phenomenon indeed. To begin with, one of the great disadvantages of leaf-shutter SLRs is the narrow light path imposed by their relatively small diameter interlens shutters, which precludes the use of really fast lenses. For example, the aperture dial on the Bessamatic goes from f/2 to f/22 (you can't set it at wider aperture settings than the lens has, natch), and most lenses in the line were considerably slower than f/2. Yet, wonder of wonders, in 1959, out comes this semi-wide-to-semi-tele f/2.8 zoom lens, which was probably the most exciting thing to happen to the Bessamatic in its entire production life. Compared to modern zooms, the image quality provided by this first, camless, optically compensated zoom is mediocre, but not atrocious. And only lately have we begun to offer significantly wider and longer wide-to-tele zooms of such remarkable speed. Furthermore, the V-Z's operating controls are a marvel of ergonomics—you can focus with your last three digits while you zoom back and forth with your thumb and forefinger on the grippable "zoom collar." Ironically, the only modern two-touch zoom capable of a similar feat was the 40-80mm f/2.8 Minolta with concentric control "gearbox" on the right-hand side.

Where does all this leave us and our intrepid reader who shoots flash pictures in broad daylight? Well, if he's interested in a plain, original model Bessamatic with 50mm f/2.8 Color-Skopar in clean condition it leaves him out about $125. If he insists on gloating to his friends about his "obsolete," mid-60's SLR with full finder readouts, a Deluxe model will set him back $175-200, similarly equipped. And if he lusts after the world's first zoom for still photography in series production, he'll have to plunk down about $200 more. As for the rest of us, we can look forward to the next installment on the Voigtlander Ultramatic, an SLR which took leaf-shutter automation to then-untold heights and then promptly flopped on its face in the marketplace.

Voigtländer Ultramatics: Too much too soon?

Auto and match-needle exposure, instant-return mirror and diaphragm plus full finder information in an early-60's SLR? Alas, it was too good to be really reliable.

Although my discursive narrative style might lead you to believe otherwise, I have actually evolved a few rules for writing this column which have (usually) kept me out of major trouble in dealing with such arcane historical tidbits as the knurling patterns on rewind knobs, the metallic composition of neckstrap lugs, and the sundry needles and arrows of outrageous viewfinders.

Perhaps the most useful of these unspoken precepts—and the one most difficult to adhere to—comes under the general heading of "Don't trust anybody if you can help it." It goes like this: Never, ever provide specific details about a camera model unless you're holding the very machine in your hot little hands and can verify the facts personally. "Follow this dictum," I mutter to myself, "and at least your mistakes will be your very own, not some other photo-historical nitwit's."

As you've probably gathered by now, there were two tiny little nit-picky errors that appeared in the last Voigtländer Bessamatic epic, and both resulted from rely-

Grand, comprehensive, and noisy, the Ultramatic was world's third auto SLR.

ing on published "facts." First, a sin of omission: The Voigtländer Bessamatic m (not "M" as printed) was indeed a "meterless Bessamatic Deluxe" as claimed, but it also had a full-focusing screen sans central focusing aids while all others of its ilk had non-focusing Fresnel screens with central split-image rangefinders and clear focusing collars *a la* Contaflex. Error number two concerns the shutters used in this column's Voigtländer Ultramatics. They are not "Synchro-Compur X units with no M sync" as reported, but are labeled Synchro-Compur V (the Voigtländer script "V" from their ancient logo, natch) and they not only have M and X sync, but built-in self-timers as well, all settable via a little "MXV" tab on the left side of the camera (see photo). Now these may not strike you as major slips, but I assure you they've already resulted in a dozen mildly outraged epistles from Voigtländer fanatics. Well, I suppose it's a compliment to be read with such diligence.

State-of-the-art in '63

Turning now to the camera in hand—literally—we have one of the more fascinating and even brilliant products of early-60's West German technology, the original Voigtländer Ultramatic of 1963, a leaf-shutter SLR that prompted MODERN's testers (March 1963), to ask in the vernacular, "What's left to add?" Indeed, while the Ultramatic is large, loud, and none too flexible optically, it's got just about every feature a 20-year-old non-electronic SLR could hope for, and some useful items lacking on most of our current automatons.

Undoubtedly, the original Ultramatic's single most important technical feature is exposure automation of the shutter-preferred type, but it wasn't the first SLR to have it. That honor goes to the rare, clever, and mechanically unreliable Savoyflex Automatique of 1960, made by Royer in France. The second such creation was the renowned Contaflex Super B which aced out the Ultramatic by

one year, having been introduced in 1962. But while Voigtländer may have been a close third in the leaf-shutter auto SLR sweepstakes, it surely made up for it by being the most comprehensive.

The Ultramatic's grand features are paralleled by its imposing appearance. It's a tad over 4 in. tall, 5½ in. wide and weighs in at a hefty 2 lb., 5½ oz. with 50mm f/2 Septon (seven-element) lens. Its bright satin chrome finish is very good, and its stylish contours and distinctive selenium meter grid on the front of the prism housing give it a regal air. Its price was pretty regal, too—$365 with f/2 lens back in '63, which is equivalent to roughly 900 battered 1981 bucks.

Although the Ultramatic's majestic lens surround stirs visions of a wide-diameter lens mount, such is not the case. Press in the lens-release tab under the lens as you turn the lens clockwise, then lift off the lens, and you'll see that the Ultramatic's smallish, three-lobed bayonet is identical to the Bessamatic's. In fact, Ultramatic lenses will fit and couple perfectly on the Bessamatics—but only those lenses with an identifying yellow dot on the back will meter-couple properly with the Ultramatics. Just outside the actual mount area, nestled in arcuate grooves, are two little tabs. The one on the left (see photo) controls the aperture-stop-down mechanism, and the one on the right transfers the pre-set aperture from the camera to the lens.

The mount's the same as Bessamatic down to aperture-stop-down tab (see text).

All right, enough component ogling; here's how the Ultramatic's exposure automation operates. At the rear of the lens surround are two large scales that rotate concentrically with respect to the lens axis (*a la* Nikkormat FT). The forward ring, which has a knurled gripping surface on its underside, is the aperture ring, and it's calibrated from f/2 to f/22 with a further click-stopped setting (past f/22) denoted by a red "A." Directly behind the aperture ring is the shutter-speed ring with marked speeds of 1-1/500 sec. plus B. To change shutter-speed settings, you grab onto two knurled ears on the side of this ring, and to change film-speed settings (ASA 12-3200) you push in on a small knurled tab on the underside of this same ring, grab the self-same ears with thumb and forefinger, and turn it until a red delta lines up with the proper digits on the ASA scale near the lower left area of the lens. Now that we've set the ASA and set the aperture ring to "A," we're ready to meter. Choose and set a reasonable shutter speed, bring the camera to eye level, and all of a sudden you begin to appreciate how advanced this camera really is.

Since the chrome "nose" above the selenium meter grid contains a little prism which reflects *both* the aperture and shutter speed set into a little window above the finder screen, you know by observing the red "A" atop the white "60" that you're in auto-exposure mode and shooting at 1/60 sec. The aperture that the camera will automatically select for the lighting conditions is read out by a needle and crescent-shaped scale on the left side of the screen. In the middle of the scale are f/stop digits ranging from 2 to 22, and there are red areas above and below the numerical scale to denote over- and underexposure. Mount a lens slower than f/2 and the bottom red area moves up to cover the non-usable apertures—classy. What if you want to meter semi-automatically? It's a cinch—just make the settings you desire, with your eye still up at the viewfinder, and the Ultramatic's meter will continue to read out the camera-suggested aperture for the shutter speed and ASA you've set.

The joys of obsolete metering

Since the original Ultramatic is obviously not a through-lens-metering camera, some exposure compensation provision had to be made for using filters. Voigtlander's system is a dilly. Atop the right side of the camera, an inch above the long-throw, single-stroke wind lever, is a round filter-compensation control marked with red dots plus 1.5, 2, 3, 4, and 5. The detented red-dot position provides no exposure compensation, and you just set the appropriate filter factor before mounting a filter over the lens. Furthermore, as soon as you dial in any compensation, a black circle appears in the upper left-hand corner of the finder to warn you of the fact—a feature absent in most contemporary SLRs. Obviously, you can use the filter factor dial as an underexposure-compensation control if you wish, but in back-lit situations there's an easier method with the Ultramatic—simply take a close-up reading of your subject, lock it in by pressing the oddly-shaped, front-mounted shutter button part way in, back up and finish taking the shot. Such are the joys of "outdated" trapped-needle systems of exposure automation.

As soon as you follow through with your shutter finger, two additional characteristics of the Ultramatic become instantly apparent. One is wonderful, the other rather distasteful, and both are inextricably intertwined. To lead off with the good news, the Ultramatic was the very first leaf-shutter SLR to be blessed with an instant-return mirror

and instant-reopening (to full aperture) diaphragm. And while it's been argued for decades that these features offer only psychological advantages, they will nevertheless be appreciated by those weaned on modern SLRs. Unfortunately, the mechanical complexities and resultant clatter associated with these pleasant features sometimes hardly seem worth it. The '63 Ultramatic's loud and protracted ker-clunk must be heard to be believed, and its hint of tinniness—combined with the camera's noisy, ratcheted-but-single-stroke-only wind mechanism—does little to further the camera's quality image.

Counting down from 20 to 36

But to revel once again in the Ultramatic's niceties, all you have to do is load a roll of film: To open the double-locked back you must first move a knurled tab (it's near the upper left-hand edge of the camera) to the right and the rewind knob will pop up. Now pull up sharply on the knob (which is surmounted with a cute color-coded film-type reminder dial) and the back swings open toward the right. Inside, in addition to the usual features are a large plastic take-up spool with a single, wide opening but a very efficient film-grabbing tang, and a film roller to the left of the pressure plate to ensure smooth film take-up. Direct your attention to the bottom of the camera and you'll find yet another ingenious bit. The subtractive film counter on the left, which curiously advances as you fire the shutter, has two windows. Press and twist a textured fingertip control and you can select either a 36-exposure or 20-exposure countdown—a pointed answer to that poignant question. "How can you have a self-zeroing, exposure counter that doesn't count up from zero?" At any rate, if it's counting you can be pretty confident that the film is running through the camera—because it won't work without film in the camera! Rewinding is equally ingenious. There's no rewind button or lever—just release the rewind button as mentioned and the sprocket shaft is declutched and free to turn in reverse.

A less rotten Zoomar

As mentioned before, the optical range of the Bessamatic/Ultramatic series ranged from 35-350mm, including the improved version of the 36-82mm f/2.8 Voigtländer-Zoomar (the original one was pretty rotten). When you add all the little accessories—the right angle finder, left-handed shutter release, tripod and microscope adapters and myriad filters and close-up lenses—you have a fairly comprehensive system even by current standards. Regrettably, the Ultramatic was difficult to repair (intricate disassembly was required just to get at the shutter mechanism); the instant-return mirror, with its plastic stop, proved to be of dubious reliability; and the prism often suffered from desilvering with resultant finder woes. However, the second (and final) model of the Ultramatic "series" was designed to alleviate at least some of the problems while simultaneously updating the metering and viewing systems.

A metering breakthrough

The Voigtländer Ultramatic CS of 1965 shares honors with the Contaflex Super BC (introduced in the same year) as the first SLR of any kind with through-lens metering and full finder readouts (aka a full information finder). In the interest of mechanical reliability, the instant-return mirror and quick-return diaphragm found in the original model were deleted, but to make up for it, the CS incorporated a CdS metering system making "full-area integrated readings" off the viewing screen, and a full-focusing non-Fresnel-pattern screen with diagonal split-image rangefinder in the center. As a logical consequence of through-lens metering, which can usually compensate automatically for any filters placed over the lens, the filter-factor compensation control found on the original model became a modern-type compensation control providing up to plus- or minus-one-stop compensation, but virtually all other features were identical to those found on the 1963 model.

Triple lock is a dilly (see text).

Second and last Ultramatic, the CS, had behind-lens CdS meter, but no instant-return mirror or diaphragm.

Two exceptions: The CS has a rectangular pull-out battery compartment for a PX-13 or 625 battery on its back, a green battery check button to the right of the rewind knob and (yes, it's true) a *triple lock* on its hinged back. To open the CS you must first push a small round button on the back upward in the direction of the arrow; then, as you are doing so, push a knurled tab to the right, and finally,

pull up smartly on the popped-up rewind knob. Your chances of executing this sequence by accident are about one in a billion. Incidentally, the CS finder was adequately bright, and the camera was easy to focus (providing the prism did not desilver!) despite its lack of Fresnel assistance (the finder optics did include a condenser lens), but the meter was, curiously, about a stop *less* sensitive than the selenium meter fitted to the original version. Despite its mechanically simpler design, high price (also $365 with 50mm f/2), and seemingly robust construction, the CS didn't fare much better than the original Ultramatic in the reliability, durability or popularity departments. Too bad, for in many ways they were the most advanced auto-exposure SLRs of the brief era before the introduction of the Konica Autoreflex in 1967 (the first widely available auto-exposure SLR with focal-plane shutter). Certainly they're no slouches optically, and their modest sales success has made good, functioning examples fairly uncommon today.

For the record, the selling prices of the featured Ultramatics (both in very good cosmetic and operating condition) are: Original model with 50mm f/2.8 Color-Skopar lens, $200; Ultramatic CS with 50mm f/2 Septon lens, $275. Of course, user-collectors will have to add the price of a genuine leather case (about $30) to the above, since both Ultramatics are proud exemplars of the neckstrap-lugless Voigtländer tradition! Many thanks to Bernd Minderjahn of Profoto of New York for furnishing the brace for our delectation.

The Zeiss Ikoflex saga, part 1

The Zeiss Ikoflex Saga, Part 1. Wherein a leading German camera maker tries to emulate or outdo the most famous TLR.

Ever since I was a youthful and itinerant old-camera hunter, skulking through seedy neighborhoods amongst the pawnshops, asking too many silly questions of wizened and knowledgeable old camera salesmen along New York's "camera row," I have fancied Zeiss Ikoflexes. Actually, like many "serious photographers" before me, I have really coveted those matchless examples of well-integrated and meticulously executed TLR-dom known as Rolleiflexes—but the Ikoflex, in many cases, offered the same optics, shutter and basic features for less money. And after all, the legendary firm of Zeiss-Ikon which made them had its own panache, so you didn't have to suffer the ignominy of toting a "cheap" camera in order to save money. Regrettably, though the Ikoflexes surely offered fine construction and were beautifully made and finished, there is something ineffably clunky about most models—something not found in spec sheets but in hands-on shooting that might indicate that the cameras were designed by engineers instead of photographers. Indeed, by and large, these noble twin-lens beasts were never a resounding success in the marketplace (at least in the U.S.), nor is their general reputation up to their actual picture-taking performance. But it was not ever thus—in fact just before the Second Great Unpleasantness, the Zeiss Ikoflex was, from somewhat humble beginnings, at the pinnacle of its prestige and mechanical development. So let's hark back to those bleak Depression days when the house of Zeiss-Ikon unleashed what is perhaps the strangest Ikoflex of them all, the (for lack of a better designation) Original.

Although postwar Zeiss Ikoflexes have justly been called unabashed Rolleiflex take-offs, this can hardly be said of the original Ikoflex of 1934. A more "different" configuration for a twin-lens reflex designed for 120 roll film would be hard to imagine, and most of the camera's controls are situated precisely where you wouldn't expect them. To get the basic specs out of the way, our "Original" is fitted with an 80mm f/4.5 Novar-Anastigmat lens (a so-so triplet), an unmarked Sucher-Anastigmat viewing lens, and an everset, interlens leaf shutter with speeds of 1/25-1/100 sec. plus T and B. The shutter release is a little milled tab just above the "I" in the Ikoflex nameplate, while both apertures (to f/22) and shutter speeds are set with milled tabs below the lens.

So much for the conventional stuff—now the fun begins. Visually, the most distinctive feature of this model is the art deco, "elongated hexagonal" lensboard, but even more fascinating is the way it focuses. Grab a little knurled-tip lever on its left-hand side (in shooting position) and move it downward to focus closer. Distances (down to a marked 3.6 ft.) are read out by a rotating wheel atop the lensboard, which is surmounted with what must be the world's most illegible depth-of-field scale (in deference to its age I'll presume the digits and lines were once enameled in white). For those of you who wonder about such trivia, the fact that this camera's focusing scale was calibrated in feet rather than meters indicates that it was intended for export, as confirmed by its left-hand finder-hood flap with an exposure table in English.

As long as we've mentioned the focusing hood, let's state that the original Ikoflex set one trend that was to continue among prewar Ikoflexes—its focusing hood was

Distinctively different in shape and design, the original "art deco" Ikoflex had two frame counters, but why?

of the old fashioned "four-flap" type instead of Rollei's more convenient "front and back sections," which could be closed with one hand. Now that our hood is open for viewing, let's flip up the hinged magnifier and take a peek at the viewing image. Yes, by today's standards it's miserably dim, with much fall-off at the edges, but that's really no worse than most roll-film TLRs of the era.

Naturally I've saved the best for last, and in this case it's the loading procedure. As you might surmise from examining the original Ikoflex's bulging sides and side-mounted covered red window, this is one of the few roll-film TLRs to feature side-to-side (rather than top-to-bottom or vice-versa) film transport. To achieve this, the Zeiss-Ikon engineers used a film insert system similar to that found on many box cameras, but it's actually quite effective. Press in a small silver button about an inch below the

A bottom loader, original Ikoflex had pull-down film holder section (right) with hinged spool retainers and pressure plate, wind lever on bottom. Cast-alloy body (left) is hell for strong.

finder hood release bar on the back of the camera as you grab hold of two nubbins on the side of the camera body with your other hand, and the whole thing emerges giving you a clear view of the camera's die-cast alloy body. Atop the insert itself are two hooks which engage spring-loaded catches inside the camera body, and two hinged spool retainers. Place a fresh roll of film and an empty spool in the clearly marked chambers, click the spool retainers closed, lift the hinged pressure plate and thread the paper leader (black side in) over the thin rollers on either side of the film aperture and onto the empty spool, bring the pressure plate back down over the film, click the film holder back into the body and you're ready to go.

Knobless nicety

Where is the film-advance knob, you ask? There isn't any, but on the bottom front of the camera, integral with the film holder section, is a spring-loaded lever that moves side to side. Wind the film until number "1" appears in the red window, then push a small lever under the wind lever to the right and the two(!) frame counters, one atop each of the bulging side sections, will read "1." Obviously, there's no double or blank exposure prevention in a camera with an everset shutter, and the film-wind lever doesn't stop automatically when you reach the next exposure, but the Ikoflex's semi-auto frame counter nevertheless was an improvement over ye olde red window. What's the necessity of having two such frame counters? The one on the left, marked "Met" for "metal spool," was designed to count 620 film, while the right-hand counter was calibrated for the thicker 120 spool! At any rate, the original Ikoflex, in adddition to being peculiar, is also heavy and quite rare. I'd peg the current value of our very-good-condition example at about $200.

Later, in 1937 to be exact, Zeiss-Ikon brought forth the

Conventional and competent, Ikoflex II of 1937 had first-rate shutter and optics, but somewhat dated features.

Ikoflex II which, if less audacious and more Rollei-ish than its predecessor, was at least a much better camera. This model was fitted with a very good 75mm f/3.5 Zeiss Tessar lens in 1-1/500 sec. (plus B) Compur-Rapid shutter, a 75mm f/3.5 viewing lens, and it has a large diameter focusing knob near the center of its left side, a feature Rollei wouldn't have until shortly after the war. Even more importantly, the II incorporated true double-exposure prevention—you had to wind the film to the next exposure before you could fire the shutter. As you can guess from its classic TLR shape, the model II also had conventional bottom-to-top film transport with a standard film-wind knob on the right side.

Although the Ikoflex II was very nicely made and quite handsome in an understated way, it had few features to compete with the legendary Rolleiflex Automat introduced in the same year. Its major claim to fame was a shutter-release button conveniently placed at the right front corner of the finder hood. Also its lever-controlled aperture and shutter speed settings adjacent to the taking lens, with small readout windows above the lensboard front section were (in addition to being a left-handed homage to Rollei) much better placed for swift picture taking. Where the Ikoflex II was deficient was in those little conveniences that separate good cameras from great ones. The II's shutter still had to be cocked manually with a little lever below the taking lens, so there was a little window about ¾ in. behind the shutter button to tell you what was going on—if the film wasn't wound it would show white, but if it was wound to the next exposure it would show red. Why? Because if you couldn't press the shutter button you wanted to know whether it was the film wind or shutter-cocking lockout that was preventing you from doing so. Compare this to the Rolleiflex Automat, which has automatic first frame positioning and counter coupling (the Ikoflex did not), crank wind, and automatic parallax compensation in the finder! Of course the Ikoflex II (at $95 in New York) was cheaper and it was an excellent picture taker, and 10 or 20 bucks was certainly an important consideration back then. Withal, the Ikoflex II was in many ways the most successful of its breed, as a camera and in the marketplace, so there *are* virtues to the conservative, derivative approach. Oh yes, I almost forgot, today an Ikoflex II in very fine shape is worth about $150.

One shall not lead

Shortly after the Ikoflex II made its debut, there was (would you believe) the Ikoflex I of 1938, which was produced almost unchanged until shortly after World War II. It's usually found with a 75mm f/3.5 Novar lens and a Compur (not Compur-Rapid) 1-1/300 sec. shutter. If that isn't strange enough for you, I have it on good authority that the model II I just told you about was demoted from being the model III when the camera I am about to describe was introduced! Maybe those wily Germans had called the original model the 1 after all, but that doesn't fully explain the pre-war Ikoflex nomenclature mess. At any rate, the Ikoflex III of 1939 was undoubtedly the greatest of the Ikoflex generation even if it wasn't the finest in terms of optical performance. Ikoflex die-hards who insist that their TLRs are as good as anything those upstarts from Braunschweig ever made usually bring up this model in their defense, and a glorious machine it is, too.

As expected, there's a family resemblance between the Ikoflex II and its posher, much-more-expensive cousin. The focusing knob (larger, but still with adjacent depth-of-field scale) is amidships on the left, the shutter release

A majestic masterpiece, Ikoflex III of 1939-40 had Rollei beat on lens speed, rapid-fire action, but not on overall design integration. It's rare.

(now a lever instead of a button) is up near the right front corner of the finder hood, and the lens and shutter-speed controls run in arcuate grooves on the side of the taking lens. However the whole "presence" of the model III is of another order entirely—you're cognizant of holding the premier roll-film TLR creation of one of the world's greatest camera companies—and its appearance with viewing hood erected is imposing, to say the least.

Futuristic features

The Ikoflex III's features are equally impressive. It's fitted with an 80mm f/2.8 Zeiss Tessar lens (which stops down to f/22), has a self-returning, spring-loaded film-wind crank on the side which advances to the next frame in one swift downward stroke of the right thumb, and this action simultaneously cocks the shutter. The film counter (about an inch behind the shutter release) features automatic first-frame positioning (after you line up the arrow on the paper backing with dots on the sides of the film aperture) and is self-zeroing. However, you can't turn the crank continuously after the twelfth exposure as you can

on a Rollei, so there's an end-of-roll indicator below the crank to let you know when the paper backing is on the roll and you can open the camera.

Although the Ikoflex III's lens is a half-stop faster than the Rollei's of the same era, you had to pay for it in two ways (besides money). The larger-diameter optic meant that the Compur-Rapid shutter had a top speed of only 1/400 sec. rather than 1/500 sec. Also, it was not a stellar performer, particularly at wide apertures, as Rollei found

Five easy features: Below spring-loaded crank is film-end-signal window; above it is auto frame counter. In front of counter is shutter-release lever; below it and forward is self-timer control.

out when they fitted it to the ill-starred Rolleiflex of 1949. But the Ikoflex III had something else going for it besides mere optics. Lift the finder hood and magnifier and glance downward and you'll see a viewing image, provided by the 80mm f/2.8 Teronar viewing lens, that is reasonably bright even by current standards (although it does fall off in brightness at the corners). Now glance through the rear "sports-finder" eyepiece at the back of the hood, and you'll comprehend the purpose of that beautiful sexy mirror on the front of the finder hood. What you see before you, friends, is a genuine Albada viewfinder, which is like a true *reflected* frameline that looks like a *projected* frameline. Now focus the camera closer and notice how the frameline moves downwards. That's right—while the Ikoflex III lacks the Rollei's superb parallax-compensated focusing image or its eye-level focusing mirror (which let you focus at eye level, but upside down and laterally reversed!), it certainly has the most splendid sports finder ever fitted to a twin-lens reflex. Other amenities include a self-timer (set by pushing up a lever to the right of the finder lens) and a "shutter cocked" indicator (to the left of the taking lens).

Not lightly taken

One feature that is hardly ever mentioned in referring to the Ikoflex III is its light weight. While it's no featherweight, at just a smidgeon over 1 kilo (2.2 lbs.), it is obvious that Zeiss-Ikon went to great metallurgical pains to keep their large, deluxe TLR easy to tote. They also spent great effort on the camera's detailing and finish, which can only be described as exquisite. Of course, such pains don't come cheaply, and the Ikoflex III originally sold in New York for a princely $199 back in '39. Today, the Ikoflex III borders on being rare, and the magnificent model pictured sold recently for $550. In my view, even the Ikoflex III, for all its panache, was never so well integrated a photographer's camera as the Rolleiflex Automat and its successors. But it certainly stands as a monument to the persistence, mechanical ingenuity, and dedication of Zeiss-Ikon's engineers.

Many thanks to Ken Hansen Photographic Inc. of New York (and to Ken personally) for providing the early Ikoflexes used in this column, and a bouquet to Thomas A. Beckett of the *New York Times* for lending us his pristine Ikoflex III.

Rangefinder Nikons and SLRs from Leitz

Rangefinder Nikons and SLRs from Leitz prove that finesse and quality are variegated virtues.

Despite my rapidly approaching 40th birthday (Feb. '82 —please, no cards to remind me) and the onset of middle-age spread, I am seldom given to mawkish sentiments about my declining years or the folly of youth. But there are times when such thoughts are unavoidable, as when contemplating the incredulous expressions of teenagers when you tell them that you first "saw" the Lone Ranger on radio, or when, as I did just yesterday, of explaining to a young pro photographer that yes, Nikon really built their original reputation on a very fine, if mostly derivative, series of rangefinder 35s in the 50's. It is indeed a tribute to Nikon's engineering and marketing prowess that today people think "SLR" when you mention their name. Leitz probably wishes people would think the same

Stodgy precision? Sorta, but original Leicaflex of '65 had renowned "Leica feel," performance to match, and a very bright viewfinder which focused only in the center!

when hearing the prestigious name "Leica," but they don't. That's what happens when you've been producing the world's premier rangefinder camera since the early 30's and only deigned to allow your SLRs to be addressed likewise since '77 (the Leica R3).

This brings me to the subject of the original Leicaflex of 1965, a camera that appears much better in retrospect than when it first debuted. (If Nikon rangefinder fans will bear with us for a while, we'll conclude with a few delicious examples of this breed.) Why the lukewarm reception? Many reasons. Leica fans more or less expected an SLR from Leitz to be a combination M-series body with a Visoflex III tucked into it and then some. What they got was a magnificently crafted "tank" of a camera with a separate, external CdS meter port instead of behind-lens metering, and a brilliant aerial image viewfinder, but with focusing restricted to a central microprism circle, and no depth-of-field preview. It was clear that this dated design was served up by a group of ultraconservative engineering perfectionists having a fine disregard for the demands or economies of the marketplace. "You want an SLR from Leitz?", they seemed to say, "We'll give you what we think is best, and you'd better like it." Such a magisterial-bordering-on-arrogant attitude might prevail in Europe, but it hardly carried the day in the U.S., and relatively few Leicaflexes (at $585 per copy with 50mm f/2 Summicron-R lens) were sold over here.

Still, quality without compromise has its virtues. And while the 3.7-in. high, 5.9-in. long, 2.2-in. wide body of the original Leicaflex appears ungainly, and its weight of 34.5 oz. (with 50mm f/2 lens) would seem excessive, it begins to grow on you after you've shot a few rolls with it. For one thing, the body's distinctive "rounded, elongated trapezoid" shape contours quite nicely to human digits, and the camera's considerable heft imparts a feeling of solidity. Then there's the finder, with one of the most

Shape of SLRs to come? In a way. Leicaflex's palmable, rounded contours parallel those of current compacts.

brilliant viewing images extant thanks to an extremely fine (but non-focusing) Fresnel outer area, and a large central microprism circle incorporating one of the finest patterns ever seen in such a device. True, the prism is fixed, the screen non-interchangeable, and you're forced to focus in the center of the screen and then recompose if necessary, but the finder must nevertheless be counted among the Leicaflex's plus points. Below the viewing image is a horizontal shutter-speed scale with cutout numerals from 1 to 2000 plus B and black index line, and along the right side of the viewing area there's the moving meter needle, a lollipop-shaped match-needle pointer, and dots to indicate maximum and minimum metering range. Yes, the Leicaflex meters at wide-open aperture, and you needn't remove it from eye level to find out what shutter speed you've set.

Aside from its superb finish and general air of overdesign, the Leicaflex's interior is quite conventional—the heavy cast-alloy back is hinged (a first for Leitz) and the hinge itself is a study in overkill. Equally ordinary are the ASA dial under the rewind crank (ASA 12-3200), the self-timer lever (next to the mirror lock-up lever) on the front, and the rewind button on the bottom. True, the battery check button next to the CdS meter port on the front of the prism housing, and the round battery chamber cover on the opposite end of the prism's front plate are a bit unusual, but these are minor points. However, the controls clustered around the shutter release are all, in their own quiet way, quite remarkable.

Best SLR shutter release ever?

First of all, the large (1-in. diameter) heavily knurled shutter-speed dial is placed very conveniently around the shutter release, and the horizontal travel, rubberized cloth, focal-plane shutter itself does provide a top speed of 1/2000 sec., and an electronic flash sync speed of 1/100 sec., instead of the usual 1/60. The concentric film-wind lever is not ratcheted, and its throw is moderate (120°) plus 60° from tucked-in to standoff position), but its action is but-

tery smooth even with film in the camera. The crowning glory is, as you might expect the shutter release itself, a model of super-smoothness and predictability. And the mirror-flipping action is surely among the smoothest and most jar-free to be found on any 35mm SLR (though possibly the camera's weight is equally responsible for damping out any shake).

Coupled to this mechanically superb machine are an excellent and accurate (though not extremely sensitive) meter, and a fine quality 50mm f/2 Summicron lens (six elements, non-multicoated, but equal to any of its competitors). As you'd expect, the focusing helical is silky smooth, and all engravings are superb (though the original lens's red-on-black footage markings were none too legible in dim light). In short, the original Leicaflex coupled uncompromising design with uncompromising quality, qualifying it as one of the best "user collectibles" currently available. Oh yes—while the original Leicaflex is finally starting to "take off" pricewise it is still, relatively speaking, in the doldrums. Granted, $400 for a near-mint, perfectly functioning example with lens will buy you a lot of mechanically competent, technically advanced contemporary machinery, but it's still small potatoes for a superbly finished mechanical masterpiece that will function with current Leica R3/R4 lenses and can be adapted to take rangefinder Leica optics as well.

More than a Japanese Contax, Nikon S of '52 offered precision at low cost.

Turning now to the legendary rangefinder Nikons, let's back up a bit and see just what it is that Nippon Kogaku had wrought. Remember we're back in those nasty days just after WWII, when Japanese camera manufacturers were getting their inspiration from the well-established Europeans rather than from the latest in micro-electronics. So, enter the Nikon designers, desiring to concoct a first-class, interchangeable lens rangefinder 35. Where would they get the world's best combined range/viewfinder? From the renowned Contax II of 1936, and they would lift it from Zeiss complete with focusing via a finger wheel adjacent to the right-hand (moving image) window, using a lens mount virtually identical to the Contax also. Indeed, the rotating, 3-lobed bayonet with spring-loaded (actually a notched flat spring) mounting catch and outer 3-lobed bayonet (beyond the moving focusing scale on the front of the mount) was such a perfect copy that wide-angle Contax lenses (shorter than 50mm) could actually be used on rangefinder Nikons sans modification (a tiny difference in the back focus prevented longer Contax lenses from being used, but Nikon offered slightly revised "C" labelled lenses for Contaxes).

So far, the original Nikons would seem to be nothing more than Japanese Contaxes, but here's where a bit of straightforward genius comes in. The one feature of the Contax that no savvy camera maker in his right mind would steal is the shutter mechanism. Why? Because as clever as the Contax's vertical-travel, metal roller blind shutter was and is, it's overly complex, difficult to manufacture, and, in effect, less reliable than the more conventional horizontal cloth focal-plane shutter found in the classic rangefinder Leica (and the original Leicaflex). Ergo, Nikon's engineers decided to go with the Leica shutter in their Contax-ish body, creating what many regard as one of the finest rangefinder 35s the world has ever seen.

Since I was unable to snare either the original Nikon I or Nikon M (introduced in 1948 and 1949 respectively), let's just say that the "I" is the rarest Nikon rangefinder model (current value about $450) and is identified by its non-standard 24 × 32mm format, frame counter numbered past 40, and lack of flash sync. The model M is much more common and is basically the same as the model I, but provides the standard 24 × 36mm format and has a frame counter numbered to 36. Both these models closely resemble the model S, which was introduced in 1952, and was almost identical to the model M but had flash sync built in (up to 1/20 sec. on X; 1/40 sec. or faster with FP bulbs) and a double sync cord receptacle on its upper, front left-hand corner. Since the Leica-type shutter has separate fast and slow-speed gear trains and dials, The Nikon had its slow-speed dial concentrically around and just below the rotating fast-speed dial.

conventional knurled knob, and the film take-up spool is non-removable. The range/viewfinder has a greenish-tinted viewing image with contrasting pinkish rangefinder patch and compares favorably with the somewhat larger Contax II finder. Perhaps more prescient was the general fit, feel and finish of the Nikon, which, incredibly, were the equivalent of the more expensive German camera. Of course, it was the Nikon's lenses, particularly the fabled 50mm f/1.4 Nikkor, that were largely responsible for creating Nikon's image of quality, and here it's a question of small improvements creating great legends. The original 50mm f/1.4 Nikkor-S lens was perhaps a tad better than the 50mm f/1.5 Summarit from Leitz, about equal to the remarkably good (for its day) 50mm f/1.5 Sonnar from Zeiss, and a teensy bit faster than either one. In addition, the early Nikkor was amazingly consistent from lens to lens, indicating a great deal of hand assembly and subsequent quality control.

By the time the second classic rangefinder Nikon, the S2 began to roll off the production line in 1955, Nikon had already established an enviable reputation for optical and mechanical quality among the world's photojournalists. And while the S2 hewed quite closely to the original Nikon rangefinder concept, improvements were numerous. First and foremost, the S2 had a much larger viewfinder window, providing 1:1 life-size viewing (a feature lacking on even the exquisite Leica M-3) and a fixed bright-line finder. Shutter speeds on the dials (now black with white digits) went up to 1/1000 sec., and flash sync delay via a single PC contact was settable for X (at 1/50 sec.) or FP bulbs using a flash sync dial beneath the new folding rewind crank. Finally, the camera now had a ratcheted, single-stroke wind lever, and the removable back was now locked with a single bottom lock, with a film-speed reminder dial where the second lock used to be. I have

A usable classic, Nikon S2 of '55 now fetches $300 with 50mm f/1.4 Nikkor.

Rarest rangefinder Nikon? Last model S4 sold only in Japan. Current price: $1,000.

Incidentally, the Nikon S's back is removable a la Contax with a twist lock on either end, film advance is via

always regarded the Nikon S2 as a benchmark among 35mm rangefinder cameras and perhaps the first clear indication that the Japanese were about to wrest the leadership role from the Germans in camera technology, design, and marketing (the S2 was advertised using Joe Ehrenreich's timeless slogan—"Advance, Focus, Shoot," highlighting the camera's logically placed controls). Yes, the finish is gorgeous, the controls operate with silken precision, and the damn thing is a visual work of art. But I still can't stand the pressed, hollow bottom wind lever which is the only chintzy bit on the whole glorious camera. I guess I'm getting old.

How to *Sell* your camera

Do you want a swift and convenient transaction or maximum dollar return?

While potential camera *buyers* have been continually deluged with short and lengthy articles, entire magazines, and even books designed to turn tyros into knowledgeable purchasers, those of us faced with *selling or trading* our photographic treasures have been virtually ignored. Since the vast majority of cameras *are* eventually sold or traded in by their owners, this "information gap" has resulted in much wailing and gnashing of teeth and not incidentally, a steady stream of anguished letters to yours truly. To remedy this intolerable oversight I hereby present my fearless and (hopefully) comprehensive guide to selling your camera(s). But before we begin delving into the inner recesses of this complex and fascinating subject, kindly bear one large fact in mind: All of the following methods of sale (or trade) have distinct advantages and disadvantages. If they didn't, the other methods wouldn't exist, at least not in a (relatively) free-market economy. The trick is to select the method of selling or trading that best suits your particular situation.

To sell or not to sell?

Obviously, there are many valid reasons for selling your faithful 1968 Rexoflex even if it has proven reliable and still functions perfectly. Maybe you want an SLR with more modern features, such as auto-exposure and dedicated flash capability, or perhaps you're taking the plunge and switching to a camera system with a non-compatible lens mount or even to a different format altogether. But, as always, it pays to think before you act. For example, maybe your Minolta SR-T 101 isn't new and shiny, but it can serve as an excellent back-up to your newly acquired Minolta XG-M and will even do some things the latest automatic model won't (like provide a full range of shutter speeds with a dead battery). So before you sell it or trade it in, consider how it would or could fit into your present picture taking system. The same thing holds true for non-system cameras in many cases, particularly if they offer unique features. I recently toyed with the idea of unloading my near-mint Yashica-Mat 124G for a paltry $75 (a bit less than its wholesale value), but when I considered that I ran about 40 rolls of 120 film through it last year and then examined the enhanced technical quality of my 11 x 14s shot on the 2¼ x 2¼ in. format, I decided to keep it. Likewise the actual value of many old folding and box cameras, fixed-lens rangefinder 35s, and non-meterized 35mm SLRs is often so low that it may pay to save them for a budding young photographer in your family, or to donate them to a local charity organization's flea market.

Why not trade it in?

Presuming you've decided to unload your camera in some manner, why not do what most people do and trade it in on the new camera of your dreams? The big advantage of this method—and it shouldn't be underestimated in your mental calculations—is convenience. You simply present your used camera for the dealer's appraisal, negotiate a fair trade-in value, apply that value to the price of the new camera, and pay the difference. It's neat, clean, swift, and utterly devoid of lingering details.

The main disadvantage of this ubiquitous selling method—and don't forget that trading in is just another form of selling—is that it's a poor way of maximizing the dollars you obtain for your camera. Or, to put it another way you *do* ordinarily pay for the convenience of trading in your camera by receiving less for it than you would probably get by selling it to a private individual. How much less do you get? Well, that depends on numerous factors, including the particular dealer, the type of camera, whether it's a discontinued model, a "slow" or "hot" seller, etc. But typically, a camera worth $100 on a trade-in against the actual selling price (not the list price!) of a new camera can be sold for roughly $150-175 on the open market.

Does this mean that the majority of camera dealers are truly greedy, or worse? Emphatically not—they're simply operating on the sound business principles of profit and loss, and attempting to minimize the latter. For example, the aforementioned cameras maybe worth $100 on a trade-in because it's three years old, isn't the latest model, is in cosmetically good (but not excellent) condition, and originally cost the dealer $200 when new. Since you paid $250 for it as a brand-new camera, a $100 trade-in may seem like a rip-off, but consider the following facts:

(1) Your camera may have concealed damage that's not apparent at the time of the dealer's cursory check. If so, it will have to be repaired at cost to the dealer before the camera can be sold.

(2) Unless the dealer sells your used camera "as is" at a substantially reduced price, he'll have to guarantee it for anywhere from 30 days to one year and/or offer a 10-day money-back return privilege to the buyer. This may entail extra costs.

(3) With new camera models being introduced more frequently, and genuine technical advances often present in newer models at the same cost as (or only slightly higher than) the models they supersede, discontinued or older models may depreciate in value more rapidly. This is particularly true if a given camera is a current production model when you sell it to the dealer, but is discontinued before the dealer has a chance to sell it to another buyer.

In short, taking in used cameras is an even riskier business than buying them for personal use, and the only practical way for the dealer to bring his risk down to manageable proportions is to offer the seller a lower price or trade-in value.

Or sell it to a dealer?

What about selling your camera to a dealer directly, for cash on the barrelhead? Well, this may be useful if you must have instant cash to meet a mortgage payment or keep the wolf from the door but it's not usually financially rewarding. Without the incentive of a new camera sale to mitigate the previously mentioned financial risks involved, you'll probably get only about half the retail value of your camera—roughly $75 in cash versus $100 on the trade-in already discussed. You'll often get a higher percentage of the retail value on such items as rangefinder Leicas and current, top-of-the-line SLRs that are in short supply, but the convenience of a straight cash sale to a dealer is seldom worth the dollar loss.

There's one type of sale involving a dealer that ought to be more popular than it is—selling on consignment. The basic principle is quite straightforward—you leave your camera at the dealer's store (make sure you get a receipt for it!) and he sells it for you. When the camera is sold, the dealer notifies you of its selling price, shows you the sales receipt and takes a percentage of the sale—typically 10 to 20 percent—for his services. Using our well-worn example, if your camera sells for $150 and the dealer charges 15 percent, you get $127.50 in cash, which is a lot better than a $100 trade-in or $25 less than that in greenbacks.

While the merits of this system sound almost too good to be true, it's not without its foibles. For one thing, many large, urban camera stores and camera departments don't accept cameras or anything else to be sold on consignment because they object to the "loose ends" and extra bookkeeping involved. Some stores will, however, make exceptions for steady, longtime customers, particularly when you're trying to sell a rare high-priced or classic camera as opposed to a more pedestrian item. If you're friendly with the owner of a smaller local camera emporium, there's a

good chance you can convince him to sell your camera on consignment and, financially speaking, it sure beats most other methods of selling through a retail establishment. But bear in mind that it may take quite a while to sell your camera in this way, and there's no guarantee that it'll be sold at all. In fact, some stores will place your camera on their shelves for a limited period only—often 60 to 90 days. If it isn't sold by then you get it back and are faced with your original dilemma.

Before we leave the subject of selling to and through camera stores, a few final words of caution. While the vast majority of stores are honest and forthright in their trade-in and selling practices, there is a small percentage of outfits that engage in sharp and shady dealings. To guard against getting stung, it's essential to establish at least a ballpark figure for the retail value of the camera you're selling, and in the case of trade-ins, the going price of the camera you're buying as well. The easiest way to get a line on your camera's value is to shop around various stores selling used equipment and see what it's selling for around town. If your town or the nearest metropolis is too small to permit such a luxury, you can peruse newspaper ads in the "Articles for Sale" section of the classified, pore over the numerous used camera ads in *Modern Photography* and the new "Readers Bulletin Board" classified ad section, check out the local "pay-for-the-ad-when-you-sell-it" paper, etc. Remember that asking prices are only a rough guide to actual selling prices, which are apt to be somewhat lower. The local paper, particularly the Sunday edition of metropolitan dailies, is a good source for new camera selling prices as well, as are *Modern Photography* and other photo magazines, local advertising flyers, and sale prices displayed at camera stores and departments. While some experienced camera traders advise buyers to negotiate a cash price for a new camera and then present the trade-in camera as an afterthought, my advice is to do just the opposite, but not to let on that you're aware of the camera's local "discount" selling price. If you then ask the dealer how he calculated the final trade-in price and he starts off with a new camera selling price that's way out of line, you know you're dealing with a sharpie who has artificially inflated the value of your trade-in! Of course the obvious advantage of knowing the value of both pieces of merchandise is being able to judge what kind of deal you're getting whether the dealer is honest or not. And don't overlook the possibility of haggling to obtain the deal you had in mind. In many retail stores and in certain localities, it's considered poor form to haggle over the established selling prices for new merchandise, but at trade-in time a bit of old-fashioned bargaining is often accepted. In any case you won't be arrested for it, and monetarily it's worth a try.

It pays to advertise . . .

This brings us to the grand and glorious subject of advertising your cameras for sale, or more specifically to the pros and cons of the various methods of doing so. No matter what form it takes, an ad is essentially a written proclamation that you have something to sell, and it may be enhanced by an enticing but *absolutely factual* description of the item in question. By all means include all relevant information such as brand, model, lens speed and focal length, basic features, and asking price. Some sellers favor listing a highish "asking price" to allow the buyer reasonable room for bargaining, while others furnish a minimum non-negotiable price using the form "$300 firm." Both approaches are useful and workable, and which one you use depends largely on your personal style and willingness to engage in the ancient ritual of bargaining. I suggest you avoid the practice of listing no price and substituting the phrase "best offer." The subliminal message you're sending to potential buyers is that you either don't know what your camera is worth or that you'll take anything you can get. Most people are turned off by the idea that they're "bidding" on your equipment. In any case, reasonable asking prices may be obtained by the same method as ballpark selling prices discussed earlier.

What can you legitimately do to entice customers to respond to your ad? Well, if your camera is "hardly used," in "mint" or "excellent" condition, is genuinely "rare" or a "classic" it doesn't hurt to say so, but you'd better be honest or you can wind up looking pretty foolish. By all means list accessories that will be useless to you once the camera is sold—they can only increase its value and/or appeal. And if you sell your camera along with additional lenses as well as cases, filters, etc., make sure to list it as an "outfit," which indeed it is. Sometimes a catchy phrase, bold type, capital letters, or a slightly altered word order compared to other similar ads will get a better response, but don't overdo the cuteness and cleverness. Do list your phone number(s) and the hours when you can (or would prefer to) be reached; don't give out your address unless a local party says he's coming over at a stated time or a distant party says he's sending a check.

But where to advertise?

As with every other aspect of the camera selling game, every one of the advertising media covered below has its good points and its difficulties. We'll go into some detail on those publications that charge for placing an ad (or when you sell the advertised item), but keep in mind that there are some free ways of advertising your wares. Community bulletin boards can be particularly effective if they're strategically located in large offices, well-attended houses of worship, town halls, camera repair shops, supermarkets, etc.—and they're absolutely free. Type or print your notice (neatness counts). Some bulletin board advertisers cut the bottoms of their ad cards into little strips imprinted with their phone numbers, which strikes me as a clever idea. Clearly, even a heavily perused bulletin board is no match for the average newspaper when it comes to reaching potential buyers, but most folks who read your ad will live or work in your area so you can arrange to "show and sell" your equipment without too much hassle.

Which medium fits your message?

Local newspapers offer several advantages as a camera-advertising medium. As mentioned, they almost always reach a larger audience than community bulletin boards and other informal methods, but respondents to your ad will more than likely be within convenient driving distance, so you can consummate the sale expeditiously.

Although small "home town" weeklies offer cheaper rates than daily papers covering larger areas, I recommend choosing a local paper with a circulation of say, at least 50,000—the $10-20 they charge for a one week ad is usually worth the extra bucks. Personally, I've found running an ad for a week is more effective than a one-time Sunday insertion, but the latter is cheaper. Some inveterate camera sellers I've spoken with report good success with this latter method.

Why not go national?

Nationally circulated papers and photographic magazines offer you the largest possible audience for your camera ad, and those publications aimed specifically at photo enthusiasts provide you with the highest percentage of camera buyers. Targeting your ad this way is extremely effective and, as you'll see, it need not be any more costly than other media. The biggest problem with national advertising media is that the handful of buyers anxious to purchase your "mint classic" Nikon F may call you from other states or clear across the country! And while such calls may produce useful exchanges of information and even decisions to buy, few buyers are willing to hop in the next plane just to get a glimpse of your $279 SLR and give you the requisite dollars for it. Granted, such "flights of fancy" are fairly common among folks dealing in multi-thousand-dollar rare Leicas and the like, but for "ordinary" transactions, long distances between sellers and buyers pose problems.

The "Catch-22" is this: Barring such noble concepts as mutual trust, friendship, loyalty among camera buffs, and fundamental human decency, you, the seller would be a fool to send your Contarex PDQ off to some chap who calls you on the phone promising to pay for it, and he'd be an idiot to send you a check for similar reasons. Is there any way out of this dilemma? Not entirely—even a C.O.D. package must be paid for before it's opened, and you might send him a brick if you didn't mind having a potential mail fraud conviction hanging over your head.

Of course, this piece is written for the benefit of the sellers, so my advice to you camera hawkers out there is to send your camera(s) via UPS, either C.O. D. or *after having cashed* the buyer's check. If you're not a totally untrusting soul you can send the camera out upon receipt of a cashier's check, bank check, or U.S. Postal Money Order (the last being the safest). Sad to say, I cannot recommend that you entrust your parcel to the tender mercies of Parcel Post—but if you do, pack it especially well, include address info *inside* as well as outside the package, and insure it for its current market value. UPS parcels are automatically insured for up to $100 loss, so you may want to add extra insurance to cover more expensive cameras. Do use bubble wrap or styrofoam for packing, good strong tape for sealing, and sturdy boxes for shipping. Print addresses in indelible ink and/or cover them with transparent tape. Where does all this leave the hapless buyer? Well, despite my previous cynical remarks, only a tiny percentage of people advertising cameras for sale are rip-off artists, and many sellers bend over backwards to satisfy their "customers." In general, the seller sends out the camera with the understanding that the buyer has a 10 day money-back return privilege if he doesn't like it, finds that it's not in the condition described, discovers defects, etc. Other arrangements, such as "as is" sales, should be made explicitly clear at the time of sale, and you as an honest seller are honor bound to comply with them. In other words, *don't spend the money you receive* until you're absolutely sure your buyer is satisfied!

Exactly what are these national camera-ad media, you ask? Obviously they include such estimable publications as *Modern Photography*, other photo magazines and *Shutterbug Ads*. The last is, to my knowledge, the only nationally circulated monthly newspaper devoted almost entirely to advertising photographic items. It also contains a few columns on various camera topics and photographic events as well as readers' letters.

While *Shutterbug Ads* has a current circulation of only about 20,000, this 11-year-old publication has an audience composed almost entirely of rabid camera fans seeking to buy and sell cameras and other photo equipment. It is, therefore, an effective medium in which to advertise your camera. While "conventional" cameras comprise a fair percentage of its hundreds (thousands?) of individual ads, *Shutterbug* has a collector's flavor, with a preponderance of small ads for collectible and classic cameras sprinkled throughout its listings, and such exotica as large-format cameras, old lenses and lots of Leicas, Contaxes, rangefinder Nikons and Canons and lenses for all of the above spicing up its 96 or so yellow 10½ x 13½ in. pages. It also includes full-page, half-page, etc., ads by dealers and traders.

Another plus for *Shutterbug* is its low ad rate—12¢ per word for subscribers, 24¢ per word for non-subscribers. Subscriptions cost $10 per year (12 monthly issues) via third-class mail, $35 per year via first class. Condition of advertised items must be described according to *Shutterbug* standards using such phrases as SA new, SA Mint, SA Excellent, etc. and sold on a 10-day money-back basis. Publisher Glen E. Patch reports that over the years only a minute smattering of "bad apples" have surfaced among *Shutterbug*'s sellers and buyers, and that only two advertisers have been convicted of mail faud— an amazingly good performance.

Advertise in MODERN

This brings us to *Modern Photographys*'s new "Readers' Bulletin Board." At a cost of $18.50 for a 10-word reader ad (including name and address or name and phone number for free) an ad in MODERN reaches a readership of about 1½ million photo enthusiasts (based on a monthly circulation of 665,000). As with a newspaper ad, the total price of the advertised item(s) should be at least four to five times the cost of the ad for it to be a sound expenditure, but it's a highly effective way to advertise a wide variety of current items as well as collectibles. In addition, you're not limited to listing a single item, although the "featured" camera should appear first. The above rate applies to readers' ads only; additional words are $2.50 each and, at present, similar ads in most other American photo publications cost over three times as much.

Catching the flea-market syndrome

Needless to say, direct sale, trade-ins, and ads hardly exhaust the ingenious ways in which cameras can be sold—there are local events such as garage sales, flea markets, swap-and-shop meets and auctions to titillate the seller's (and buyer's) fancy. All these methods are especially suitable if your closet is cluttered with an assortment of old folding cameras, superseded Polaroids, 8mm movie cameras and projectors and the like. If they're too common and (relatively) new to be collectible, but have limited or no real trade-in value, you can turn them into cash by hawking them directly at your own garage sale, horning in on a friendly neighbor's garage sale, or unloading them at the next local flea market. If you have enough stuff to sell, consider renting a table or space yourself and displaying your photographic wares prominently. If not, perhaps your buddy has rented a table and would be willing to let you place your cameras thereupon. Even if you have an SLR or 2¼ camera worth 100 bucks or more, feel free to set it out with a price tag on it—nobody's forcing you to sell it if you don't get an amount close to your asking price.

Another selling technique that's worth a shot is to contact your local photographic society, camera club, etc. to find out the date of their next "swap and shop" event. As with flea markets, you can usually rent or pool a table at a modest cost, and if the event is large enough and well advertised, you can rest assured that hordes of beady-eyed cameraphiles will descend upon you and may buy the camera(s) you're selling. While much of the merchandise will inevitably fall into the "antique and classic" category, usable non-collectible cameras often move briskly at such affairs too. Indeed, if you join the local camera club, you may very well be able to "advertise" your cameras for sale by the oldest known method—word of mouth—which is almost always free and doesn't depend on your waiting for special events to occur.

This brings up the fascinating subject of auctions, which are probably the second most ancient method of advertising and selling things photographic and otherwise. Well publicized auctions devoted exclusively to photographic items are good places to sell almost any kind of photo equipment, and you usually receive cash. However, bear in mind that the auctioneer takes from 10-25 percent of the selling price, and you have no assurance that your item will sell at the price you had in mind. Some auctioneers will allow the seller to set a floor or minimum price, particularly on rare or unique items, or will allow the seller the first bid; but practices vary widely so it's essential to check in advance. Yes, you can sell your cameras at small, local "general merchandise" auctions, but you're not likely to get as much as you could by advertising or selling them yourself. This is particularly true of usable "bread and butter" cameras like late model SLRs. Finally, you *can* do well by selling rare antique cameras at the posh acution houses (like Parke-Bernet and Christie's) that run "photographica" auctions from time to time, but I recommend them only if your treasures are worth in excess of $5,000 or so. Less grandiose photographic collections are probably best sold at well-publicized local photographica auctions held under the auspices of a camera or photo-historical society.

Of course, while many serious photographic collectors could care less whether their rare 19th century shutters work properly or not, the same is emphatically not true of the boy who purchases your year-old SLR or faithful twin-lens reflex. And while individual sellers are not ordinarily responsible to guarantee what they sell, it's poor form to try to pawn off non-functional equipment on unknowing purchasers. No, this doesn't mean that you should spend $35 to fine-tune the shutter and exposure system of a four-year old SLR that's been taking good pictures, but it does mean that any camera you don't specifically sell "as is" should be functioning satisfactorily unless you tell the buyer otherwise.

Now that we've examined many, if not all, the ins and outs of "private" camera selling and its various pitfalls and nuances, are you clutching your camera in shaking hands as you rush off to the dealer to trade it in? That's just fine, for then I've succeeded in conveying the basic fact that the additional cash you get by selling on your own is often not worth the time, trouble, and inconvenience involved. However, after having sold scads of cameras using almost all the methods described herein, I can report that selling your own camera can be financially rewarding, challenging, and even fun. The secret message in this is *"caveat venditor"*—let the seller beware.

Can you profit from the current "bear market" in collectibles?

Jasonomics, or how you can profit from the current price bust in photographic collectibles and have fun doing it.

Despite my frequent sarcastic allusions to beady-eyed camera collectors and their technological and financial acquisitiveness, I can truthfully say that I never bought a single one of the 250 or so cameras I own because I thought it was a good investment. This is not to say that I've confined my collecting pursuits to worthless junk, just that my primary and tertiary motivations in acquiring cameras have always centered around semiromantic imponderables. Give me a camera that's cute, elegant, ugly, weird, or bristling with mechanical doodads and I'll find some way to buy it; tell me that I can turn a 300 percent profit on it in a year's time and I'll smile the wistful smile of the pure of heart and turn my wallet elsewhere.

Now the problem with this idealistic approach is other people. When my wife, in-laws, or well-meaning but overly rational friends have backed me into a corner by comparing the great and noble avocation of camera collecting to playing long shots at the track or buying diamonds from street vendors, I've been forced to fight back. Indeed, I have occasionally proclaimed with the force of

passion that amassing collectible cameras is a good investment. When pressed by fiscal mavens like my brother, I'll admit that goldmining shares or Treasury bills are probably a better way to accrue assets, but they're certainly a lot less fun. Besides, until quite recently my camera collection surely appreciated more rapidly than an ordinary savings account or U. S. Savings Bonds.

Has the bottom, then, fallen out of old cameras—leaving veteran collectors with their film exposed, so to speak? No, nothing as dramatic as all that, but, along with other more conventional collectibles like stamps and coins, classic cameras have certainly taken a financial beating in the last year or two and many individual items have actually decreased in value. Don't feel too bad though; even such well-heeled groups as classic car buffs have seen their Rolls-Royces and Bentley's selling at bargain prices lately. Indeed, the only staple collectible I know of that has resisted substantial price erosion of late is rare books.

All right, what are the underlying reasons for the general decline in the value of collectibles, and how do they affect the classic camera market? To begin with, the entire decade of the 70s was a period of rampant, often double-digit inflation, and one of the last things you want to hold onto in such an economic climate is cash. If you stuffed your dough under your matress or left it in a savings account at

5¼ percent interest, its value steadily eroded, so clever folks—and, later, just plain folks—decided to hedge. Basically, hedging against inflation takes two major forms: (1) Investing in something like bonds or money market funds that pay a higher rate of interest than the going rate of inflation, or (2) Buying some physical commodity such as real estate, gold coins, Chinese porcelain or rare Leicas, betting that the scarcity and intrinsic value of such items will cause their ongoing price rise to outpace inflation. Obviously, the above is a vast oversimplification of a large and complex subject, but it's worth noting that when enough people take approach number 2, the result is a self-fulfilling prophecy—they rapidly bid up the value of the most sought-after collectibles.

Meanwhile, the money market maniacs are busy withdrawing their savings and buying up billions in high interest paper, the federal government tolerates huge budget deficits while maintaining a tight money policy, and we find ourselves in the middle of the deepest recession since the Depression. If there's one word that characterizes our present situation it's "illiquidity," a polite way of saying your money is tied up in something other than spendable cash. True, if your credit rating is "triple A" you *can* borrow money at astronomical interest rates, but most of us cameraphiles can't compete with the U. S. Treasury or AT&T, so we're effectively squeezed out of the credit market. Faced with a dire need for cash, many of us will glumly turn to the magnificent old Contax IIa outfit with all those Zeiss lenses and finders resting in our top drawer. (And you were wondering why they call economics the dismal science.)

It's a truism that economics, like the weather, affects everybody, and you may rest assured as you trudge sadly to the camera shop to unload your prize collector's item, that other enthusiasts and de facto collectors are in precisely the same oarless boat. And since camera collecting is one of the small capitalist niches in our multi-agglomerated "gover-business" society where the immutable law of supply and demand still functions, the effect of all those folks unloading their high priced classic cameras over a short period of time is inevitable—prices tumble. But, here's the catch: Not all cameras suffer equally in this period of retrenchment. Some weather the financial storms quite nicely, even advancing modestly (though usually at a lower rate than inflation), while others are so decimated in value that they're quite difficult to sell at any price.

Now before I plunge into the gory details of the current classic camera biz, let me reiterate that the joys of camera collecting clearly transcend mere monetary gain. And while many of us are spurred on in "the endless hunt" by such visions as a whole plate Daguerreotype camera emerging unscathed from a Vermont hayloft for 15 bucks, we soon discover more important things, like bits of history preserved and quaint mechanical solutions to outdated problems that plagued our grandfathers. Nevertheless many of us have considerable sums tied up in ancient picture-taking machines, so herewith a detailed analysis of the bad news.

To make an arbitrary but useful distinction, I would divide the universe of collectible cameras into three parts: (1) Universally prized collector's pieces: These would include such items as well-known but rare special-purpose, limited-production 19th-century cameras and very early cameras that may be more aptly described as museum pieces than as collectibles. Added to this prestigious list would be very-low-production Leicas such as the factory-gold-plated Luxus, Compur shuttered model B's, and the half-frame Leica "72," the original 4¼ x 6cm Ermanox with f/1.8 or f/2 lens, the original "Kodak" of 1888, the Stereo Graflex 5 x 7, etc. Clearly only the crème de la crème would merit inclusion herein.

(2) High class collectible cameras: This glorious but somewhat more pedestrian bunch would include the bulk of *attainable* collector's heartthrobs like the rangefinder Nikons, most popular series-production Leicas, the Kodak Ektra system, the Hasselblad 1600F, the original Rolleiflex of 1929, the Gami 16, etc. Where does this leave such estimable creations as the original Latvian Minox, the Leica MP, the Hansa Canon of 1936 and the Rolleiflex Automat of 1937? I'd unhesitatingly put the first three in group 1, and the more plentiful Rollei in group 2. Remember, the first group is reserved for very desirable items that are also scarce.

It would be tempting to call group 3 "everything else," but I dislike wastebasket categories, especially those that would lump together such diverse entities as the redoubtable Minolta Autocord and the ugly-but-lovable Argoflex. I'll sidestep this dilemma by calling category 3 Middle-class collector's items (with apologies to the *petit Bourgeoisie*). The untouchable and unmentionable fourth class *lumpen proletarian* cameras, include such cheapies as plain-Jane roll-film folders, run-of-the-mill box cameras of the 30s through the 50s, most Argus 35s, and such brand names as Spartus, Perfex, and Imperial. As my loyal readers know, I have a soft spot in my heart for these neglected waifs of cameradom, and I exclude them from my "financial report" for a very simple reason—most were priced so low to begin with that no clear "profit and loss" picture has emerged, and they seldom represent much of a financial investment in any case (too bad if you just bought one for 75 smackers).

Okay, now that you have these arbitrary and non-watertight camera categories loosely in mind, how has the Great Recession affected them? Well, as you probably guessed, the tippy-top cameras in category 1 have fared the best, with little if any price slippage (down 10 percent at worst), and many showing modest gains. Why? They're virtually irreplaceable, still highly desirable, and most are owned by rather wealthy folks who aren't forced to sell them. People who own items like these are not the type to "buy high and sell low."

Even cameras in the second "high-class" category have fared rather well in these bleak economic times. While the trend is definitely on the down side, a typical loss compared to the peak value period of 1980 is a 10 to 20 percent, and few collectors who have bought such cameras have actually sold them for fewer dollars than they paid. Of course, breaking even dollarwise can represent a loss, but we haven't exactly seen the market flooded with "class 2" cameras either, since they're often difficult to replace and most collectors hang onto them. Clearly the cameras that have taken the worst beating are in the vast "middle class" of nice-but-ordinary collectibles. Kidding aside, the category is aptly named; most of the people with substantial holdings in it are themselves middle-class, and they're the ones who've been forced to prune or liquidate their collections to obtain some discretionary cash, or even to pay for necessities. Typical dollar losses based on the peak value period of 1980 run from 25 to 35 percent, and unfortunately large numbers of collectors bought "high" in the 1978-80 period and sold "low" fairly recently. While few individuals have actually lost more than a few hundred to a thousand bucks in this "entertaining hobby," dealers specializing in collectible cameras report sales are definitely off for the great bulk of "middle-class" cameras, while cameras in the top categories are holding their own saleswise.

Hopefully this is all very interesting in its own right, but what does it mean for all you mild-to-wild collectors out there? Obviously, it means that you should keep mum about your camera collection when people tell you what a killing they just made in soybean futures, but it also means that this is a lousy time to sell your collectible camera if "maximizing your return" is what you have in mind. In short, hang tight until times improve, appreciate your cameras for the mechanical-optical marvels they are, and can the notion of short-term economic gain. However, if you're lucky enough to have the requisite bucks, now is a great time to buy collectible cameras that will be much more expensive and much less obtainable should the light ever materialize at the end of the tunnel.

For all you brazen, counter-cyclical types determined to invest in classic cameras as well as enjoy them aesthetically herewith is Schneider's compact guide to sources and methods of doing so:

(1) Haunt large, well established urban camera stores with substantial used-equipment inventories. Make friends with knowledgeable salesmen you find; leave your card and make your wants known.

(2) Scour local flea markets, garage sales, church bazaars, country auctions, etc. Be prepared to pay less than camera store prices for what you find, as it will seldom be guaranteed and may have concealed damage.

(3) Try small, local camera stores in urban, surburban, and rural areas. Long-established places are likely to have caches of old merchandise on display or even down in the basement. You may never get to experience the breathless joy of searching through a 50- or 100-year-old store's basement "junk room" as I've done on a few occasions, but it doesn't hurt to ask.

(4) Advertise that you are a camera collector and ancient cameras will seek you out with anxious sellers attached. Many savvy collectors print up cards stating their specialties or just "old cameras"; others leave "contact cards" on any free bulletin boards they run across, and some of the most successful collectors place long running ads in local papers.

(5) Subscribe to and advertise in the *Shutterbug Ads* (P.O. Box F, Titusville, FL 32780). Subscriptions run $10 a year via third class mail in the continental U. S. and $35 via first class, while ads are only 12¢ a word (minimum $2) for subscribers. This thick, large-format monthly newspaper of photographic ads (plus a few folksy columns and bunches of nit-picky letters) is practically indispensible to the serious collector, and reading it assiduously will give you what is perhaps the clearest picture of today's ever fluctuating market in photographic collectibles. No, I don't own shares in this enterprise—in fact they send me my complimentary subscription third class!

Filter Sizes for Collectors' Cameras

With the widespread interest in collecting and using older cameras, the question of finding the correct size filters and similar lens attachments for these models can be troublesome. Generally, you can find the correct size filters eventually *if* you know what size you need. Unfortunately, these sizes are not always listed and, while you can take your camera with you to try to find the right fit, it is more convenient to carry a chart such as this the next time you go shopping. Sizes listed are for slip-on mounts which fit on the outer rim of the lens barrel. In some cases, such as with the Contax cameras, where screw-in type lens attachments are also available, the size of the screw-in attachment is listed in parentheses.

Camera and/or Lens		Filter Size
Agfa Karat	50mm f/2.8 Xenar	31.5mm
Argus C-3	50mm f/3.5 Cintar	41mm
Bee Bee (6 × 9 cm)	105mm f/4.5 Tessar	32mm
(9 × 12 cm)	135mm f/4.5 Tessar	42mm
Contax	50mm f/2 Sonnar	42mm (40.5mm)
	50mm f/1.5 Sonnar	42mm (40.5mm)
	85mm f/2 Sonar	51mm
	135mm f/4 Sonnar	42mm (40.5mm)
Dollina	50mm f/2 Kenon	32mm
Dolly	75mm f/2.8 Tessar	37mm
Kodak Recomar (6 × 9)	105mm f/4.5 Kodak	31.5mm
(9 × 12)	135mm f/4.5 Kodak	42mm
Exakta B	75mm f/3.5 Exaktar	32mm
	75mm f/3.5 Tessar	28.5mm
	75mm f/2.0 Biotar	51mm
Kine Exakta	50mm f/2 Kenon	32mm
Ikoflex II	75mm f/3.5 Triotar	28.5mm
	75mm f/3.5 Tessar	28.5mm
Ikoflex III	80mm f/2.8 Tessar	37mm
Ikonta and Super Ikonta A	75mm f/3.5mm Tessar	32mm
Super Ikonta B	80mm f/2.8 Tessar	37mm (40.5mm with adapter)
Ikonta and Super Ikonta C	105mm f/3.5 Tessar	37mm
Juwel A (9 × 12)	150mm f/4.5 Tessar	42mm
	165mm f/4.5 Tessar	51mm
Korelle Reflex	75mm f/2.9 Radionar	37mm
	75mm f/2.8 Tessar	37mm
Leica	35mm f/3.5 Elmar	36.5mm
	50mm f/3.5 Elmar	36.5mm
	50mm f/1.5 Xenon	43mm
	73mm f/1.9 Hektor	43mm
	90mm f/4 Elmar	36.5mm

Camera and/or Lens		Filter Size
Linhof	105mm f/3.5 Xenar	42mm
	105mm f/3.5 Tessar	42mm
	150mm f/4.5 Xenar	42mm
	210mm f/4.5 Xenar	60mm
Master Reflex	80mm f/2.8 Tessar	40mm
Maximar (6 × 9)	105mm f/4.5 Tessar	32mm
(9 × 12)	135mm f/4.5 Tessar	42mm
Minolta Autocord	75mm f/3.5 Rokkor	28.5mm (Rollie Bayonet Size I)
Nikon S2, SP	50mm f/1.4 Nikkor	44.5mm
Primarflex	135mm f/2.8 Biotessar	60mm
Rolleicord Ia	75mm f/4.5 Triotar	28.5mm
Rolleicord II	75mm f/3.5 Triotar	28.5mm (Rollei Bayonet Size I)
Standard Rolleiflex	75mm f/3.5 Tessar	28.5mm
Voigtlander Brilliant	75mm f/7.7 Voigtar	29mm
Voigtlander Superb	75mm f/3.5 Skopar	29.3mm
Weltini	50mm f/2 Xenon	32mm

Press Cameras and View Cameras

Below are some of the lenses commonly used on press and view cameras, and which are quite often sold separately for mounting on a specific camera.

Ilex	5½-in. f/4.5 Paragon	43mm
	6½-in. f/4.5 Paragon	43mm
Wollensak	127mm f/4.5 Raptar	38mm
	162mm f/4.5 Raptar	44.4mm
	190mm f/4.5 Raptar	54.5mm
Zeiss	135mm f/3.5 Tessar	51mm
	150mm f/3.5 Tessar	51mm
	180mm f/4.5 Tessar	51mm

Collectible Camera Price Guide

Note: See Index on page 212 for page references for cameras not listed herein.

Manufacturer	Model	Comments	Price
Agfa	Clack	120 box camera	$10-15
	Billy	120 folder, Compur shutter	40-50
	Karat	35mm rfdr., f/2.8 Solinar	60-70
		35mm rfdr., f/2 Solagon	75-90
Aires	Airesflex	2¼ square TLR	
		75mm f/3.5 Coral	60-75
		75mm f/3.5 Nikkor	125-150
	Aires III L	35mm rfdr., f/1.9	75-90
	Aires III C	35mm rfdr., f/1.9	80-100
	Aires V	35mm rfdr., interch.	
		45mm f/1.5 Coral	150-175
	Penta	35mm SLR, fixed f/2.8	50-75
	Viscount	35mm rfdr., f/1.9	65-75
Alpa (Pignons S.A)	Alpa Reflex (original)	35mm SLR	
		50mm f/2.8	200
		50mm f/1.8	225
	Alpa Prisma Reflex	35mm SLR	
		50mm f/1.8 or f/1.9	225
	Alpa 4	35mm SLR, 50mm f/1.8	200
	Alpa 7	35mm SLR, 50mm f/1.8	200
	Alpa 9d	35mm SLR, 50mm f/1.8	225
	Alpa 10d	35mm SLR, 50mm f/1.9	250
Ansco	Karomat	35mm rfdr., 50mm f/2	65-85
	Karomat	35mm rfdr., 50mm f/2.8	50-60
	Super Memar	35mm rfdr., 50mm f/2	60-70
	Super Memar	35mm rfdr., 45mm f/3.5	40-50
	Super Memar	As above, with LVS scale	40-50
	Regent	35mm, scale focus, f/3.5	35-45
	Super Regent	35mm rfdr., 50mm f/3.5	40-60
	Super Regent LVS	As above, with LVS scale	45-65
	Automatic Reflex	2¼ TLR, no flash sync	125-150
	Automatic Reflex	2¼ TLR, with flash sync	135-175
	Memo	Half frame 35mm f/6.3 lens	50-60
Argus	C3	35mm rfdr., interch. 50mm f/3.5 Cintar	25-45
	21	35mm leaf shutter, removable lens (50mm f/3.5)	25-40
	C4, C4R	35mm rfdr., 50mm f/2.8 Cintar	35-50
	C44, C44R	35mm rfdr., interch. 50mm f/2.8	90-110
		with 50mm f/1.9	90-110
	Argoflex E, EM	2¼ square TLR, sync	25-40
	Argoflex EF	2¼ square TLR, with sync	25-40
	A, AF, A2F	35mm scale focus, 50mm f/4	20-30
	CC	35mm scale focus, built-in meter, 50mm f/4.5	25-40
	21	35mm scale focus, removable 50mm f/3.5	25-40
	A-Four	35mm scale focus, 44mm f/3.5	15-25
	C-Twenty	35mm scale focus, 44mm f/3.5	20-30

Manufacturer	Model	Comments	Price
Argus	C33	35mm rfdr., 55mm f/3.5 or f/2.8 accepts coupled meter	$25-40
	V100	35mm rfdr., 52mm f/2.8 or 48mm f/2, made in Germany	35-50
	Autronic	35mm rfdr., 50mm f/3.5, auto exposure. Compur shutter	45-60
Asahi Optical	Asahiflex IIa	35mm SLR, waist-level, 50mm f/3.5 or 58mm f/2.4	150-175
	Pentax S	35mm SLR, eye-level, rapid-wind lever, 58mm f/2.2	135-150
	Pentax K	35mm SLR, 1/1000 sec. top speed, 55mm f/1.8	125-140
	Heiland Pentax H-2	35mm SLR, 55mm f/e lens, non revolving shutter dial	60-80
Beauty	Canter	35mm rfdr., f/2.8 lens	35-45
	Canter	35mm rfdr., f/1.9 lens	40-50
	Beautyflex	2¼ TLR, 75mm f/3.5 lens	50-60
Bell & Howell	Foton	35mm rfdr., interch. lenses, built-in spring motor, T/2.2 Cooke Amotal lens	500-650
	Infallible	127 roll-film camera, auto exposure	70-85
Canon (price with std. 50mm f/1.8)	Hansa Canon	35mm rfdr., 50mm f/3.5 Nikkor	1000-1200
	II-B	35mm rfdr., interch. 50mm f/1.9, 1/500 sec. top speed	175-200
	III	35mm rfdr., interch. screw-mount lens 1/1000 sec. speed, no sync	150-185
	IV	Same as III, but has flash sync, 50mm f/1.8	135-175
	III-A	Same as IV, but no flash sync, has film speed indicator	135-160
	IV-S	Same as model IV, but has film speed indicator	150-170
	IV-S2	Same as model IV-S, but has lock on slow speed dial	150-175
	II-D	Similar to model III-A, but has 1/500 sec. top speed	135-150
	II-F	Similar to model IV-S2, 1/500 sec. top speed, flash sync	125-140
	II-S	Same as model IV-S2, but 1/500 sec. top speed sync for high & low speeds	125-140
	V	Rapid-advance trigger in base, hinged back no folding rewind lever	175-250

Manufacturer	Model	Comments	Price
Canon	Vt Deluxe	Same as model V, but has folding rewind crank	$185-250
	L-1	Similar to Vt Deluxe, but has top-mounted wind lever	150-200
	VI-T	35mm rfdr., auto parallax comp, trigger on bottom	185-275
	P	Similar to VI-T sans 3-position finder, has top wind	130-145
	Canonflex	35mm SLR, 50mm f/1.8	150-175
	Canonflex RP	35mm SLR, 50mm f/1.8, 1/2000 sec. top speed	160-185
	Canonflex RP	35mm SLR, fixed prism, no split-image rfdr., 50mm f/1.8	120-135
Graflex, Inc.	Ciro 35	35mm rfdr., 50mm f/3.5	20-35
	Ciro 35, model R	35mm rfdr., 50mm f/4.5	20-30
	Ciro 35, model T	35mm rfdr., 50mm f/2.8, ½-1/400 sec. shutter	25-40
	Ciro-Flex B	2¼ TLR, no flash sync. Alphax shutter, 85mm f/3.5 Wollensak lens	35-55
	Ciro-Flex D	Similar to model B but has MF flash sync.	40-60
	Ciro-Flex C	Similar to model B with 1-1/400 sec. Rapax shutter, no flash sync.	50-70
	Ciro-Flex E	Similar to above, but with MF type flash sync.	55-75
	Ciro-Flex F	2¼ TLR, 83mm f/3.2 Wollensak Raptar lens, 1-1/400 sec. Rapax shutter, MFX sync.	60-75
	Graflex "22" 200	2¼ TLR, 85mm f/3.5 Graftar lens, Century shutter with speeds 1/10-1/200 sec., B, T	45-60
	Graflex "22" 400	Identical to above, but has 1-1/400 sec., plus B & T Graphex MX shutter	50-70
	Graflex "22" 400F	Identical to model 400, but has 83mm f/3.2 Optar lens, MFX sync at all speeds	55-75
Hasselblad Ab	Hasselblad 1600F	2¼ square SLR, interch. bayonet mount lenses, interch. film backs and focusing hoods, top shutter speed 1/1600 sec., with 80mm f/2.8 Ektar	425-575
	Hasselblad 1000F	Similar to 1600F but has top shutter speed of 1/1000 sec., with 80mm f/2.8 Tessar	375-525
Ihagee Kamerawerk (with normal lens)	Exakta I	35mm SLR, waist-level finder 50mm f/2.8 or 58mm f/2 lens, M sync	125-150
	Exakta II	Same as Exakta I but has flip-up magnifier	100-135
	Exakta V	Similar to model II, with 2	

Manufacturer	Model	Comments	Price
Ihagee Kamerawerk	Exakta V	sets of flash contacts, re-movable finder	$75-100
	Exakta VX	Similar to model V, but has film transport warning signal, hinged removable back	75-100
	Exakta VX IIa	Similar to VX with gear-set exposure counter, safety cover on shutter release	85-125
	Exakta VS IIb	Similar to VX IIa but has geometric shutter speeds, no finder-removal button	80-110
	Exakta VX 1000	Similar to VX IIb but has instant-return mirror	85-125
	Exakta VX 500	Simplified version of VX 1000 with shutter speeds 1/30-1/500 sec.	65-85
	Exakta A	Roll film SLR; 2½×1⅝ in. format on 127 film, interch. lenses, focal-plane shutter 1/25-1/1000 sec. plus B & T, with 75mm f/3.5 Tessar lens	70-90
	Exakta B	Similar to above, but with com-bined film wind and shutter cocking, slow speeds to 12 sec., with 80mm f/2 Biotar	125-165
	Exakta C	Same as model B, but has plate/sheet film adapter, auxiliary rear groundglass, with 75mm f/2.8 Tessar lens	150-200
	Exakta Junior	Same configuration as model A, but non-interch. 75mm f/4.5 lens slow speeds to 1/25 sec.	100-125
	Square Exakta	2¼ square SLR for 120 roll film, interch. bayonet mount Tessar lens, same basic shape as 127-film models but larger, wind lever on bottom	275-400
Eastman Kodak Co.	Ektra	35mm rfdr., interch. lenses, interch. film backs, 50mm f/1.9 or f/3.5 Ektar lens	325-450
	Retina (original model, 1934)	35mm scale focusing folder, 50mm f/3.5 Xenar lens, 1/300 sec. shutter	75-100
	Retina (1935)	Same as original model but has 1/500 sec. Compur shutter	60-90
	Retina (1936)	Same as above, but has film-advance release on top, accessory shoe	60-90
	Retina I (1937)	Similar to above, but has 50mm f/3.5 Ektar lens, T and B shutter settings	60-90
	Retina I (1948)	Similar to above but has 50mm f/3.5 Xenar lens,	

Manufacturer	Model	Comments	Price
Eastman Kodak	Retina I (1948)	no accessory shoe	$60-90
	Retina II (1937)	35mm rfdr. folder, separate range/viewfinder windows, 50mm f/2.8 or f/2 Xenon	65-95
	Retina II (1948)	35mm rfdr. folder, combined range/viewfinder window coated 50mm f/2 Xenon lens	80-110
	Retina IIA	Same as model II (1948) but has top-mounted film-advance lever	80-110
	Retina IIIc	35mm rfdr. folder, internal bellows, front-component interchangeable 50mm f/2, 2-range exposure meter	150-200
	Retina IIc	Similar to above (bottom-mounted wind lever) with 50mm f/2.8 Xenon, no meter	75-110
	Retina IIIC	Similar to Retina IIIc, but has single range meter with no hinged cover	175-240
	Retina Reflex	35mm SLR, front-component interchangeable 50mm f/2 built-in, non-coupled meter	65-85
	Retina Reflex S	35mm SLR, fully interch. 50mm f/1.9 or f/2.8, coupled meter	70-90
	Signet 35	35mm rfdr., combined range/viewfinder, 44mm f/3.5 Ektar lens	30-50
	Signet 40	35mm rfdr. thumb-type film advance, 46mm f/3.5 Ektanon	30-45
	Signet 30	35mm rfdr. with 44mm f/2.8 Ektanon	25-40
	Signet 50	Similar to model 30 but has built-in exposure meter	25-40
Konica (Konishiroku)	Konica (original model of 1946)	35mm rfdr., collapsible 50mm f/3.5 lens, no sync	50-65
	Konica I	35mm rfdr., same as above but has flash sync., 50mm f/3.5 or f/2.8 lens	50-65
	Konica II	35mm rfdr., recessing lens mount, dbl. exposure prevention, curved chrome front 50mm f/2.8 lens	75-85
	Konica IIA	Similar to model II, but has 48mm f/2 lens, full sync	75-85
	Konica III	Has self-timer, vertical, left-handed film advance, self-timer, 48mm f/2	65-90
	Konica IIIA	Similar to III, but has 1:1 bright frame finder with parallax comp. frameline, 50mm f/1.8 or f/2 lens	75-100

Manufacturer	Model	Comments	Price
Konica	Konica IIIM	35mm fixed lens rfdr. type, built-in meter with fold-down cell above finder, optional single-stroke film advance with half-frame mask, 50mm f/1.8 lens	$80-110
Ernst Leitz, GmbH	O-Series Leica	Prototype of 1923, 35mm scale focusing, 50mm f/3.5 Leitz Anastigmat lens	5,000+
	Leica A	First production model, 35mm scale focusing, non-interch. lens	
		With Leitz Anastigmat 50mm	3,000+
		With 50mm f/3.5 Elmax lens	2,500+
		With 50mm f/3.5 Elmar lens	300-500
		With 50mm f/2.5 Hektor lens	400-575
	Leica B	35mm scale focusing, 1-1/300 sec. Compur shutter, 50mm f/3.5 Elmar lens	
		With dial-set shutter	2,500+
		With rim-set shutter	2,500+
	Leica C	35mm scale focusing, interch. 50mm f/3.5 Elmar lens	
		In original mount	750-1,000
		In standard mount	250-400
	Leica D or II	35mm rfdr., interch. 50mm f/3.5 or f/2.5, no slow speeds	250-450
	Leica E or Standard	35mm scale focusing, std. interch. mount, pull-up rewind knob, with 50mm f/3.5	200-350
	Leica F or III	35mm rfdr., interch. lens, slow speed dial on front, swiveling diopter control on eyepiece, 1/500 sec. top speed, with 50mm f/3.5 lens	200-350
	Leica G or IIIa	Similar to model III above but has 1/1000 sec. top speed	150-250
	Leica G or IIIb	Similar to IIIa but has diopter control for eyepiece on top, range- and viewfinder eyepieces close together, with 50mm f/2 lens	175-300
	Leica IIIc	Similar to IIIb but has longer (5⅜ in.) die cast body with 50mm f/3.5 or f/2 lens	150-250
	Leica IIId	Nearly identical to IIIc, but has self-timer to right of low-speed dial, 50mm f/3.5 or f/2 lens	200-375
	Leica IIIc K model	Has K stamped on shutter curtain and after serial no., usually in gray finish	1,000-1,200 without lens
	Leica IIc	Similar to late model IIIc but lacks slow shutter speeds, with 50mm f/3.5 Elmar	150-275

Manufacturer	Model	Comments	Price
Ernst Leitz, GmbH	Leica Ic	Similar to IIc but lacks rangefinder, has two accessory shoes, with 50mm f/3.5 Elmar	$150-250
	Leica IIIf	35mm rfdr., interch. lenses, has flash sync delay dial under top shutter dial, with 50mm f/3.5 Elmar	
		Black sync delay numerals	125-200
		Red sync delay numerals	150-250
	Leica IIf	Similar to IIIf but has round blanking disc in place of slow shutter dial	125-200
	Leica If	Similar to IIf but has no rangefinder, two accessory shoes, sync socket in slow speed blanking disc, with 50mm f/3.5 Elmar	150-200
	Leica IIIg	35mm rfdr. interch. screw-mount lens, finder frames for 50mm and 90mm focal lengths, self-timer, film speed dial on back, with 50mm f/2.8 Elmar	600-900
	Leica Ig	Similar to IIIg, but lacking rangfinder, has two accessory shoes, no self-timer	800-900
	Leica M3	35mm rfdr., bayonet interch. lenses auto-keying finder frames for 50, 90, 135mm lenses, self-timer, with rigid 50mm f/2 Summicron	
		With single stroke wind	600-700
		With two-stroke film wind	575-675
	Leica M2	Similar to M3 but has finder frames for 35, 50, and 90mm lenses, no self-timer, with rigid 50mm f/2 Summicron lens	450-650
	Leica MP	Pro model of M3 double stroke, MP serial number, without lens	5,000-6,000
	Leica Ml	Same as M2 but without rangefinder, self-timer, field frame selector, without lens	750-1,000
	Leica M4	Similar to M2 and M3, but has angled rewind crank, field frames for 35, 50, 90, and 135mm lenses, rapid load system, with 50mm f/2 Summicron lens	700-1,000
	Leica M2-R	Same as M2 but has self-timer, R serial number prefix, with 50mm f/2 Summicron lens	900-1,100

Manufacturer	Model	Comments	Price
Ernst Leitz, GmbH	Leica M5	35mm rfdr., bayonet interch. lenses, built-in, behind lens meter, shutter dial overhangs top, with 50mm f/2 Summicron lens	$700-1,000
	Leica CL	Compact Leica with CdS meter cell behind lens, vertical shutter dial has speeds of ½ to 1/1000 sec., with 40mm f/2 Summicron lens	550-700
	Leica 72	Looks like IIIf, but provides 18×24mm format on 35mm film, made in Midland, Ontario, Canada, without lens	7,000-8,000
	Leica FF or 250	35mm rfdr., interch., lenses, has enlarged chambers on sides for 33 ft. long rolls yielding 250 exposures, without lens	5,000-6,000
	Leica MD	35mm scale focusing, no rfdr. or viewfinder, scientific camera is otherwise similar to Ml, without lens	700-750
	Leica MDa	Similar to M4 but has no rfdr., viewfinder, field frame selector, or self-timer, without lens	600-650
	Leicaflex (original model)	35mm SLR, central focusing area in finder, CdS port on front of prism housing, with 50mm f/2 Summicron-R lens	375-550
	Leicaflex SL	Similar to Leicaflex (original) but has behind-lens CdS meter, full focusing screen, with 50mm f/2 Summicron-R lens	450-750
	Leicaflex SL2	Similar to Leicaflex SL but has flatter body contour, hot shoe, meter scale illumination button, with 50mm f/2 Summicron-R lens	550-800
Minolta	Minolta 35, Model II	35mm rfdr., focal-plane shutter, interch. screw-mount lens, hinged back, with 45mm f/2.8 or 50mm f/2	70-85
	Minolta A	35mm rfdr., non-interch. 45mm f/3.5 Rokkor	40-50
	Minolta A2	35mm rfdr., non-interch. 45mm f/2.8 Rokkor	40-60
	Minolta Super A	35mm rfdr, interch. lens, leaf shutter, bright finder frames for 35mm, 50mm fields, 50mm f/2 or f/1.8 lens	70-85
	Minolta V2	35mm rfdr., non-interch. 45mm f/2 Rokkor, leaf shutter with 1/2000 sec. top speed	65-80

Manufacturer	Model	Comments	Price
Minolta	Minolta Autowide	35mm scale focusing, 35mm f/2.8 lens, coupled exposure meter	50-65
	Minolta SR-2	35mm SLR, autodiaphragm 50mm f/1.8 Rokkor lens	60-75
Miranda Camera Co.	Miranda Standard	35mm SLR, 1-1/500 sec. shutter, eye-level prism, 50mm f/1.9 Miranda lens	60-75
	Miranda A	35mm SLR, 1-1/1000 sec. shutter, rapid-wind lever, 50mm f/1.9 Miranda lens	60-75
	Miranda C	35mm SLR, same as Miranda A but with instant-return mirror, 50mm f/1.9 lens	65-80
	Miranda D	35mm SLR, similar to Miranda C, but no self-timer, exposure counter in between film advance and shutter dial, 50mm f/1.9 lens	60-75
Nikon (Nippon Kogaku)	Nikon I	35mm rfdr., interch. bayonet mount lenses, 24×34mm format, exp. counter numbered past 40, 50mm f/2 or f/1.4 Nikkor, 1/500 sec. top shutter speed	200-350
	Nikon M	Similar to Nikon S below, but has 24×34mm format, with 50mm f/1.4 Nikkor lens	175-250
	Nikon S	Same features as model I, but has full flash sync, standard 24×36mm format, auto frame counter, with 50mm f/1.4 Nikkor lens	150-225
	Nikon S2	Similar to model S but has film-wind lever, 1:1 viewfinder, folding rewind crank, with 50mm f/1.4 Nikkor lens	175-275
Olympus	Olympus 35S1-2.8	35mm rfdr., non-interch. 48mm f/2.8 lens, no bright frame in finder	35-50
	Olympus 35S-1.8	35mm rfdr., non-interch. 42mm f/1.8, bright frameline in finder with auto parallax compensation	45-70
	Olympus S2 f/2.8	Similar to model above, but has no self-timer, 48mm f/2.8 lens	40-60
	Olympus S2 f/2	Similar to model above, but has self-timer, 42mm f/2 lens	45-65
	Olympus Wide S	Similar to Olympus 35S-1.8 but has 35mm f/2 lens, no self-timer	65-90

Manufacturer	Model	Comments	Price
Olympus	Olympus Wide E	35mm scale focusing with bright frame finder, built-in exposure meter, 35mm f/3.5 lens	$35-45
	Olympus Auto B	35mm rfdr., non-interch. 42mm f/2.8 lens, coupled exposure meter	40-55
	Olympus Electroset	Similar to Auto B but has 42mm f/1.8 lens	50-70
Robot-Berning & Co.	Robot I	35mm scale focusing with spring motor drive, 24×24mm format, 37.5mm f/2.8 lens in interch. screw mount	85-150
	Robot II	Similar to model I, but has chrome finish, finder adjustable for right angle view, speeds down to ½ sec. only, 40mm f/1.9	100-175
	LW Robot	Similar to model II, but in black finish only with tall "double spring" motor, usually with Luftwaffe insignia, without lens	250-350
	Robot IIa	Accepts standard 35mm cartridges or Robot cassettes, has double flash contacts on front, otherwise similar to model II, 40mm f/1.9	125-200
	Robot Junior	Same as IIa, but no finder adjustment for right-angle view, with 38mm f/2.8	100-175
	Robot Star I	Similar to model IIa, but has rewind handle for winding film back into standard 35mm cartridge, 38mm f/2.8	110-185
	Robot Royal 36	35mm rfdr., interch. breech-lock bayonet mount lenses, std. 24×36mm format, spring motor drive for auto wind or bursts, 45mm f/2.8 Xenar or 50mm f/2 Sonnar lens	
		With f/2.8	200-300
		With f/2	250-375
Rollei (Franke & Heidecke)	Rolleiflex Standard (1939)	Similar appearance to Automat (1937) but first frame set in ruby window, lever set f/stops, speeds, with 75mm f/3.5 Zeiss Tessar	110-150
	Rolleiflex (1949)	Similar to Automat (1937) but has coated 75mm f/3.5 Xenar or Tessar, X-sync only	85-115

Manufacturer	Model	Comments	Price
Rollei (Franke & Heidecke)	Rolleiflex (1951)	Same as above but has built-in magnifier showing entire groundglass, 75mm f/3.5 as above	$85-115
	Rolleiflex (1954)	Similar to above but with auto first frame positioning, LVS scale, large focus knob with film type indicator 75mm f/3.5 lenses as above	90-125
	Rolleiflex 2.8	Similar to Rollei (1951) but has 80mm f/2.8 Tessar or Biometar lens	90-125
	Rolleiflex 2.8C	Similar to above but with 80mm f/2.8 Xenotar or Planar lens, no LVS	150-175
	Rolleiflex 2.8D	Similar to above but with cross-coupled LVS, no meter, 80mm Xenotar or Planar	170-195
	Rolleiflex 2.8E	Similar to above, but has auto depth of field indicator, aux. 36-exp. counter, built-in meter or provision for same, lenses as above	275-350
	Rolleiflex 2.8E2	Similar to above, but with removable focusing hood, meter or provision for same, lenses as above	275-375
	Rolleiflex 3.5E	Similar to 2.8D, but has 75mm f/3.5 Xenotar or Planar lens	250-350
	Rolleiflex 4×4 (1931)	TLR for 4×4cm format on 127 roll film, lens accepts push-on accessories, Compur shutter with 1/300 sec. or 1/500 sec. top speed, 60mm f/2.8 Tessar	250-300
	Rolleicord I	Before 1934 came only with nickel-plated body; after 1934 only with leather, co-vered body; only Rolleicord with exp. counter on left Triotar f/4.5 lens	75-125
	Rolleicord IA	Similar to Rolleicord I but has auto film stop, accepts plate and 35mm adapters, Triotar lens	65-115
	Rolleicord II	Has bayonet mount for over-lens accessories, eye-level focusing, Xenar or Triotar lens, other features same as IA	60-90
	Rolleicord III	Similar to model II, but has coated Triotar or Xenar lens, no film window, safety lock on back latch	65-95

Manufacturer	Model	Comments	Price
Rollei (Franke & Heidecke)	Rolleicord IV	Similar to model III, but has MX sync. selector lever, no release button in film-transport knob with coated 75mm f/3.5 Xenar lens	$75-110
	Rolleicord V	Similar to model IV, but has cross-coupled LVS, larger focusing knob, MXV sync selector lever, film speed indicator, with 75mm f/3.5 Xenar lens	85-140
	Rolleicord Va	2¼ TLR, accepts kits for 5 different format sizes with interch. film counters; has focusing knob on left, with coated 75mm f/3.5 Xenar lens	150-185
	Rolleiflex (Original)	2¼ TLR using 117 or conv. to 620, film-wind knob, ruby window on back, with 75mm f/4.5 or f/3.8 Tessar lens	125-175
	Rolleiflex Standard (1932)	2¼ TLR for 120 film; lever below lens cocks, fires shutter, wind crank, with 75mm f/4.5 or f/3.8 Tessar	110-150
	Rolleiflex Automat (1937)	2¼ TLR, 120 film, cpld. film wind/shutter cocking crank, no ruby window, with 75mm f/3.5 Xenar or Tessar lens	125-165
	Rolleiflex 4×4 (1938)	Similar to 1931 model but has f/stop/shutter speed window atop viewing lens, bayonet mount around taking lens, 60mm f/2.8 Tessar lens	275-350
	Rolleiflex 4×4 (1957)	TLR for 4×4cm format on 127 roll film, gray finish, knob wind, 60mm f/3.5 Xenar, cross-coupled LVS lens	150-225
Voigtlander	Prominent	35mm rfdr. interch. bayonet lenses, top knob focus, with 50mm f/2 or f/1.5	110-185
	Prominent II	Same as above with bright frame finder	125-200
	Vitessa (1950)	35mm rfdr., collapsible lens on bellows, hinged doors, plunger advance, with 50mm f/2 Ultron lens	135-180
	Vitessa (1951)	Same as above with full MX flash sync, accessory shoe, 50mm f/2 lens	140-185
	Vitessa L	Same as above with cross-coupled LVS, built-in exposure meter	
		With 50mm f/2.8 lens	135-185
		With 50mm f/2 lens	150-190

Manufacturer	Model	Comments	Price
Voigtlander	Vitessa N	Same as Vitessa (1950) but with 50mm f/3.5 Skopar lens; latest version has LVS	$120-150
	Vito I	35mm scale-focusing folder, with 50mm f/3.5 Skopar lens	
		With Prontor shutter	35-45
		With Compur shutter	50-60
	Vito II	Same as above with optical finder flush with top, round shutter-release plunger, 50mm f/3.5 Color-Skopar lens	50-60
	Vito IIa	Same as above with rapid-advance lever, pull-out rewind knob, accessory shoe, 50mm f/3.5 Color-Skopar lens	55-65
	Vito III	35mm rfdr. folder, combined range/viewfinder, film type indicator, 50mm f/2 Ultron lens	125-165
	Vito B	35mm scale focusing, rapid-wind lever, Pronto or Prontor shutter, 50mm f/3.5 or f/2.8 lens	45-65
	Vito BL	Similar to Vito B but has built-in meter, 1:1 finder	50-70
	Vito BR	Similar body to Vito BL, but had coupled rfdr., 50mm f/2.8 lens, only	50-70
	Vitomatic I	Similar to above, but has built-in coupled exposure meter, no rfdr., 1:1 finder, exposure counter on bottom	45-65
	Vitomatic II	Similar to Vitomatic I, but has coupled range/viewfinder	60-75
	Dynamatic	35mm scale focusing, auto exposure control with low-light warning, rapid-wind lever, 50mm f/2.8 Lanthar lens	45-65
	Dynamatic II	Similar to above, but with coupled range/viewfinder, f/stops visible in finder	60-75
Zeiss-Ikon	Contaflex twin-lens reflex	35mm TLR, interch. lenses, built-in meter, ½-1/1000 sec. shutter	450-600
	Contaflex I	35mm SLR, non-interch. 50mm f/2.8 lens, no exp. meter	70-100
	Contaflex II	Same as model I with built-in meter	75-100
	Contaflex III	35mm SLR, front-component-interch. 50mm f/2.8, no meter	85-110
	Contaflex IV	Same as model III with built-in meter	85-115
	Contaflex Alpha	Similar to model III with 45mm f/2.8 Pantar lens	65-90

Manufacturer	Model	Comments	Price
Zeiss-Ikon	Contaflex Beta	Similar to model IV with same lens as model III	$65-90
	Contaflex Rapid	Similar to model III, but has rapid-wind lever	85-110
	Contax I	35mm rfdr., interch. lenses, shutter speed/wind knob on front, 50mm f/3.5 or f/2	200-300
	Contax II	35mm rfdr., interch. lenses, combined range/viewfinder, finger-wheel focus on top, 50mm f/2 or f/1.5	100-150
	Contax III	Same as model II, with built-in coupled exposure meter	85-125
	Contax IIa	35mm rfdr., similar to model II, has M or MX flash sync	150-250
	Contax IIIa	Same as model II but with built-in coupled meter	150-225
	Contessa 35 (1950)	35mm rfdr. folder with 45mm f/2.8 lens, built-in meter	125-175
	Contessa 35 (1960)	35mm rfdr., 50mm f/2.8 lens, Pronto 1/30-1/250 sec. shutter, built-in meter	45-75
	Contessa-Matic	Similar to Contessa 35 (1960) with match-needle metering	50-80
	Ikonta 35	35mm scale focusing;	
		With 45mm f/3.5 Novar	35-50
		With 45mm f/2.8 Tessar	45-60
	Contina I (1952)	Similar to Ikonta 35 with Prontor SV or Compur shutter	50-60
	Contina II (1952)	35mm rfdr. folder	
		With Novar lens	60-75
		With Tessar lens	75-100
	Contina I (1955)	35mm scale focus, non-folder, with Novar or Novicar lens	35-50
	Contina II (1955)	35mm scale focus, similar to model I (1955) with built-in meter	40-60
	Contina III	Similar to Contina II (1955) with component-interch. 45mm f/2.8 Pantar lens	50-65
	Tenax I	35mm scale focusing, rapid film wind/shutter cocking lever, folding optical finder, 35mm f/3.5 Novar lens	65-85
	Tenax II	35mm rfdr., interch. bayonet lenses, rapid-wind lever on front, 24×24mm format, 40mm f/2.8 Tessar or 40mm f/2 Sonnar lens	
		With 40mm f/2.8	150-200
		With 40mm f/2	200-300

Manufacturer	Model	Comments	Price
Zeiss-Ikon	Ikoflex I	2¼ TLR for 120 roll film, body shutter release; early version has focusing lever, later version has focus knob, Klio or Compur shutter	
		With 75mm f/3.5 Novar	$50-65
		With 75mm f/3.5 Tessar	65-80
	Ikoflex Ia	Similar to above but with auto dbl. exposure prevention, auto exposure counter, "Extra-brite" screen	
		With 75mm f/3.5 Novar	65-80
		With 75mm f/3.5 Tessar	75-90
	Ikoflex Ic	Similar to Ib, but with built-in meter	
		With 75mm f/3.5 Novar	65-80
		With 75mm f/3.5 Tessar	75-90
	Ikoflex Ib	Improved version of Ia with magnifying lenses on shutter-speed and f/stop windows, folding body shutter release, with 75mm f/3.5 Tessar	65-80
	Ikoflex II	2¼ TLR with Compur-Rapid I-1/500 sec. shutter, uncoated 75mm f/3.5 Tessar, no sync	60-70
	Ikoflex IIa (1950)	2¼ TLR, coated 75mm f/3.5 Tessar, Comput-Rapid 1-1/500 sec. shutter, X sync speeds and f/stops lever set	75-90
	Ikoflex IIa (1953)	Similar to above, but has f/stop/shutter speed window above viewing lens, with 75mm f/3.5 Tessar lens	80-100
	Ikoflex III	2¼ TLR with crank film transport, uncoated 80mm f/2.8 Tessar, Albada sportsfinder, 101/400 sec. Compur shutter	300-450
	Ikoflex Favorit	2¼ TLR, knob wind, f/stop and shutter-speed wheels, built-in meter, cross-coupled LVS, with 75mm f/3.5 Tessar lens	135-175

Index